UNDERSTANDING THE ENVIRONMENT AND SOCIAL POLICY

Also available in the series

Understanding social security (second edition)
Issues for policy and practice
Edited by **Jane Millar**

"*This updated second edition brings together some of the leading writers in the field to provide a critical analysis of the recent changes to the social security system.*"
Dr. Liam Foster, Department of Sociological Studies, University of Sheffield
PB £21.99 (US$36.95) **ISBN** 978 1 84742 186 9 **HB** £65.00 (US$99.00) **ISBN** 978 1 84742 187 6
344 pages February 2009
INSPECTION COPY AVAILABLE

Understanding equal opportunities and diversity
The social differentiations and intersections of inequality
Barbara Bagilhole

This book challenges the official discourse that shapes the debates on Equal Opportunities and Diversity (EO&D) at national, regional and European level.
PB £21.99 (US$36.95) **ISBN** 978 1 86134 848 7 **HB** £65.00 (US$99.00) **ISBN** 978 1 86134 849 4
272 pages April 2009
INSPECTION COPY AVAILABLE

Understanding social welfare movements
Jason Annetts, Alex Law, Wallace McNeish and Gerry Mooney

The book provides a timely and much needed overview of the changing nature of social welfare as it has been shaped by the demands of social movements.
PB £19.99 (US$35.95) **ISBN** 978 1 84742 096 1 **HB** £65.00 (US$99.00) **ISBN** 978 1 84742 097 8
304 pages June 2009
INSPECTION COPY AVAILABLE

Understanding human need
Hartley Dean

"*Hartley Dean's book certainly meets a need: he expertly summarises debates over what human needs are, how they relate to happiness and capabilities, and what they entail for human rights and social policies. An invaluable book.*" Ian Gough, Emeritus Professor of Social Policy, University of Bath
PB £21.99 (US$34.95) **ISBN** 978 1 84742 189 0 **HB** £65.00 (US$89.95) **ISBN** 978 1 84742 190 6
240 pages February 2010
INSPECTION COPY AVAILABLE

Understanding social citizenship (second edition)
Themes and perspectives for policy and practice
Peter Dwyer

"*A second edition of this excellent book is most welcome. Dwyer's understanding of social citizenship is second to none and this new edition provides an updated discussion and assessment of all the practical and theoretical issues that students need to know about this important area of study.*" Nick Ellison, University of Leeds
PB £19.99 (US$32.95) **ISBN** 978 1 84742 328 3 HB £65.00 (US$85.00) **ISBN** 978 1 84742 329 0
280 pages June 2010
INSPECTION COPY AVAILABLE

For a full listing of all titles in the series visit www.policypress.co.uk

www.policypress.co.uk

INSPECTION COPIES AND ORDERS AVAILABLE FROM:
Marston Book Services • PO Box 269 • Abingdon • Oxon OX14 4YN UK
INSPECTION COPIES
Tel: +44 (0) 1235 465500 • Fax: +44 (0) 1235 465556 • Email: inspections@marston.co.uk
ORDERS
Tel: +44 (0) 1235 465500 • Fax: +44 (0) 1235 465556 • Email: direct.orders@marston.co.uk

UNDERSTANDING THE ENVIRONMENT AND SOCIAL POLICY

Edited by Tony Fitzpatrick

First published in Great Britain in 2011 by
The Policy Press
University of Bristol
Fourth Floor, Beacon House
Queen's Road
Bristol BS8 1QU
UK

t: +44 (0)117 331 4054
f: +44 (0)117 331 4093
tpp-info@bristol.ac.uk
www.policypress.co.uk

North American office:
The Policy Press
c/o International Specialized Books Services
920 NE 58th Avenue, Suite 300
Portland, OR 97213-3786, USA
t: +1 503 287 3093
f: +1 503 280 8832
info@isbs.com

British Library Cataloguing in Publication Data
A catalogue record for this book is available from the British Library.

Library of Congress Cataloging-in-Publication Data
A catalog record for this book has been requested.

ISBN 978 1 84742 379 5 paperback
ISBN 978 1 84742 380 1 hardcover

The right of Tony Fitzpatrick to be identified as editor of this work has been asserted by him in accordance with the 1988 Copyright, Designs and Patents Act.

The statements and opinions contained within this publication are solely those of the editor and contributors and not of the University of Bristol, The Policy Press or the Social Policy Association. The University of Bristol, The Policy Press and the Social Policy Association disclaim responsibility for any injury to persons or property resulting from any material published in this publication.

The Policy Press works to counter discrimination on grounds of gender, race, disability, age and sexuality.

Cover design by Qube Design Associates, Bristol
Front cover: photograph kindly supplied by www.alamy.com
Printed and bound in Great Britain by Hobbs, Southampton
The Policy Press uses environmentally responsible print partners.

FSC
www.fsc.org
MIX
Paper from
responsible sources
FSC® C020438

Contents

List of figures, tables and boxes

Figures

Tables

Boxes

Detailed contents

Notes on contributors

Nikolay Angelov holds a PhD in Economics from Uppsala University, Sweden, and since 2006 he has been a post-doctoral researcher there at the Department of Economics. His main research interest is in microeconometrics. In particular, he has worked on discrete choice models with applications to educational choice and firm mergers. He has previously done work on time-series analysis, more specifically unit-root testing.

Michael Cahill is Reader in Social Policy at the University of Brighton, UK. He is the author of *The new social policy* (1994, Palgrave), *The environment and social policy* (2002, Routledge) and *Transport, environment and society* (2010, Open University Press). With Tony Fitzpatrick he edited *Environmental issues and social welfare* (2002, Blackwell) and *Environment and welfare* (2002, Palgrave Macmillan). He is currently the reviews editor for the journal *Social Policy and Administration*.

Alan Carter holds the historic Chair in Moral Philosophy at the University of Glasgow, UK. Previous chairs held have included Adam Smith, Francis Hutcheson and Thomas Reid. Previously, Professor Carter taught at the University of Colorado at Boulder, Heythrop College (University of London) and University College Dublin. He has been a Visiting Professor at the University of British Columbia and the University of Bucharest. Working principally in political philosophy, moral philosophy and environmental philosophy, he is the author of over 60 articles in academic journals and three books, including *A radical green political theory* (1999, Routledge).

Philip Catney is Lecturer in Politics at Keele University, UK. His research interests are in the areas of environmental policy, urban regeneration, British public policy and political economy. He is co-editor of *Sustainable brownfield regeneration* (2007, Blackwell) (with Tim Dixon, Mike Raco and David Lerner) and has had articles published in many journals, including the *Journal of Environmental Policy and Planning*, *British Politics*, *Public Administration*, *Environmental Hazards* and the *Journal of Environmental Management*.

Timothy Doyle is Professor of Politics and International Relations at Keele University, UK, and also Professor of Politics and International Studies at the University of Adelaide, Australia. His most recent works include *Environment and politics* (2008, with D. McEachern, Routledge), which has been translated into Korean, Turkish and Hindi, *Beyond borders* (2008, edited with B. Doherty, Routledge) and *Crucible for survival* (2008, edited with M. Risely, Rutgers University Press). He has been an environmental and human rights activist since the 1980s, is founding co-editor of the *Journal of the Indian Ocean Region* and founding director of Human and Environmental Security for the Indian Ocean Research Group in New Delhi and Perth.

Tony Fitzpatrick is Reader at the University of Nottingham, UK. He is the co-editor of the journal *Policy & Politics* and was the principal editor of the three-volume *International encyclopaedia of social policy* (2006, with Nick Manning, Gill Pascall, Huck-ju Kwon and James Midgley, Routledge). His other recent books include *Applied ethics and social problems* (2008, The Policy Press), *Voyage to utopias* (2010, The Policy Press) and the second edition of *Welfare theory* (2011, Palgrave). He has published extensively in journals such as the *Journal of Social Policy*, *Environmental Politics*, the *International Journal of Social Welfare* and *Economy & Society*. Three of his books have been translated into foreign languages, including Japanese and Korean translations of *Freedom and security* (1999, Macmillan).

John Hannigan is Professor of Sociology at the University of Toronto, Canada. He is the author of *Environmental sociology* (2006, Routledge) and *Fantasy city* (1998, Routledge). The latter was nominated for the 1999–2000 John Porter Award of the Canadian Sociology and Anthropology Association. *Environmental sociology* has been translated into Chinese, Japanese, Korean and Portuguese. He is presently working on a new book for Polity Press, *Disasters without borders* (2012).

Sherilyn MacGregor is Lecturer at the University of Keele, UK. She co-edits the journal *Environmental Politics* with Professor Andrew Dobson and her recent publications include *Beyond mothering earth* (2006, University of British Columbia Press), and many chapters and articles in journals such as *Ethics, Place and Environment* and *Ethics and the Environment*.

Susan Molyneux-Hodgson is Senior Lecturer in Sociology and Director of Research Training for Social Sciences at the University of Sheffield, UK. Her work is in the field of science studies and she publishes in both the sociology of science literature and in interdisciplinary and engineering journals. She has particular interests in water and society issues, and more generally in processes of scientific knowledge production. In 2007 she co-edited *Policy reconsidered* with Zoe Irving (The Policy Press).

David Phillips was Reader in Social Policy at the University of Sheffield, UK, and is now involved with non-governmental organisations (NGOs) specialising in sustainable development and education in West Africa. His research interests include the quality of life, 'social quality', social cohesion and social exclusion. *Quality of life* (2006, Routledge) has been translated into Japanese and his most recent book (co-authored with C.K. Chan and K.L. Ngok) is *Social policy in China* (2008, The Policy Press).

Claire Quinn is an ecological social scientist with over 10 years' experience working on interdisciplinary projects in Africa and the UK. Her research interests concern the links between ecological and socioeconomic processes in the management and conservation of natural resources. She currently works as Lecturer in Natural Resource Management in the Sustainability Research Institute at the University of Leeds, UK. Her research focuses on the distribution of property rights in multi-resource systems and the implications for management; and livelihood vulnerability and adaptation to environmental change in agricultural communities.

Carolyn Snell is Lecturer at the University of York, UK, having previously worked as a Research Associate for the Stockholm Environment Institute. Her research interests include water and fuel poverty, people and their local environment and sustainable schools. She is the author of *The impact of Local Agenda 21 in England* (2009, VDM Publishing House Ltd) and has published in many journals, including the *Journal of Youth Studies, Local Environment, Journal of Urban Regeneration and Renewal* and *Policy Studies*. A co-authored 2006 paper in *Transport Research Review* won the Charley V. Wootan Award in recognition of a paper of outstanding merit.

Glenda Verrinder is Senior Lecturer at La Trobe University, Australia. Prior to this she worked in various roles within the health sector of metropolitan and rural Victoria. Her current teaching, research and publications reflect her interest in population health with respect to health promotion and ecological sustainability. She is the co-editor of *Sustainability and health* (2005, with John Grootjans, Jan Ritchie and Valerie A. Brown, Earthscan) and co-author of *Promoting health* (2010, with Lyn Talbot, Elsevier Australia).

Maria Vredin Johansson holds a PhD in Economics from Umeå University, Sweden. She began her career at the Swedish National Road and Transport Research Institute, working with economic valuations of time and lives for transport analyses. In 2001 she was a post-doctoral researcher at the University of Sydney, Australia. Since 2003 she has worked as a researcher at Uppsala University, Sweden, mainly focusing on environmental economics. In 2008 she also started working at the National Institute of Economic Research in Stockholm, where she evaluates environmental policy instruments to provide an evidence-based foundation for Swedish environmental policy.

Stephen M. Wheeler is Associate Professor at the University of California at Davis, USA, and has previously taught at the University of New Mexico and UC Berkeley. Author of *Planning for sustainability* (2004, Routledge) and co-editor of *The sustainable urban development reader* (2008, with Timothy Beatley, Routledge), his research interests include sustainable development, planning for climate change, urban design and built landscapes of urban regions. Professor Wheeler's awards include the 2009 William R. and June Dale Prize for Excellence in Urban and Regional Planning.

Acknowledgements

I am grateful to the series editor, Saul Becker, for inviting me to take this project on and to the reviewers of the original proposal and the draft chapters. Thanks, as always to The Policy Press, especially Emily Watt. I am also grateful to to the contributors who were always professional, encouraging and helpful. There was only one contributor who was a complete pain: rude, lazy and frequently stupid. There is no way in the world I ever want to work with this person ever again. Unfortunately, it was me.

Acronyms and abbreviations

BCA	basic capital asset
CCPI	Climate Change Performance Index
CDM	Clean Development Mechanism
CFCs	chlorofluorocarbons
CO_2	carbon dioxide
DALYS	disability adjusted life years
DWP	Department for Work and Pensions
EJ	environmental justice
EKC	environmental Kuznets curve
EM	ecological modernisation
EU	European Union
GDP	gross domestic product
GEF	Global Environment Facility
GGND	Global Green New Deal
GHGs	greenhouse gases
GNP	gross national product
IMF	International Monetary Fund
IPCC	Intergovernmental Panel on Climate Change
LEED	Leadership in Energy and Environmental Design
LETS	Local Exchange Trading Systems
MDGs	Millennium Development Goals
NGOs	non-governmental organisations
NHS	National Health Service
OECD	Organisation of Economic Co-operation and Development
POPs	persistent organic pollutants
ppm	parts per million
R&D	Research and Development
SUV	sports utility vehicle
UN	United Nations
UNCED	UN Conference on Environment and Development
UNDP	United Nations Development Programme
UNEP	United Nations Environment Programme
UV	ultraviolet radiation
WCED	World Commission on Environment and Development
WHO	World Health Organization
WTO	World Trade Organization
WTR	work time reduction
WWF	World Wildlife Fund for Nature

Introduction

Tony Fitzpatrick

Environmental issues are central to the political, social, economic and moral challenges of the 21st century, although public debate regarding the scale of those challenges remains fairly rudimentary. Governments have been slow to react for many reasons, some of them less forgivable than others. It is true that the problems we face are unprecedented, leaving us without a template for reform and making it extremely difficult to achieve the long-term, global agreement and action that is needed. Yet at the same time, too many governments have been the willing prisoners of their pasts, disinclined to break with the reassuring attitudes and habits of old. Politicians and electorates have locked themselves into a circular culture of mutual denial, each taking the other's lack of urgency as an excuse for its own inertia and apathy. Those wishing to sleep through the ecological alarm bells gleefully seize upon any scientific mistakes made when estimating future increases in global warming. Thus, while, since the late 1980s there have been various international protocols and a spreading consciousness of environmental risks, we continue to daydream, disregarding the shouts and warnings of even the most optimistic and pragmatic commentators.

How severe are the environmental problems we face? How steep is the decline of essential natural resources? How quick is the rise of global warming and how durable will its effects be? What are the short- and long-term impacts on society? Who are the most vulnerable groups? How should we respond to these dilemmas? Can we rely on relatively modest reforms (improved technologies, new forms of market regulation, etc)? Or do we need to make more substantial changes to our institutions, our systems of governance, our social cultures, our very understanding of what it is to be human? How quickly must we act? How late is it already? This book explores these questions, coming at them from a particular direction.

Relevance of social policy

In the UK, 30% of national income, or about two thirds of government spending, is directed towards welfare services. Some European countries spend more, some less. This means that much of what Europeans are asked to vote for (or against) during elections concerns social policies. Levels of welfare expenditure fluctuate across the rest of the world. Yet relatively few countries now deny that, however organised and funded, governments have a social and moral responsibility to ensure the provision of basic needs like housing, healthcare and education, including protection against economic contingencies (such as unemployment) and personal contingencies (reductions of income during periods of incapacity, long-term illness, childcare and old age). Although a diversity of welfare systems, cultural values and political goals exists, social policies are deeply embedded within most societies and economies.

There are always difficulties in trying to offer a simple yet sophisticated definition of social policy. The term bears differing connotations in different national and, increasingly, post-national contexts. In some countries it is instantly recognisable; in others, it means little until you mention its bigger, older cousins such as 'public policy' or 'political economy'. For academics and researchers, social policy denotes an interdisciplinary patchwork of multiple elements: politics, sociology, philosophy, law, criminology, economics, social work, psychology and cultural studies.

Since you have to start somewhere, the contributors to this book were asked to consider 'systematic public interventions relating to social needs, well-being and problems'. By and large, when this book mentions 'social policy' it is referring to the subject of academic and non-academic research and public debate; when 'social policies' are mentioned reference is being made to actual government services, systems, reforms and interventions. Contributors were also advised, however, not to censor their own disciplinary and geographical understandings of what these might involve. In short, this book incorporates the core concerns and understandings of social policy while acknowledging that a diversity of views and conceptualisations is inevitable and indeed desirable.

We immediately face a paradox, then. Social policies are essential to the very societies and economies that are slowly having to wake up to environmental imperatives. Yet the literature that encompasses both subjects remains thin on the ground (see, for example, Khakee et al, 1995; Huby, 1998; Cahill, 2001; Cahill and Fitzpatrick, 2002; Fitzpatrick and Cahill, 2002a; Fitzpatrick, 2003a). There are several reasons for this.

First, it could be that many of the relevant debates are hiding beneath other discipline-specific headings. Academic researchers tend to be highly specialised creatures who may fail to make connections between, or offer translations into, other disciplinary idioms. Second, social policies have traditionally been the 'handmaiden' to politics and economics. There is still a widespread view that once you have worked out the hard-headed details of political and economic organisation then other, 'softer' forms of public administration can follow on behind. Yet we surely cannot understand a green economy without attending to green social policies too. Finally, it is almost certainly the case that social policy and government policies have contributed to the denial mentioned above. Some of the daydreams we have indulged in have been welfare state daydreams. Sometimes for good reasons. If people need jobs, it can be argued, then let us grow the economy and worry about climate change later. However, this culture of deference and deferment now has to change.

That said, pick up social policy books these days and you will increasingly find some mention of the environment, often connected to discussions concerning globalisation, social risks and international development. The environment is now regarded as important to social policy researchers, teachers, practitioners and policy makers to an extent that it was not, even recently, in the 1990s. Yet such publications will often 'smear' the environment onto other subjects, like spreading another layer on top of a multistorey cake. To some extent this is understandable. Social policy is a vast, interdisciplinary field with lots of ideas, developments, proposals and vulnerable groups vying for attention. But the premise of this book is that sustainability is the *sine qua non* of everything else. If we don't get this right, we don't get the chance to make anything else right either.

Conversely, books, articles, reports, and so on dealing with the environment, green politics, ecological economics and so forth have usually neglected social policies. Again, this is understandable. In addition to climatology and other physical sciences, it seems especially important to question what we produce and consume (economics), why we do so (philosophy) and how we govern production and consumption (politics). To the extent that it registers at all, social policies tend to be buried under the rubric of 'public policy' or 'public services'. This has been the case within government itself where the prevailing orthodox – 'ecological modernisation' (see below) – has also set the agenda for discussions of public sector goods and services.

But even politics and public policy books tend to neglect the significance of *social* policy. One of the world's leading authorities, Michael Kraft (2011: 220), has said:

> Money spent on the environment is not available in the short run for other social purposes such as education and health care.

True, Kraft is distinguishing here between the short and the long term. Nevertheless, this either/or reference to '*other* social purposes' suggests a failure of imagination, even when it comes to short-term trade-offs, since money *can* be spent twice. For instance, measures to eliminate fuel poverty have both social and ecological benefits (see Chapter Seven).

Thus, we need to turn environmentalism and social policy from distant acquaintances into firm friends and it seems we need to do so with some urgency. Fortunately, the conversation is becoming noisier.

First, it is now practically impossible to discuss policies without reference to global agencies, agreements and networks, and, of course, ecological problems require global solutions. That said, second, green politics typically stresses the dangers of *neoliberal* globalisation and offers an alternative: a global coordination of *local* organisations and initiatives that highlights the human scale ('small is beautiful') of values that free markets can capture only imperfectly. In objecting to the emptying of localities by distant, top-down bureaucracies and unaccountable, impersonal corporations, environmentalism's reference to community and neighbourhood accords with the decentralising strategies of the 'new localism'. Third, the environmental values of precaution, sustainability and stewardship parallel the recent attention paid to care and obligation, expanding our understanding of citizenship and responsibility to encompass future generations, non-human animals, non-sentient beings and ecosystems. Finally, environmentalists have long argued that welfare cannot be accurately measured by national income accounts, such as gross domestic product (GDP), and that 'quality of life' is more than, and may be threatened by, material prosperity, rampant consumerism and competitive individualism (Jackson, 2002). The recent interest within social policy research in happiness, well-being and status equality is therefore welcome.

So, there are many congruities between environmentalism and social policies. As the United Nations Development Programme (UNDP) (2007: 14) puts it:

> Social protection programmes can help people cope with [climate change] risks while expanding opportunities for employment, nutrition and education. In Ethiopia the Productive Safety Net Programme is an attempt to strengthen the capacity of poor households to cope with droughts without having to sacrifice opportunities for health and education. In Latin America conditional cash transfers have been widely used to support a wide range of human development goals, including the protection of basic capabilities during a sudden crisis. In

southern Africa cash transfers have been used during droughts to protect long-run productive capacity.

But there are also potential incongruities. Some of these may simply require patient research and negotiation to resolve. For instance, while green technologies and markets offer many job-creating opportunities they may also contribute to those socioeconomic developments which have disrupted working-class communities over the last few decades, for example the shift away from mass manufacturing towards new service economies of flexibility and re-skilling.

But other incongruities are deeper. Although more scepticism than previously is now directed towards the ethos which has powered the development of modern societies (the assumption that well-being equals material affluence and economic growth), most environmentalists call for a rethink much deeper than governments and electorates seem currently willing to go. Addictions to short-termism, possessive individualism and acquisitive competition are deeply ingrained within our cultural psyches. If we cling to those cultural and socio-psychological habits whatever the cost then we may only succeed in slamming a narrowing window of opportunity down on our heads.

These dangers and opportunities concern social policy in two respects. First, modern welfare institutions developed within and according to the expectation that economic growth would continue indefinitely. Whatever goals it was meant to serve (redistribution, stability, social control, etc) the role of social policies was either not to threaten such growth or, wherever possible, to promote it. Central to the political arguments of the last three decades has been the question about whether and to what extent 20th-century welfare reforms achieved this. Second, the size and the scale of social expenditure in most developed economies means that, whatever measures are taken to address ecological problems, reorganisation of social policies will be crucial. Obviously, this means potentially major changes to what the state does and why. A mixed economy of welfare demands a mixed economy of eco-welfare too.

This book therefore derives from the assumption that there is an enormous amount of work to do in understanding the relationship between environmentalism and social policy – in all its positive and negative aspects. It is concerned to explore, consolidate and strengthen existing synergies, without ignoring the fundamental incongruity just outlined. The book draws in contributors from many countries and from many of the subjects out of which social policy is composed. As an introductory book, offering primers to a vast series of debates, it emphasises breadth while guiding readers on to further, more specialist understandings of each subject.

Scientific basics

What is the nature of the challenge? The entire book deals with this question – see Chapter One especially – but let us outline the basics here.

I hate to hit you with statistics this early on but it's unavoidable. According to the Intergovernmental Panel on Climate Change (IPCC) (2007: 37), whose reports every six or seven years are the most authoritative available, in pre-industrial times there were 280 parts of carbon dioxide (CO_2) for every million molecules of dry air. By 2005 this had risen to 379 parts per million (ppm) and by the time you are reading this book concentrations will be at least 390ppm (they are rising about 2ppm every year, with the rate of increase accelerating).[1] Doesn't sound like much, does it? 390? Unfortunately, compared to pre-industrial times, it means we have already experienced an average rise in global temperatures of approximately 0.8°C, with another 0.6°C almost certain to happen whatever we do and an additional 0.6°C after that also very likely. Again, doesn't sound like much? Yet 2°C is widely regarded as the upper limit beyond which global warming becomes dangerously unmanageable. Hansen et al (2008: 218) argue that we are already within the 'danger zone'.

According to the IPCC (2007: 48) the health status of millions of people, especially in developing countries, is going to be affected through increases in malnutrition, diarrhoeal and infectious diseases, and cardio-respiratory diseases due to higher concentrations of ground-level ozone in cities. Furthermore, even a rise of 0.8°C has led to increasing and disastrous incidents of hurricanes, floods, wildfires, droughts, deforestation, species extinction and heatwaves, all of which particularly affect the poorest. At 1.5°–2°C these will certainly be joined by severely rising sea levels, irreversible ice sheet loss, mass species extinctions, larger and more frequent droughts and famines, rainforest collapse, coral reef devastation, acidic oceans and mass ecological migration (and possibly ecological wars) as levels of potable water and crop yields decline. The consequences that might follow from increases of 3°–5°C, or even higher, can only be estimated. The world has not experienced such temperatures for 30–50 million years:

> ... human releases of carbon dioxide are possibly happening faster than any natural carbon releases since the beginning of life on earth. (Lynas, 2008: 236)

Take the following example. Until the late 19th century it was widely thought that there was a polar sea at the North Pole, one it would be possible to sail across. By the summers of the 2030s this may turn out to be eerily prescient. According to some scientists it might already be too late to save the Arctic ice from melting entirely during the summer and the Greenland ice sheet already faces a 50% chance of unstoppable melting, even if global warming is stabilised at 2°C. In short, even with the best scenarios, we face greater changes to our ecosystem than it has sustained for tens and possibly hundreds of thousands of years:

> Continued growth of greenhouse gas emissions, for just another decade, practically eliminates the possibility of near-term return of atmospheric composition beneath the tipping level for catastrophic effects....The stakes, for all life on the planet, surpass those of any previous crisis. The greatest danger is continued ignorance and denial, which could make tragic consequences unavoidable. (Hansen et al, 2008: 229)

> ... the ability of many ecosystems to adapt naturally will be exceeded this century. In addition, multiple barriers and constraints to effective adaptation exist in human systems. Unmitigated climate change would, in the long term, be likely to exceed the capacity of natural, managed and human systems to adapt. Reliance on adaptation alone could eventually lead to a magnitude of climate change to which effective adaptation is not possible, or will only be available at very high social, environmental and economic costs. (IPCC, 2007: 65)

Sustainability

To avoid the worst possibilities we need a politics based around the principle of sustainability. Environmentalists identify a disjunction between what we demand of the world and what the world is capable both of supplying (resources) and absorbing (pollution). If the demands we make are significantly larger than the planet's 'coping capacity' then ours is an unsustainable existence. Sustainability therefore implies reducing human demands and/or increasing the coping capacity of the Earth so that this disjunction is repaired.

But, as even the above figures make clear, sustainability has many dimensions. It implies *slowing* the rate of growth in emissions, *halting and stabilising* emissions so that global warming levels off and then *reducing* emissions so that global warming itself eventually reverses towards a level which can be maintained and which is not detrimental to humans, animals, future generations or the very ecosystem itself. And sustainability is also concerned with preserving a certain stock of non-renewable natural resources and replenishing the stock of renewables.

Even if a definition of sustainability can be agreed there are many scientific variables, conceptual debates and legitimate disagreements about the socioeconomic implications of the above. Therefore, sustainability is a political principle that can be thought of as a 'portal', an entrance into a series of debates. Its meaning and implications both can and should imply a degree of openness just as the contestability of other principles – liberty, democracy, equality – does not stop societies from valuing and trying to embody them; indeed, a wide degree of disagreement may be essential to any society claiming to *be* free, democratic or equal. It is the same with sustainability. The necessity of acting rapidly and meeting important targets should not be used to justify an illiberal, moralistic, intolerant, authoritarian approach. The principle of sustainability is, then, not an inflexible reference point and is certainly not shorthand for a 'green utopia'.

That said, if you claim that climate change is not occurring, or is occurring but is not attributable to human activity, then you won't find much sympathy here. There are legitimate debates to be had about the science. We should be open to such debates as science is, by definition, a potentially fallible enterprise. We are dealing with probabilities. But this does not mean we should give undue attention to global warming deniers. Furthermore, social scientists are fond of using the term 'social construct' to underline the extent to which 'facts' are assemblages of social categories, discourses, interpretative frames, paradigms and understandings (see Chapter Two). Yet nor should we use a constructionist veil to bind our eyes. Furedi (2002) regards the green movement as exemplifying the contemporary culture of anxiety, and its politics of fear, by exaggerating and demonising the risks we face. Yet the fact that many in the West feel anxious at exacerbating global warming does not imply that global warming is a mere projection *of* anxiety.

Varieties of green thought

Therefore, as with any ideological family, there are squabbles, arguments and occasional schisms between the members. Most environmentalists are likely to agree with the encapsulation of sustainability that has just been offered, but will also take it in many different directions, some of which are difficult to reconcile. How, then, can we reflect such differences while continuing to identify a core of green thinking?

There have been so many attempts over the years to chart the varieties of ecological thought that a comprehensive summary is not attempted here. However, by adapting one of the most influential attempts (Dryzek, 2005), let us plot some key perspectives.

Survivalists:
- Those who anticipate the worst and so advocate radical and drastic action to curb the most extreme events and ensure that humans can adapt to a world substantially different to today's. The politics of survivalism is often fatalistic, draconian and authoritarian.

Modernisers:
- Ecological modernisers are generally optimistic about environmental problems, recognising their seriousness but arguing that existing institutions and practices – economic growth, representative democracy, etc – are sufficient and can be adapted to cope with them. Modernisers therefore look to administrative, technical and technological solutions to global warming.

Social radicals:
- Social radicals are concerned with the social causes and impacts of climate change. If global warming is human-made then we ought to address its socioeconomic, cultural and moral origins. For socialists and Marxists this means attending to capitalist systems of production with their economic and material inequalities; for feminists it means challenging masculinist, patriarchal habits of domination, oppression and control.

Deep ecologists:
- Deep ecologists argue that only through a fundamental break with existing moral values and social philosophies can we cope with the challenges ahead. We need to rethink how we see ourselves and our place in nature. Humans have disrupted the natural and need to reinsert themselves into its web of biological interdependency.

Democratic pragmatists:
- Although, like social radicals, they recognise the social contexts of environmental issues, democratic pragmatists are less likely to recommend drastic changes to socioeconomic institutions. Instead, democratic reform possesses the necessary resources. Through improved forms of consultation and dialogue, popular opinion can be mobilised to demand transformations to our governing systems and social–moral assumptions.

Market liberals:
- Those who believe that unregulated markets will enable us to cope with ecological risks. Because the price mechanism makes scarce resources more expensive, demand for them is reduced so that (a) they are preserved, and (b) innovative technologies and industries develop as a way of using

these and other resources. Interference with markets makes it *less* likely that we will tackle global warming.

Conservationist conservatives:
- Sometimes driven by a dislike of industrialisation, consumerism and modernity, this label describes those who combine a love of nature and the land, often in patriotic and nationalistic terms, with an 'organic' politics of limits and stewardship. The more ambitious forms of green ideology might, if anything, disrupt our attempts to live within our means.

We could extend this list to include bioregionalists and animal welfare groups, for instance; and we could break each of the above categories down to reflect the differences that such headings smooth over. However, as an indicative summary of the last half-century of green thinking it can stand. If we now construct two axes – contrasting left versus right and radicals versus reformists – we come up with the following taxonomy.

Figure i.1: *A green political taxonomy*

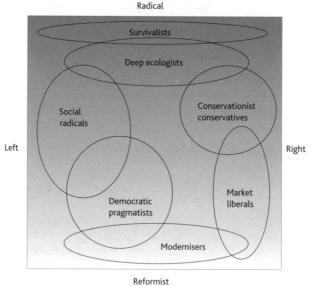

What we have captured here is an additional texture in green thought, from 'deep green' at the top of the box to 'light green' at the bottom (represented here by shading from dark to light). The distinction discriminates between those who prioritise sustainability above all else, and only regard value systems and political ideas as useful if they contribute to that environmental imperative; and those who seek synergies between green and non-green ways of thought, concerned to make sustainability consistent with other important objectives and principles. We can also see that each category overlaps with at least one other. For example, modernisers stretch across the political spectrum and may encompass democratic pragmatists and market liberals. Few people belong to just one group, in other words, and many may identify with several. You should of course feel free to play around with the figure, rearranging and even substituting the headings based on your own reading of the environmental literature.

Of its nature, social policy is a subject concerned to analyse and prescribe practical changes to political and economic systems. It may certainly be interested in the deeper foundations that concern deep ecologists, for instance, but is ultimately motivated by the question, 'how can we make this work?'. However, this does not necessarily imply limiting ourselves to the light green spectrum and you will find here many ideas that are socially radical in inspiration. For although welfare systems attract widespread political support they are more closely representative of a broad centre-left politics and this is reflected in the stance of the book's contributors. Overall, it is probably true to say that this publication is concerned with the darker shades of light green thinking and the lighter shades of dark green thinking.

The road from 2012

Nothing would please me more than for you to read these pages in 20 years time and think, 'thank God we came to our senses'. *Can* we act quickly and radically enough? Yes. The window of opportunity is still open, even if the gap it presents is closing steadily. *Will* we act quickly and radically enough? I have no idea.

As this book goes to press major international discussions are in progress about what should succeed the first phase of the Kyoto Protocol. Coming into effect in 1997 this committed most developed nations, by 2012, to reductions in greenhouse gas (GHG) emissions of 5.2% below their 1990 levels. Ongoing discussions relate not only to the fact that phase one ends in 2012 but also to a general perception that it failed. Perhaps that is too harsh of me. Perhaps Kyoto1 was rather like a mock examination where you test yourself in preparation for the real one. Unfortunately, our failure in the mock exam has made it harder to succeed next time around.

True, we know far more now than we did when the Climate Convention was negotiated in 1992; and it is also true that climate change denial at the level of government is much less in evidence than it once was. Still, if we have struggled to achieve even the modest goals of the Protocol then the gap between what we ought to do and what we seem able and willing to do is painfully wide. How do we reduce that gap? What elements of Kyoto1 should we retain or abandon? And can we move fast enough since we might have, at best, barely a decade left to avoid the worst climate change scenarios?

When preparing this book I had hoped to report that the first substantial discussions on moving beyond Kyoto1 gave grounds for optimism. Yet at the Copenhagen Summit in December 2009 all that was settled was the *agreement* to limit global warming to the 2°C threshold mentioned above. No action plans, nothing that was legally binding, just an aspiration. This was very little. If this inaction had been directly due to the financial crisis of 2008–09 then, paradoxically, things might currently look rosier. Yet while the recession aided those who believe that action to address climate change should be delayed – always tomorrow, always once we are just a little bit richer – the actual reasons for Copenhagen's failure are deep rooted and precede the economic crisis.

'We all have a responsibility for fixing the environment,' pleads the West. 'Yes,' reply developing countries, 'but you broke it and so the first and principal responsibility for fixing it is yours'. Add into the mix the usual playground politicking, national self-interest, economic horse-trading and business-as-usual instincts, and hey presto! The distance we have to travel lengthens the longer we take to depart.

During the American Civil War observers would sometimes notice that the closer they were to a battle the quieter it sounded. This is because of a phenomenon known as 'acoustic shadows', where noise fails to carry because of wind currents and various obstructions. We are dangerously close to a battle now but choose to hear only some of the reverberations. Noise levels are set to rise. The question is, will we be adequately prepared for them when they do?

Understanding the environment and social policy will be published shortly after the follow-up Mexico Summit of December 2010 and you will need to judge for yourselves whether that conference has set us on the right path or not.

The book

How to use this book

Summary boxes:
*   contained within each chapter these offer quick summaries of relevant material (such as this one!). Overviews and chapter summaries are also included.
Questions for discussion:
*   the chapters contain questions at the end that you can use to review your understanding of each topic.
Key further reading and useful websites:
*   the chapters also contain suggestions for further reading and the addresses of some useful websites you might wish to consult.
Glossary:
*   at the end of the book short definitions of key terms are provided and, within the chapters, these are highlighted in **bold** when they first become essential to the narrative.

Standard introductory textbooks to social policy can be highly diverse but tend to focus on some or all of the following:

*   Criminal justice
*   Cross-national comparisons, international factors and globalisation
*   Culture, media and social identity
*   Economics and expenditure
*   Education
*   Family
*   Health and healthcare
*   History
*   Housing
*   Law and legislation
*   Mixed economies of welfare
*   Policy making, governance and administration
*   Political theories, concepts and ideologies
*   Social care, social services and social work
*   Social inequalities, social divisions, distributions and poverty
*   Social security and income maintenance
*   Vulnerable groups
*   Work and employment.

If environmental issues are altering the parameters of social policy then presumably they carries implications for each of the above. Yet the ecological agenda reconfigures these topics while according greater priority to some more than others. The following chapters therefore incorporate many of the above themes, if not necessarily in ways that correspond precisely to standard social policy texts. For instance, there is no distinct overview of social security but discussions relevant to income maintenance do appear in Chapters Three, Six, Seven and Eleven. Housing is explored in the context of fuel poverty and urban planning (Chapters Seven and Nine, respectively) and education within Chapter Twelve. The book incorporates evidence from many countries and takes account of development issues (see Chapters Four and Thirteen especially) but is largely addressed to audiences in the affluent West. The book reviews the main debates in a fashion that seems appropriate but also insists you see it as the start of a (hopefully) long conversation.

This is because other publications in the *Understanding Welfare* series usually have a distinct literature on which to draw. This book, however, is more speculative. We cannot review 'eco-social policies' because there are few examples of such policies in existence. The agendas of environmental and social policy are only slowly coming together and the aim of this publication is to help them on their way. But it cannot offer a comprehensive overview of what barely exists yet.

So do not expect to find a blueprint for a 'green welfare state'. Even assuming that the social policies of the future can be described in such terms there are likely to be many institutional forms adopted. Without precedents or templates we are having to feel our way. Instead, this book raises key questions, both examining and assessing some of the provisional responses that have been given to those questions so far. We need to act urgently but also thoughtfully.

Synopsis

As such, contributors were asked to outline and explore the key challenges faced within their respective subjects and to explain and assess the key responses that have been, or can be, proposed and implemented. Within this broad parameter each contributor has then summarised their subject according to how the relevant debates and literatures currently appear to them.

In Chapter One, Susan Hodgson and David Phillips present the essential environmental challenge by examining the causes of climate change and presenting some of the main scientific data. They then review the key implications of climate change on weather events and related phenomena and analyse the principal solutions that have been proposed.

In Chapter Two John Hannigan discusses three major explanations for the environmental crisis: the limits to growth, the treadmill of production and the consumerist ethic. He considers the pros and cons of each while discussing the concepts of sustainable development and sustainable consumption. He concludes by considering how such concepts are socially constructed, especially in terms of the policy-making process.

Chapter Three then introduces social policy into the picture. I outline the principal criticisms made of social policies by environmentalists and then review some of the responses researchers and policy makers have made to the environmental agenda. The chapter then investigates a range of global warming targets, explores the parameters of a green economy and outlines the basics of an eco-social policy agenda.

Given that social policy deals with interventions at the interface of society and state, Philip Catney and Tim Doyle, in Chapter Four, then offer a detailed analysis of the state's role in the creation of the environmental crisis and consider what a 'green state' might imply. They draw what they call the 'Global South' into the discussion and suggest that, in many respects, developing nations have much to teach affluent countries about how to synergise social, welfare and environmental imperatives.

Having outlined the main challenges we face the book then turns more firmly to the various conceptual and institutional resources we have available to us.

We begin with moral philosophy. In Chapter Five, Alan Carter discusses the distinction between consequentialist and deontological moral theories, arguing that we should take temporally and geographically distant future persons into account, as well as sentient non-human animals and the Earth's ecosystems. He concludes that any convincing environmental ethic will include anthropocentric, zoocentric and ecocentric perspectives. In Chapter Six I also offer a pluralistic account when looking at political philosophy, specifically debates concerning justice. I offer a framework for understanding the concept of 'environmental justice' by arguing that none of the familiar philosophies provide an exhaustive account of it.

The book then begins to consider a series of institutional and policy arenas that represent key sites within which issues of environmental and social policy may be said to intersect. Indeed, the work begins in Chapter Six where I explore some of the more radical proposals for translating environmental justice and social justice into actual policy reforms. Chapter Seven then turns more to existing practices. It explores the types, the governance and the contexts of established environmental policies. It also offers a case study of fuel poverty in order to learn lessons from one topic where environmental and social policy agendas are slowly beginning to converge.

Glenda Verrinder then pursues this theme with reference to health in Chapter Eight. She establishes that the prerequisite for human health is a healthy ecosystem and therefore appropriate built and social environments also. For the most part, she insists, international policies have failed to impede the widening gap in health inequalities between the most and least deprived. In an extensive review of initiatives stretching back decades she concludes that national and international policies need to cut across different sectors in order to protect the health of the Earth and its people

Chapters Nine and Ten then turn to issues of urban planning, habitation and mobility. In Chapter Nine, Stephen Wheeler reviews the key questions and problems facing cities, looking specifically at land use, housing policy, housing design, transport, infrastructure and public spaces. He outlines some key developments around the world and summarises the planning difficulties faced by the developing world. Michael Cahill then focuses on transport. Chapter Ten explains how the car in particular has transformed social space and relations, creating significant health hazards and new forms of exclusion.

We then turn to debates concerning social participation. Chapter Eleven looks at the literature on 'green jobs' and employment issues. Nikolay Angelov and Maria Vredin Johansson show how the green sector of the economy possesses a potential for both high levels of employment and a capacity to generate high levels of revenue. Sherilyn MacGregor then investigates the connections between citizenship, care and environmental policy in Chapter Twelve. By understanding each in relation to the others, she proposes, we may become more able to shift towards sustainable ways of living and interacting.

Finally, in Chapter Thirteen, Carolyn Snell and Claire Quinn offer an overview of global, development issues. They review the main challenges for sustainable development, the key initiatives in international decision making over recent decades and, as illustrations, describe and assess two environment-related programmes.

The concluding chapter then summarises where all of this takes us and suggests further questions for debate and research.

Note

[1] Carbon dioxide (CO_2) emissions are a useful and familiar shorthand for understanding what is at stake. But you should also be aware that scientists work with other, slightly different yardsticks too. The greenhouse gases (GHGs) include CO_2, methane, nitrous oxide and halocarbons; collectively, these are termed 'carbon dioxide equivalents' (CO_2e).

one

The environmental challenge

Susan M. Hodgson and David Phillips

Overview

This chapter presents the main arguments relating to climate change. It outlines:

- the causes and some of the implications of climate change;
- the main solutions that have been proposed;
- issues of biodiversity, water provision, waste and resource depletion.

Throughout, we aim to show how these challenges constitute *socio-technical problems* that need to be addressed.

Introduction

What counts as an environmental problem changes over time. Yet few would deny that current environmental challenges are many. In this chapter we aim to provide an overview of major environmental challenges of direct relevance to students and researchers in the social sciences. The primary focus is on global climate change, as many other challenges relate, directly or indirectly, to this issue. For example, concerns about biological diversity can arise directly from the destruction of habitats; habitat destruction, however, could be the result of land management policies aimed at increasing the production of plant stuffs to make biofuel (an alternative to fossil fuels). At the same time, the shift towards biofuels has led to food production problems: for example, land is being used to farm plants for fuel rather than plants for food, thereby affecting food supplies and costs. Also, climate change effects result in some crops becoming no longer suitable for certain environments. Thus, a wide range of environmental issues is actually intertwined and forms a complex web of concerns. Additionally, matters of the environment and socio-political concerns are rarely easy to separate and what may look like a potential technical or social solution to an environmental problem may reinforce existing, or create new, environmental and social problems.

What is global warming?

The Earth's temperature has not been constant in the past. Indeed our planet has gone through several periods of global cooling and global warming as it has moved in and out of what we call 'ice ages'. Why, then, is so much attention being paid now to the phenomenon of global warming if it is something that has happened before? This is because some of the warming that is taking place now is believed to have different causes from previous warmings; it is what the textbooks call 'anthropogenic', which means it has been caused primarily by human activity, unlike previous global temperature shifts which were due entirely to natural causes. The scientific consensus is that human activities have been warming the world and it will continue to get hotter for the next hundred years or so, irrespective of whatever we choose to do now. *Figure 1.1* charts the annual and five-year average changes in temperature, from the mid–19th century onwards.

Predictions suggest that if we change our behaviour for the better immediately, then the increase in warming will be kept under control to some extent; if we carry on in the same way as we do now then the warming will increase and the consequences will be dire, at least for a large proportion of the world's population.

Summary box

The term 'global warming' refers both to (a) the anthropogenic increase in the temperature that has already taken place on the Earth's surface and near-surface air and oceans, and (b) its continuation into the future.

In the past the term has been extremely controversial; it is only recently that some pundits and a few governments – particularly the USA – have accepted its existence, and some commentators still prefer to use the less dangerous-sounding term 'climate change' (Henson, 2008: 6; Houghton, 2009: 13). Arguably, 'climate change' *is* a more appropriate term because the anticipated effects are not just in temperature, but also in other aspects of the climate, such as changes in rainfall patterns.

Figure 1.1: Increases in global temperatures

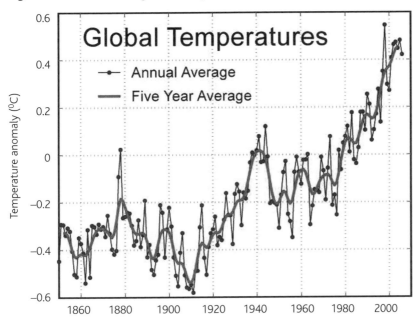

Source: Image created by Robert A. Rohde/Global Warming Art, from publicly available data.

Causes

The climate can change due to a number of reasons, including shifts in the Earth's orbit and the sun's intensity. Anthropogenic warming is to do with greenhouse gases (GHGs). GHGs were given their name because the atmosphere is like a natural greenhouse that keeps the Earth warm: without any GHGs the Earth would be 35°C colder (Maslin, 2004: 4). Naturally occurring GHGs in the atmosphere include water vapour, carbon dioxide (CO_2), ozone, methane and nitrous oxide and their level had been relatively stable for thousands of years.

Recently, the world has been getting hotter. Over the same period the composition of the Earth's atmosphere has been changed by increased human activity that produces CO_2 particularly by burning fossil fuels (in power stations, cars, lorries, ships and aeroplanes, etc), cement production and deforestation. *Figure 1.2* shows the percentage contribution from different sectors of human activity to overall GHG emissions, and to the three main individual gases (CO_2, methane and nitrous oxide).

Figure 1.2: *Annual greenhouse gas emissions by sector*

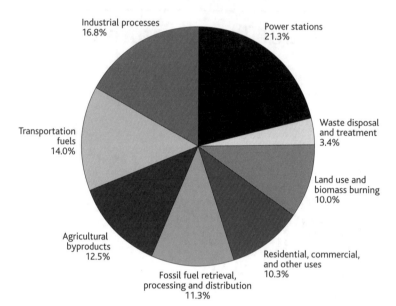

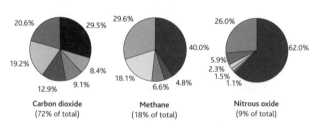

Source: Image created by Robert A. Rohde/Global Warming Art, from publicly available data

These human-made CO_2 emissions account for 72% of the added greenhouse effect to date (Houghton, 2009: 35). Once CO_2 is in the atmosphere it stays there for thousands of years before dispersing. Indeed the world's most prestigious and influential body researching global warming, the Intergovernmental Panel on Climate Change (IPCC) (2007: 17), warns that

> ...both past and future anthropogenic carbon dioxide emissions will continue to contribute to warming and sea level rise for

more than a millennium, due to the time scales required for removal of this gas from the atmosphere.

The IPCC (2007: 10) also tells us that:

> Most of the observed increase in global average temperature since the mid-20th century is *very likely* due to the observed increase in anthropogenic greenhouse gas concentrations.

The conclusions on climate change are endorsed by all the national academies of science in the major industrialised societies (see, for example, The Royal Society, 2005). The IPCC's use of the term 'very likely' rather than 'certain' here is a reflection of the uncertainty inherent in all scientific work, genuine scientific caution and of the complexity of the phenomenon under study. Most other scientific commentators are more forceful. For example, The Royal Society (2008: 11) (the UK's national academy of science) states: 'Our scientific understanding of climate change is sufficiently sound to make us highly confident that greenhouse gas emissions are causing global warming'. This can be seen graphically in **Figure 1.3**, which shows CO_2 emissions as being stable at around 260–280ppm (parts per million) in the atmosphere for a period of around 10,000 years, rising

Figure 1.3: *Changes in greenhouse gases from ice core and modern data*

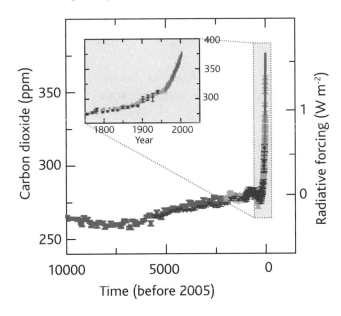

Source: IPCC (2007: 3)

to around 300ppm in the early 20th century and then rapidly rising to over 350ppm at the beginning of the 21st century and 387ppm in 2008 (IPCC, 2007: 3).

How bad is global warming?

So, it is clear that the Earth *has* been getting hotter. According to the IPCC (2007: 5),

> ... warming of the climate system is unequivocal as is now obvious from observation of increases in global average air and ocean temperatures, widespread melting of snow and ice, and rising global average sea level.It would seem plausible that if human activities have added to global warming then reversing these actions should, in a few years time, lead to its reverse: global cooling. Unfortunately this will not happen. We noted above that once CO_2 gets into the atmosphere it stays there for a considerable time. Carbon dioxide is, of course, absorbed by vegetation, especially forests, and by water, for example, seas. The issue is that the increase in GHGs being emitted into the atmosphere now outstrips the capacity of forests and seas to absorb them. The consequences of this are truly awesome:... the climate change that takes place due to increases in carbon dioxide concentration is largely irreversible ... atmospheric temperatures do not drop significantly for at least 1000 years. (Solomon et al, 2008: 1704)

The IPCC (2007: 5) also notes that global warming had increased by 0.74°C (± 0.18°) over the 100 years between 1906 and 2005 – or 0.074°C per decade – and had increased by nearly double that rate in the last 50 years, at 0.13°C per decade. Eleven of the 12 years between 1995 and 2006 rank in the 12 warmest years ever recorded and 20 of the 21 hottest years ever measured were in the past 25 years (Gore, 2007: 48).Looking to the future, the IPCC's mid-range estimate of an average global increase this century of 2°–3°C leads The Royal Society (2008: 10) to predict that the Earth will experience a larger climate change than it has had for at least 10,000 years. The IPCC presents six scenarios for the future in its latest report. In the least pessimistic scenario, if all feasible steps are taken to minimise global warming, then it is anticipated that by 2100 the Earth will be between 1.1°C and 2.0°C hotter. The most pessimistic scenario, where we all carry on as normal and emissions rise in line with expected rises in energy demand, is that temperatures will rise by more than 6°C. The most probable outcome is somewhere between these two, with average temperatures rising by around 4°C by 2100 (Giddens, 2009: 21).

Houghton's definitive text on global warming reminds us that the difference in average global temperature between the coldest part of an ice age and the warm periods in between ice ages is only about five or six degrees: 'we can see that a few degrees in this global average can represent a big change in climate' (Houghton, 2009: 13-14).

But what are the effects of these few degrees of extra warmth and what will the effects be of further warming? The effects will be various and include:

Sea and ice temperatures:
Temperature increases have been measured even at depths of 3,000 metres and the average ocean temperature has increased over the past 130 years by 0.65°C at the surface (Maslin, 2004: 49). At first sight, this does not appear to be a major change but the average figure hides dramatic differences: for example, in the 24 years between 1982 and 2006 temperatures in the Baltic Sea, North Sea and South China Sea all rose by more than 1.2°C (Giddens, 2009: 20). Average Arctic temperatures rose at double the global rate over the past hundred years and the Arctic could be ice-free by 2030.

Sea level:
A significant proportion (up to 80%) of the temperature rise is absorbed by the oceans, expanding the water and contributing to increases in the sea level. Between 1880 and 2000 it rose by 200mm (see ***Figure 1.4***). The average annual sea level rise throughout the 20th century was 0.17mm; between 1962 and 2003 it rose to 1.8mm; and between 1993 and 2003 it reached 3.1mm.

There has also been widespread melting of glaciers and ice caps particularly in Greenland and Antarctica, which has also contributed to sea level rise (Houghton, 2009: 179). Since 1978, Arctic sea ice has shrunk by 2.7% per decade and the Arctic ice cap is now less than half the size it was 50 years ago. The situation in Greenland is perhaps even more troubling; although its contribution to the rise in sea level has so far been less than that of Antarctica, observations in 2008–09 have identified rapid melting in the Greenland glaciers and fears have been expressed of rapid acceleration leading to a 'tipping point' (Houghton, 2009: 177-9). If the whole Greenland ice sheet melted, this would trigger a globally catastrophic rise in sea levels of 7 metres (23 feet) (Henson, 2008: 88). Even if these specific catastrophes do not occur, sea levels are still set to rise by at least 18–38cm by 2100 even on the least pessimistic of IPCC's scenarios – and up to 50cm on the most pessimistic scenario (Giddens, 2009: 21).

Figure 1.4: *Rise in sea level, 1880–2000*

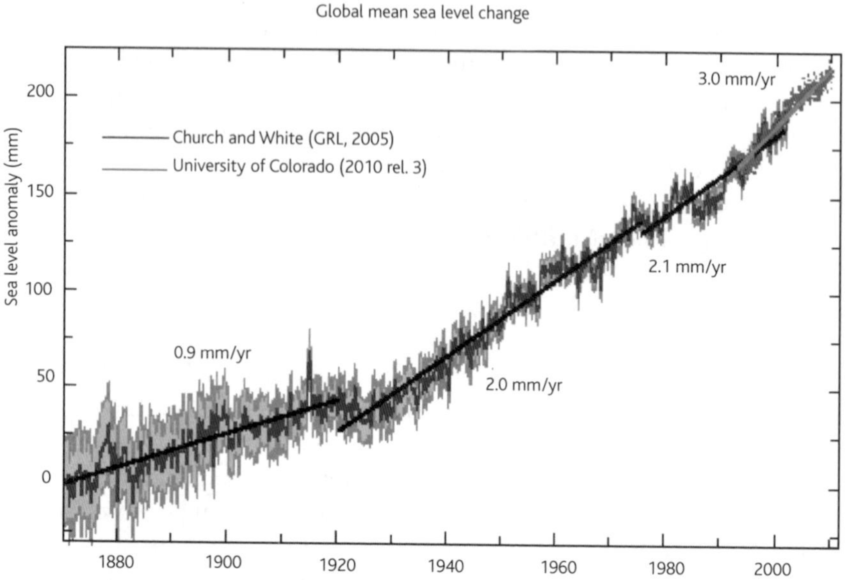

Global mean sea level change

Church and White (GRL, 2005)
University of Colorado (2010 rel. 3)

Source: Church and White (2006)

Permafrost:

Temperatures have increased by 3°C since the 1980s and the maximum area covered by seasonally frozen ground has decreased by around 7% in the northern hemisphere since 1900 (IPCC, 2007: 5). Permafrost holds substantial quantities of methane that are swiftly released when it melts. Al Gore, in his influential talk and video *An Inconvenient Truth*, drew attention to the possibility of this leading to abrupt and substantial increase in global warming – another tipping point (Gore, 2007; Preuss, 2008).

Rain and drought:

Long-term trends in precipitation (that is, rain, sleet, snow, etc) are much more variable than those in temperature – there have been increases in rainfall in eastern areas of North and South America, northern Europe and northern and central Asia. On the other hand, drying has occurred in the Sahel, Mediterranean and parts of southern Asia. More intense and longer droughts have been observed since the 1970s, particularly in the tropics and sub-tropics. Frequency of heavy precipitation has increased over most land areas (IPCC, 2007: 5). The IPCC (2007: 15) predicts a further 10–20% reduction in precipitation in the Sahel by 2090.

Heat and cold:
Not only has the average temperature gradually but inexorably increased but it has also been subject to much more volatility. Widespread changes in extreme temperatures have occurred over the past 50 years: fewer cold days, cold nights and frosts, more hot days, hot nights and heatwaves. There has also been increased intense tropical cyclone activity in the north Atlantic since the 1970s (IPCC, 2007: 5).

'Type two' events:
Type two changes are different from the gradual but inexorable changes that take place over years and decades – type two events are sudden and are triggered by 'tipping points'. For example, current phenomena such as El Niño, hurricanes and typhoons would become unpredictable and wreak exponentially greater havoc than before (Giddens, 2009: 25-7).

Ocean acidification:
The oceans are significant absorbers of atmospheric CO_2. As the concentration of CO_2 increases in the atmosphere, so the amount absorbed into the oceans increases and this leads to changes in the acidity of the water. Even though the changes in ocean chemistry appear small (a decrease from pH 8.2 in pre-industrial times to pH 8.1 currently), the effects on marine life and ecosystems are huge, including the destruction of coral reefs and the reduced capacity for sea creatures to develop shells and skeletons.

Summary box

Effects of climate change
Most of the following are inevitable to some extent; the scale of the effects will depend, in part, on the amount of climate change the planet experiences:

- weather events becoming more severe and unpredictable;
- increased flooding and increased drought in different areas;
- ice-cap melting;
- rising sea levels (from ice melting and from water expansion);
- oceans becoming more acidic.

Consequences

Giddens (2009: 1) uses shock tactics to confront his readers with the enormity of the consequences of climate change:

> This book is about nightmares, catastrophes – and dreams....
> It is about SUVs – Sports Utility Vehicles or 4x4s. The book
> is a prolonged enquiry into a single question: why does
> anyone, anyone at all, even for a single day longer, continue
> to drive a SUV? For their drivers have to be aware that they
> are contributing to a crisis of epic proportions concerning the
> world's climate.... In case it isn't obvious, I hasten to add that
> SUVs are a metaphor. If I can put it this way, we are all SUV
> drivers because so few of us are geared up to the profundity of
> the threats we face.

The Royal Society (2008: 10) expresses the same sentiments in a much
more measured and prosaic way, but nevertheless focuses on the stark
consequences of global warming for the most disadvantaged and vulnerable
people in the world:

> The impact and pace of this change would be difficult for
> many people and ecosystems to adapt to ... [but] the impact of
> climate change will fall disproportionately upon developing
> countries and the poor – those who can least afford to adapt.
> Thus a changing climate will exacerbate inequalities in, for
> example, health and access to adequate food and clean water. It
> is this exacerbation of inequality and massive increase in social
> injustice that is a central consequence of climate change. In a
> similarly pessimistic mood, Giddens (2009: 22) comments that,
> 'The IPCC says that resource-based wars could dominate the
> current century'.

As noted above, many of the effects of global warming are being felt
already and many others are inexorably in train: even if we completely
stopped producing CO_2 now – which will not happen – the increased CO_2
concentrations in the atmosphere will not go away and it would take several
hundred years to get back to pre-industrial levels (Houghton, 2009: 47).
   Although the overall effects of global warming are relatively clear (as
noted above), it is not easy to be specific about the precise consequences or
locations of the changes that are taking place. According to Lewis (2006: 1),

> ... this is because the Earth is an integrated system consisting of
> a network of sub-systems ... each linked by various processes
> ... in complex ways.

This complexity causes him to hedge his bets about whether the Earth will be overtaken by a sudden catastrophe. He makes the important point that it is not just the complexity of the world's *natural* systems that renders it impossible to make robust predictions but it is also their interactions with global political and social systems. The European Union (EU) Commission is more specific than Lewis in its predictions for Europe, which include the following potential effects:

- *Agriculture and fisheries:* increased risk of crop failure through extreme weather; reduction in soil fertility through depletion of organic matter; threats to fisheries from severe effects on coasts and marine ecosystems.
- *Energy:* hydro-electric power will be affected both negatively and positively; negatively by the impact of drought in southern Europe leading possibly to a 25% reduction; and positively in northern Europe by melting glaciers leading to an increase.
- *Infrastructure* will come under severe threat, particularly in low-lying urban areas through flooding.
- *Tourism* will suffer in Alpine regions through snow loss and in Mediterranean regions through excessive temperatures.
- *Water:* as well as the flooding danger from too *much* water, the increased stress placed on water supplies from too *little water*, particularly for irrigation and drinking, will be a major issue in southern Europe with 'Europe's high water stress areas expected to increases from 19% today to 35% by the 2070s' (CEC, 2009a: 4-5).

Responses

Houghton (2009: 16) is unequivocal that something *has* to be done: '"wait and see" is an irresponsible response'. Interestingly, the Commission of the European Communities (CEC, 2009a: 6) claims that in the medium to long term it will be cheaper to act to address climate change than to do nothing and then try to pick up the pieces once the negative effects of global warming are felt. Similarly, using IPCC figures, the British government estimates that timely action will cost between 1% and 5.5% of gross domestic product (GDP) (closer to 1% if action is swift) whereas inaction will cost between 5% and 20% in consumption terms (see Chapter Three, this volume).

The Royal Society (2008: 11) is specific on what should be the two main strands of concerted international action:

> The science clearly points to the need for nations to take urgent steps to cut greenhouse gas emissions into the atmosphere, as

much and as fast as possible, to reduce the more severe aspects of climate change. We must also prepare for the impacts of climate change, some of which are already inevitable.

The first of these options is known as **mitigation**, the second as **adaptation**. There is also a third possibility that might make some difference: that is, the intervention of **geo-engineering**. Finally, from a deep environmental (and perhaps unrealistically utopian) perspective, there is the goal of **conservation**. These four approaches are now dealt with in turn.

Mitigation

Mitigation is perhaps an unfortunate word to have come into common usage in relation to reducing GHGs, because it has several varying meanings. The most apt are perhaps:

> To moderate or reduce in strength (heat, cold, light, etc), esp. so as to make more bearable; to temper the severity of (a climate). (*Oxford English Dictionary*, OED)

These appropriately refer to cutting GHG emissions. Some of its other everyday meanings, however, are very close to the notion of adaptation, for example, 'to alleviate or give relief from', 'to lessen the trouble caused by', 'to abate, make less oppressive', 'to reduce the severity of' (*OED*). All of these could appropriately refer to dealing with the consequences of global warming. It needs to be borne in mind that all references to mitigation here, and in all the sources referred to here, refer to *reducing* the level of GHG emissions. Lewis (2006: 2) summarises mitigation as:

> The basic solution to climate change is obvious but rarely articulated: most fossil carbon must not get into the atmosphere. Currently the only proven way to do this is to leave most fossil fuels in the ground. That is, no new oil fields, no new coal mines.

Governments are already responding to this challenge, for example, by returning to the construction of new nuclear power stations and supporting the expansion of areas such as biofuel production. Funding is being put into the development of technologies to capture and store CO_2, for example, by adding technological interventions onto existing power stations and factories, or by diverting CO_2 from its point of production into storage facilities underground. Industry is also responding by increased investment in alternate energy sources such as wind and aiming to produce more energy efficient technologies. Individual people are being asked to cut down on energy usage too. Groups have emerged that aim to tackle climate change and related problems; for example the Transitions Network (TN, 2009) aims to drastically reduce emissions through re-localisation and to address the depletion of fossil fuels through increasing social resilience.

Although it is simple to say what needs to be done, the politics involved, from carbon trading schemes for industry to promotion of individual behavioural change, are not straightforward.

Adaptation

Even if mitigation is as successful as it can possibly be, and this is, of course, so exceedingly unlikely as to be beyond the realms of reasonable anticipation, then we will still have to find ways of living with the extent of climate change that is already present in the system. At its most extreme this might mean abandoning large areas of low-lying land – for example much of the Netherlands and the delta area of Bangladesh – leading to the relocation of tens of millions of people. Less extreme measures include massive increases in flood defences, water conservation, changes in agriculture, disease prevention and medical care (particularly in relation to malaria and other climate-sensitive and water-borne diseases) and intervention to protect threatened species (CEC, 2009a).

The EU Commission's impact assessment identified three major options for adaptation:

- 'grey' infrastructure approaches based on engineering science including design of the built environment to withstand extreme events;
- 'green' structural approaches including increasing ecosystem resilience, halting biodiversity loss and restoring water cycles;
- 'soft' non-structural approaches including land use controls and economic incentives to reduce or prevent disaster vulnerability.

Central to these 'soft' approaches are water and land use policies to maintain eco-systems that are optimally resistant to climate change and minimise adverse effects of potential disasters particularly in relation to human well-being and health and the protection of property (CEC, 2009a: 5).

But even these extensive approaches, in themselves, are seen only as *necessary* but not *sufficient* for successful adaptation, 'They require more careful management of the underlying *human systems*' (CEC, 2009b: 6; original emphasis). The emphasis here on management of human systems is a chilling reminder of the sheer extent and depth of the social-psychological challenge facing people in the economically developed world in adapting to the changes in lifestyle and indeed 'life view' necessary to cope with both mitigation and adaptation to global warming. The Commission also identifies the ethical requirement for any EU strategy to be socially fair, both in the EU itself and its constituent countries but also between the world's developed and developing nations (CEC, 2009b: 7).

Geo-engineering

Here the approach to reducing atmospheric CO_2 levels involves massive feats of engineering, some on a global scale. Possible examples include removing gases from the atmosphere and solar radiation management. Several different proposals have been put forward for removing CO_2 from the atmosphere (see The Royal Society, 2009). One is to find a way to remove it mechanically and store it either underground or in the oceans. Another is to find a way of removing it directly from the atmosphere, for example via 'synthetic trees' (Rees, 2003: 56-7; Henson, 2008: 332). Solar radiation management – reducing the amount of sunlight getting to Earth – can be undertaken chemically or mechanically. Chemically induced reductions in solar radiation take place naturally when sulphuric particles are emitted by volcanic eruptions. Mechanical approaches include the suggestion to use giant mirrors located in space to reflect the sun's rays away from the Earth.

Overall, geo-engineering propositions have a seductive attraction as a 'technical fix'. However, there is a real danger that time and resources spent chasing after a perhaps impossible technological approach might just be wasted in a dangerous distraction from the real-world tasks of reducing carbon emissions and adapting to a changed climate.

Conservation

The ultimate solution to the problem of global warming is that of 'ultra-mitigation' or conservation whereby, following Lewis's (2006) prescription (noted above), we must leave most fossil fuels in the ground and have no new coal mines, no new oilfields, no new gas fields. Conservation of natural resources, along with substantial contraction of consumption, is an essential requisite of the deep environmental approach associated with strong notions of sustainability (Fitzpatrick and Cahill, 2002b). This approach sees an intrinsic value in nature that must be sustained at all costs (Phillips, 2006: 104).

It is interesting to note that Giddens (2009: 55), although castigating all SUV (sports utility vehicle) owners, draws the line at conservation – he will have none of it:

It [conservation] is a value that has a certain aesthetic quality to it. It is very possibly important to the good life, but it has no direct relevance to climate change.

Policies and politics

Kyoto Protocol

The definitive event in the beginnings of the development of international policy and concerted action on global warming was the Kyoto Protocol of 1997. Its purpose was to firm up the commitments made by virtually all the world's countries in 1992 at the United Nations (UN) Earth Summit which pledged to stabilise GHGs 'at a level that would prevent dangerous anthropogenic interference with the climate system' (Henson, 2008: 15).

There were two major problems with the Kyoto Protocol. The first is that it was only a *very small* beginning: the goal was for industrialised nations, on average, to cut their annual GHG emissions by 2012 to 5.2% below their level in 1990. This works out at 29% below what they would otherwise have been if they had continued rising. At first sight this seems to be rather ambitious but put in perspective it is not so:

It appears that few, if any, of the world's big economies will meet their Kyoto targets by 2012. Even if they did, it would only make a tiny dent in the world's ever-increasing output of greenhouse gases. Reducing greenhouse gas emissions by a few percent over time is akin to overspending your household budget by a decreasing amount each year: your debt still piles up, if only at a slower pace. (Henson, 2008: 17)

The second problem is the continued reticence among many countries for actually doing anything about global warming. The Protocol required ratification by enough industrialised countries to represent 55% of the CO_2 emissions of the developed world and it took a full seven years after the signing of the Protocol for it to be enacted (Kyoto Protocol Status of Ratification, 2006). Australia only ratified it in 2008 and Kazakhstan in 2009. Up to recent times the least enthusiastic country, and thus the biggest stumbling block to the full implementation of the Kyoto Protocol, has been the US, which at the time of writing had still not ratified Kyoto. Even though it has less than 5% of the world's population, the US is responsible for about 25% of total global warming (Maslin, 2004: 118–19).

Progress towards meeting targets

This can be answered in one word: dismal. Not a single country in the world is on target to meet its contribution to keeping the increase in CO_2 emissions at a maximum of 2°C above pre-industrial levels – every country in the world is going to overshoot. Germanwatch (2008: 1) is scathing about progress and, in sheer disgust, refused to award any of the first three positions of its Climate Change Performance Index 2009:

> ... [it] therefore does not have any winners this year.... Position four to ten ... are made up by Sweden, Germany, France, India, Brazil, the United Kingdom and Denmark.

Anderson (2009: 1) agrees with this appraisal and is extremely pessimistic about the future:

> Current global emission trends and the absence of meaningful political leadership by even the most climate-progressive nations, suggests that there is now very little hope of staying below the 2°C threshold between 'acceptable' and 'dangerous' climate change.

Nevertheless, some countries, particularly Sweden and Germany, and to a lesser extent the UK, are making some progress. Sweden has an effective carbon tax with a significant bite, so much so that when it was introduced, income tax was cut by half to compensate. Between 1990 and 2005 its economy grew by 44% but its GHG emissions went down by 9%. Germany leads the world in micro-generation of energy from renewable sources: it has 'feed-in tariffs' where householders and small businesses get paid for generating their own energy and inputting it to the national grid. The price is highly subsidised and fixed for 20 years so Germany is far ahead of any other country in micro generation (Giddens, 2009: 74).

The EU

There is a bright spot – albeit dimly lit – on the climate change horizon. The European Union (EU) is the most strongly committed governmental body of all in trying to deal effectively with global warming. It is in a uniquely advantageous position in being a relatively strong supranational governmental body and is almost continental in its scope. The EU Commission gives the following rationale for acting at European rather than national level:

The EU has a particularly strong role when the impact of climate change transcends the boundaries of individual countries (eg river and sea boundaries and bio-geographic regions). Adaptation will require solidarity among EU Member States to ensure that disadvantaged regions and regions most affected by climate change will be capable of taking the measures needed to adapt. Moreover, coordinated EU action will be necessary in certain sectors (eg agriculture, water, biodiversity, fisheries, and energy networks) that are closely integrated at EU level through the single market and common policies. (CEC, 2009a: 6)

The EU is taking active steps to meet the target of stabilising global temperatures at no more than 2°C above pre-industrial levels (Anderson et al, 2007: 1). In 1997 the EU agreed unilaterally to reduce its GHG emissions by 20% by 2020, increasing it to a 30% cut if other developed countries agreed to do the same (Giddens, 2009: 193). It also created a legally binding emissions trading scheme in 2003, covering industries which are major sources of GHG, including power stations, refineries and a substantial number of large factories which together account for about half the CO_2 emissions in the EU. This was the first large emissions trading scheme in the world and its inception was rather bumpy – the initial emissions allocations were set far too high and there was a considerable amount of avoidance and misinformation going on – but it has now started to reduce emission levels (Anderson et al, 2007: 6).

Nevertheless, in spite of this success, according to Hulme et al (2009: 23), existing European policies are not sufficient to meet the 2°C target. In order to meet its own targets, they claim that EU climate policy entails reduction of GHG emissions by 60% to 80% by 2050 and that this will require increased European integration and the full 'Europeanisation' of policies relating to climate change.

The EU has made another bold innovation in aiming to get 20% of its energy from renewable sources by 2020 including 10% of petrol and diesel used in transport from biofuels. Anderson et al (2007: 11) are deeply suspicious about this on three counts. First, it is over-ambitious: 'well beyond what is either technically possible through current or envisaged levels of blended fuels, and probably also beyond Europe's capacity to supply its own needs'; second, it will probably result in an increase in food prices; and, third, it might even *add* to GHGs if the biofuels are grown on reclaimed wetlands or cleared forest areas.

The UK

Prior to 2008 the UK did not have a particularly auspicious record in legislation regarding global warming, although (ironically) its CO_2 emissions were relatively low because of Margaret Thatcher's conflict with the National Union of Mineworkers which led to large-scale closure of coal mines and the 'dash for gas' – a fuel contributing much less to global warming (Giddens, 2009: 80). Thus the UK is on target to meet its Kyoto Protocol targets of a reduction of 12.5% in GHGs over its 1990 level by 2012. In 2008 the Climate Change Act was passed. This targeted 80% reduction in GHGs by 2050 and is also aiming for a 26% reduction in CO_2 emissions by the 2018–22 budgetary period. The latter aim will be a considerable challenge to meet because the UK is unlikely to meet its intermediate target of a 20% reduction by 2010.

Developing nations

Developing countries are caught in a dilemma in relation to global warming. It is clear that they are the countries which will suffer the most from the impacts of global warming already set in train by the developed countries, but they are also being warned that any attempt on their part to join the club of developed nations by expanding their economies must be constrained in order to minimise carbon emissions (Giddens, 2009: 9). And such constraints would make it impossible for them to grow their economies to a level matching the developed world. Pepper (2005: 15) claims that EU policies towards the developing world through its Sixth Environmental Action Programme (2001–10) are underpinned by assumptions that western affluence levels can be universalised in environmentally sustainable ways. He disagrees, claiming that such growth would require the resources of another two or three planets.

Giddens (2009: 9) is unequivocal in insisting that poorer nations must have the right to develop even if this raises emissions sharply for a while. He calls this the *development imperative* and this is not only for moral reasons:

> The consequences of climate change will worsen the enormous tensions that already derive from global inequalities, with implications for the world as a whole.

Copenhagen Summit

The UN Climate Change Summit held in Copenhagen in December 2009 was anticipated to produce a step-change in how countries would address environmental concerns. The output of weeks of face-to-face negotiating and the attendance of numerous world leaders was an 'accord' rather than the legally binding climate change agreement that many had wanted. The accord, drafted by the US, China, Brazil, India and South Africa, speaks only of reducing gas emissions to limit additional temperature rise to 2°C above pre-industrial levels. There was no agreement on how to achieve these limits in concrete terms. A fund to support poorer nations through the worst effects of climate change and to support research on sustainable energy technologies was also proposed. Not all countries have signed up to the accord and it remains to be seen whether it has any efficacy. At the time of writing, the next UN climate conference will be in Mexico City (December 2010) and once again there are high hopes that a legally binding agreement will be reached.

Other environmental challenges

Although discussion of climate change currently dominates, other environmental challenges are pressing. Many of these are the result of human exploitation of the planet, and are concurrent with global population growth, increased urbanisation and associated demands on power and resources. Others emerge as a result of potentially ill-conceived solutions to problems of energy supply demands and climate change itself. We outline briefly some of these other relevant concerns.

Resource depletion

Natural resources include such things as water, timber, minerals and fossil fuels. We could include in this list 'less obvious' resources such as soil, which might seem ubiquitous but that are being degraded and depleted at a phenomenal rate. Some of the items that the natural world provides may be available on a sustainable basis – being replenished as quickly as they are used up – while others are being used up and a point will be reached where they are no longer available to be used. Fossil fuels fall into this latter category as resources like coal, oil and gas are not replaceable. By most estimates, we have already reached, or will reach in the very near future, a *peak* in the supply of oil and gas. This peak, first described by geophysicist Marion King Hubbert in 1956, is the point after which supplies will decline and never pick up and is arrived at from a calculation based on a number of factors, including a trade off between reserves which exist and those that are economically viable to exploit. Although the many models that have predicted the year of occurrence of 'peak oil', since Hubbert's original calculations, are open to much debate and occasional controversy, as a non-renewable resource, a non-returnable peak in oil is inevitable at some point. World supplies of many of the minerals used in the manufacture of everyday products are also finite, yet arguably, at the current time, it is the effects of their extraction and use in products (and end-of-life waste) that are more environmentally problematic. Suffice to say, much of the fabric of modern life is founded on supplies of materials that are not ultimately renewable. This has huge implications for the ways in which societies currently consume.

Waste and pollution

As well as the waste produced through everyday consumption in people's lives, the extraction and processing of resources, other industrial processes and agricultural processes all produce large quantities of waste material. This waste also constitutes an environmental challenge, whether by volume or the often-polluting nature of the material. Plastic refuse waste has been found in large quantities in the middle of the Atlantic Ocean, disrupting shipping and wildlife. As well as producing CO_2, the burning of fossil fuels produces other gases and small particles that act as pollutants. Agricultural chemicals, used as fertilisers, pesticides and so on affect not only plant and animal life but can also impact on soil quality and enter water courses.

Water

Two key issues with water supply are (a) increasing demand from society and (b) unevenness of supply. Demand is increasing in both the domestic and industrial spheres, while the places in which water is available are not necessarily the same as those with the demand. There are places in the UK that receive rainfall that comes into the technical category of a 'desert'. While access to clean water is clearly a major issue for developing nations, when access is coupled with the energy-intensive water treatment methods used in the developed world, the supply of clean water to everyone presents a challenge. The likely increases in extreme weather events as a result of climate change are predicted to lead to more droughts in parts of the world and more flooding events in others.

Biodiversity

Multiple plant and animal species are potentially at risk of extinction and while Giddens has argued that these should perhaps not be saved unless they contribute essential services to humanity, the fact is that the way biological diversity contributes to the health of the planet and all its occupiers is not that well known. So there are potentially large risks in making choices in what to preserve and what we are prepared to lose. The Millennium Ecosystem Assessment was a huge programme to measure the effects on human well-being of changes in ecosystems. Although the techniques of assessment that were used are open to sociological critique (Hodgson et al, 2007) the results are unequivocal in anticipating huge problems for humanity when ecosystems are irrevocably degraded.

The fragmentation of habitats, the encroachment of human settlements (particularly as human population grows and further resources demands are created), agricultural intensification (including overfishing and selective breeding of crops and food animals) and climate change all contribute to the loss of biodiversity and other ecosystem changes.

Summary box

Environmental challenges beyond climate change
- Current consumption behaviours are unsustainable.
- Society is using up non-renewable resources.
- Population growth is increasing pressure on the environment in multiple ways.
- Biodiversity is being lost due to human action.
- Waste and pollution is increasing due to human action.

Justice, equality and human rights

The task for social policy scholars, researchers, students, commentators and policy makers is therefore immense. One way to make sense of this challenge is via the issue of social justice (see Chapter Six, this volume). Three facets are central: inequality between developed and developing countries; inequality within countries; and intergenerational issues. The first two are dealt with throughout the book, but especially in Chapters Seven and Thirteen. A philosophical account of intergenerational issues is given in Chapter Five so, here, we offer a few comments pertaining more to the policy literature.

Intergenerational issues

The major intergenerational issue is whether the present generation passes on most of the cost of its contribution to global warming to future generations. Anderson (2009: 2) puts it in strong terms:

> We are today faced with a dilemma. Do we continue to pay lip service to the issue of climate change, and hope future generations will understand our preference for barely-veiled hedonism over stewardship? Or are we prepared to respond genuinely to the scale of the challenge we have brought upon ourselves.

However, the responsibility of current generations toward future generations needs to be understood in terms of the use of all non-renewable resources, not just fossil fuels and their link to climate change.

Fitzpatrick (2001: 506) constructs a new temporal framework for social policy based on intergenerational justice. He posits the notion of *sustainable justice*: 'reconciling the interests of present and future generations of the least well-off requires the design of a new property regime'. He notes that social policy seldom has a time frame more than two generations away (that is, grandparent, parent, grandchild) and that this is mostly confined to pension issues. To fit in with environmental concerns it needs to have a much longer time span. He makes the sobering claim that,

> Unless we develop a concept of 'sustainable welfare' we might awake in a world either where distributive justice today is bought at the expense of tomorrow or where existing inequalities ossify forever due to the recalcitrance of the affluent and the fragility of the ecosystem. (Fitzpatrick, 2001: 507)

Lundqvist (2001: 466) points to the problems inherent in awakening our generation to these dangers:

> Present citizens may be reluctant to accept limitations on what they have come to view as indispensable individual freedom of choice, particularly because sustainable development is not something they will actually experience during their lifetime [and] the political credibility of arguments and measures aimed at changing consumption behaviours may not look too convincing to individual citizens.

Anand and Sen (2000: 2030) bring all these facets together under the banner of an ethical universalism recognising the shared claim of all people, present and future, to have the basic capability to lead worthwhile lives:

> Not working towards guaranteeing these basic capabilities to the future generations would be scandalous, but in the same

way, not working towards bringing those elementary capabilities within the reach of the deprived in the present generation would also be outrageous.

Conclusion

We have presented a range of environmental challenges that societies must confront. Many of these challenges are related to each other, often in intricate ways, rendering the societal responses that may be required as less than straightforward. Arguably, we need to dissolve the current divide between environmental policy making and welfare decision making (Hodgson and Irving, 2007).

While climate change is currently the most prominent issue in the public and political conscious, other environmental concerns remain highly important and a focus on climate change at the expense of other environmental issues would be a mistake. The range and reach of environmental challenges present policy analysts and the public at large with a complex landscape. Several attempts to reach global agreement on action have yet to demonstrate change for the better. Yet, as we know from policy work and global action in response to ozone depletion in the 1980s (Christie, 2001), responding to scientifically uncertain and complex environmental problems is indeed possible.

Chapter summary

The chapter has discussed:

- the causes of climate change;
- the main implications of climate change on weather events, flooding and drought, the ice-caps, sea levels and acidification;
- the main solutions that have been proposed (mitigation, adaptation, geo-engineering, conservation);
- the Kyoto Protocol;
- a variety of other environmental challenges;
- questions of intergenerational justice.

Questions for discussion

- Do you see the effects of environmental problems in your local area?
- What changes might a more erratic climate make to your everyday life?
- Does the fact that all science involves levels of uncertainty mean that we do not need to worry about climate change?

- To what extent can climate change be understood as both a local and global problem?
- Should policies on climate change and other environmental matters be set at national, regional or global levels? Why?

Key further reading

Giddens, T. (2009) The politics of climate change, Cambridge: Polity Press.
Henson, R. (2008) *The Rough Guide to climate change*, London: Penguin.
Houghton, J. (2009) *Global warming: The complete briefing* (4th edn), Cambridge: Cambridge University Press.
Stern, N. (2007) *The economics of climate change*, Cambridge: Cambridge University Press.

Useful websites

Graphics that present the data on global warming in a variety of forms can be found at: www.globalwarmingart.com/wiki

Intergovernmental Panel on Climate Change (IPCC) produces the scientific reports that monitor the state of climate change: www.ipcc.ch/

Millennium Ecosystem Assessment (MEA) assessed the consequences of ecosystem change on human well-being: www.millenniumassessment.org/en/index.aspx

The Montreal Protocol was the agreement on limiting depletion of the ozone layer and included a global ban on certain chemicals: http://ozone.unep.org/

The Sustainable Development Commission (SDC) is the UK government's independent watchdog on sustainable development: www.sd-commission.org.uk/

Transitions Network is a global social movement, with some sites in the UK, aimed at addressing climate change and other environmental problems in an integrated way, particularly through processes of 'relocalisation': http://transitiontowns.org/TransitionNetwork/TransitionNetwork

United Nations (UN) Climate Change Conference, December 2009, Copenhagen: http://en.cop15.dk/frontpage

two

Social challenges: causes, explanations and solutions

John Hannigan

Overview

Environmental policy making involves a search for explanations and solutions that are both ecologically valid and politically feasible. This quest is complicated by incompatibility between a political imperative that mandates continuous economic growth and an environmental ethic that warns against such untrammelled expansion. This chapter discusses three major models and explanations for the environmental crisis:

- limits to growth
- the treadmill of production
- consumerist ethic.

While in agreement that a failure to curtail current levels of development will spawn ecological disaster, they differ:

- over where and why blame should be assigned;
- in their recommended course of action;
- in their understanding of social equity as a barrier to sustainability.

With regard to this latter point, this chapter discusses the concepts of sustainable development and sustainable consumption. It concludes by considering how such concepts are socially constructed, especially in terms of the policy-making process.

Introduction

In one of the first systematic discussions of its type, US political scientist and government adviser Lynton Caldwell (1970 [1963]) wrote that effective public decision making regarding natural resources and the environment is seriously hampered by the dissimilarity between two intellectual tendencies or viewpoints: the market and the environment. The polarities of ecology and the market induce a fundamental conflict, in the political and business spheres especially. 'The search for common denominators of environmental policy that are both ecologically valid and politically feasible', he proclaimed, 'has become a major task of environmental administration today, and will be for a long time to come' (1970 [1963]: 12). By 'ecologically valid', Caldwell meant that the natural world, including its human inhabitants, must maintain a constant state of 'moving equilibrium' or 'dynamic balance'. By the early 1970s, it was obvious that this equilibrium was being critically disturbed, necessitating the formulation of a proactive public policy to protect the quality of the environment.

But how, first of all, is the environmental crisis to be explained?

Three explanations

There are three main explanations of this 'environmental disturbance' and the substantial challenge to society that it poses: *limits to growth*, *the treadmill of production* and *the consumerist ethic*. While these approaches are in some ways interlocking, nonetheless, each provides an identifiable diagnostic leading to a distinctive set of policy options. For a summary see **Table 2.1**.

Limits to growth

According to the limits to growth interpretation, our planet is in peril due to an escalating mismatch between human population growth and available material resources, notably, fuel, food and water. Writing in 1970, the same year that Caldwell made his observation, US population biologists Paul and Anne Ehrlich (also 1968) warned that human over-population posed a serious threat to terrestrial life. Employing a metaphor popular at that time, the Ehrlichs (1970: 3) came to the conclusion that 'Spaceship Earth is now filled to capacity or beyond and is running out of food'. Futurist John McHale (1970) calculated that the world population would double in 30 years to around six billion, and reach a staggering 30 billion by 2070. Cause for alarm about the population explosion resides in the possibility that food supplies, energy and housing will grow at a lesser rate over this time period. On the final page of his book, McHale asks three questions:

Table 2.1: *Three explanations for the environmental crisis*

Explanation/approach	Environmental crisis is the result of:	Role of the state	Environmental inequities are primarily:	Recommended course of action
Limits to growth	... escalating mismatch between human population growth and available material resources	Authoritarian	... intergenerational	Reduce global population levels, especially in less developed nations
Treadmill of production	... constant and unstoppable pressure from industrial expansion	Contradictory: both promoter of economic expansion and environmental regulator	... class-based; distributional	De-accelerate treadmill; democratic ownership and control over production
Consumerist ethic	... wasteful and polluting effects of an extravagant and materialistic lifestyle	Disengaged; government needs to be a catalyst and facilitator of change	... global; disparity between the wealthy North and the poor South in their access to resources	Reduce rate of consumption; reshape household practices so they are simpler and more ecologically sustainable

What are the physical limits and constraints in the overall ecosystem? What are the relevant human limits? What are the irreplaceable resource limits?

One influential attempt to answer these questions was the Club of Rome project, named after its sponsors, an international think-tank founded by the Italian management consultant Aurelio Peccei. The research employed World3, a computer model of global population growth and economic development constructed by members of the Systems Dynamics Group at the Massachusetts Institute of Technology. Employing seven different scenarios, patterns and trends of population growth, industrial output, resource availability and depletion, pollution and food production were projected from 1970 levels all the way to the year 2100, as were rates of growth between 1900 and 1970. The first volume summarising the results, *The Limits to Growth* (Meadows et al, 1972), was a general, non-technical report written to apprise policy makers and the public of the project's general objectives and conclusions (Meadows and Meadows, 1973: vi). The book was widely noticed and became a key reference point in environmentalist writing throughout the 1970s.

The researchers came to several major conclusions (Meadows, 1973: 42-4). First, exponential growth in population and material output can be expected to constitute the dominant force in socioeconomic change in most contemporary societies. Second, current growth rates of both of these are unsustainable. Third, two contrasting scenarios are introduced here. Optimally, we will recognise the seriousness of the situation and take immediate and drastic action to bring population and the finite resources of the environment into a state of equilibrium. If this is not done then an *overshoot* of the limits of growth will occur followed by uncontrolled decline. Fourth, technological solutions alone are not enough as these can only serve to postpone the decline. Rather, technological improvements must be accompanied by changes that decrease the social, economic and political factors causing growth. Finally, remedial action should begin immediately; each year of delay significantly reduces the probability of attaining a desirable state of global equilibrium. This pessimistic scenario constitutes a classic *outbreak-crash model*, raising the spectre of nothing less than the collapse of civilisation and the advent of an exhausted and polluted planet (Harper, 2001: 293).

Guiding this discussion and 'serving as a springboard for exploring policy options' (Durham, 1995: 250) is a simple representation of the human causes of environmental change called the **I=PAT equation**. Originally developed in 1971 by Paul Ehrlich and environmental scientist and science adviser (to US President Obama), John Holdren, the $I=PAT$ model has become a standard representation of the relationship between population, human welfare and environmental impacts. 'A' for affluence is measured by gross domestic product (GDP), which in turn, comprises three different components: (1) personal consumption, (2) government consumption and investment and (3) gross private domestic investment. 'P' signifies population size, while 'T' refers to the damage done by technological development. The dependent variable is 'I' (environmental impact). Consumption levels have been steadily rising since the beginning of the 20th century (except for a brief dip during the Second World War). Combined with increasing population levels, spiralling consumption causes a corresponding increase in 'withdrawals' from the natural environment and increased environmental degradation.

Brulle and Young (2007: 526) have pointed out that the *I=PAT* model, influential as it has been as a research tool, is essentially a 'simple accounting framework'. It is vital, they say, to move on and 'develop a more robust empirical model of the fundamental driving forces of the elements of the IPAT model'. One weakness is that the three prime variables are treated as being independent. While this allows for the formulation of different policy approaches aimed at different societies – population control in southern nations, curbs on technology and consumption in northern countries (Harper, 2001: 267-8) – it precludes the possibility that the components are both interactive *and* part of a wider pattern of causation.

In the 1968 bestseller *The Population Bomb*, Paul Ehrlich advocated an international policy research programme to set optimum population-environment goals for the world and to devise methods for reaching these goals. One major goal was population control, both domestically (in the US) and abroad. At home, he recommended instituting a package of financial rewards and penalties, notably adding US$1,200 for each child above two to a family's taxable income. Additionally, he suggested setting up a federal Department of Population and Environment with the power to take whatever steps were necessary to establish a reasonable population size in the US and to put an end to the steady deterioration of our environment. Abroad, he envisioned establishing political machinery for 'area rehabilitation'. This meant that the developed nations, through the agency of the United Nations (UN), should instigate a programme involving simultaneous population control, agricultural development and forced industrialisation. Ehrlich acknowledged that these initiatives might be too draconian to be politically acceptable, but countered that even a partial adoption would help immeasurably. Such schemes are decidedly 'authoritarian' and 'depend on the Malthusian assumption of economic scarcity' (O'Sullivan, 2008: 52). At a 1970 meeting in New York City, Barry Commoner, author of the bestselling book *The Closing Circle*, accused Paul Ehrlich of harbouring totalitarian ideals, especially with reference to his call for compulsory population control (cited in Olson, 2009: 62).

Recently, the limits to growth approach has re-emerged. Citing population figures that recall those presented by McHale, the Optimum Population Trust, a leading think-tank and campaign group in the UK whose patrons include James Lovelock and Sir David Attenborough, conclude that our planet barely has room for five billion people – the present population is approaching 6.8 billion (Adam, 2009). In 2008, a group of concerned environmentalists in Europe established the International Lindau Group. As with the Club of Rome in the 1960s, the Lindau Group was convened in response to mounting concerns over the uncharted role of human-induced global material flows, and the economic ramifications of their unchecked growth. Ecological disruption is on the rise, they warn, as are global natural resource consumption, population and violent natural catastrophes. The Lindau scholars outline a programme, the adoption of which, they claim, would do much to head off this crisis. Their '10 basic conditions for approaching sustainability' include: 'dematerialising' human economic activities and reducing the environmental impacts of resource use; pioneering 'radical eco-innovations' that will both re-conceptualise existing technological and economic systems and capture the markets of the future; and adopting a toolkit of economic instruments – environmental taxes, trading schemes that give explicit prices to the use of natural resources and the emission of pollutants. The Lindau Group insist that there is a case for the creation of a major new public institution that generates, validates and publishes relevant data and information, carries out policy analysis, gives policy support and rewards outstanding ecological performance and resource productivity.

The limits to growth model positions human folly as a major contributing factor to the looming ecological crisis. Nations of the North are indicted for their reckless squandering of natural resources, rampant consumerism and irresponsible development policies in the southern hemisphere. However, no concerted structural analysis is proffered, and the political dimensions of human/environment interactions are virtually neglected (Durham, 1995: 249). Little is said about social power and social relations, property ownership and questions concerning different levels of consumption by different classes hardly come into the picture (Dickens, 2004: 121). Ultimately, responsibility for taking action is unfairly placed on the shoulders of southern nations with high birth rates rather than on middle-class people in the high-consumption nations of the North (Martell, 1994: 38). The Optimum Population Trust, Monbiot (2009) asserts, glosses over the fact that population growth rates are slowing down almost everywhere and that those with the most children use relatively few resources.

The treadmill of production

The treadmill of production explanation assigns cardinal responsibility for environmental deterioration to the competitive character of capitalism and the role of the state in lubricating industrial growth (see Chapter Four, this volume). John Bellamy Foster, a leading interpreter of the ecological dimensions of Karl Marx's thought, puts it this way:

> In what follows, I will argue that we must begin by recognizing that the crisis of the earth is not a crisis of nature, but a crisis of society. The chief causes of the environmental destruction that face us today are not biological, or the product of individual human choice. They are social and historical, rooted in productive relations, technological imperatives, and historically conditioned demographic trends that characterize the dominant social system. (Foster, 1999: 12)

One especially influential model of 20th-century political economy and capitalist production can be found in the writing of the US environmental sociologist Allan Schnaiberg. Schnaiberg et al (2002) outline a post-1945 US production system that changed its relation to the environment in two fundamental respects. First, the modern factory, with its mass production methods, requires ever-greater quantities of raw materials or material inputs to run its machinery. These *withdrawals* from ecosystems lead to a process of accelerated natural resource depletion. Second, modern factories use many more chemicals and chemical-intensive processes to transform raw materials into finished products. This produces a second set of environmental problems, which Schnaiberg terms *additions* to the ecosystems.

At the core of Schnaiberg's model is the concept of the *treadmill of production*. By this he means a constant and unstoppable pressure for industrial expansion that feeds off itself. Rising profits are invested in new, still more productive technologies. This supports still greater production expansion and requires greater withdrawals of natural resources. It also leads to increased amounts of toxic waste and other additions to the environment.

If the treadmill is to hum along efficiently, consumer demand needs to be constantly stoked and shaped. This is the brief of the advertising industry, which is expert in creating social and psychological needs for status, identity and excitement. The captains of industry are also complicit, insofar as they dictate that their products will necessarily have a short life before wearing out and having to be replaced (known as 'planned obsolescence'). Consumers are basically powerless; their tastes and desires are shaped by industry itself.

According to Schnaiberg, politicians and civil servants are vital players in the project of sustaining this treadmill. Collectively, they prefer growth to 'stagnation' in order to ensure tax revenues and, in the case of the former, enhance the likelihood of re-election (Buttel, 2003: 88). This translates into social and economic policies that subsidise and support private capital accumulation and economic expansion, ranging from tax breaks and loopholes to watered-down labour and environmental regulation. The state, he concludes, shares an orientation that revolves around a belief that 'economic criteria remain at the foundation of decision-making processes' (Schnaiberg et al, 2003: 423).

Nevertheless, the state often finds itself caught in a whirlpool of contradictory pressures. On the one hand, it routinely acts as a facilitator of capital accumulation and a promoter of development and economic expansion. At the same time, government agencies are expected by the public to play the roles of environmental mediator and regulator, especially in conflicts over natural resources. This creates a constant tension and incompatibility.

Two notable features of the contemporary political-economic landscape exacerbate this 'double-bind' (Schnaiberg et al, 2002). First, treadmill organisations strenuously resist environmental regulation. Second, where public pressure occasionally leads to the successful passage of environmental legislation, treadmill producers reach into their toolkit for indirect forms of resistance. Thus, they press for amendments to dilute the legislation in order to minimise its impact on their operations. Broadly speaking, state environmental policies are largely restricted to regulating ecological additions (pollution control) rather than regulating ecological withdrawals (resource extraction).

Schnaiberg and his colleagues argue that the nation-state looks to technological innovation as a way out of this dilemma. Technological changes, they suggest, allow for solutions that seemingly 'reduce environmental degradation without bankrupting the economic enterprise or the nation's tax revenues' (Gould et al, 1996: 17). For example, to battle high carbon emissions, US energy secretary Steven Chu favoured such measures as constructing fast neutron reactors that could burn nuclear waste and replacing the electricity grid with a 'smart grid' that would be compatible with small-scale generators (McKie and Helmore, 2009).

As we have seen, the treadmill of production requires an ever-rising and uninterrupted flow of consumption, which it delivers through advertising. Nonetheless, consumption is not identified here as the prime force in producing environmental degradation. Schnaiberg is quite clear about this, quashing any suggestion that he alter the central concept in his model to 'the treadmill of consumption'. His model

> ... of socio-environmental dynamics emphasizes production rather than consumption.... Decisions about types of technologies, the use of labor and volumes of production are made outside the realm of consumer decision-making. (Gould et al, 2004: 300)

Not all academic commentators agree with this privileging of production over consumption. Eric Olin Wright (2004: 318) calls Schnaiberg's continual stress on producers as pivotal actors 'misleading', noting that marketability, which depends on consumer demands, plays a central role in the treadmill model.

Wright also interrogates the treadmill model on its failure to specify an alternative. Schnaiberg and his team make some 'fairly vague allusions', he notes, to an *ecological synthesis* that 'would extend the state's substantial control over ecosystems without regard to issues of profitability and wages/employment' (Gould et al, 2004: 305). Yet there is no attempt to explain how this might be done in a capitalist society or whether a truly green capitalism is possible. Wright demands that the authors of the treadmill model 'at least sketch the implicit vision of that alternative rather than leave it in a black box' (Wright, 2004: 320).

Consumerist ethic

Some analysts do accord the individual consumer a more central position. Sutton (2004: 134-50) points out that such theories make several key assertions. First, it is conspicuous consumption rather than the workplace that provides people with their core sense of individuality and identity. Second, consumer demand drives the production process rather than the reverse. This is reflected in the demise of Fordist, mass assembly line production methods in favour of more flexible post-Fordist methods designed to cater to niche markets. Third, social conflicts are less likely to be production-based, as is the case with localised labour management disputes, and more inclined to be global, symbolic and brand-related, for example in consumer boycotts or campaigns against overseas sweatshops.

In pondering whether the good life can be secured in a more ecologically sustainable manner, Kate Soper (2005: 58) concludes:

> ... when looked at from this perspective, global environmental problems are very clearly recast as problems of human consumption, and in a two-fold and interconnected way.

The first problem here is the huge disparity between rich and poor in their access to resources, while the second is that consumerism depends on an ever-enhanced consumption of material goods and luxury services. The two problems connect 'in the sense that pressures for a more egalitarian distribution of resources between rich and poor are unlikely to be applied unless and until the "good life" is reconceived along different and altogether less consumerist lines' (Soper, 2005: 59). In contrast to the limits to growth perspective, the prime directive here is not to reduce the overall level of societal consumption through slowing down population growth and reducing global population levels (Sutton, 2004: 135). Instead, what counts is re-shaping consumer practices so that they are simpler, more 'stripped down' and less wasteful. Citing a recent paper by David Satterthwaite (2009), Monbiot (2009) argues that the $I=PAT$ formula is wrong and total environmental impact should be measured as $I=CAT$: consumption $\times$ affluence $\times$ technology. Note, however, that affluence here seems to describe individual consumption rather than the three components of GDP utilised in the original $I=PAT$ equation.

Peter Dickens (2004) states the case against 'the consumer society' in considerable detail. Drawing on data from a large-scale (24,000 adults) survey of consumption habits, carried out by the British Market Research Bureau, Dickens spells out what constitutes an 'extravagant', materialistic lifestyle, as opposed to a more enlightened, 'body-centred', green lifestyle. The former is associated with a new dominant professional class who engage to an above-average extent in a number of leisure activities and consumptive practice (high levels of alcohol intake, frequent holidays abroad, regular consumption of bottled water, golfing and skiing) that are environmentally damaging. Even when they embrace activities that promise a healthier body – windsurfing, jogging, working out at the gym – Dickens (2004: 131) says they are doing so in order to 'perpetuate their income-earning capacity over a relatively long time' through keeping fit. By contrast, a smaller proportion of the middle class engage in a number of leisure pursuits designed to cultivate their spiritual and physical well-being – climbing, skating, camping, doing yoga – that are more environmentally neutral. Dickens especially worries about the wasteful and polluting activities of the dominant professional class because they 'act as a beacon to the less economically successful'.

Rather than singling out the managerial and professional classes, Cahill (2002: 161) casts the 'ideology of consumerism' as a long-term process that crucially coalesced in the 1950s among the British working class. With full employment and a welfare state consensus, a 'work-and-spend ethic' prevailed. This featured a household crammed with labour-saving appliances: washing machines, tumble dryers, dishwashers. One consequence here was a spike in energy consumption – by the late 1990s energy used in the home accounted for 30% of the UK's total energy consumption (Stokes, 1999, cited in Cahill, 2002: 164). Freed from the drudgery of domestic chores, people embraced sundry forms of leisure from television viewing to motorcycle racing. In the US, the spectacular growth of suburbia and the government-financed highway-building binge of the 1960s and 1970s put the car at the centre of the emerging consumer society. One negative result was air pollution. A car-centred culture enshrined a worldview that glorified speed and power, privileged the individual over the collective and consigned public transport use to the poor and the socially marginal.

Given the prevalence of the consumerist ethic, policy measures that advocate a cleaner, less polluting version of the status quo are insufficient. Recently, the Obama administration in the US announced new, tough automobile-emission standards that are forecast to improve fuel efficiency by an average of 5% per year, starting in 2012. While this promises to generate a raft of environmentally friendly effects – a reduction of greenhouse gas (GHG) emissions by 900 million tonnes through 2016 and a drop of 1.8 billion barrels of oil consumption by 2016 – it postpones, and, perhaps precludes, people making major changes in their lives that would challenge the dominance of consumerism.

This consumerist ethic can be overstated. In his *Guardian* column, Monbiot (2009: 19), playing the role of the provocateur, asks 'So where are the movements protesting about the stinking rich destroying our living systems? Where is the direct action against super-yachts and private jets? Where's Class War when you need it?'. Statements such as this reflect the acute distaste that many political radicals have always had for elites and for consumerism. Yet, in affluent countries, goods consumed by households and individuals represent only a relatively small fraction of energy and material use, compared to the contribution of industrial and agricultural production (Lock and Ikeda, 2005: 42). Furthermore, designating the individual consumer as the principal agent of change may not be wise. As Sanne (2002: 273-4) points out, this obscures how consumer choice is affected by an array of *structural* factors in society. In addition to the corporate marketing machine that lubricates the treadmill of production, these factors include working life conditions, urban structure and everyday life patterns.

On a macro-level it has been suggested that the rise of environmental consciousness in the 1970s was closely linked to the emergence of a *post-materialist* ethic. Drawing on Abraham Maslow's 'hierarchy of needs' (1954), political scientist Ronald Inglehart (1977) proposed that the generation born in the immediate aftermath of the Second World War adopted a brand new set of values and attitudes. Unlike their parents, who weathered the tough economic times of the Great Depression, followed by the privations of wartime, this younger generation was raised in a situation of untrammelled economic growth and prosperity. As a result, they were more inclined to tend to matters pertaining to spiritual growth, democratic participation and quality of life than were those focusing primarily on the attainment of financial success and security. Accordingly, post-materialists could be expected to be more concerned about the state of the environment. While Inglehart's thesis found some resonance in western Europe, it fitted less well in other parts of the world. In particular, post-materialist values alone are not sufficient to explain the existence of poor black environmentalists in the US or third world environmentalists who lack both economic security and formal education (Humphrey et al, 2002: 184-5).

Sustainability

Each of these models has its strengths and weaknesses. In their prescriptions for social and policy reform in particular, what they all engage with, and disagree about, is the meaning and implications of **sustainability** (see Chapters One, Three, Eight, Thirteen and also the Introduction, this volume).

From the late 1980s onwards, consideration of the environmental challenge has been blanketed in a discourse of 'sustainability'. The impetus for this was the 1987 publication by the World Commission on Environment and Development (WCED) of *Our Common Future*, popularly known as the **Brundtland Report** after Commission chair Norwegian Prime Minister Gro Harlem Brundtland. Famously, the Report defined sustainable development as 'development that meets the needs of the present without compromising the ability of future generations to meet their own needs' (WCED, 1987: 43).

In proposing the concept of 'sustainability' or 'sustainable development', the Commission was attempting to transcend (or perhaps sidestep) those debates that saw an ethos of unlimited economic growth as problematic (Dale, 2001: 3). It is fully possible, the authors of the report venture, to continue indefinitely with socioeconomic development 'without exhausting the world's resources or overburdening the ability of natural systems to cope with pollution' (Yearley, 1996: 96). In stark contrast to the limits to growth perspective, the authors of the Brundtland Report assert quite unambiguously that, 'Growth has no set limits in terms of population or resource use beyond which lies ecological disaster' (WCED, 1987: 45).

Unfortunately, the report never spells out how continuous growth is to occur without triggering ecological Armageddon. By attempting to frame sustainable development within a discourse of 'ideological neutrality', the Brundtland Report

> ... offers no clear vision of an ideal end state, whether green utopia or otherwise, and no set of political or economic arrangements is specifically promoted. Instead, sustainable development involves a *process of change* in which core components of society – resource use, investment, technologies, institutions, consumption patterns – come to operate in greater harmony with ecosystems. (Carter, 2007: 212)

Environmental critics of the Brundtland Report do overlook one of its central briefs, however: to address the deteriorating economic situation of the poorer countries of the Global South. The phrase 'development that meets the needs of the present' in the official definition of sustainable development refers to 'the essential needs of the world's poor, to which overriding priority should be given' (WCED, 1987: 43). Arguably, this trumps the North's demand for environmental protection. In contrast to previous environmental policy approaches, the Brundtland Report, together with subsequent blueprints for implementing its recommendations such as **Agenda 21**, the action plan for sustainable development adopted at the 1992 Rio Earth Summit, highlight the interdependence between environmental and developmental issues.

Two key features inform this 'poverty–environment nexus' (Carter, 2007: 218). First, environmental damage from global consumption falls disproportionately and most severely on the poor, especially those in southern regions. Second, in a struggle to survive, the poverty-stricken and landless people in the South are forced onto marginal, ecologically fragile lands and into damaging practices such as engaging in deforestation in order to obtain firewood. Thus, without first addressing poverty, strategies to come to grips with global environmental problems are inherently flawed.

To simultaneously address the imperatives of poverty and environmental sustainability a dual-track strategy is recommended. Until they reach a certain basic standard of wealth, the poorer countries of the South are permitted to opt out from international agreements that mandate carbon reduction. Giddens (2009: 64) describes this contraction and convergence principle as 'a necessary point of connection between the two types of development'.

Sustainable consumption

While the Brundtland Report does not specifically direct how citizens of northern countries might act, individually and collectively, to reduce poverty and environmental degradation in the South, Agenda 21 is more forthcoming by introducing the concept of **sustainable consumption**. Sustainable consumption is defined as the use of goods and services that meets basic needs and aspirations for a better life in the present, while respecting the limits of the Earth's ecosystems and not mortgaging the choices of future generations. When sustainable consumption entered the international policy arena in Agenda 21, 'this was the first time in international environmental discourse that over-consumption in the developed world was implicated as a direct cause of unsustainability' (Seyfang, 2005a: 139).

In the quarter century since sustainable consumption made its debut, there have been many opinions on how best to achieve the twin aims of 'reducing the direct impact of Northern consumption on scarce resources and improving the social and economic lot of the communities who supply those resources' (Carter, 2007: 219). One noteworthy treatment of this can be found in *Prosperity without Growth?*, a major policy report written by Tim Jackson, Economics Commissioner of the Sustainable Development Commission in the UK (2009).

In the last quarter century the global economy has doubled while an estimated 60% of the world's ecosystems have been degraded. If the level of affluence currently enjoyed by citizens in OECD (Organisation for Economic Co-operation and Development) nations is to be achieved, the global economy would need to be 15 times larger than the present one by 2050 and 40 times larger by the end of the century. At these levels, unless environmental impacts are somehow 'decoupled' from economic growth, ecological disaster is inevitable. There is no evidence as yet, Jackson (2009) finds, of decoupling taking place on anything like the scale and speed which would be required to avoid increasing environmental devastation. Looking to the future, in a world roughly a quarter larger than at present, carbon intensities would have to drop at a rate 16 times faster than they have since 1990 in order to stabilise the climate. This assumes a standard of income commensurate with 2% growth on the average European Union (EU) income today. 'The truth is', Jackson (2009: 8) concludes, 'there is yet no credible, socially just, ecologically sustainable scenario of continually growing incomes for a world of nine billion people'.

Is the situation hopeless then? Jackson (2009: 10) thinks it is, unless we adopt a different kind of macro-economic structure. Such a model would have to dismantle 'the iron cage of consumerism', not an easy task since material goods 'are so deeply implicated in the fabric of our lives'. Jackson reasons that if consumerism is powered by a relentless competition for status then only a more equal society will counteract this. Furthermore, the government must assume the reins of leadership and fundamentally revise 'the social logic of consumerism'. How this is to be achieved is not entirely clear. Jackson foresees 'prosperity without growth', where people turn away from shopping to pursue 'an alternate hedonism', described as 'sources of identity, creativity and meaning that lie outside the realm of the market'. However, the examples given (small-scale 'intentional' communities such as Findhorn in Scotland, or the 'transition town' movement, which aims to raise awareness of sustainable living and equip citizens for the dual challenge of peak oil (see p 35) and climate change through establishing community gardens and local currencies) appear unlikely to be rolled out any time soon on a mass level.

Seyfang (2005a) distinguishes between 'mainstream policy frameworks' and 'alternative strategies' for sustainable consumption. The former treats sustainable consumption as a market-based tool for change where the customer is sovereign. If there is sufficient demand for 'green' cleaning products or 'fair trade' coffee, then business will sell them – or at least that is the assumption. Seyfang disputes this on several grounds. For instance, many major consumption decisions are made out of the public eye, well away from market pressures. Thus, the purchase of construction materials for public infrastructure projects and provisioning contracts for the armed forces are both outside of regular retail markets. Furthermore, the international system of tariffs and other trade barriers can block the free flow of green imports. Even where corporations offer more environmentally friendly products, they may subvert any chance for success – this is what seems to have occurred with the electric car. Consumers may lack accurate information about what they are purchasing. An alternative strategy for sustainable consumption involves the 'radical re-organising' of economies to be more localised, decentralised and smaller-scale. Examples are localised food chains, non-market exchange mechanisms and community currency initiatives (see Chapter Six, this volume). However, like Tim Jackson's 'alternative hedonism', these represent only a small niche in the consumer market.

Social constructions and policy processes

It is clear that the gravity and sources of, and potential solutions to environmental problems are subject to considerable interpretation and debate. This chapter has shown how and why three explanatory models differ considerably in their diagnosis of what has caused the 'environmental crisis' and their prescription for what should be done to mitigate it. This realisation has given rise to a *social constructionist* approach to environmental risks and problems. According to the constructionist perspective, social understanding, knowledge and perception of both nature and environmental risk is inherently subjective, 'shaped and constructed by cultural, social, economic, political and psychological factors' (Burchell, 1998: 8).

Hannigan (2006) argues that environmental claim makers must successfully complete three sets of tasks (assembling, presenting, contesting) if they are to generate public visibility and secure political support for their issue of choice. The task of 'assembling' environmental claims concerns the initial discovery and elaboration of an incipient problem. At this stage, it is necessary to engage in a variety of specific activities: naming the problem, distinguishing it from other similar or more encompassing problems, determining the scientific, technical, moral or legal basis of the claim, and gauging who is responsible for taking ameliorative action. This occurs primarily within the realm of science.

Once a problem or issue has been identified and scientifically validated, it must be firmly situated on the public agenda. As Hilgartner and Bosk (1988) note, the arenas through which problems are defined and conveyed to the public are highly competitive – not all issues catch on or are given a high profile. Extensive and positive media coverage is crucial. One reason is that politicians *think* that the media shapes the public's perception of what is important and potentially act on this premise, especially if this appears to relate to government performance (Gavin, 2009: 765-6). Even where an environmental problem leapfrogs onto the media agenda, there can be conflicting interpretations or ways of 'framing' the situation.

In the late 1970s and early 1980s, some media sociologists (Altheide, 1976; Tuchman, 1978; Gitlin, 1980) coined the terms *frame* and *framing* to describe how news stories are 'constructed'. Frames represent a way of structuring and contextualising the tidal wave of data and information that swirls around us daily. They constitute 'organising devices' that assist both the journalist and members of the public to make sense of issues and events, thereby injecting them with meaning (Hannigan, 2006: 81). Similarly, a framing perspective has become central to the sociology of social movements. Here framing is treated as a strategy used by social movement organisation leaders to package their message and connect it to existing public concerns and perceptions (known as *frame alignment*). Frames that possess a measure of continuity over time are known as *story lines*. At a broader level, *discourse* is 'an interrelated set of story lines which interprets the world around us and which becomes deeply embedded in societal institutions, agendas and knowledge claims' (Hannigan, 2006: 36). Frames, story lines and discourse are key building blocks in the social construction of environmental issues and problems.

While scientific support and media attention constitute a vital part of the claim package, the problem is principally contested within the arena of politics. Within the social sciences, there is a critical mass of literature on 'agenda setting' that assists us in understanding why some issues achieve a high profile and inspire an official response, while others do not. Pralle (2009: 782) identifies three broad 'agendas' in democratic political systems. The *public agenda* refers to sets of issues that are most salient to citizens and voters. The *governmental agenda* consists of issues that are under discussion in legislatures and in bureaucratic agencies. Finally, the *decision agenda* is a narrower set of issues about which the government is poised to make a decision. In a perfect storm, all three agendas are aligned, legitimacy is achieved and official action is taken. Normally, however, the three agendas are out of sync. For example, electoral restructuring and tax reform may be paramount in official circles, while the public agenda emphasises the need for tougher laws governing juvenile offenders.

The agenda-setting literature favours explanatory models that allow issues to move up and down in importance over time. One seminal piece of work here is Anthony Downs' (1972) *issue-attention cycle*. This depicts fluctuating concern over the environment as determined by a combination of salient events and media attention. Downs observes that the cycle proceeds through five sequentially occurring stages:

- pre–problem stage;
- alarmed discovery and euphoric enthusiasm;
- realising the cost of significant progress;
- gradual decline of intense public interest;
- post–problem stage.

Another influential schema is John Kingdon's (1995) 'streams' model of agenda setting. The latter conceptualises the rise and fall of issues on governmental and non-governmental agendas as a product of the interplay of three largely interdependent streams or policy processes: problems, policies and processes. Occasionally, a window of opportunity ('policy window') opens up. If alert 'policy entrepreneurs' seize the moment, they can direct a merger of the three streams, increasing the chances that an issue will receive serious attention by policy makers (Pralle, 2009: 784).

Conclusion

Nearly three decades after he argued that the environmental challenge to modern society requires the cultivation of environmental public policy as 'a vast multi-disciplinary field of inquiry' (1970 [1963]: 23), Lynton Caldwell revisited the issue. Caldwell (1997: 9-10) notes that the difficulties presented by environmental problems as a policy area 'are distinctive in complexity and ramification'. These difficulties can be mitigated, he argued, if there were to be a shared public interpretation of the causes of and remedies for 'environmental impairment'. Public perceptions vary, he observes, from:

- the *incidental* (environmental 'disruptions' are isolated phenomena that occur as the result of human error or carelessness), to
- the *operational* (environmental problems are inadvertent caused by misdirected policy, flawed programme planning and bureaucratic intransigence), to
- the *systematic* (environmental degradation and, potentially, collapse, are the result of the priorities of a modern technological society that are economistic, growth-oriented and unsustainable).

While they differ in emphasis and interpretation, each of the three approaches to the environmental challenge discussed in this chapter are more or less consistent with the third level of interpretation cited by Caldwell. To a greater or lesser extent, each of these interpretations plugs into the paradigmatic discourse of sustainability. Where they differ is in their treatment of equity and social inclusion/exclusion.

The limits to growth model dwells on the notion of 'intergenerational equity', that is, the danger that we are robbing future generations of a planet with clean air and water, diverse species and an adequate supply of natural resources. The treadmill of production model favours a class-based distribution model of vulnerability (Gould et al, 2004: 298) to toxic effluents. Blue-collar workers live adjacent to or downstream of community pollution, while their managers, who long benefited to a greater extent from the expansion of the treadmill, live away from the polluting enterprises. Only through democratic ownership and control over production, we are told, will social and ecological problems be ameliorated. The consumerist ethic model focuses on the disparities between the wealthy northern nations and the poor South. The preferred course of action is for the middle class to act responsibly, drastically reducing its 'ecological footprint' by shopping and travelling less, buying food locally and generally living a simpler life.

More broadly, the challenge to society has been framed as an equity imbalance in applying the principles of sustainability. As Pickvance (2009: 329-30) notes, the Brundtland Report defines sustainable development as having three elements: economic, environmental and social. Taking as his illustration the construction of sustainable housing policy in the UK, he argues that there is a real danger that the 'social' dimension is being shunted aside 'rather than be pursued using complementary concepts such as inequality and affordability'. This is a key issue in understanding the link between environmental policy and social welfare. Paradoxically, those most likely to damage the Earth's ecological health are located at opposite poles of the income spectrum: the wealthy because their affluent lifestyles are likely to lead them to consume disproportionately; the poor because they are driven by desperation to engage in activities such as stripping bare tropical forests for firewood. In envisaging a green society, policies need to be developed that moderate the former, while providing some level of hope and basic security to the latter.

Chapter summary

Efforts to understand why the global environment is under siege have become mired in a slough of conflicting interpretations. This chapter has summarised and critiqued these models and explanations.

Some have pointed to unchecked population growth, which, they claim, is outstripping available resources such as food, fuel and water. A second school of thought insists that the prime cause of environmental disruption is the dynamic of production, which assumes the form of a 'treadmill' and which cannot be halted without dismantling the dominant economic system. And some argue that the prime villain is overconsumption by the affluent, especially in the North.

All three explanations implicitly, if not explicitly, recognise that a sustainable society is unlikely to emerge in the absence of some redress of basic social and economic inequities.

Questions for discussion

- To what extent is a focus on population growth an alarmist explanation that blames poor people in poor countries for having too many children?
- How can we step off the 'treadmill of production'?
- Do you think that consumer habits can become green or must we try and develop post-consumerist ways of living and interacting?
- Can there be such a thing as 'sustainable growth'?

Key further reading

Dickens, P. (2004) *Society and nature*, Cambridge: Polity Press.
Hannigan, J. (2006) *Environmental sociology* (2nd revised edn), London and New York: Routledge.

Harper, C.L. (2001) *Environment and society: Human perspectives on environmental issues*, Upper Saddle River, NJ: Prentice Hall.

Humphrey, C., Lewis, T. and Buttel, F.H. (eds) (2002) *Environment, energy and society: A new synthesis*, Belmont, CA: Wadsworth.

Sutton, P.W. (2004) *Nature, environment and society*, Houndsmills: Palgrave Macmillan.

Useful websites

American Sociological Association: http://envirosoc.org/

For a resource page dealing with Environmental Sociology, see:
www.socialresearchmethods.net/Gallery/Neto/Envsoc1.html

Challenges for social policy[1]

Tony Fitzpatrick

Overview

This chapter explores the principal challenges that all welfare systems face. It:

- reviews the main criticisms of environmentalists towards existing social policies;
- discusses the relationship between poverty and the environment;
- examines some 'environmental pioneers';
- investigates several global warming targets and strategies;
- explores the broad parameters of a green economy;
- outlines basic questions for an 'eco-social policy' agenda.

Having explored the broad social dimensions of environmental issues we narrow our focus onto social policy – both as an academic subject and a set of government activities – beginning with the principal critiques of its assumptions and practices which have been offered by greens.

Three critiques

Obviously, much depends on which environmentalists we are talking about (see the Introduction, this volume; also Jordan, 2010: Chapter 5). In general terms, however, most would assent to some version of the following.

Productivism and over-consumption

Environmentalists oppose social policies and welfare systems that are unsustainable. The basic idea is that a finite planet cannot support endless appropriations of its resources and unlimited contamination of its ecosystems. Some types of growth are less damaging than others but, for greens, only that growth which is consistent with, and preferably enhances, the coping capacity of the Earth is justifiable. Both ends of the political spectrum therefore stand accused. The Right treat rising material prosperity as the central justification for capitalism and free markets, the job of social policies being to assist markets by maintaining social order and enforcing the disciplines that unregulated markets require. Many on the Left have thought it best to champion social justice by emphasising a painless form of redistribution where basic needs are met by directing ever-higher levels of growth in appropriate directions, through horizontal redistribution and modest forms of vertical redistribution. In short, 'productivism' can be said to underpin all welfare regimes, whatever their political complexion.

Another charge, therefore, is that social policies *contribute* to unsustainability. By perpetuating the ideologies of productivism, welfare systems help to fuel more unsustainable growth. One implication is that welfare reforms tend only to address what environmentalists regard as the surface symptoms of social problems and miss the fact that the roots of many problems lie in ecological degradation and injustice. For instance, environmentalists note the extent to which poor health is caused by economies that place profits ahead of physical and mental well-being. 'Productivism' is therefore the assumption that economic growth is infinite and should take priority in all our economic, social and public policies (Fitzpatrick, 2003b, 2007a; Jackson, 2009; Paehlke, 2010: 246-7). Productivism is also a habit of the mind. Chapter Two emphasised the dangers of an irresponsible consumerism, a possessive individualism in which we measure our status (and that of others) in terms of income, wealth and possessions. This 'acquisitive impulse' leads us to demand more, more and more, when there is now numerous evidence that well-being is only partially related to material accumulation (Fitzpatrick, 2011: Chapter 1). However, this does not mean that greens should adopt a puritan anti-consumerism. There are forms of fair trade and fair consumption that can be promoted without requiring a massive (and unrealistic) revolution in habits. Instead, green consumerism implies a 'balanced diet': less self-indulgence but not a life of self-denial either. This is *post*-materialism but not *anti*-materialism.

Thus, sustainable growth (sometimes called 'zero growth') does not imply 'no growth' (see also Miliband, 2007); it means that growth has to remain within the physical limits of the Earth's capacity (Daly, 1996: Chapter 1;

Meadowcroft, 2005: 11-12; Simms, 2009: 210-18). You should only take out what you can put back. As such, sustainable growth won't be about adding quantity to our possessions but about adding quality to our lives and communities. This does not mean condemning people to penury, but it does mean finding other ways for them to create and exchange value. For instance, a 'caring society' is one where people use resources only insofar as they replenish them, nurture rather than discard, recognise their natural and social interdependencies and form convivial systems of association, organisation and progress.

National and short-term scales

And this means *all* humans. Dryzek (2008: 336) observes that social policy remains centred on the 'sovereign nation-state', whereas environmentalism demands (a) dynamic, non-state forms of interdependent activity, (b) local governance, for example, in the form of deliberative democracy, and (c) coordinated global action. It is possible to question Dryzek's contrast since the development and analysis of 'global social policies' is increasingly evident. Still, environmentalism does possess a distinct agenda of its own and it may well be that environmental governance will overtake and supersede existing forms of welfare governance. One implication is that social policy has to think more about the longer term. At present, governments are at best concerned with the short to medium term, for example, even thinking about substantial pension reform generally only takes you two generations into the future. A green politics says that our responsibilities extend much farther (Fitzpatrick, 2003b: Chapter 7).

Therefore, an 'eco-social' policy agenda has a steep hill to climb. Yes, we are apparently addicted to growth and materialist notions of prosperity but, beyond this, environmental problems are unprecedented, affect a global arena, occupy a longer timescale and are subject to collective unpredictability. It is no surprise that people find it difficult to make links between London and Mozambique, or between their own behaviour and mass flooding, or between 2010 and 2110. And even if they do, deciding how to reorganise our assumptions and practices is difficult.

Employment, work and insurance

Another critique proposes that social policy is too heavily based on wage earning as a source of economic security, moral value, social identity and communal participation. The 'employment ethic' is essential to modern society. In questioning it, many environmentalists are arguing not for the abolition of employment but for a recognition that security, value, identity and membership derive from far wider sources and activities. So rather than 'work' being equated with 'employment' we should recognise a broader spectrum of participative and socially valuable contributions. This requires a revised politics of time (Fitzpatrick, 2004), one which, as we have already mentioned, makes room for care (see Chapter Twelve, this volume). The welfare states that appeared in the middle of the 20th century were based on male, full-time, full employment, for only if employment was high (and the numbers of benefit claimants low) could social expenditure be maintained at generous levels. Yet while welcoming the social benefits of full employment, and arguing that ecological measures can generate 'green collar jobs', environmentalists also point to the ecological diswelfare created by existing employment attitudes and practices.

And if the employment ethic is challenged, then what happens to other assumptions? Social insurance, for instance, is based on the notion that socioeconomic security – the collectivisation of risks – can and should derive from labour market participation. It may not be possible to anticipate that *this* individual will experience unemployment or long-term illness, but across a population we can reasonably estimate that $x\%$ of people will encounter such contingencies. When it comes to climate change, however, *collective unpredictability* becomes central (Gough, 2008). We cannot simply use actuarial tables to calculate risks to individuals because the circumstances we all face are themselves subject to transformation and uncertainty. And the longer we delay implementing radical reforms the costlier the consequences and the more difficult it becomes to mitigate. In other words, our own (in)actions are as much a cause as they are an effect of collective unpredictability. If so, then job- and wage-based forms of insurance alone may no longer offer the secure bridge, linking the past, present and future, that their architects anticipated.

Centralisation and participation

The final main critique concerns the degree of control and autonomy currently possessed by individuals. The allegation is that existing forms of social organisation and welfare provision underestimate the extent to which citizens can be self-organising. The state is interpreted largely as too distant and impersonal a set of institutions (see Chapter Four, this volume). Representative democracy is thought to encourage a passive, consumerist attitude towards the common good, one that minimises the level of political participation in favour of a party political elitism. In terms of social policy, this state centralisation is thought to encourage the 'clientalisation' of welfare, where well-being is something we receive from experts and bureaucrats, and rarely something that people collectively generate for themselves. The price has been an over-arching collectivism that allows little space for bottom-up provision. Note that most greens reject a neoliberal ethos of market choice, minimal states and Victorian self-help, because they are committed to notions of social justice that this ethos contradicts. Thus, greens envisage new social policy processes and outcomes where the state provides a universalistic framework which makes greater room for civic associations and policy communities that would control funds and so reduce the distance between the users and producers of services (Offe, 1996; see Bulkeley and Newell, 2010: 74-86). In short, green social policies seem to require a greater degree of decentralisation and the emergence of a newly empowered 'welfare citizen'.

The above is far from exhaustive but does capture the basics of the environmentalist challenge. We now need to explore some responses that researchers, campaigners and policy makers have made to them. In the next section we explore a topic central to social policy research and in the following we highlight those welfare states that might be thought of as environmental pioneers.

Poverty

Chapter Seven offers a case study designed to explore the effects on vulnerable groups of environmental policies. Here, our questions are more general:

- What is the relationship between poverty, social exclusion and ecological conditions?
- To what extent are environmental solutions consistent with solutions to poverty?

It seems clear that, in developed and developing countries, there is a 'vicious cycle' between (1) poverty and exclusion, and (2) ecological decline (UNDP: 2007: 8).[2] People in poverty and exclusion are most vulnerable to the negative effects of global warming (Johnson et al, 2008) which then exacerbate many aspects of their deprivation: a kind of eco-poverty and eco-exclusion. Bads such as inadequate resources and opportunities, less purchasing power, poor communal facilities and higher levels of stress and illness all invite 'environmental deprivations' to join what Wolff and de-Shalit (2007) call a 'cluster of disadvantages'. For instance, while some may benefit from warmer winters any gains will probably be dwarfed by higher numbers of the elderly poor (who are most likely to experience ill health) suffering further ill health due to summer heatwaves. Poor housing raises fuel bills, making individuals less able to afford carbon taxes and other costs (such as insurance needed to protect against extreme weather events), so reducing their income further. Unless environmental policies are sensitive to such clustering, therefore, to the way in which disadvantages reciprocally reinforce one another, then they may make a bad situation worse.

> Climate change also has implications for the 'feminisation of poverty':... in the heat wave in Europe in 2003, the excess mortality for women was 75% higher than that for men at all ages.... In response to climate change and other environmental problems, households are expected to do more waste recycling, or more environmentally sensitive purchasing.... This added burden is likely to fall more on women than men, to add to the existing double or triple burden (paid work, care of dependents, housework) already felt, particularly by women in low-income households. After an extreme weather event, these added responsibilities are compounded. For example, it tends to be women who deal with the impacts of flooding: caring for children when schools are closed; caring for vulnerable relatives; and putting homes and families back together again once the waters have receded.... Women are significantly under-represented in environmental decision-making in government, industry and the scientific community.... (Johnson et al, 2008: 20)

Despite this, the advocates of social justice and environmental sustainability have all too often spoken past one another and so blunted their influence on policy makers. Thus, anti-poverty groups and agencies have been slow to connect the dots; for example, although it makes reference to topics like food and fuel, the Child Poverty Action Group (CPAG) lacks a specific ecological focus (see, for example, Flaherty et al, 2004; also Gordon and Townsend, 2000; Hills and Stewart, 2005; Pantazis et al, 2006; Dorling et al, 2007). This partly explains why the actions needed to combat climate change have so often been missing. Only in recent years have anti-poverty and green organisations really begun to work together systematically, for example, the Make Poverty History campaign. Inspiration for such campaigns may have derived from the environmental justice movement. The term 'environmental justice' originated in the US as a claim that people who are poor and/or members of minority groups experience the greatest risks of environmental deprivation that then help to perpetuate the cycle of socioeconomic poverty and cultural discrimination (Rosenbaum, 2008: 131-8). Thus, landfills and incinerators are most often sited in low-income communities, with obvious and adverse consequences for health, because the inhabitants typically possess little power and influence to resist them. Poorer children are exposed to higher toxin levels because they are more likely to play in streets or near to industrial plants and waste disposal sites. The affluent can also afford to move away from sources of pollution. Research in other countries reveals similar findings (Seyfang and Paavola, 2008: 674). In the UK, children from poorer communities are five times more likely to be killed in road accidents than children from affluent ones; and half of all carcinogenic emissions occur in the top 20% of deprived wards (Adebowale, 2008: 263).

The environmental justice *movement* therefore developed as a means for challenging this vicious circle of multiple deprivations, building alliances with anti-poverty lobby groups and contributing to a green movement that had previously been dominated by middle-class white people. As a result, the US government now requires federally funded planning projects to take account of, and listen to, underrepresented communities. Others have thus taken inspiration from such campaigns. Where sustained innovations are made, evidence suggests that deprived communities can simultaneously raise their social *and* environmental quality of life (Johnson et al, 2008), turning the vicious cycle into a virtuous one. Such progress counters the view that is evocatively expressed in the title of Burningham and Thrush's (2001) report: *'Rainforests are a long way from here'*. However, we should not assume that social and environmental objectives will always sit comfortably together. Consider the following. Roberts (2009) found that, due to their deprivation, the poorest 20% of UK households emit, on average, 60% less carbon dioxide (CO_2) per year from their energy and car use than the richest 20%. (The disparity would be greater if it took account of air travel and other emissions.) Funding emissions reductions purely from higher energy bills would be regressive, therefore. The poorest would be asked to pay proportionately more for the pollution created mainly by the affluent. However, poor households do emit more than the *global* average. We therefore need to protect them while lowering the country's overall carbon emissions. Hills (2009: 331-8) confirms that domestic fuel taxes are regressive, and while compensatory measures can be taken (by raising benefits and tax credits) a third of the poorest would still lose. First, not everyone is eligible for means-tested transfers and not everyone who *is* eligible actually claims them. Second, taxes are particularly severe on those whose homes lack insulation and other efficiency measures.

What Hills highlights is, then, a major problem for social policy. Ecological problems demand radical, integrated and immediate action. Yet the variables affecting the distribution of income and wealth are so considerable that effective action is difficult to take. If Hills is correct, should we (a) accept a certain amount of distributional regression that hurts some of the poorest or (b) avoid introducing carbon taxes until we can be reasonably sure of minimising any regressive effects? The problem is that (a) risks perpetuating poverties and exclusions, while (b) lengthens the period of transition to a low-carbon society, since it takes time to correct the problems of ineffective redistribution and thermal inefficiency. Both involve uncomfortable trade-offs between social and environmental goals. Much depends on our strategies and targets. If we cannot or will not speed up the political and policy process then we commit our descendants to dangerous increases in global warming. Or, if we prefer to avoid those levels then we are going to have to bite the bullet now. At present, we are headed towards a global warming of more than 2°C (see below).

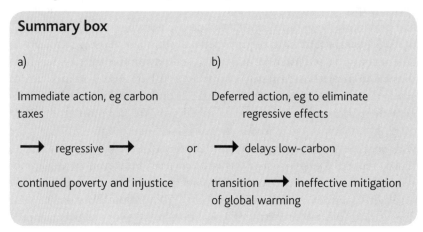

Summary box

a)

Immediate action, eg carbon taxes

→ regressive →

continued poverty and injustice

b)

Deferred action, eg to eliminate regressive effects

or → delays low-carbon

transition → ineffective mitigation of global warming

So, while social and environmental *injustices* often go together, ensuring the mutuality of social and environmental *justices* is not easy. Turning vicious cycles into virtuous ones, in a transition to green and socially just societies, involves extremely difficult decisions about what we should and should not value.

Environmental pioneers

What responses have policy makers made to the challenges and critiques outlined above? Which welfare states are the environmental pioneers?

The Nordic countries typically come at, or close to, the top of league tables that rank environmental performance; Sweden and Norway make the top 10 in two widely respected indexes (the others ranking in both lists are Switzerland and France). Frequently, the pioneers are also the most egalitarian countries with generally low rates of poverty (Friberg, 2008). This correlation gives rise to some big questions.

(1) Is social egalitarianism the *sine qua non* of ecological sustainability?
(2) Do the Nordic nations constitute a template for eco-social policies?

Various commentators will respond to question (1) in the negative. These may be conservatives or neoliberals who, while genuinely committed to sustainability, resist what they see as a state centralisation (Anderson and Leal, 2001). Other commentators may be sympathetic to centre-left politics but nevertheless deny that sustainability requires a single political model. Giddens (2009) believes that tackling climate change is an example of *post*-ideological politics.

My view is that, if anything, ideological politics is stronger than ever but, nevertheless, we ought indeed to encourage a 'green pluralism', since it is neither desirable nor possible to overturn the sheer scale of institutional-cultural, moral, political and historical diversities that are found around the globe. A green laggard like the US is unlikely to be converted to redistributive social democracy any time soon; but that does not preclude it following other routes to an environmental consensus. The arch individualist and naturalist Thoreau (1995: 207) urged his countrymen to '... be a Columbus to whole new continents and worlds within you, opening new channels, not of trade, but of thought'. That said, nor should we downplay the example that certain countries set for us. *Figure 3.1* takes the most egalitarian nations – according to the United Nations Development Programme's (UNDP) (2009) **Gini coefficients** – and cross-references these against the 2008 Environmental Performance Index (EPI).[3] As you can see, the more unequal the country the lower it scores on the EPI.

Figure 3.1: Top 20 green countries by Gini coefficient

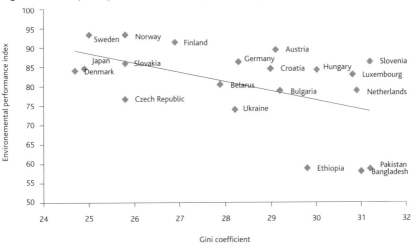

This is reinforced by *Figure 3.2* where, again, among the most developed nations, the more unequal the country the less well it typically performs on the EPI.

Figure 3.2: *Top 20 countries in the UN's 'Very High Human Development' Index*

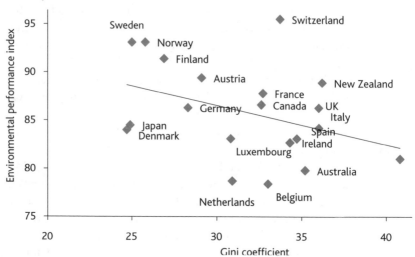

And in *Figure 3.3*, the worst-performing countries on the EPI are, on average, much more unequal than the best-performing ones.

The correlation is weaker in *Figure 3.4*, which takes the top 20 from the EPI list and cross-refers the Gini coefficient data. But although some of the best-performing countries, for example, Switzerland, have higher levels of inequality, overall the best-performing countries have a coefficient of approximately 35 or less.

We should hesitate to draw strong conclusions from this quick exercise. And even if equality is good for the environment, social democracies do not provide the only egalitarian template. With its six decades of post-war Conservative government, Japan performs respectably. Other factors are relevant too. Giddens (2009: 88) observes that the best-performing nations are often as concerned with energy security as climate change. Also, the worst performing countries are frequently characterised by severe economic underdevelopment, wars, civil conflict, famine and disease. But while a certain amount of economic development is important, it is not the only factor driving sustainability (see the discussion in Chapter Thirteen of the environmental Kuznets curve). In short, what matters is politics, good governance and, for the most developed nations, some commitment to socioeconomic equality. This does not necessarily demand a *social democratic* egalitarianism but we would also be unwise to treat the Nordic record as unremarkable or just lucky.

Figure 3.3: *Top 20 and bottom 20 countries on the EPI*

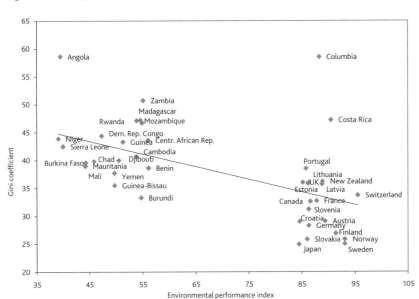

Figure 3.4: *EPI Top 20*

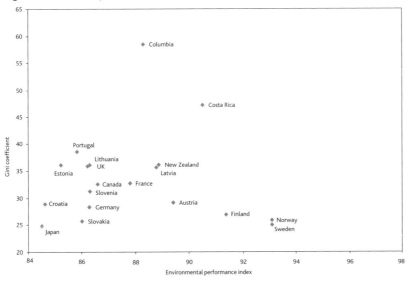

This takes us to question (2). What is it that the Nordic countries are getting right? If social and environmental policies need to converge, what lessons can we learn?

We need to tread carefully here. Norway's aim to become the first nation to reduce its greenhouse gas (GHG) emissions to zero (by 2030) is in part made possible by its being the world's fifth largest oil exporter. Geography also matters. Norway is well placed to generate most of its electricity from hydroelectric power.

Nonetheless, the relative successes of Sweden and Norway are in large part due to their inviting non-state organisations, groups and movements into the policy process, although Lundqvist (2004: 176-80) believes that in Sweden such organisational networks have squeezed citizen-centred participation out of the picture. This is not equivalent to successive UK governments' enthusiasm for voluntary and charitable organisations, often deriving from hostility towards the public sector. In Sweden and Norway the relationship is more 'horizontal', open, deliberative, mutual and interactive.

So, Dryzek et al (2003: 22-7, 139-41) observe that in Norway groups are tightly integrated into a corporatist, policy-making system. Leaders, ministries and administrators have taken environmental problems seriously and continuously since the 1970s and green groups have been partners within this process of development. They characterise this as an 'active and inclusive' state: *active* in that the state helps to connect organisations to the policy process, and *inclusive* because it is open to interaction with numerous organisations. There are differing emphases within the literature. Dryzek et al (2003: 75-8, 171-4) suspect that Norway has allowed its environmental organisations to be co-opted too much into the political arena, undermining the counterweight to the state that independent actors should provide. However, this characterisation has been disputed by Grendstad et al (2006). They agree that Norway has an inclusive polity, or what they call a 'state-friendly society', in which there is a close structural, attitudinal and behavioural relationship between state and society. But they propose that Norway also possesses a 'local community perspective' that implies a blurred distinction between town and country, humanity and nature, and represents the kind of counterweight which prevents the state from becoming too dominant. In any event, it seems clear that countries like Norway possess a higher degree of reciprocal trust, loyalty and support between policy makers and citizens than can be found elsewhere. The lesson for other countries is therefore double-edged. We can always envisage political parties, institutions, policy makers and other actors within the state-political apparatus becoming more open to civil society influences. However, trust is an intangible and elusive moral and emotional value that cannot be created overnight. Some argue that 'high-trust' societies are more likely to be historical cause and effect of universal, egalitarian and solidaristic welfare states (see Fitzpatrick, 2005: 61-3; Offer, 2006: 125-7). Such cultures cannot be quickly and easily engineered. This perhaps suggests that structural reform to encourage greater participation in the policy process will not pay full dividends until, over the long term, the political culture itself evolves.

However, it may be that alternative forms of high trust can be promoted. The UK lacks universalism, solidarity and vertical redistribution in its welfare schemes but perhaps its more individualistic system carries a radical potential nonetheless. With some notion of user empowerment at least on the agenda (Taylor-Gooby, 2009), it is not unreasonable to imagine translating such empowerment into forms of democratic coproduction that are less imitative of private sector and consumerist practices (see, for example, Gannon and Lawson, nd; Wainwright, 2009).

This accords with Meadowcroft's (2008: 331-2) view that existing political ideologies, social institutions and welfare regimes are shaping the design and implementation of environmental policies. Lundqvist (2004: 205-7) believes that the development of Swedish environmental policies is indebted to the institutional relationships and egalitarian cultures of its welfare state. If synergies can be strengthened and incongruities resolved we might expect this layering to evolve into an integrated, 'de-layered' state-economy-society ecological apparatus. In short, there are lessons to be learned from environmental pioneers like Norway and Sweden; namely, the importance of participative inclusivity and equality within the policy process. However, since cultural values are also vital other nations may have to pursue alternative methods, for creating high trust and low poverty, to the Scandinavian model.

What is the way forward for social policy, then? The answer to this depends to a large extent on how ambitious we ought to be. In combating global warming what targets and timescales should we aim for?

Ramps and launch pads

Two considerations appear relevant. First, there is some doubt that we should set international targets and timescales, believing that this distracts attention from the do-able. However, while setting a target and delivering on it are distinct activities, it is difficult to see actions being effective without something to aim for. Second, we are dealing with uncertainties. For instance, in **Table 3.1** there is an 18% chance of global temperatures rising by 3°C (above their pre-industrial level) if CO_2e stabilise at 450ppm (parts per million). This increases to 69% if CO_2e rise to 550ppm. This kind of research is helpful, but we should never forget we are dealing with probabilities, with some influential voices insisting the Intergovernmental Panel on Climate Change (IPCC) is too conservative in its estimates (see, for example, Hansen et al, 2008).

Table 3.1: Probabilities of temperature rises at varying levels of CO$_2$e

CO$_2$e ppm	2°C	3°C	4°C	5°C	6°C	7°C
450	78%	18%	3%	1%	0%	0%
500	96%	44%	11%	3%	1%	0%
550	99%	69%	24%	7%	2%	1%
650	100%	94%	58%	24%	9%	4%
750	100%	99%	82%	47%	22%	9%

Source: Stern (2009: 26)

With that in mind, and because I don't want to get lost in intricate details, I will use *Table 3.2* as a useful reference point and hope you will forgive me for smoothing over some of the complexities. This table utilises the IPCC's global warming scenarios that have already been introduced in Chapter One.

Table 3.2: Six global warming scenarios

Category	CO$_2$ concentration at stabilisation (2005 = 379ppm)	CO$_2$ equivalent concentration at stabilisation including GHGs and aerosols (2005 = 375ppm)	Peaking year for CO$_2$ emissions	Change in global CO$_2$ emissions in 2050 (% of 2000 emissions)	Global average temperature increase at equilibrium above pre-industrial level
	ppm	*ppm*	*Year*	*%*	*°C*
I	350-400	445-490	2000-15	−85 to −50	2.0-2.4
II	400-440	490-535	2000-20	−60 to −30	2.4-2.8
III	440-485	535-590	2010-30	−30 to +5	2.8-3.2
IV	485-570	590-710	2020-60	+10 to +60	3.2-4.0
V	570-660	710-855	2050-80	+25 to +85	4.0-4.9
VI	660-790	855-1,130	2060-90	+90 to +140	4.9-6.1

Source: Adapted from IPCC (2007: 67)

A policy ramp?

Some believe we should not panic because slamming on the socioeconomic brakes would be as dangerous as global warming itself (Lomborg, 2007). Since a 2°C rise is probably inevitable and since humans are ingenious at devising solutions to problems, an over-reaction would drain vital resources. Instead, we should grow now so that we can sustain more effectively later. Nordhaus (2008: 166) proposes a 'policy ramp':

In a world where capital is productive, the highest-return investments today are primarily in tangible, technological, and human capital, including research on and development of low-carbon technologies. Nordhaus (2008: 103, Table 5-7) therefore proposes that by 2100 we can afford to allow carbon emissions to rise to Point A in *Figure 3.5*.[4]

Figure 3.5: *Four recommendations for CO$_2$e stabilisation*

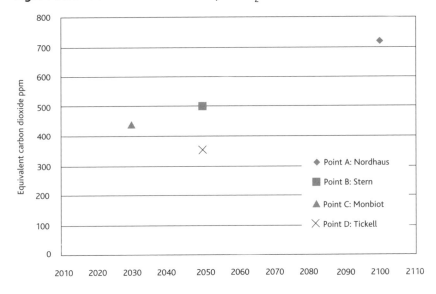

The policy ramp appears to correspond to the lower end of Category V in *Table 3.2*. Nordhaus would undoubtedly object to this characterisation. He believes his policy ramp would involve a temperature increase of just 2.6°C by 2100 and 3.4°C by 2200. The problem is that Nordhaus risks underestimating the rise in temperature that his preferred strategy would create (his projections are much more optimistic than the IPCC's), and even if they are correct, should we invite a temperature rise of 3.4°C anyway? As we add more GHGs to the atmosphere, we may reach a tipping point beyond which *any* mitigation becomes much harder to effect. This is known as 'positive feedback' (Lovelock, 2007: 44-5): warming can, by itself, create more warming. Nordhaus (2008: 28-9, 194), in fact, acknowledges that his economic model is highly uncertain after 2050 but argues that ecosystem complexities should be ignored for the sake of the model. Better, he believes, to work with assumptions 'more consistent with today's market real interest and savings rates' (Nordhaus, 2008: 191). But according to the **precautionary principle** we ought to plan for the worst-case scenarios.

Compare two possibilities. In one we overestimate the severity of global warming, while in another we underestimate it. According to the precautionary principle, and so long as we protect the most vulnerable, being over-cautious on the basis of an over-estimate is better than being under-cautious on the basis of an under-estimate. If we are wrong, at least with the former we lose a little whereas with the latter we risk losing a lot. This does not mean preferring inaction to action or refusing to interfere with nature, as Giddens (2009: 57-61) misleadingly puts it, but of minimising the harm we can reasonably anticipate.

I am therefore going to assume that social policies should incorporate a lower discount rate than Nordhaus recommends. **Discounting** refers to the means by which we gradually devalue future costs and benefits against present ones. A high rate means prioritising the interests of the present generation. But if my argument about the precautionary principle holds then we ought to apply a lower discount rate. This factors the interests of future generations more directly into today's policy-making decisions (for a longer discussion, see Fitzpatrick, 2003b: Chapter 7). What might this imply?

A policy launch pad?

Stern (2007, 2009) and Garnaut (2008; also, IPCC, 2007: 69) have argued that the developed world should aim to cut carbon emissions by 80% by 2050 in order to stabilise CO_2e at around 500-550ppm. This would create a temperature rise of approximately 2°-3°C and so corresponds to Category II and the lower range of Category III in **Table 3.2**. Stern's contribution in particular has highlighted the risks of delaying mitigation since, according to his figures, the cost of cutting carbon emissions (2% of global gross domestic product [GDP] by 2050) is much less than the cost of inaction (5%-20% of GDP by 2050). Stern thus recommends stabilisation of CO_2e emissions at Point B in **Figure 3.5**.

Although Stern is more ambitious than most governments to date, his approach has been criticised by some as too conservative. Monbiot (2007a: xii-xiii; see also Simms, 2009: 207-8) objects to Stern's use of cost-benefit analysis – indeed, many of those who make room for such analysis do not believe that it should be the dominant method for weighing environmental options (Kraft, 2011: 223; see Rosenbaum, 2008: 144-58). Monbiot's preferred alternative is for cuts in CO_2e of 90% by 2030 so that emissions are stabilised at about 440ppm (Point C in *Figure 3.5*) (see also Walker and King, 2008: 96-100; Lynas, 2008: 251-9). Tickell (2008: 29) reviews a range of expert literature and argues that we should aim for a complete cessation of GHGs in order that concentrations can be eventually stabilised at 300-350ppm – Point D. Monbiot and Tickell and others are, at the very least, recommending Category I in *Table 3.2* and, indeed, seem to go further.

Which should we prefer? Because I promised to void complexities, let me propose that the zone encompassing Points B, C and D constitutes the region, the broad target and timeline, for which we should aim, taking into account what is both politically feasible and ecologically necessary at the present time. In other words, something corresponding to Category I, with Category II as a hopefully avoidable, upper limit. This is to argue for radical emissions cuts over the next 20-40 years, bringing the social and environmental agendas together and moving heaven and earth to avoid, or at least minimise, the trade-offs mentioned on pages 67-8.

Transition

If this is the aim then the transition we need to achieve resembles something like *Figure 3.6*.

Although the various sectors are dealt with throughout the book, society has been dealt with in Chapter Two, the state is discussed in Chapter Four and green values are the theme of Chapters Five and Six. The missing link is the economic one and so it is to this that we now turn.

A green economy

What kind of economy might a 'launch pad' require? The following are typically mentioned as examples of mitigation and adaptation strategies (Walker and King, 2008: Chapters 10-11). But note that no policy instrument can *automatically* deliver sustainable growth. The latter depends ultimately on the values and motivations of the actors who deploy them.

Rationing

One popular idea concerns '**contraction and convergence**' (Monbiot, 2007a: 44-6; Tickell, 2008: Chapter 4). The world can only afford to emit x tonnes of carbon in any one year. Therefore, we should divide x by the number of people on the planet during that year and whatever figure that calculation generates represents a 'carbon allowance' for each individual. Obviously, the value of x depends on the sustainability targets and timelines we select, with fewer emissions being permitted in later decades. Also, countries with lower per capita emissions than x are allowed to emit *more* carbon until x is reached, in contrast to developed economies that have to initiate cuts to descend towards x. Countries therefore converge on one another as, over time, overall global emissions contract.

Figure 3.6: *An eco-social transition*

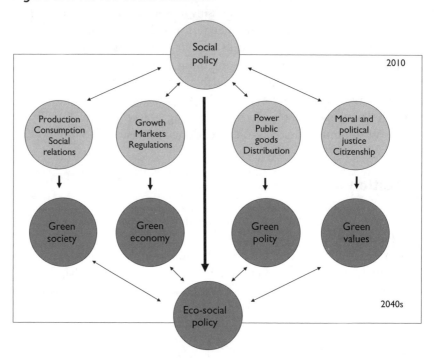

To try and remain within the limits of x we might distribute permits. These could be distributed as an annual carbon allowance. The problem with such a system would be its incredible complexity. It is a 'downstream' solution, targeting the point at which GHGs are released into the atmosphere. We might simplify the scheme so that such permits cover just purchases related to energy and transportation. By and large, however, we ought to emphasise the 'upstream', that is, the point of production. This means targeting producers. Obviously, if we do so correctly, then the cost of carbon will be incorporated into the prices that consumers will end up paying anyway 'at the end of the pipe'. So, how should we distribute permits to producers?

Since giving them away at no cost has proved to be a failure (see Chapter Seven, this volume), many propose that permits be sold in a global carbon market. How should the price of those permits be determined (Stern, 2009: 102-11)? We might elect to sell a flexible number of permits at a fixed price. This is equivalent to introducing a carbon tax. The problem is that taxes for different goods and services are difficult to coordinate internationally and they cannot *always* reflect the actual amount of pollution that is subsequently generated. Another approach is to auction a fixed number of permits at a flexible price. This way, the quantity of the emissions is 'capped' in a quota system by a global authority. The problem is that those prices may swing to the point where they are either worthlessly low or else dangerously high.

Presumably, the solution is to have both. In a hybrid **cap-and-trade** scheme, quotas solve the problems associated with taxes and vice versa. This hybrid solution dominates debates about the greening of the economy. As Nordhaus (2008: 164) observes, it would possess quantitative limits strong enough to guide firms and countries while also being able to reduce price volatility, uncertainty and 'perverse' incentives for corruption and game playing.

Regulation and innovation

But markets are never enough. Left alone, they displace the costs and consequences of production and consumption elsewhere. For instance, if car manufacturers had to factor the full social costs of driving – involving healthcare, pollution, waste, accidents and stress – into prices then cars would become prohibitively expensive and profits would fall. Such costs therefore shift onto others as 'negative externalities': public services (which cope with the deaths, ill health, injuries and disabilities created by car-dependent economies), the global poor (the most vulnerable to global warming) and the ecosystem (in higher rates of species extinction, for instance) and future generations. Prices, then, do not reflect costs and so we over-consume natural resources and erode the planet's coping capacity.

Regulations are needed to factor negative externalities into market processes, for example, through energy taxes, clean-up surcharges and higher quality standards. This relates back to the oft-quoted maxim that we need to impose more tax on what we do not want (pollution) and less on what we do (jobs). We review some specifics on pages 81-2 and in Chapter Seven.

None of which is to propose that regulations and technological innovations by themselves will deliver miraculous solutions (Simm, 2009: 26-8). Regulations can misfire and even the best technologies may produce unintended consequences – the efficacy of technologies depends on the individuals, institutions and corporations who operate them. Still, few will argue that they have no role to play in a green economy.

Adaptation

Adaptation to cope with global warming which is already heading our way will be a crucial aspect of a green economy. For instance, the World Health Organization (WHO) (2002: 71–2) estimated that in 2000, 154,000 deaths and 5.5 million DALYS (disability adjusted life years) occurred due to climate change. We explore global adaptation below. What of developed nations, however (Stern, 2007: Chapter 19)?

To date, two events have been prominent: heatwaves and floods (Walker and King, 2008: Chapter 4, 90–2). It seems clear that the 2003 European heatwave and the 2005 New Orleans flood may be symptomatic of more frequent extreme weather events to come. In Europe (IPCC, 2007: 50) climate change will magnify regional differences with greater rainfall and snowfall in the north and severe, more frequent droughts in the south. Cities in floodplains – think of the Netherlands – and in already warm climates may be at risk. There are now increased risks of inland flash floods, more frequent coastal flooding and increased erosion (due to storms and sea level rise), accelerating glacial retreat in mountainous areas, reduced snow cover and extensive species loss. In southern Europe, high temperatures and drought will make it a less attractive destination for emigrants due to further heatwaves, wildfires, reduced water availability and crop productivity. The WHO estimates the 2003 heatwaves to have cost 70,000 lives.[5] By the 2040s half of all summers may well be hotter than 2003, with elderly people being at particular risk (Lynas, 2008: 58–63). Tourism will be affected – because reduced snow cover means less winter tourism in the Alps and heatwaves less summer tourism around the Mediterranean – as will agriculture, fisheries and energy (changing water flows will affect both nuclear and hydroelectric plants).

Adaptation strategies at the European Union (EU) level are beginning to emerge to provide both forward planning and coordination of local and national adaptation policies. These include water, coastal zone, forest and soil management, protection of biodiversity and disaster management measures within the emergency services (Giddens, 2009: 167–9). It is difficult to place an exact price on adaptation. Stern (2007: 472–4) estimated future costs as anywhere between US$15 billion to US$150 billion per annum across OECD nations. We return to this later.

These, then, are crucial components of a green economy. To be consistent with a launch pad strategy we will have to move much faster and farther in each respect than we are currently managing.

Questions for an eco-social agenda

I have made two crucial claims. First, that while we have much to learn from the green pioneers it is unrealistic to expect the world to convert to Scandinavian social democracy. Green politics has to encompass diversity and plurality. Yet there are surely limits to what is acceptable, given the scale of the challenges we face. Thus, the second claim was that a launch pad strategy should be adopted. Countries need to say to one another: however you get there, get there! So, eco-social policy should embody what I will shortly call 'gestalt governance'. Some elements of the shift towards sustainable growth are essential and non-negotiable, while some are important but more matters of local discretion.In what follows I will not labour the distinction, however, my main aim being to ask some key questions which all of us – politicians, policy makers, researchers, citizens, practitioners, activists – are going to have to ask if social and environmental policy agendas are to converge. These questions link to the themes of previous sections, as well as to those covered in other chapters, and are simply intended to frame and (like the 'Questions for discussion') assist further reflection. In addition I will elucidate some current thinking, including my own.

1. How can social policies help to achieve sustainable/zero growth?
If the argument of pages 62-8 holds then, properly designed and implemented, social policies have a crucial role to play in getting us there by breaking into the vicious cycle of poverty/exclusion and ecological decline. Carbon taxes and quotas will be essential to the rationing and regulation of a green economy, making it more expensive to pollute and more attractive to preserve. But because, as we saw, carbon taxes are regressive, we will need redistributive counterbalances.

For example, much has been made of personal carbon trading (House of Commons, 2008; Capstick and Lewis, 2008). With a personal allowances scheme those who consume more of their allowance would have to purchase surplus permits from those who consume less. Since the poorest generally emit less carbon than the affluent, could redistribution be built into a cap-and-trade system? We could distribute higher allowances to low-income individuals since they may find it financially harder to make the adjustment to a low carbon economy (Garnaut, 2008: 388), requiring deeper cuts in the allowances of the affluent.But recall that the overall emissions of developed nations have to contract and, obviously, we already possess distributive schemes, for example, minimum wages, tax thresholds, tax credits and benefits.Thus, it may or may not be worth building extensive redistribution into cap-and-trade.We need to pilot the proposal and assess its merits in the light of other priorities, including the trade-offs mentioned on pages 67-8.

2. How can social policy reforms contribute to 'domestic adaptation'?

Some adaptation within welfare services is already under way. In Britain this includes ensuring that infrastructures can cope with the effects of heat, gales and floods (Johnson and Simms, 2007: 7). In short, the kind of energy and building efficiency measures discussed in Chapter Seven can and should also apply to 'welfare state buildings': decentralised electricity, combined heat and power, renewables, and so on. Furthermore, central capital grants are needed to assist with such building and energy adaptations. So, to meet government targets (a 60% reduction in emissions below 1990 levels by 2050) the NHS will need to reduce its net annual emissions by 600,000 tonnes of CO_2. Unfortunately, while energy efficiency in NHS buildings has improved, overall consumption has been rising so that government targets are not being met. This does not bode well for more ambitious, launch pad cuts. One problem is that energy efficiency and energy reduction are distinct. If I buy a car with double the normal fuel efficiency and use the money I save to buy my wife a car too then our overall fuel consumption has not decreased. Could the NHS therefore adapt to a proper cap-and-trade scheme?

A case could be made for allowing welfare services to reduce carbon emissions at a slower rate than the rest of society, on the grounds that we should not risk compromising provision for basic needs. This slower rate would presumably need to be compensated by applying a faster rate elsewhere. Set against this, is the EU's estimate that in 2000 there were 370,000 premature deaths due to air pollution, costing €80 billion to €150 billion per annum.[6] As such, with the NHS and other services occupying such a large part of social activity, there are perhaps greater benefits to be had by *not* exempting them from cap-and-trade targets. One well-publicised way to ensure that consumption reduces is to pour such savings into preventative healthcare so that fewer people turn up at the doors of the NHS. This ambition of turning an ill health service into more of a well health service is good for individuals and for the environment (see Chapter Eight, this volume).

All of that said, there is presumably still a case for allowing certain welfare services to breach their targets under certain circumstances. In the event of heatwaves on the scale of 2003, for instance, the priority should surely be to provide care rather than worrying about carbon (or indeed budgetary) targets. A formula permitting such 'selective exemptions', consistent with a cap-and-trade scheme, would need to be worked out.

3. How can we achieve a political economy of care?
It is difficult to imagine a green society that does not promote a care ethos. With social policy having been at the forefront of 'politics of care' debates, and since many welfare services should (theoretically) embody that ethos, then social policies will be central to a caring society. Yet we should not assume that the meaning and implications of care are automatic. Care means something in a conservatively religious society that it would not necessarily mean in a secular, cosmopolitan one. We deal with care in Chapters Six and Twelve.

4. How can we distribute political power more effectively?
For Sen (2009: 248-52), green policies must enhance the capabilities of individuals (their freedoms, powers and opportunities) through a redistribution of political power. We have seen that the environmental pioneers of Norway and Sweden possess open and inclusive systems, ones indebted to the high levels of trust and equality within their welfare systems. Such redistribution also means giving greater control vis-à-vis social policies, so that there is less of a distinction, and greater communication, between the producers and users of services. As with care, social policy has been at the forefront of recent debates. Nor should we forget the political importance of cultural representation. The environmental justice movement has been very effective at demonstrating how ecological degradation is linked to the devaluing of disadvantaged people.

5. How can we re-learn the habits of thinking collectively and communally?
The relatively affluent are more able to protect themselves from some socio-ecological shocks — such as rising energy and food prices; but in socioeconomic cultures which are highly possessive, short-termist and competitive, they may also 'individualise' environmental problems and prefer personalised solutions, for example, private insurance, which neglect the common good. A dissociation between the environmental and the social is both cause and effect of political systems unable to translate one vocabulary into another, for example, green political parties continue to be thought of as 'single issue'. Social policies may have become increasingly privatised and consumerised, but they retain the residue of an earlier age when we were not so quick to deny and run away from our shared vulnerabilities, mortalities and interdependencies. The welfare state stores the social memories of what Bauman (2005: Chapter 3) calls a 'community of fate'.

6. What kind of employment and labour market should we prefer?
Is a green society a post-employment society where waged work occupies a less central role than at present and which is more decentralised and

participative? Many think so. However, whether this implies a 30-hour week – or 20 hours or 10 hours – is likely to be an evolving target. Possible examples of post-employment schemes are discussed later in Chapter Six, and for specific discussions of working-time reductions see Little (2002) and Coote et al (2010).

7. How can social insurance systems be adapted to cope with collective uncertainties?
As urban areas along the coast and in flood-prone areas become vulnerable to rising water levels, and as storms become more severe, what should the government's responses be? Giddens (2009: 169-75) supports a strengthening of current developments. He says we need to avoid:

• placing unsupportable burdens on the state (hence private insurance should predominate, with the state picking up additional costs);
• moral hazard (where people leave themselves vulnerable because they know they have a safety-net to fall back on); and
• inequalities (where only the affluent can afford insurance premiums).

Yet surely there is a case here for some kind of social insurance scheme working in tandem with the private insurance industry. Social insurance pools risks, ensures the poorest are covered but does not necessarily invite moral hazard since participating households can be required to take adequate protection measures. This is another issue that requires large-scale research and piloting.

8. How can we mobilise political support and public opinion?
Unfortunately, welfare reforms have for a long time appealed to self-interest and images of others which, in portraying them as lazy scroungers exploiting the hard working, devalue them and make it easier to cut their benefits. Social-environmental politics cannot ignore self-interest but it is unlikely that the new sense of moral and political justice we need will come from self-interest alone.

Thus, it is easy enough to call for a decoupling of well-being from affluence and property ownership (Jackson, 2009), but myopia and self-interest remain powerful motivators. There are deep problems in trying to wean people away from the growth ethos with its culture of material consumerism and waste. We have spent so long identifying status and value with being advantaged within a system of massive inequalities. So, the development of post-material values may involve living with and reconciling some conflicting imperatives as we effect the transition to a new way of living, working, relating and thinking. Whatever your critique of the present, the future starts from where you are and not just where you want to be.

9. What forms of political, welfare and environmental governance do we need?
In short, we need everyone to join the same fleet, sailing in the same approximate direction at the same approximate speed, while also being able to carve out their own social spaces (Meadowcroft, 2005: 20-1). This is the self-assembly (LEGO® or Meccano®) model of governance. You do not get to determine the components or the basic rules of construction, but within those institutional parameters freedom and autonomy reassert themselves. People can be nudged paternalistically, through the use of incentives and institutional re-engineering, to act in ways that are good for them and others without this necessarily inhibiting their freedoms (Thaler and Sunstein, 2008).

And this applies to national as well as personal habits. A transitional period therefore may imply a form of 'gestalt governance' which embraces both unity and diversity, globality and locality, centralisation and decentralisation, structure and fluidity, the top-down and bottom-up, the directive and consensual, command and deliberation, states and networks, vertical bureaucracies and horizontal associations and partnerships. Thus gestalt governance tries to reconcile two objectives. Green politics has to make room for diversity while also promoting a hegemonic shift in the terms of political discourse, one that learns lessons from the environmental pioneers. Today's conservatives are likely to be conservative tomorrow too, but they also need to become *green* conservatives. Green politics and social policies therefore have to travel along several ideological and moral tracks which more or less point in the same direction.

10. How can we promote global justice?
Global trade has arguably worsened environmental conditions, because of **food miles** for instance. But opposing it involves more than simply challenging 'evil' multinational corporations and the like. It also pertains to our own expectations and habits. We all collude, to some extent, in unfair and self-destructive practices. Do we want to be shoppers in a global supermarket or people who enhance rather than squander their inheritance?

The global and transnational characteristics of social policies and policy debates have multiplied in recent years. The fact that developing countries bear the brunt of a worsening environment supplies another reason why social policies must (Heltberg et al, 2010):

• reduce poverty levels – according to the UNDP (2005: 4), US$300 billion would abolish extreme poverty (perhaps 10% of the cost of the Iraq War);

- share out the proceeds of past growth more equitably – and so return what was often stolen, for example, through slavery;
- help with adaptation (Stern, 2007: Chapter 20).

I have suggested previously (Fitzpatrick, 2008a: 218-25) that poverty relief requires a level of assistance that is expensive but, at 3% of GDP, far from ruinously so. Indeed, this is higher than some experts in the field recommend (Pogge, 2008: Chapter 8). If a Global Adaptation Fund were to be added to an anti-poverty scheme then how much are we talking about?

I am going to ignore the considerable synergies between anti-poverty and ecological adaptation because I want to deliberately over-estimate the sums involved. My purpose is to show that even exaggerated figures would not cripple developed nations, although they would certainly require some readjustment of our priorities.

Stern (2009: 179) estimates that global adaptation would cost £75 billion per annum, although if we add this to his figures for halving deforestation and improving public energy Research and Development (R&D) then the total comes to US$130 billion. Tickell (2008: Chapter 6) mentions a figure of US$200 billion per year. However, given my deliberate over-estimations, perhaps we should take his higher figure of US$1 trillion (including funds for clean energy and emergency relief) as a useful reference point (see also Simms, 2009: 199-200). This, Tickell argues, corresponds very closely to the amount that would be raised via a cap-and-trade permits auction, most of it flowing from developed to developing nations. Is it affordable? In 2009, the annual GDP of OECD nations stood at US$43-$44 trillion. Therefore, US$1 trillion represents approximately 2.3% of that total. If we add this percentage to the 3% just mentioned then we end up with a redistributive fund of approximately 5.3% of rich nations' GDP. This is certainly higher than existing targets and spending, but hardly debilitating. And since I have deliberately over-estimated the sums involved the actual percentage is probably much lower.

Thus, my earlier conclusion is likely to hold: global distributive justice will not bankrupt the West because, while it is expensive, it is not ruinously expensive. It will require us to make some decisions about the balance between domestic social and private expenditure, but this should hardly be beyond the bounds of ingenuity, not given the events during and following the 2008 financial crisis. You would be surprised what humans can adapt to when necessity beckons. As such, perhaps reorganising our economies around the principle of sustainable growth would not be quite the shock to the cultural system that some environmentalists and most anti-environmentalists portray it as being. We may need to 'downsize' our economies and find things to value other than transient consumer goods, but sustainable societies of the late 21st century and beyond would not necessarily be unrecognisable to us.

This is all a back-of-the-envelope snapshot based on existing wealth, obviously. Have I over-estimated the sums involved or might I even have under-estimated them? Are Stern's calculations correct? What would happen if we add his estimate regarding emission stabilisation (2% of annual GDP by 2050) to my exaggerated figures? And what are the likely effects of the 2008 financial crisis?

And yet, in response to such doubts we surely encounter a familiar moral *and* financial thought: whatever the cost, the cost of not acting is almost certain to be considerably higher.

The cost of acting

- 3% of GDP: global poverty reduction (see Fitzpatrick, 2008a: Chapter 11)
- 2.3% of GDP: Global Adaptation Fund
- 2% of GDP: Stern's estimate of the cost to global wealth by 2050.

Even with exaggerated figures we see that while the cost of acting is considerable, it is not debilitating.

Conclusion

There are many environmental challenges which social policy has to face: philosophical, moral, political, social, humanitarian, cultural and economic. I do not pretend to have covered them all in this chapter, only to have sketched the basics of an eco-social agenda. Interpreting and completing the portrait is a collective, long-term endeavour.

Notes

[1] Many thanks to Ian Gough for commenting on an earlier version of this chapter.
[2] In what follows I assume that poverty refers to relative poverty and deprivation, and therefore to exclusion from what is widely held to be a socially decent way of life. Since developing countries are covered in Chapter Thirteen (see also Tobin, 2010), I leave them to one side here.
[3] See http://epi.yale.edu. Similar results can be found by using the 2010 Climate Change Performance Index (CCPI) published by Germanwatch (www.germanwatch.org), although it covers fewer countries. Nonetheless, if you plot the CCPI of 30 OECD (Organisation for Economic Co-operation and Development) countries against the UNDP's Gini coefficients then, here too, the lower the inequality the higher the environmental ranking.

[4] Note that Nordhaus talks of CO_2, which I have here converted into its corresponding CO_2e figure so that easy comparisons can be made.
[5] '10 facts on climate change and health' (www.who.int/features/factfiles/climate_change/facts/en/index2.html).
[6] European Commission, MEMO/05/334, Brussels, 21 September 2005.

Chapter summary

This chapter has:

- outlined the environmentalist criticisms of social policy;
- debated the relationship between poverty and environmental problems;
- explored the lessons that might be learned from environmental pioneers;
- investigated a range of emissions targets, recommending a 'policy launch pad' strategy;
- explored the parameters of a green economy;
- outlined basic questions for an eco-social policy agenda.

Questions for discussion

- To what extent might the welfare state have contributed to global warming?
- Which elements of the existing welfare state appear to be most compatible and least compatible with a green economy?
- How might we cope with collective uncertainties?
- How successful are ongoing attempts to 'green' the welfare state?
- To what extent can the traditional goals of social policy, for example, reducing poverty, be made consistent with new ecological objectives?
- Do environmental challenges imply a radical new agenda for social policy?

Key further reading

Cahill, M. (2001) *Social policy and the environment*, London: Routledge.
Cahill, M. and Fitzpatrick, T. (eds) (2002) *Environmental issues and social welfare*, Oxford: Blackwell.
Fitzpatrick, T. (2003a) 'Environmentalism and social policy', in N. Ellison and C. Pierson (eds) *New developments in British social policy*, Basingstoke: Palgrave.
Fitzpatrick, T. and Cahill, M. (eds) (2002) *Environment and welfare*, Basingstoke: Palgrave.
nef (2008) *A Green New Deal*, London: nef.
Special Issue of the *Journal of European Social Policy* in 2008, vol 18, no 4.

Useful websites

Glossary of climate change terms: www.epa.gov/climatechange/glossary.html

Collection of resources relating to environmental justice and environmental racism: www.ejnet.org/ej/

New Economics Foundation (nef): www.neweconomics.org/

four

Challenges to the state

Philip Catney and Timothy Doyle

Overview

This chapter explores the 'turn to the state' in green political thought. After often being considered complicit with environmentally damaging processes, the state is now being reconceived as an institution in which the core activities of government are focused on environmental protection as much as on managing the economy or administering welfare policies.

This 'turn to the state' is considered through the experiences of governance and state restructuring in both the North and the South.

Finally, we show how the emergence of 'global governance states' in the Global South has raised concerns over their accountability and led to the imposition of largely post-materialist interpretations of sustainability and welfare.

Introduction

Before launching into our analysis it is worth pausing to offer a brief definition of how the (non-ecological) state has traditionally been defined. Richards and Smith (2002: 39) identified six features which any modern state possesses.

Six features of the state

- The state exercises sovereignty.
- State institutions are recognisably 'public', in contrast to the 'private' institutions of civil society.
- All states depend for their existence on institutions.
- The state is a territorial association – it exercises jurisdiction within geographically defined borders, and in international politics is treated (at least in theory) as an autonomous entity.
- The state is an exercise in legitimation: its decisions are usually (although not necessarily) accepted as binding on its citizens because, it is claimed, it reflects the interests of society.
- The state is an instrument of domination: it possesses the coercive power to ensure its laws are obeyed and its transgressors punished.

There have been sustained challenges to the very definition of what constitutes the state – its boundaries and functions – over the past 30 years or so. The traditional definition listed in the box above is firmly ensconced within *Westphalian* thought, with an emphasis on the concept of the nation-state: state and national boundaries coincide with defined territories in real terms of space, place and national identity. In more recent times, what are sometimes called more *post-modern* and/or *neoliberal* and/or *globalised* interpretations of the state have challenged this orthodoxy, leading to more amorphous and disparate understandings of state forms, including cross-boundary and cross-sectoral interactions and interpretations. While research into states has changed considerably over the past generation, democratic reforms and innovations have not necessarily matched the degree of state restructuring. Later in this chapter, we show how these structural and democratic tensions have been greater in the Global South than in the Global North as, in the case of the former, these newer, globalised notions of governance have been even more *hollowed out*.

Green theory and the state

In environmental political thought, the state has long been treated with considerable suspicion (see also Chapter Eleven, this volume). Green theorists have been quick to identify the state as a source of environmental degradation, as well as social domination. Yet green political thought is currently in the process of revising this position in order to recognise the importance of the state for securing effective action on a range of environmental challenges. In this chapter we explore how a number of green theorists have sought to 'bring the state back in' as an institution that has a potentially constructive and positive role to play in securing more sustainable forms of social, economic and political organisation. These theorists have sought to steer the movement away from hostile stances to the state, to recognising the continued importance of states in the contemporary world and the possibilities that may exist for state reform so that environmental and social welfare goals are more effectively promoted.

The type of state that has been utilised within these discourses has variously been termed the 'green' (Eckersley, 2004), the 'ecological' (Meadowcroft, 2005) or the 'global green governance' state (Doyle and Doherty, 2006). These terms are, respectively, normative, analytical and critical in meaning and intent, and are discussed below. In the archetypal green state, the core activities of government are focused on environmental protection as much as on managing the economy or administering welfare policies. The 'welfare of the Earth' challenges old categories, arguing for a more holistic concept of welfare for all, both human and non-human.

Green critiques of the state emerged during the late 1960s when Keynesian welfare states were the norm across industrialised states. In many European states the administration of policies such as welfare was undertaken at a national scale with some form of national-level economic planning. For many green theorists, the national scale was too large and placed too great a distance between those making decisions and those affected by them. At a national scale, green theorists claimed, decision makers were too far removed from the ecological consequences of the decisions that were made centrally (Paterson et al, 2006: 137). As we will show later, this critique still resonates in the 'global governance states' of the Global South.

Furthermore, anarchistic and certain libertarian strands of the green movement objected to every single one of the six features identified by Richards and Smith (2002). The anarchist theorist Murray Bookchin (2005: 200) argued:

> In restructuring society around itself, the State acquires superadded social functions that now appear as political functions. It not only *manages* the economy but *politicizes* it; it not only *colonizes* social life but *absorbs* it. Social forms thus appear as State forms and social values as political values. Society is reorganized in such a way that it becomes indistinguishable from the State. Revolution is thus confronted not only with the task of smashing the State and reconstructing *administration* along libertarian lines; it must also smash society, as it were, and reconstruct human *consociation* itself along new communal lines.

In place of a centralised and bureaucratic state, eco-anarchists such as Murray Bookchin wish to see a return to small-scale forms of social organisation, such as communes, based on ecological bioregions. Their argument is that truly sustainable forms of society can only be achieved when hierarchies such as the state are removed and replaced with more cooperative forms of governance. For these theorists, the local offers the *natural* scale at which social organisation and welfare distribution can be organised in a democratic and participative manner. Green political theorists from this tradition place considerable emphasis on self-reliance, on participation and on small units, which implies a welfare system of local services run by local residents for one another (George and Wilding, 1994). Yet, as Paterson et al (2006: 144) observe, these ideas – while gaining considerable support from beyond their obvious followers – have not gone uncontested in the green movement. One of the key arguments against their proposals is that the small-scale forms of social organisation proposed would find it near impossible to effectively deal with ecological problems that have a global character (Paterson et al, 2006: 144). The sheer number of small-scale communities would defeat attempts to produce the necessary collective action.

However, while the green movement has often been antagonistic in its reading of the state, this does not mean that it has only advocated localism as a political strategy; the global scale has been a site of considerable activity by environmental movements. In part this is driven by a tendency in the green movement to reject the arbitrary division of the world into competing states.

Although accepting the need for a state controlled directly by its citizens, a further salient critique comes from eco-Marxists. They assert that aside from being viewed as an instrument of capitalist military, economic and cultural domination, the state only intervenes to prevent environmental degradation where it poses considerable threats to the maintenance of the capitalist system and, even then, only intervenes to secure the interests of business and the continuation of processes of capital accumulation (Hay, 1994; Paterson, 1996: 159). Furthermore, other analysts have suggested that the division of the world into separate states creates competition between them to exploit the environment for financial gain, especially when negative ecological externalities are inflicted on populations beyond the state (Pirages and DeGeest, 2004: 214).

Some of the radical schools of thought outlined above would no doubt view attempts to rehabilitate the state within environmental thought as the triumph of 'light green' sustainable development discourses – which advances the possibility of forms of economic growth that are compatible with environmental protection (see below) – rather than 'deep green' radical visions of an ecologically sound future development. We argue in this chapter that the scale and severity of the social, economic and environmental challenges already facing states in the Global North, but particularly in the Global South, necessitates an urgent rethinking of the nature of environmentalism and the role of the state in order to secure welfare for present and future generations. We argue, by contrast, that the state *per se* is not the problem, but that a key barrier to the achievement of this welfare is the issue of governance; namely, how to create a capacity for states (particularly in the Global South) to respond to processes of internationalisation and neoliberalisation.

Welfare and the politics of growth

The issue of growth is a potentially problematic one for greens (see Chapters Two and Three, this volume). Over the 20th century, the provision of welfare became the primary concern of politics in industrial countries (Meadowcroft, 2005: 3). The politics of many states was defined by the extent to which political actors felt that government should be involved in the provision of welfare. Broadly speaking, while social democrats advanced claims for greater state action to address welfare concerns, neoliberals advocated more residual forms of support and a minimal state (Turner, 2008: 140-66). To a greater or lesser degree, this debate structured the terrain of political debate for the entire century. Both left and right tacitly agreed that constantly rising rates of economic growth were essential for funding the additional welfare burdens placed on the state. This is what is often termed the 'logic of industrialism' (Pierson, 2006: 92-94).

While political parties competed on the platform of satisfying the rising economic aspirations of their electorates, the green movement sought to open this assumption to scrutiny, and to highlight the ecological costs imposed by the constant pursuit of growth (Porritt, 1984). As Chapter Two makes clear, the green movement emerged in the context of the 'limits to growth' debates in the early 1970s, and as a response to the neglect of ecological concerns by mainstream parties (see Meadows et al, 1972). Broadly speaking, the green movement argued that the pursuit of economic growth – or more precisely, the wrong sorts of economic growth – has done little to improve the quality of life, welfare and well-being of people (Pierson, 2006: 93).

Yet a reduction in economic growth and consumption rates, it is often argued, would limit the degree to which the state can make public welfare provision. Already, welfare states in the Global North are confronting a number of **post-industrial** challenges such as low levels of economic growth, ageing populations and changing family structures (Pierson, 2001).

States are hence required to push further for economic growth (and, indirectly, social welfare), potentially at the expense of the environment. For example, while the UK government has made considerable progress in terms of ecological modernisation of the past two decades (see below), the economic imperative has intervened to push anti-environmental agendas, such as the growth of air travel, to secure inward investment and promote growth (Barry and Paterson, 2004). Analysts from a sustainable development perspective have critiqued this trade-off between economic growth and environmental protection, arguing that the state can pursue forms of economic growth that are compatible with environmental protection (Dryzek, 2005).

Sustainable development is often criticised for its ambiguity. This ambiguity has given rise to a panoply of discourses that interpret sustainability in a variety of ways within and across nations (see Lafferty and Meadowcroft, 2000). The dominant interpretation of sustainable development comes in the form of **ecological modernisation** (EM) (see the Introduction, this volume). EM can be understood as an attempt to resolve the traditional tension in environmental politics between striving for economic growth and protecting the environment. Instead of seeking to replace capitalism with some other alternative system of socioeconomic organisation, EM suggests that governments, corporations and civil society can seek to promote economic growth but that they must take greater responsibility for protecting the global environment from further damage. The Brundtland Report (WCED, 1987) supported this interpretation of sustainable development by arguing that continued economic growth could support environmental protection, as well as promoting social development (Doyle, 1998). EM is typically interpreted as taking a variety of forms, from weak EM (low levels of reform to the state with limited changes to prevailing models of political economy) to strong EM (a fundamental reconsideration of state structures to open up the policy processes to greater citizen participation and a fundamental reorientation towards an ecologically sensitive capitalism) (Christoff, 1996; Barry and Paterson, 2004).

Summary box

Ecological modernisation (EM)

EM first emerged in the 1980s. Its advocates argue:
* it is possible to decouple economic growth from environmental harm;
* the application of new technologies and the redesign of institutions can reduce or better manage the amount of raw material throughput, energy use and waste generation that modern societies produce.

EM has been an influential discourse, utilised in UK environment policy over the past two decades. Both Revell (2005) and Barry and Paterson (2004) argue that the UK has embraced the weak version of EM. Politicians from both Conservative and Labour parties have utilised the language of EM in their speeches on the environment. At a time of increased ecological awareness, the 'win–win' (Revell, 2005) philosophy of EM enables politicians to offer policy solutions to these threats that also contribute to economic growth. The influence of EM over UK environmental policy can be seen in the increased use of market-based policies. For example, the Climate Change Levy was introduced in April 2001 as a tax on energy delivered to non-domestic users. The overall aim of the Levy, which is applied to electricity, gas, coal and liquid petroleum gas for non-domestic users, was to increase energy efficiency and reduce carbon emissions. The implications of a more carbon-friendly society are well-documented (see Salih, 2009).

Towards a green welfare state?

Since the modern environmental movement emerged in the late 1960s, increasing scientific information and more active lobbying by environmental parties and pressure groups have combined to produce a growing ecological awareness in the citizenry of many states. As a result, the past two decades have witnessed the development of more coherent strategies in states to meet commitments undertaken as part of international agreements such as the Montreal Protocol (1989), Rio (1992) or Kyoto (1997), or as the result of concerted lobbying action by green social movements (Dryzek et al, 2003). Smaller states in Europe such as the Netherlands, Sweden and Norway, have moved more rapidly to integrate environmental concerns with core state functions (Meadowcroft, 2005: 4). Indeed, most developed states have seen the development of specific ministries or agencies dedicated to the environment, as well as national action plans to guide future efforts.

While many environmentalists considered states, at best, as a blockage to environmental protection and, at worst, playing a critical role in generating environmental crises, more recent contributions have sought to 'bring the state back in'. For example, Eckersley (2004), Meadowcroft (2005), Doyle and Doherty (2006) and Giddens (2009) all highlight the essential role that the state will play – and in some cases is already playing – in structuring responses to climate change and other environmental crises. For these authors, the state remains the essential political unit through which effective action needs to take place, albeit in the context of international regimes and agreements. These authors argue that the state possesses both the financial and coercive means, as well as the political legitimacy, necessary to create the context for effective action on climate change. In short, the state, however imperfect, still provides a powerful and legitimate presence in world affairs when confronted by the increased power of transnational corporations in these globalised and neoliberal economic times (Meadowcroft, 2007).

The normative

For Eckersley (2004: 241), the development of greener states and societies has been inhibited by three developments: the anarchic state system, global capitalism and the bureaucratic rationalities of the administrative state. However, while she finds some trends that offer hope of a transition to greener forms of socioeconomic development, for example, greater environmental multilateralism and ecological modernisation, she argues that a fundamental transformation to a truly green state cannot be achieved within the framework of **liberal democracy**. She observes:

> Liberal democracies continue to construct decisions to invest, produce, and consume as essentially private matters, unless such decisions can be shown to cause direct and demonstrable harm to identifiable agents (which is never an easy matter). (Eckersley, 2004: 241–2)

A clean and sustainable environment is a public good which is critical for ensuring our ability to produce and reproduce our daily lives (Dobson, 2006: 222). Eckersley (2004: 242) argues, however, that liberal democratic (capitalist) states focus on the individual's freedom and privileging of *private* goods, which deflect attention away from the social and economic structures that 'shape and limit the horizons of individual choice (including environmental choices), and more so for economically marginal social classes and groups'. She advances a vision of an ecological state acting as a 'public ecological trustee', protecting public goods essential to creating a truly sustainable order such as public transport, biodiversity and life support systems (Eckersley, 2004: 12). While she recognises that the emergence of 'green consumerism' has challenged the traditional boundaries between public and private spheres, she argues that this is a poor substitute for a critical dialogue in public fora:

> Any management regime that seeks to relinquish public control of environmental quality can no longer provide any security against private interests prevailing over the public interest. (Eckersley, 2004: 95–6)

For Eckersley, 'free market environmentalism' is insufficient to meet the challenges posed by environmental hazards. Only through extending the public sphere and advancing new forms of democracy which win the support of traditionally marginalised groups can a truly effective ecological order be brought into being. This focus on marginalised groups is broad. Eckersley argues that an ecological democracy would focus more on the rights of those potentially affected by ecological risks, rather than the rights of the individual. Like Hayward (2005), Eckersley believes that environmental rights should be constitutionally guaranteed by the state, for people within and beyond the boundaries of the state. Hence Eckersley (2004: 247) seeks to break apart the nexus of citizenship, democracy, territoriality and sovereignty that is at the heart of liberal democratic theory and replace this with more flexible and localised forms of sovereignty, albeit with national and transnational linkages.

While Eckersley may seek to dispense with liberal democracy, she does not advocate the complete removal of representative forms of democracy. While she advocates the extension of participation through greater popular deliberation, she notes that it is unfeasible to expect all affected parties to be able to deliberate together *en masse* (Eckersley, 2004: 132). Therefore she supports retaining political representation, but making it as diverse as possible so as to encourage and facilitate 'enlarged thinking'. This diversity is not just in the sense of political recruitment from across social groups (along the lines of class, 'race', gender, region and so on), but also in the sense of bringing diverse viewpoints into the public sphere that can challenge accepted political nostrums. Furthermore, as noted above, she argues that representatives must be obliged to consider how their decisions affect social and ecological communities both within and beyond the state.

The analytical

Dryzek et al's (2003) analysis of the green state is different (see Chapter Three, this volume). It is based less on normative arguments than on empirical analysis of the ways in which states are being transformed in response to the mobilisation of environmental movements within different states. Examining the interactions between states and civil societies in four developed western nations (the US, the UK, Germany and Norway), Dryzek et al show how different patterns of greening of the state are taking place. Paterson et al (2006: 150) observe:

> Combined, the analyses of Eckersley and Dryzek et al provide powerful arguments which suggest that the 'green anarchist' position is over-stated; that while there is much which is clearly

anti-ecological in contemporary state practice and structures, these should be regarded as historically contingent rather than structurally inherent features of statehood.

Positive reform to the state is possible to make it a useful ally in attempts to bring about a more just and sustainable society. For some, like Meadowcroft (2005: 4), the shift to a green state will be an incremental process, similar to how the welfare state emerged in many countries.

Internationalisation

While green theorists have begun to set out the broad contours of a green state, the thorny issue of how welfare commitments can be met in such a state has to some extent been side-stepped. The EM thesis suggests that it is possible for states that are greening to decouple economic growth from ecologically damaging practices. But the post-industrial pressures confronting advanced welfare states (see Pierson, 2001) would not simply dissolve due to ecological reforms. Furthermore, in the context of climate change, the ambit of welfare will potentially need to *expand* to meet the more basic survival needs of populations in both the Global North and the Global South. As Hirst (2001: 129) succinctly put it:

> In the circumstances of unchecked climate change, territorial states with inclusive policies that attempt to protect all citizens will become more not less necessary. States will use public funds to acquire scarce resources and will ration them, and they will use public action to cope with the direct physical consequences, such as flood and drought.

The state in developed countries continues to command considerable financial, organisational and coercive resources through which to guide societal development inside its boundaries, and remains the key unit of decision making on the international stage (Meadowcroft, 2007). For example, while the European Union (EU) has done a great deal to advance the environmental agenda over the past few decades, it remains the responsibility of member states to decide on the appropriate means of implementing (or not implementing) the decisions agreed at the supranational level. In addition, the state remains at a critical scale for legitimising the types of difficult collective decisions that are needed for environmental improvement. As already noted, despite the apparent weaknesses of the state to address complex, long-term cross-boundary social and environmental problems, it provides a more stable counterweight to both the fluidity and lack of citizen responsibility found in marketplaces and civil society. It is for these reasons that a number of analysts continue to assert the importance of the state in attempts to ameliorate environmental concerns.

It should be noted here that the focus on the state is not always to dismiss the contribution of international institutions and global governance in advancing the ecological agenda. For example, the EU has been an important actor in environmental policy diffusion across its constituent member states. John Gummer, the former UK environment secretary (1993–97), estimated that as much as 80% of British environmental legislation in the 1980s and 1990s was derived from requirements of EU law (McCormack, 2002: 135). It has promoted programmes such as emissions trading and burden sharing agreement. While the EU failed to successfully broker a deal between the US and China at the Copenhagen Climate Conference in December 2009, it has committed itself to a 20% emissions reduction below 1990 levels by 2020 (although had an agreement been reached, this figure would have been 30%).

Overall, then, this focus on the 'green' state should not be taken as a replacement for efforts at the international scale. Rather, in the context of debates over the capacity of the state to respond to environmental and associated social welfare concerns, this perspective seeks to reassert the state's importance in helping to negotiate and implement agreements that emerge from international institutions. Yet the actual capacity of the state to meet the obligations of international treaties and self-imposed domestic goals is uncertain. It is to this question of coordination and capacity in the modern state that we now turn.

Redefining state capacities in a neoliberal world

Over the past three decades, the state has undergone significant transformation in both the developed and the developing world. Instead of using the term *government* – by which we now understand the traditional institutions and processes of government – it is more common for political analysts to refer to **governance**. While governance can also be a synonym for government, it is now widely concerned, as Pierre and Stoker (2000: 32) observed, 'with creating the conditions for ordered rule and collective action'. Governance theory focuses on the changing form of state power in the context of the process of globalisation, the increasing power of market forces and the 'hollowing out' of the state's functions which, it is claimed, has led to the capacity of the state to exert hierarchical control being increasingly supplanted by complex patterns of multi-organisational collaboration and informational social networks. In the post-governance state, 'heterarchy' replaces hierarchy; control of organisations is replaced with subtler, more negotiated and consensual methods of steering.

Similarly, Kooiman (1993, 2003) promotes the idea of a 'centreless society' in which governance becomes an interactive process and where the state operates alongside a constellation of private and societal actors in order to achieve collective goals. The process of governing societies has shifted from being state-centric to a more variegated and multifaceted process of governance. The resulting increased tensions between a static 'territorial space' and dynamic 'functional space' causes many governance problems in terms of legitimacy and public accountability, challenging the very definition of the state given at the beginning of this chapter. Thus, the challenge is to accommodate and, if necessary, adapt the traditional systems of representative democracy associated with 'old' government within these systems of 'new' and multilevel governance. The basic assumption of this literature is that the agency open to governments in developing and implementing public policies has reduced.

In Britain, a number of central government policy decisions have contributed to the emergence of governance. Inspired by **neoliberal** theory that downplayed the importance of government and hyped up the role of the market, the Conservatives under Margaret Thatcher and John Major sought to alter the size of government through the deregulation, contracting out and privatisation of state functions (Hood, 1991). In addition, the sovereignty of states has also been eroded through the increasingly international nature of economic activity. The establishment of international trade organisations such as the World Trade Organization (WTO), the World Bank and the North American Free Trade Association, alongside closer EU integration, has further diminished the authority of the central state. As we will show later with reference to the Global South, the power of transnational capital and international development organisations has considerable influence over the policies directed towards a whole range of policy issues, including social welfare and the environment.

Summary box

Governance
Governance is a descriptive label used to capture the changing nature of governing. Although definitions abound, it is commonly used to stress the complexity of policy making, implementation and accountability between a variety of state and societal actors at a variety of spatial levels (supranational bodies, central governments, state or devolved administrations, county and/or district authorities, plus quasi-governmental organisations). It points to a shift from hierarchical, territorial modes of government based on the dominant position of the

nation-state to more functionally based systems of governance, such as policy networks. The rise of governance is often claimed to have 'hollowed out' the state, reducing the capacity to act exclusively on behalf of national governments.

The extent to which the state has lost its capacity, however, is contested. For some, the effects of globalisation have been exaggerated (Hirst and Thompson, 1999). Similarly, many of the reforms inspired by the 'new public management' may have reduced the size of the state but it is questionable whether it has actually reduced the capacity of the state to implement change. In fact, it may even be that these forms have actually *increased* the steering capacity of the state in the Global North (Meadowcroft, 2007). Governance theorists assert that when faced with complex, multidimensional policy challenges, from climate change to welfare provision, states need to work in collaboration with actors from across society (for example, subnational governments, business, non-governmental organisations [NGOs] and other parts of civil society) or beyond it (supranational institutions such as the EU or transnational NGOs). In order to achieve its policy goals, the state must build coalitions in order to mobilise resources and change individual behaviour in significant ways. One key institutional mechanism for achieving collaboration is partnership (see Selin and Chevez, 1995; Poncelet, 2001). The concept of partnership in the environmental field was popularised by the Rio Earth Summit and the Agenda 21 programme (see Doyle, 1998).

An associated change in the ideas of how to manage environmental problems has been the development of 'cooperative management regimes' that seek to develop negotiated solutions with actors and agencies from across the various tiers of government and the different spheres of society (Meadowcroft, 1999). This increase in public–private cooperation chimes with the concept – associated with sustainable development – of developing more participatory arrangements that bring together actors from across 'the broad areas of social life' (Meadowcroft, 1999: 231). As well as actors from the public and private sectors, this can incorporate NGOs and other organisations from civil society that represent environmental groups and community action groups (Meadowcroft, 1999: 252). Significantly, these collaborative regimes also imply that the risks associated with environmental and welfare policies are shared.

Environmentalism and welfare in the Global South

Sustainable development suggests that we need to have greater regard for the welfare of future generations so that they can enjoy similar resources and opportunities to the ones we presently enjoy (Doyle and Risely, 2008). This aspect of sustainable development is one more prevalent in the increasingly **post-materialist** environmental discourses of the Global North than the South. In much of the post-materialist literature, the welfare of non-humans is considered (Hay, 2004). Indeed this new ground in considering the rights and welfare of 'other nature' is quite inspirational and, indeed, at the forefront of radical green thought. But, despite recognising the benefits to all inhabitants of the globe – both human and non-human – within a more holistic and inclusive view of the welfare of the Earth, this conceptual framework can also be quite negligent of welfare issues in the Global South as it often lumps Homosapiens together as one entity, further diffusing welfare differences between the global *haves* and the *have-nots* (see also Chapter Thirteen, this volume).

As George and Wilding (1994: 162) observed,

> Greenism was one of several post-industrial concerns of primarily the affluent world which could afford to worry about the future of planet Earth or the position of women. The Third World had the more immediate and pressing problem of how to feed its people and stave off starvation for millions of its citizens.

In a similar vein, Doyle (2008: 311) has observed that the policies of development institutions and international environmental NGOs are dominated by the rationalities of post-materialist approaches to environmental protection and welfare (see below). Strongly premised on Maslow's (1954) 'hierarchy of needs', post-materialists such as Inglehart (1990) argue that having largely fulfilled its more basic needs of safety and security, parts of advanced industrial society are able to pursue 'higher' activities – such as love and a sense of belonging (or even the rights and welfare of future generations) – beyond the politics of present-day and material existence. While these values arguably dominate environmental thought in the Global North, the Global South still wrestles with the more basic needs of survival for those actually living on the planet, rather than those who might at some time in the future.

Global governance states

Whereas in the Global North the state retains considerable autonomy against extra-territorial actors due to its still substantial resources, the Global South has witnessed a magnification of the processes of governance, in part because of the even greater limitations on the capacity of the state in this part of the world. Here, the emergence of forms of governance between states (including northern states acting in the South), global environmental NGOs, private companies and the World Bank has seen the emergence of what Doyle and Doherty (2006) term 'global governance states'. Duffy's (2006) examination of transnational environmental management in Madagascar showed how the increasingly strong relationships between the government of Madagascar, several northern governments, global environmental NGOs, private companies and the World Bank through the development of a donor consortium has reshaped the nature of state–civil society interactions to reduce the separation between the two. In Madagascar, this consortium contains key donor institutions such as the World Bank, USAID, the governments of Germany, Japan, France, Switzerland, as well as NGOs such as the World Wildlife Fund (WWF), the Wildlife Conservation Society and Conservation International (Doyle, 2008: 318). Of course, in terms of representative democracy, questions arise in relation to the legitimacy of these NGOs and other private parties within this *consortium state*.

In these global governance states, sovereignty is not delineated by the nation-state's geographical boundaries but is constructed through the requirements of donors and interactions between the consortium's participants. In particular, the World Bank and its policies are identified as a key shaper of state sovereignty. The incorporation of NGOs in such consortia makes these organisations just as much part of sovereign, global governance states as national governments.

The three green NGOs in the Madagascar Donor Consortium are all wildlife welfare-oriented although, incredibly, they also direct a lot of the national *human* welfare policy making in Madagascar, both environmental and non-environmental, including the national poverty reduction strategy. Central to this approach are the 'the debt-for-nature swaps' and the establishment of wildlife corridors. The green voices of the South are deafeningly silent here. As Doyle and Doherty (2006) observe, the development of the green state may not actually lead to democratic change at all as some analysts assume, or may simply lead to the implantation of free market policies in a given society.

Fagan's (2008) research on the development of the environment and civil society in post-conflict Bosnia-Herzegovina illustrates how national-level NGOs developed in response to the ecological conditionalities of donor consortia. This top-down development of NGOs in response to the provision of funding – largely from the EU – skewed the priorities of the emergent civil society away from representing the social and environmental aspirations of local people, and instead aimed to promote organisations that could effectively deliver the priorities of funders. This steering was achieved through the linking of funding with conditionalities. Harrison's

(2004) study of the World Bank's policies in African states showed how these conditions generally include priorities such as developing a pluralist, democratic system of governance which is coupled with neoliberal policy prescriptions. Often these neoliberal social and economic policies and conditionalities do away with the welfare infrastructure of the state, further hollowing out its welfare function. The intention of these prescriptions is to replace the 'failed' governance structures of the state requiring aid with those more commonly found in the prosperous Global North.

The difficulty with this form of restructuring is that, as Doyle (2008: 318-19) observes:

> ... with a lack of continuous funding, one set of top-down NGOs is replaced by others better positioned to achieve success under the latest round of funding, creating an orientation towards external funders and away from representing local people. There is no support offered to lasting administrative and social structures that would allow citizens to decide and implement appropriate management structures, as indigenous networks are shunned.

Furthermore, Chapin's (2004) analysis of the funding of three more established and long-standing NGOs – WWF, Conservation International and the Nature Conservancy – demonstrate how their funding arrangements became intermeshed with the vested interests of transnational capital. As with their national-level counterparts, transnational NGOs have found that funding is increasingly dependent on other parts of the governance state, leading to competition between them. Furthermore, these 'big players', Chapin argues, have sought to expand their operations within developing countries, leading to the decimation of local organisations.

Donors assert an apolitical version of democracy that sees environmental NGOs as mere service providers for the donor organisations (Fagan, 2008), rather than as representing local people affected by the policies promoted by the World Bank among others (Harrison, 2004). This disconnection between international elite organisations in the global governance state and the societies they are supposed to serve can lead to the development of interpretations of sustainability and welfare that do not achieve widespread support in the countries in which they are implemented. For example, the increasing shift in the Global North towards post-materialist values on the environment and welfare has been mainstreamed into the concerns of international environment NGOs, although the more essentialist and human survivalist concerns of the Global South remain on the policy periphery. In this vein, Duffy takes issue with Conservation International and the Wildlife

Conservation Society as 'fortress conservation' organisations, meaning that they support policies that would exclude people from designated wildlife zones in order to protect the welfare of non-human nature. This post-materialist 'fortress' approach sees people as environmental degraders, and seeks wilderness parks devoid of human imprints: 'a romanticised view of a stunning wilderness and an aura of extraordinary biodiversity' (Duffy, 2006: 738). In this manner, the welfare of the non-human *other* is pursued in post-materialist fashion.

Summary box

Global governance states: Madagascar

Duffy's (2006) analysis of transnational environmental management in Madagascar showed how increasingly close relationships between states, global environmental NGOs, private companies and the World Bank have produced 'governance states' where NGOs such as WWF and Conservation International work so closely with the interests of transnational capital and nation-states that they often become part of the donor consortiums that have a large influence over national policy making. This has led to the imposition of 'Global North' interpretations of environmental sustainability and welfare over the immediate concerns of indigenous people.

Conclusion

This chapter has described key differences in the very manner in which the environment/welfare nexus is experienced and understood in both the Global North and the Global South. In the case of the former, environmental issues have been usually construed as post-materialist and/or post-industrialist. As the case of Madagascar illustrates, post-materialists see environmental welfare (through the rhetoric of sustainable development and EM) as something largely separate from humans (for the welfare of the 'rest of nature'). This sometimes manifests itself in discussion of the welfare of 'other species' or in arguments that insist that once the 'welfare of the planet as a whole' is pursued, then the welfare of humans will necessarily follow. When welfare is considered in the human realm, it is often viewed as something concerning *future generations*.

In the Global South, the day of reckoning already exists. Crucial green welfare issues are almost always purely perceived in an anthropocentric manner, and most of these intersect with basic human rights: the right to have a healthy water source, the right to shelter, the right to food sovereignty and the right to energy security. So, in many ways, any discussion of the potential emergence of a green state with welfare aspirations (and one with a global vision, a vision which crosses North–South divides) must be built on a shared understanding of what it is to be 'green' in the North and the South. Post-materialist and post-industrialist discourses do not recognise the post-colonialist realities of the Global South, where people wrestle with massive environmental debts incurred on them by centuries of exploitation by the North (the past), rather than trading in environmental footprints (the present and future).

Chapter summary

We began by defining the state and explaining why many ecological theorists have been hostile to the concept, with the state's commitment to damaging economic growth being a paramount reason.

We then saw that the traditional capitalistic state has at least partially attempted to accommodate itself to green imperatives through policy frameworks such as 'ecological modernisation' (EM). However, many commentators, like Eckersley, believe that this does not go far enough and have tried to outline what a fully 'green state' would resemble.

We then saw that governance issues constitute a key point of debate; namely, how to respond to the recent internationalisation and neoliberalisation of the state. We discussed the possible implications of this for ecological politics and proposed that the specific perspective of the Global South is at risk of being excluded from environmental analyses. In the South, welfare is usually understood as a human right, a form of community bond built on the social capital emerging from family, caste, community and other collective ties. Confronting this northern nexus between unquestioned economic expansion and welfare remains among the biggest challenges for advocates of a green welfare state.

In any genuinely emancipatory notion of a green welfare state, people must be seen as part of the environment, not separate from it. A truly ecological state has a vital role in providing key infrastructure necessary for the welfare of citizens (and non-humans) across the globe, North and South.

Questions for discussion

- Why have green theorists traditionally been hostile towards the state?
- Should liberal democracy be replaced by another form of democracy?
- How legitimate are NGOs in representing global citizens?

- How do the differing capacities of states influence what policies they adopt for sustainability?
- How is the interpretation of sustainability and welfare in the Global North different from that in the Global South?

Key further reading

Barry, J. and Eckersley, R. (eds) (2005) *The state and the global ecological crisis*, Cambridge, MA: The MIT Press.

Dryzek, J. S., Downes, D., Hunold, C. and Schlosberg, D. with Hernes, H.K. (2003) *Green states and social movements: Environmentalism in the United States, United Kingdom, Germany, and Norway,* Oxford: Oxford University Press.

Eckersley, R. (2004) *The green state*, Cambridge, MA: The MIT Press.

Hayward, T. (2005) *Constitutional environmental rights*, Oxford: Oxford University Press.

Richards, D. and Smith, M. J. (2002) *Governance and public policy in the UK*, Oxford: Oxford University Press.

Useful websites

UK Green Party: www.greenparty.org.uk/

Friends of the Earth: www.foe.co.uk/

Greenpeace: www.greenpeace.org.uk/autofrontpage

Environmental ethics

Alan Carter

Overview

This chapter begins by distinguishing between consequentialist and deontological moral theories. Reason is provided for holding that at least some consequentialist component is included within an adequate environmental ethic.

The chapter also considers whether moral consistency requires that we take into account temporally and geographically distant persons, non-human animals, non-sentient living beings, and finally, species and ecosystems within our moral deliberations.

The chapter concludes by indicating how anthropocentric, zoocentric and ecocentric perspectives might be combined.

Introduction: consequentialism and deontology

In this chapter we begin to review the philosophical dimensions that are relevant if we are to develop the substantive, enduring forms of ecological citizenship on which a sustainable society ultimately depends. This chapter deals with ethical theories and Chapter Six with political ones.

Environmental ethics concerns the question of whether or not our interactions with the natural environment, or our interactions between each other with respect to the natural environment, are subject to moral constraints or to moral requirements. But why might we hold that there are such constraints or requirements in the first place? Well, we certainly think that there are some proscriptions and prescriptions regarding our interactions with each other. It is uncontroversial, for example, that if you are an innocent, then I am morally required not to inflict gratuitous harm on you. It would be morally wrong for me to do so. And we can easily harm each other by how we interact with the natural environment. We can make it poisonous by polluting it, for example. And if we poison our environment through our daily activities, then we will harm each other.

But what is the basis for moral constraints and moral requirements? The two most prominent approaches in ethical theory are consequentialism and deontology. Consequentialism, such as utilitarianism, holds that the rightness or wrongness of our actions depends on the overall consequences. Utilitarianism, for example, holds that we should, directly or indirectly, bring about that outcome containing the greatest good. In contrast, deontological approaches hold that (at least certain) actions can be right or wrong regardless of their consequences. For example, some believe that lying is wrong irrespective of whether or not the consequences of a particular lie, or even of lying generally, are better than those resulting from telling the truth.

Many deontologists focus on rights, and many further claim that rights should never be violated (perhaps with the exception of doing so in order to avoid a disaster). Some consequentialists reject rights altogether. Others consider rights to be extremely important, but unlike deontologists, they do so because of the good consequences that result from respecting rights. For example, the world would be better if, *ceteris paribus*, everyone were happier; and people would be happier were they secure in the knowledge that they would not be gratuitously harmed. Recognising and respecting a right against being harmed gratuitously would thus make the world a better place. But note: the justification in this case is a consequentialist one. Many deontologists would, instead, take such a right to be inviolable regardless of the consequences.

In trying to frame an environmental ethic should we prefer consequentialism, deontology or should we try to effect some combination of the two? We now explore the specific themes that typically characterise debates about environmental ethics:

- future generations
- people in other countries
- non-human animals
- non-sentient living beings
- species and ecosystems.

Summary box

Consequentialism
The approach in moral theory that views the good (which refers to outcomes) as basic, and which holds that the rightness of actions is determined by the goodness of their outcomes.

Deontological ethical theories
Moral theories that view the right (which refers to actions) as basic, and which hold that the rightness of actions can be independent of their outcomes.

Utilitarianism
A consequentialist moral theory that holds that the best outcome is the one that contains the greatest good. There are two main forms of utilitarianism. Preference utilitarianism holds that the greatest good consists in the maximal satisfaction of preferences, while (classical) hedonistic utilitarianism holds that the greatest good consists in the greatest happiness for the greatest number.

Future generations

Consider the technology to which we have become accustomed. It alters the environment in ways that could result in innocents, for example, young children, being harmed, whether it is through the toxic effects of pesticides or heavy metals in inorganic fertiliser used in agriculture, the contamination of the environment by radioactive materials produced by the nuclear industry, the depletion of the planet's ozone shield by certain refrigerants or by climate change resulting from the emissions from, among other sources, industry, aviation, shipping and motor vehicles. At first glance it seems clear that those who will most likely be harmed, and harmed the most, by our interactions with the natural environment are future generations. Moreover, it also seems clear, at least at first glance, that if we do render our planet wholly unsuited to human habitation, then there will be many more people in the future who most likely will be harmed than are alive today. It is not surprising, therefore, that environmental activists have often cited the effects that our actions will probably have on future people as a major and seemingly compelling reason for moral constraints and requirements with respect to our interactions with the natural environment.

Unfortunately, matters are not so simple, for difficult philosophical problems arise the moment one considers the moral standing of future people.

One difficulty emerges because of what has been labelled the 'non-identity problem', which concerns actions that determine the identities of persons (Parfit, 1984: Part IV). For example, we normally think of harming a person as making that person worse off than he or she would otherwise have been. But now imagine that we could choose either a policy that depleted resources and polluted the environment or a policy that was non-polluting and which used only sustainable resources. There would be such a profound change in social development if a non-polluting policy were to be adopted in place of a polluting one that, in the temporally distant future at least, completely different people would be born compared to those who would have been born had the other policy been adopted.

Hence, no temporally distant future person is made worse off than he or she would otherwise have been by our adoption of a polluting policy, because without our adoption of that policy he or she would not have existed in order to have been better off. Thus it can be argued that we cannot harm temporally distant future persons by our choice of policies; and so their ostensible harms cannot justify the adoption of one policy in preference to another (Schwartz, 1979; see also Carter, 2001). And if we cannot harm temporally distant future persons, then their right not to be harmed cannot justify the adoption of a non-polluting policy in place of a polluting one. Moreover, if one were to hold that future persons have a right to an unpolluted world, then we can avoid violating that right by refusing to bring any more people into existence. And it is difficult to see how people who will never exist can have a right to anything. They are not the sort of entities who could possess rights.

Summary box

The non-identity problem

Imagine we have to flick one of two switches: red or blue. If we flick the red switch then 1,000 years from now Red people exist who experience miserable lives. However, we won't have harmed them because, had we flicked the blue switch instead, then Blue people would have been created and there would be no Red people alive to experience anything. It logically follows that nothing we do now – including global warming – can harm future generations, since without us they will never have existed (see Fitzpatrick, 2003b: 131-3).

Now, it seems likely that there will be temporally near future persons who will exist regardless of whether we choose one policy rather than the other. Hence, we *can* make such persons worse off than they would otherwise have been by our choice of policy. But if only temporally near persons count in our moral deliberations, then we would be justified in choosing policies, say the proliferation of dangerous technologies such as nuclear power, that might benefit temporally near future people at great cost to temporally distant future people, who would suffer from, say, the radioactive wastes that would be produced but who would not be worse off – according to the non-identity problem – than they would otherwise have been.

It could, of course, be objected that, even if we can make no temporally distant future person worse off than that person would otherwise have been by our choice of policies, we can nevertheless be responsible for their gratuitous suffering. And the wrongness of acting in a manner which results in gratuitous suffering provides moral grounds for adopting a policy that would *not* result in temporally distant future persons suffering tremendously. Furthermore, we might hold that making a person suffer gratuitously is one way of harming that person, even if that person is not thereby made worse off than he or she would otherwise have been. But we can also ensure that no future person suffers by refusing to bring any more people into existence. Yet that does not seem to be what is required of us morally. So, the *suffering* of temporally distant future persons seems, at least on its own, inadequate for grounding what many of us feel intuitively to be the correct moral response to the problem of future generations.

Importance of consequences

All of this seems to imply that we require some *conception* of the best world that we morally ought to bring about; for deontological considerations appear inadequate on their own, and merely identifying a bad world that must be avoided – one in which people suffer – will not suffice for determining the right course of action. In other words, we require, at the very least, some positive consequentialist component within our moral theory. Hedonistic utilitarians take the best world to be the one containing the greatest total quantity of happiness. This would justify the adoption of a non-polluting policy in place of a polluting one because a greater total quantity of happiness would result overall from many generations of future persons living in an unpolluted world, even if that required a lowering of the level of average happiness enjoyed by the present generation.

However, just as a greater total quantity of water would be found in a million bottles, each containing just one drop, than in a single bottle that is full of water, there would be a greater total quantity of happiness in a world containing zillions of barely happy people than in a world containing, say, 10 million very happy people. In other words, if we take as our yardstick for ascertaining the best world the greatest total quantity of happiness, then we seem to be led to what has been labelled the 'repugnant conclusion'

(Parfit, 1984: Part IV): for any number of very happy people, there is, at least in principle, some far greater number of people with lives that are barely worth living that counts as a better world. Of course, it may, in practice, be impossible to bring about a world of zillions of barely happy people, but this is not the point. The point is, rather, that the correct moral theory should, one would hope, be able to pick out the best world no matter what worlds we were *capable* of bringing about. But the 'total view', which holds that the best world contains a greater total quantity of happiness than any alternative, picks out a world that many find repugnant in preference to a world of 10 million happy people that many consider to be far, far better.

One way in which the 'repugnant conclusion' can be avoided is by adopting, in place of the 'total view', the 'average view', which holds that the best world contains a higher level of average happiness than any alternative. Clearly, a world of 10 million happy people has a higher level of average happiness than a world of zillions of barely happy people. But imagine a world containing a solitary psychopath, with no interest in other people. If that single person happened to be ecstatic, then that would be the world that contained a higher level of average happiness than any alternative. On the 'average view', this would be the best world. But many would insist that the world of the ecstatic psychopath is most certainly not the best world. And again, we miss the point if we object that such a world is not one that we can, in practice, bring about. For the correct moral theory should, ideally, pick out the best world regardless of whether or not we *can* bring it about. But the 'average view' fails to do that.

Many have also objected to utilitarianism in general on the grounds that it fails to take into direct account the distribution of happiness or well-being. For it is possible for there to be both a great total quantity of happiness and a high level of average happiness while some are ecstatic and others are miserable. Many regard the best world as one that does not contain extreme inequalities, at least when there would not be a significant reduction in either the total quantity of happiness or level of average happiness in making the world less unequal.

Combining the 'total view', the 'average view' and egalitarianism

One way in which we might combine all of these ethical intuitions in order to provide the basis for a reasonable moral theory is as follows. A plausible reason for why we are concerned by the 'repugnant conclusion' is that we find a small total quantity of happiness to be of disvalue. And a plausible reason for why we are concerned by the 'problem of the ecstatic psychopath' is that we also find a low level of average happiness to be of disvalue. Additionally, a plausible reason for why we are concerned by the unequal distributions of happiness that utilitarianism could sanction is that we find inequality to be of disvalue, too. And this suggests that the total quantity of happiness, the level of average happiness and equality all contribute to the overall value of a world.

But it also seems to be the case that it is more important to increase the total quantity of happiness by some fixed amount when it is small than when it is already great. And it also seems that it is more important to raise the level of average happiness by some fixed amount when it is low than when it is already high. Moreover, it seems that it is more important to reduce inequalities by some fixed amount when they are major than when they are already minor.

All of this implies that a world that contains a very large quantity of happiness and a very high level of average happiness but with major inequalities could be improved by some reduction in the total quantity of happiness and some lowering of the level of average happiness if either were the price of reducing the inequalities. On the other hand, it also implies that a world that contains a very high level of average happiness and with only minor inequalities but with a very small total quantity of happiness could be improved by some lowering of the level of average happiness and some increase in inequality if either were the price of increasing the total quantity of happiness. Furthermore, it implies that a world that contains a very large total quantity of happiness and with only minor inequalities but a very low level of average happiness could be improved by some reduction in the total quantity of happiness and some increase in inequality if either were the price of raising the level of average happiness.

Summary box

If we have large amounts of (a) and (b) but low amounts of (c) then we should raise (c) by reducing (a) and (b).

	(a)	(b)	(c)
Scenario 1	Total happiness	Average happiness	Equality
Scenario 2	Average happiness	Equality	Total happiness
Scenario 3	Total happiness	Equality	Average happiness

If all this is so, then we have reason for rejecting outcomes either consisting of a very small total quantity of happiness (the 'repugnant conclusion') or consisting of a very low level of average happiness (the 'problem of the ecstatic psychopath') or including major inequalities.

A moral theory of this general sort would also enable us to regard the adoption of certain environmentally benign policies as bringing about better outcomes than would the adoption of less environmentally benign ones. For policies which enable us to enjoy highly affluent lifestyles but which pollute the environment and destroy potentially sustainable resources will lead to future generations suffering a far lower level of average happiness than the level we in the rich countries currently enjoy. In short, only policies that reduce pollution and that encourage sustainable lifestyles would lead to the greatest total quantity of happiness across time, the highest level of average happiness across time, and the greatest equality between generations. And we have seen that there is reason for regarding each of these considerations as morally significant.

Future people revisited

But why assume in the first place that future people matter? Earlier, I noted that it is uncontroversial that we have certain moral duties to certain of our contemporaries. But to whom else, if anyone, do we owe any duties? Imagine that there were two unconscious patients in a hospital both on life support machines. Imagine that a doctor was to turn off one machine while leaving the other switched on, with the result that one of the two patients died. At first glance, this appears to be immoral. But if the doctor knew that one patient would never regain consciousness while there was a significant chance that the other would, then we would be far less certain that their action was immoral. Indeed, we might conclude that allowing the patient who would never regain consciousness to die was not immoral at all. This suggests that we hold, as a general moral principle, that we should treat persons similarly unless there is a morally relevant and morally significant difference between them that would justify differential treatment. Yet this moral principle appears to require us to extend moral consideration beyond our contemporaries and to include within our moral deliberations future persons.

It is true, of course, that future persons who do not yet exist are not suffering at present. But while it is true that the pain they will suffer if we engage in environmentally destructive acts is not occurring at this moment, it is no less true that there is pain that you will suffer in the future that is not occurring now. But the pain that you will suffer if others behave in a certain way is morally significant. Why should the pain that future people will suffer be any less morally significant? In both cases there is pain that will occur that is not occurring now. That you exist at this moment while future persons do not does not seem to be a morally relevant consideration given that the pain will occur in both cases; consider a person who will be conceived one hour from now. Imagine that in five years' time you and that child will both suffer excruciating pain. Why should the future pain of the five-year-old be excluded from our present moral deliberations while your future pain should be included simply because that child has not yet been conceived? And if that child, who does not yet exist, ought to count, then why should anyone else who will, as a matter of fact, be conceived, but who does not yet exist, not count equally? In a word, we have reason to hold that moral concern ought to be extended beyond our contemporaries.

People in other countries

It is clear that people in the temporally distant future will, as a matter of fact, suffer if we adopt polluting and resource-consumptive policies. Our being responsible for their living lives of a very low level of average happiness makes some of our present actions morally wrong, even if we have no idea who those future people will be. In short, the well-being of temporally distant future people matters morally. But it seems inconsistent to hold that the well-being of temporally distant people matters morally while disregarding the well-being of geographically distant people. Our polluting activities will reduce the level of average happiness of temporally distant future people. But those activities are also currently harming geographically distant people, especially those living in poorer countries. They are suffering droughts and flooding due to climate change resulting from our high output of carbon dioxide (CO_2), they are suffering from the effects of our dumping of toxic wastes onto their lands, and, among other things, they are suffering from the pesticides that we have banned in our own countries while exporting them to other parts of the world. What are our moral obligations to such people with respect to our interactions with the natural environment?

We have a moral duty not to inflict gratuitous harm on innocents. But do we also have a duty to *aid* them? Imagine that you are passing a shallow pond into which a small child has strayed. The child is small and will drown if you simply walk by. You can easily save the child, but there will be a price: your clothes will end up muddy. As it would be very bad if the child died but it would not be of great moral significance if your clothes ended up muddy, then it would, clearly, be morally wrong of you not to save the child's life. But you could, at no greater cost or inconvenience, save a child's life in Africa by donating to Oxfam the equivalent of the cost of a trip to the drycleaners. Yet many assume that they lack the duty to save a child in Africa, even if they accept that they do have a duty to save the life of the child in the shallow pond. But now recall the general moral principle that we noted earlier: we should treat persons similarly unless there is a morally relevant and morally significant difference between them that would justify differential treatment. What is the morally relevant and morally significant difference between the child in Africa and the child in the shallow pond that would justify moral condemnation for failing to save one but not the other? It has been argued that there is none (Singer, 1972; Rachels, 1982).

Once upon a time people did not know of the suffering taking place in other parts of the world. Moreover, long ago, there was little that one could have done to help those far away. These two considerations might, in the past, have justified our focus on only those geographically near to us. But modern communications are such that we do know of the plight of others far away, and organisations such as Oxfam make it possible for us to help them. Or we could campaign to change the policies of our own countries that result in extreme poverty abroad. We might think that we only have obligations to those of our own nationality. But what if the little child in the pond, instead of crying "Help", cried "Au secours"? Would this have made any difference to your moral duty to save her? Clearly not. We might think that in the case of the world's starving people there are many who could help, whereas in the drowning child case there is only you who can provide assistance. But if several people were standing around watching the child drown, then you would have just as much of a duty to save the child as you would have if there was no one else there. We might think that the morally relevant and morally significant difference between the drowning child and the starving children in poor countries is that there is only one drowning child that you can save on your own, but there are far too many children elsewhere in the world for you to save. But if the pond was full of drowning children and you could not save all them, then all that follows is that you should save as many as you can.

In short, there seems to be no morally relevant and morally significant difference between a child drowning in a nearby pond and a child in another country starving to death. Both are innocents, both need our assistance, and if we have a moral duty to come to the aid of one of them, then surely we have a moral duty to aid the other as well, especially when we can do so at no great cost to ourselves. This duty to aid applies not only to famine relief but also to suffering resulting from environmental deterioration. And when that environmental deterioration is the result of climate change that we have contributed towards, the duty is, arguably, even stronger or even more certain.

However, there is a powerful argument that has been presented against assisting those in poorer countries. And it is an environmental one. At present the world's human population doubles in size approximately every 41 years. Clearly, a world with finite non–renewable resources and, even more importantly, a finite capacity to act as a sink for our polluting wastes cannot support an infinitely expanding human population. It is natural, it has been argued, for the population of poor countries to rise above the carrying capacity of their lands and, when a catastrophe such as famine strikes, for it to fall back below the numbers that the land can support. Thus, there is a natural demographic cycle fluctuating around the land's carrying capacity. If food were to be provided to poor countries by richer ones, then the populations of those poor countries would simply keep on rising. And the end result would eventually be global catastrophe.

What should rich countries do in such a situation? It has been claimed that we should think of ourselves as if we were in a well-provisioned lifeboat. Poor countries are like badly equipped and overcrowded lifeboats. Swimming around in the sea are people who have left their lifeboats and are seeking admittance to a well-provisioned lifeboat. If we allow too many on board or share all our resources with those outside of the boat who need them, then we will all drown together. Isn't it better that at least those in the well-provisioned lifeboats survive? Many are repelled by this argument. But it needs stating that it is a moral one. If sharing our resources with the poor of the world meant that everyone would die, then we would be causally and morally responsible for a global catastrophe. Isn't it better to let millions starve now than to be the cause of billions dying later (Hardin, 1982)?

However, this argument for refusing assistance to those in poor countries assumes that the human population will simply keep expanding if there is enough food to feed everyone's children (see Carter, 2004). But many working on development in poor countries argue that a major cause of population growth is poverty. Poor people often lack education regarding family planning, poor women lack employment outside of the home and independence from the demands of their husbands, and poor people in societies without social provision for old age need large families not only to supplement earnings now but to take care of them when they grow old. In other words, the claim that we are morally obliged not to provide the poor with aid can be argued to be part of the problem rather than the solution. For unless we help people escape poverty there will remain a pressure on them to have large families. Moreover, the environmental impact of less rapidly growing rich countries is many times greater than that of more rapidly growing poor countries. Indeed, if we are to prevent a future global catastrophe, then it seems that what is morally required of us is to reduce our damaging effects on the environments of poor countries and on the global environment in general, and to aid the people in poor countries in the development of technologies and agricultural practices that are environmentally sustainable in the long term and that can also eliminate the poverty they presently endure.

Non-human animals

We have seen that there is reason to extend moral concern beyond the geographically and temporally near to persons geographically and temporally distant. This extension of moral concern follows from the general principle that we should treat persons similarly unless there is a morally relevant and morally significant difference between them that would justify differential treatment. Up until now we have taken it for granted that this principle, or one like it, applies only to human beings. We rear non-human animals for food and serve them up cooked for dinner. We also conduct painful experiments on them, and then 'sacrifice' them once we have finished. Yet we consider it morally wrong to do such things to humans. What, then, is the morally relevant and morally significant distinction that would justify such a massive difference in treatment?

We might think that it is the fact that we are more intelligent than non-human animals. But very young human infants are not. Yet we do not think that we should rear them for food or force cosmetics into their eyes everyday in order to test for toxicity. We might then think that human infants have a potential that non-human animals lack. But there are brain-damaged humans who possess far less potential than the non-human animals we rear for food or experiment on. Yet we think it morally wrong to mistreat such humans.

The general problem is this: take any factor that might seem to constitute a morally relevant and morally significant difference. It will have to be set at some level: for example, a certain degree of intelligence or a certain degree of potential. But wherever we set that level, either we will succeed in excluding the non-human animals that we rear for food and experiment on and equally exclude from moral concern certain human beings whom we regard as deserving moral consideration, or we will succeed in including all human beings whom we regard as deserving moral consideration and equally include within the domain of moral concern the non-human animals we rear for food and on which we conduct painful experiments.

We could simply set the boundary of moral concern by means of a biological distinction such as species membership, which is far from obviously a morally relevant and morally significant difference. But then we would have no grounds for criticising racists, who set the boundary of moral concern by means of a different biological distinction, namely racial characteristics, or for criticising sexists, who set the boundary of moral concern by means of yet another biological distinction, namely sex.

If we view sexists as immoral for arbitrarily distinguishing on the basis of sex, and if we view racists as immoral for arbitrarily distinguishing on the basis of 'race', then consistency demands that we view ourselves as no less immoral if we arbitrarily distinguish on the basis of species membership (for a consequentialist view see Singer, 1975, 1986; for a rights-based view see Regan, 1983, 1985).

If non-human animals, or at least those possessing a certain level of intelligence or susceptibility to experiencing pleasure and pain, count morally, and we have seen that there is good reason to hold that they do, then many of our interactions with the natural environment merit moral condemnation. Many of our agricultural practices would clearly be immoral, and our destruction of the habitats of non-human animals completely discounts their interests.

Non-sentient living beings

If moral concern, on pain of inconsistency, ought to be extended beyond human beings to sentient non-human animals, can we stop there, or must we include plants as well?

One argument for regarding plants as meriting moral concern runs as follows. We have interests of different kinds. We have interests in projects that we take to be so important that they define our identities, such as cultural goals or the collective pursuit of freedom or democracy. We have interests in enjoying pleasure and in avoiding pain. And we have interests in having our biological needs met, even when we are unaware of what they are. For example, we have an interest in obtaining the right vitamins even if we have never heard of vitamins. And just as it would be immoral to prevent a person from satisfying his or her most important projects (so long as doing so has no serious costs elsewhere) or to prevent a person from experiencing pleasure or forcing him or her to endure pain for no good reason, it would ordinarily be immoral to prevent a person from satisfying his or her biological needs. But not only sentient non-human animals but also plants have biological needs, too. Isn't it morally inconsistent to regard our biological needs as meriting moral concern but not those of plants? (For a consequentialist view see Varner, 1998 and Attfield, 1995; for a deontological defence of **biocentrism** see Taylor, 1986, 1995.)

It may be the case that it is morally wrong to go around killing living things for no good reason, but the above argument fails to demonstrate that it is. Recall the case of the two unconscious patients. When the doctor turns off one of the life support machines and thereby ensures that the patient's biological needs are no longer met, many of us do not consider it an immoral act, even if we would consider it morally wrong to turn off the other life support machine. What is the morally relevant and morally significant difference between the two cases? It is that one patient will regain consciousness and the other will not. In other words, it seems that a person's biological needs only count morally insofar as they play some role in the conscious, or at least potentially conscious, experiences of those whose needs they are. Plants that never were, are not and never will be conscious do differ from both human beings and sentient non-human animals in a way that does seem to be both morally relevant and morally significant.

Nevertheless, it might be argued that plants do have interests. They appear to have goals: they grow to maturity, they heal themselves when injured and they reproduce. Moreover, while we have excellences that plants lack, such as rationality, plants have excellences that we lack, such as the ability to obtain nutrients where we are unable to do so. Isn't it just a case of prejudice to value our interests and not those of plants?

However, it is far from certain that the word 'goal' or the word 'interest' has the same meaning when applied to plants as it does when applied to human beings. When we talk about our goals, there seems to be some inherent link to consciousness. And when we talk of our interests, there does seem to be something in which we are consciously interested. We might not be consciously interested in obtaining a nutrient we have never heard of, but we are consciously interested in avoiding the effects that a lack of those nutrients could produce. There may be a legitimate sense in which plants have interests. But the worry remains that when we speak of a plant having goals and interests we speak no less metaphorically than when we speak of a car engine's need for oil (see Parke, 1989).

Species and ecosystems

If the goals, interests and needs of plants are metaphorical, then the goals, interests and needs of species or ecosystems seem no less so. This is not to say that species or ecosystems should play no role in our moral deliberations. Human beings require considerable biodiversity and well-functioning ecosystems in order to survive, never mind to live well. Ecosystems supply human beings and sentient non-human animals with the planet's life support systems. In other words, they are a means to our ends, or put another way, they have **instrumental value**. Other humans also have instrumental value for us – others provide us with many of the things that we need or want. But it would be immoral to regard other humans as only possessing instrumental value. Other people deserve to be treated as ends-in-themselves and not merely as means to our own ends. In short, human beings possess **intrinsic value** as well as instrumental value, and we treat other people with disrespect when we regard them as only possessing the latter. The same, it can be argued, is the case with sentient non–human animals, for they, too, are ends-in-themselves.

Species and ecosystems certainly possess considerable instrumental value. Not only do they provide us with things we need for our own survival but they also provide us with tremendous aesthetic delight. But do they also possess intrinsic value? There is an argument that purports to ascertain that they do: the 'last person argument' (Routley, 2003). Imagine that because of some catastrophe there remains a solitary human being, who will soon die. Imagine that he chooses to destroy the last tree of its kind – a tree that, if left alone, could propagate and continue its species. Or imagine that all sentient non–human animals have died out in the catastrophe. Nevertheless, imagine that there remains a viable ecosystem. Now imagine the last human alive destroying that ecosystem shortly before he dies.

Many find either the chopping down of the last tree of its kind or the destruction of the remaining ecosystem to be morally wrong. But it cannot be so because of the instrumental value of that species to human beings or of the instrumental value of the ecosystem to sentient life forms, for there will never be another human nor, in the second case, even another sentient non–human. We might think that such acts of destruction by the last person reveal poor character. But virtues only seem to make sense within human communities. In such a scenario, there are no remaining human communities. If such destructive acts by the last person are morally wrong, then it seems that they must be wrong because they reduce the amount of value in the world. But if that value is not instrumental, surely it must be intrinsic. In which case, species and ecosystems would appear to possess not merely instrumental value but intrinsic value as well.

Some hold that species and ecosystems contain far more intrinsic value than their members (Rolston, 1988). Many are far more concerned by the loss of the blue whale (*Balaenoptera musculus*) than they are by the suffering of any individual member of that species. But if species, including species of non-sentient life forms, count for more than individual members of species, including members of sentient species, then it might be justifiable to sacrifice sentient individuals for the sake of the survival of, say, a species of plant. Indeed, some have argued that there is a deep divide between those who are concerned with the welfare or rights of sentient non–human animals and environmental philosophers who are concerned, instead, with the 'integrity, stability, and beauty of the biotic community' (Leopold, 1970: 262). (For the seminal argument driving a wedge between animal liberationists, such as Singer, and environmentalists such as Leopold, see Callicott, 1995.) Such environmental philosophers have been willing to see deer, for example, culled in order to protect wild plants. Yet some of the leading figures defending the moral standing of sentient non–human animals, on the other hand, regard the sacrifice of individual sentient beings for the sake of some collective, such as an ecosystem, to be tantamount to environmental fascism (Regan, 1983: 361–2).

One major problem within the field of environmental ethics is how to resolve these conflicting views. I shall end this chapter by suggesting one possible approach.

Conclusion: towards a pluralist environmental ethic

If human beings have interests that other animals lack (such as identity-determining cultural projects) that are morally significant, if sentient non-human animals also have interests that are morally significant, and if kinds such as species or collective entities such as ecosystems are morally significant in their own right as well, then there are bound to be conflicts between the values involved in each category.

Let us call all of the values that pertain primarily to exclusively human interests 'anthropocentric values'. We can think of **anthropocentrism** as being concerned solely with the promotion of anthropocentric values. Let us call all of the values that pertain primarily to the interests of sentient animals 'zoocentric values'. We could think of **zoocentrism** as being concerned solely with the promotion of zoocentric values. Finally, let us call all of the values that pertain primarily to kinds such as species or collectives such as ecosystems 'ecocentric values'. We can think of **ecocentrism** as being concerned solely with the promotion of ecocentric values. (Biocentrism could be thought of as an exclusive concern with the promotion of those values that pertain primarily to the 'interests' of non-sentient life forms.)

If anthropocentric, zoocentric and ecocentric values ought to be included within our moral deliberations, then we can offer a reason for why anthropocentrism, zoocentrism and ecocentrism will lead to counter-intuitive implications. At one extreme, for example, anthropocentrists will happily propose policies that will be viewed by those with wider moral sensibilities as appallingly inhumane in their effects on sentient non-human animals, and as nothing short of vandalistic in their effects on the natural environment. At another extreme, ecocentrists will happily propose policies that will likely be denounced as ecofascistic by anyone not deafened to the cries of a suffering humanity, especially of those persons living within the poorer regions of the world.

But if we remember how we avoided both the 'repugnant conclusion' and the 'problem of the ecstatic psychopath', then we might be able to see how a way forward could be possible. Recall that increasing a value seems more important the less that value is realised. Should ecocentric values ever be satisfied to a large degree while either anthropocentric or zoocentric values were not, then failing to take into account those other values sufficiently will strike us as immoral once we have realised the moral significance of each kind of value. And were zoocentric values ever to be satisfied to a large degree while either anthropocentric or ecocentric values were not, then failing to take into account those other values sufficiently will also strike us as immoral. But, moreover, when anthropocentric values are satisfied to a large degree and either zoocentric or ecocentric values are not, failing to take into account those other values sufficiently will also strike us as immoral. Indeed, the more damage that we inflict on the world's ecosystems, the more we would be advancing purely anthropocentric values at the increasing cost of ecocentric ones. And further advancing anthropocentric values when they are already realised to a considerable degree at the expense of ecocentric values that were only realised to a progressively lower degree would make our actions ever more immoral.

This would mean that the best world – the world that we ought directly or indirectly to bring about – would therefore be a world where anthropocentric, zoocentric and ecocentric values are all satisfied to a considerable degree, and the policies that we require are the ones that are best suited to that end. Anything less would merit moral condemnation.

Summary box

If there were large amounts of (a) and (b) but low amounts of (c), then we should raise (c) by reducing (a) and (b).

	(a)	(b)	(c)
Scenario 1	anthropocentrism	zoocentrism	ecocentrism
Scenario 2	zoocentrism	ecocentrism	anthropocentrism
Scenario 3	ecocentrism	anthropocentrism	zoocentrism

Chapter summary

In this chapter:

- the distinction between consequentialist and deontological moral theories was noted, and reasons were found for, at the very least, including some consequentialist component within an adequate environmental ethic;
- it was argued that moral consistency seems to require that we take into account temporally and geographically distant future persons, as well as sentient non-human animals;
- we saw, according to the 'last person argument', that species and ecosystems should also be included within our moral deliberations.

Thus, it can be argued that anthropocentric, zoocentric and ecocentric perspectives each pick out some morally relevant feature, but that each is partial. This suggests that we attempt to maximise as far as possible each kind of value simultaneously.

And this means that the policies we require are those that respect the interests of all persons, whether geographically or temporally near or far, that respect the interests of sentient non-human animals, and that respect ecosystemic integrity.

Questions for discussion

- Should distant future persons count as much in our moral deliberations as present persons?
- Do we have a duty to assist those in other countries to help protect their natural environment?
- Should humans count for more in our moral deliberations than sentient non-human animals?
- Should plants count at all in our moral deliberations?
- Do ecosystems or species only possess instrumental value?

Key further reading

Attfield, R. (1991) *The ethics of environmental concern* (2nd edn), Athens, GA: University of Georgia Press.

Des Jardins, J. (2005) *Environmental ethics: An introduction to environmental philosophy* (4th edn), Belmont, CA: Wadsworth.

Jamieson, D. (2008) *Ethics and the environment: An introduction*, Cambridge: Cambridge University Press.

Light, A., Holland, A. and O'Neill, J. (2008) *Environmental values*, London: Routledge.

Taylor, A. (2003) *Animals and ethics: An overview of the philosophical debate*, Peterborough, Ontario: Broadview Press.

Useful websites

International Society for Environmental Ethics: www.cep.unt.edu/ISEE.html

International Association for Environmental Philosophy: www. environmentalphilosophy.org/

Center for Environmental Philosophy: www.cep.unt.edu/

six

Environmental justice: philosophies and practices

Tony Fitzpatrick

Overview

In addition to ethical theories of what is right and good, environmentalists make reference to political philosophies of justice. Green philosophers have drawn on a range of established ideas in trying to develop a distinct understanding of environmental justice.

This chapter:

- contextualises and debates the concept of environmental justice by drawing on three of the most important political philosophies of recent decades: liberalism, communitarianism and republicanism, and feminism;
- explores several radical proposals for policy reform and considers the extent to which they might promote the practice of environmental justice.

Debates concerning **environmental justice** (EJ) are vast, complex and far from producing a consensus. Given the controversies that range around the term's intellectual parentage – what is **justice**? what is **social justice**? – this is to be expected. Analyses can range across a number of levels:

1. philosophical debates about the concept and meaning of EJ;
2. the political discourse of EJ, that is, not only what we do but what we say and understand about what we do;

3. EJ as an economic, social, legal and political practice which structures the distribution of resources;
4. social movements, groups and networks promoting EJ.

We cover aspects of points 3 and 4 in Chapters Three and Seven when discussing poverty. Here, I propose to concentrate more on point 1, with some attention to 2 and 3. I intend to follow Alan Carter in arguing for a pluralistic approach that offers tools of understanding which connect to older traditions of thought, clarify certain issues for the purpose of policy making and analysis, but without imagining that EJ can or should be reduced to a programmatic, easily digestible list of classifications and indicators. Most of this chapter is dedicated to reflecting the diverse complexity of philosophical debates related to justice.

Justice

If justice implies fair shares (being) and right or virtuous activity (doing), then EJ requires such beings and doings to recognise (a) the value of nature, and (b) our status as interdependent, natural beings. Unpacking even this simple definition is an immense task. Is justice primarily about needs or deserts, about rights or responsibilities? Is it a property of individuals, groups or collectivities? Is it backward-looking (a return for what has been done) or forward-looking (the realisation of desirable ends)? Furthermore, Barry (1995) distinguishes between 'justice as impartiality' (just rules are those which equal consent to be governed by equally), 'justice as reciprocity' (fair dealing, or agents rendering what is owed to others) and 'justice as mutual advantage' (acting justly for the sake of mutual reward). In addition, we have the kind of ethical perspectives reviewed in Chapter Five.

To simplify and, I hope, make sense of such debates I propose that any philosophy of justice has to provide at least basic answers to the following five questions:

1. What are the criteria of justice?
   What are the principles and justifications underpinning the rules and practices of justice?
2. Who are the subjects of justice?
   From whom and to whom should justice be rendered?
3. Why be just?
   What motives are needed for justice to be realised?
4. Where and when does justice occur?
   What are the socioeconomic, political and legal conditions without which justice cannot thrive?

5. How is justice realised?

   What political strategies and social policies are likely to produce those conditions?

We cannot review each and every aspect of these questions from each and every possible viewpoint. Instead, I propose to explore three key perspectives on justice and environmentalism (see also Dobson, 1998, 1999; Foley et al, 2005; Adebowale, 2008; Scholsberg, 2009), bearing in mind what has already been proposed: that we need a theory to be meaningful and operational while also providing an 'open space' which allows reasonable disagreement and further understandings to thrive.

Three perspectives

Others writing about EJ from a social policy perspective have defined justice rather more succinctly (see the summary box below and Chapters Two, Three and Nine, this volume, for discussions of the EJ movement).

Summary box

- Everyone has the right to a healthy and safe environment and the responsibility to maintain it.
- Everyone has the right to a fair share of natural resources and the right not to suffer disproportionately from environmental policies, regulations or laws.
- Everyone has a civil right to be able to access environmental information and to participate in decision making.
- The most vulnerable in society, in particular the poorest, should not suffer the disproportionate, negative effects of environmental omissions, actions, policy or law. (Johnson et al, 2008: 4)

- Aim for well-being for all.
- Put prevention before cure.
- Grow the core economy.
- Make carbon work for social justice.
- Make public services sustainable.
- Value what matters. (Coote and Franklin, 2009: 12-16)

These are worthwhile reference points, but they avoid philosophical debates. We might agree we have responsibilities to maintain a healthy and safe environment, and then find that we have conflicting notions of what 'responsibility' means. (For a specific discussion of citizenship see Chapter

Twelve, this volume.) Such definitions may also perpetuate a difficulty described by Dobson (2009: 127-40).

When we explore existing policy instruments we are dealing largely with attempts to change behaviour. But is there any guarantee that attitudes will alter as well? We cannot rule this out, for sure. Perhaps people can acquire habits that might, over time, change their feelings, views and values as well. But I agree with Dobson that attitudes are generally more definitive and constitutive of the 'self' than acts. That people comply with rules or respond to dis/incentives does not mean that their hearts and minds have followed too. If a traffic calming scheme is removed then some people will continue to drive slowly because they now recognise the value of doing so, but many drivers will revert to their previous habits. So, if we need greater shifts in attitudes, values and identities than existing policies are managing to effect, then we may need a more fundamental revaluation, one which does not rush through the philosophy to get to the policy. This is why 'green values' were included in **Figure 3.6** (Chapter Three).

Therefore, in reflecting on the attitudes which guide behaviour, we need to understand what it is to be just, to act with justice and therefore on the philosophical foundations of justice. Neither moral nor political philosophy can do all the work, but they can do some. And it is surely better to know what the intractable issues and questions are than to imagine that we can sweep them away by simply invoking 'environmental justice'. So, if ecological citizens need to comprehend and respect EJ, rather than merely responding to policy stimuli, then moral and political debates are indispensable (Pepper, 2007).

Liberal justice

For Rawls (1972), to determine what is just we must be impersonal, as if we are standing behind a 'veil of ignorance' where knowledge of our personal identities and interests has been stripped away. In this 'original position' we are to imagine ourselves as 'disembodied rationalities' who are unable to bias the rules and institutions of justice in one particular direction. In such impartial circumstances, Rawls contends that we should prioritise basic liberties (free speech, due process, etc) but that we would also want to ensure that inequalities (1) derive from, and are consistent with, 'fair equality of opportunity', and (2) are to the benefit of the least advantaged. Rawls therefore defends a leftist liberalism that incorporates a strong element of social equality.

By contrast, Nozick (1974) proposed a right-wing liberalism. It is misleading, he argues, to rearrange the distribution of property, wealth, and so on without appreciating how those distributions came about. It might benefit Sally if we take £50,000 from Larry and give it to her. But if Larry earned his money fairly then we are violating his rights as a free agent. So long as property was acquired and transferred without anyone else's rights being violated then the resulting distribution, no matter how unequal, is just. The means justify the ends. To apply a 'patterned' theory of justice, as Rawls proposes, will almost certainly create more harm than good. Justice is not *social* justice.

So far as I am aware there have been no sustained attempts to apply Nozick's 'entitlement' theory of justice to environmental issues. But one option is to divide the 'environmental commons' into distinct holdings that can then be possessed by, and transferred between, individuals (Hardin, 1998). In short, if people can own land then why can't there be equivalent property rights to the oceans or the air? Yet there is the well-documented difficulty of treating nature as a commodity (Husain and Bhattacharya, 2004). Given the shared, public, non-excludable nature of the commons, how could we really divide it up into property holdings? The interdependence of nature might suggest that EJ has to imply a stress on *collective* ownership and therefore collective, social notions of rights and responsibilities.

Does this take us back to Rawls? In the original position, we might decide to live in whatever society is consistent with the most sustainable natural environment. Surely, it would then be a relatively straightforward matter to make this consistent with the other components of Rawlsian justice (see Hayward, 1998: 156-60). Perhaps Rawls' list of 'primary goods' could include a right to sustainable resources (such as clean air). Perhaps all green reforms must aim to improve the position of the least advantaged. Does this approach seem reasonable?

There have been far too many critiques of Rawls to review here (see, for example, Freeman, 2007). However, some have argued that a Rawlsian theory of EJ lacks cogency. For instance, there is the non-identity problem mentioned on page 114, which highlights substantial difficulties regarding justice towards future generations. Others have argued that Rawlsian justice excludes an ethic of care (Anderson, 1999), an exclusion that would arguably compromise any philosophy of EJ (see below). The debate does not end there, obviously. For instance, Rawls arguably makes room for a notion of 'trusteeship' in which we – human members of the present generation – *are* able to speak for animals and future generations (Fitzpatrick, 2008b).

Essentially, however, if there are substantial problems with applying Rawlsian justice to environmentalism then perhaps **liberalism** *per se* cannot supply the framework for EJ that we need. Perhaps liberalism is too bound up with individualism, rationality, rights, freedom and choice, and neutrality:

- environmentalism implies a concern with the entire eco-community which cannot afford the anthropocentric perception of nature as a resource to be used, dominated and polluted;
- this therefore means seeing ourselves as human animals whose capacity to reason is just one of many faculties we possess;
- consequently, we ought to stress our obligations, not just to repair the damage we have done but to an ecology where the language of rights, contracts and reciprocities breaks down;
- thus, there are not only ontological limits to human freedom (the freedom to destroy the environment on which you depend is self-contradictory) but social and political limits (those choices that threaten the carrying capacity of the planet ought to be curtailed);
- so we cannot be neutral between different ways of living – we ought to proscribe unsustainable habits, for instance – and, instead, have to prefer those goods which are of most value to the natural environment.

But even if liberalism, Rawlsian or otherwise, cannot provide *the* foundations for EJ does this imply that liberalism has *no* role to play? Dobson (2003) argues that part of our responsibility to future generations is to ensure they have access to the broadest range of goods from which to choose, implying a degree of liberal autonomy. And Wissenburg (1998) observed that green reforms must work with the grain of people's existing preferences and choices if they are to have any success. In short, those suspicious of liberalism really need to state whether they think an ecological society can afford to be *non*-liberal and what exactly this would imply.

Communitarian and republican justice

Over the last few decades important challenges to liberalism have been made by communitarians and republicans.

Republicanism defines the good society as that which is organised around the 'public good', that is, that which embodies and summons all participants to a shared political space. This participation defines them as citizens with common interests and identities, rather than as family members or private individuals (Pettit, 1999; White and Leighton, 2008). A republican society is not an aggregation of individuals' desires but an arena of joint, contributory membership in which people act and deliberate together for the good of one other. For republicans, justice is *public* justice. Social justice therefore refers to those conditions which enable us to act as citizens of equal standing in participative and deliberative interaction with one another. This might imply the equal distribution of primary resources (property, assets, wealth) to ensure that no one becomes too powerful and that everyone's voice can be heard.

Communitarianism overlaps with republicanism but they are not identical. The former values membership of particular communities, some of which may be public and political but some of which could equally be private and self-enclosed (such as a select religious community) (Bell, 1993). Communitarians typically insist that obligations are more important than rights and that we are primarily communal beings. Discovering and achieving 'the good life' is more important than individual choice, and a person is defined by the roles and expectations they possess in the eyes of their peers. Who you are depends on how you see, and are seen by, others. Thus, there are limits to what the self is and what it can do. Communitarian justice implies the preservation of strong communities, typically by supporting families, schools, neighbourhoods, churches and all other civic associations that embed the self in its communal contexts.

In both cases there are obvious synergies with environmentalism. For republicans, the public good has to involve some component of environmental goods and values (Barry and Smith, 2008). The 'political' is not only inseparable from the 'natural', it is that through which the value of nature can be articulated, configured and thus defended. If we do not recognise the extent to which our mutual interdependency is as much about preserving the natural conditions of our existence as it is about maintaining worthwhile social relationships, then there will be no significant public sphere or public goods to bind us together *as* citizens. Unless we are also citizens of and for the environment then we cannot be citizens at all!

With communitarianism, it is surely a case of recognising how embedded we are, as highly evolved human animals, in nature (MacIntyre, 1999). This means expanding the circle of the moral community with which we identify so that it encompasses the developing world (those most vulnerable to global warming), animals, future generations (of both humans and animals) and perhaps the very ecosystem itself (as in Lovelock's 2007 Gaia ethic). Presumably a 'communitarian environmental ethic' needs to work out how the 'natural community' relates to all the other communities that provide meaning to our lives.

The weaknesses of liberalism therefore seem to have been overcome. Society is not a product of individuals *choosing* which goods to consume in blind interaction with one another, it is more that which shapes and pervades the very heart of what it is to be a person. Liberalism risks treating the self as infinitely expandable, as that which is in perfect control of its fate, and so as right to transform and even destroy anything that is not of the self.

Does this mean that republicanism and/or communitarianism offer the foundations for EJ? We ought to be careful before assenting. Essentially, there are many strands of both republicanism and communitarianism and so, presumably, many possible versions of the EJ that they would engender.

For instance, Aristotle and Thomas Jefferson remain key influences on republican thinking. Yet Aristotle never criticised the practice of slavery. And while Jefferson (2006: 114-20) hated slavery, he did so from the belief that because black people were inferior to whites the latter should be paternalistic rather than domineering. Obviously, such views are unacceptable and what this suggests is that our notion of the 'public' must constantly evolve to include those who were excluded by the mores and customs of previous ages. Indeed, it is by engaging in open, public debate that we can recognise how unjust it is to refuse to recognise the equal status of all. The very meaning of publicness, what it is to be a member of the polity, is defined by political exchanges within public spheres of action and communication. Yet this get-out-of-jail-free card might also then suggest that 'liberal republicanisms' have to be distinguished from 'authoritarian republicanisms'. And if we prefer the former, then the distance between them and certain schools of liberalism – those that support public spaces and values – is not so vast after all (Fitzpatrick, 2009, 2010).

Similar doubts relate to communitarianism. Someone raised within a backwoods, survivalist, neo-fascist community may derive a real sense of purpose and meaning from that background. Yet given the inherently bigoted and sectarian nature of such communal membership we would surely not want to value it in the same way we should value, say, a healthy, tolerant multiculturalism. We may value families, nations and churches, but those which are based on domination and oppression are qualitatively different from those which are more egalitarian, pluralistic and thus *liberal*. Here again, we may reconfigure what we mean by individualism, rights, choice, and so on but there seems little reason to ditch them altogether.

Furthermore, what would it mean to think of yourself as a member of an eco-community? Can you really see yourself as belonging to the same sort of community as people 1,000 years in the future? Can you identify yourself as a member of the same eco-community as termites? Perhaps these are silly examples. We don't necessarily have to *feel* our membership of a community in order to *belong* to it. We can recognise the contribution termites make to an ecosystem without *experiencing* them as eco-neighbours. But this proviso, too, might suggest that while we can revise and rethink our moral position this does not mean we have to entirely abandon belief systems like liberalism.

Feminist justice

Feminism has also challenged liberalism while seeming to incorporate a degree of flexibility that some republican and communitarian theorists may lack.

On the face of it this seems unlikely. Feminism is concerned with gender and many feminists have spent a great deal of time resisting the concept of 'nature' as essentialist and reductive (Butler, 1990). Men have historically been identified with culture, civilisation, the social, the political, and so on, while women have been identified with nature, with their biological capacity for reproduction and so as caregivers whose 'natural role' is one of wife, mother and domestic servant. The hierarchical dichotomy of culture/ nature and masculine/feminine lies at the heart of sexual oppression by constructing women as inferior, weak and submissive. With its emphasis on the centrality of nature, environmentalism would appear to revive a reductive category that feminists have spent decades trying to critique and dispel.

For feminism, justice implies sexual or gender equality in the workplace, in politics and in the home (Okin, 1991). As such, we must acknowledge the extent to which the apparently personal and domestic are interwoven with the public and the political. Inequalities in domestic arrangements will create and recycle those in the world of business and government, which will, reciprocally and unfortunately, perpetuate hierarchies in the home. Social justice therefore means attending to a host of issues that have been neglected: childcare, parental leave, working-time arrangements, equal pay, equal representation and so on.

Liberalism therefore stands condemned because, unwittingly or otherwise, it has treated the 'masculine' as the paradigm of what it is to be an individual: competitive, calculating, acquisitive, self-sufficient. But republicanism and communitarianism have also been criticised. The former may be so concerned with 'the public' that it fails to problematise 'the private', neglecting the subtle processes that continue to exclude women from political activity (Pateman, 2008). The latter can be accused of resurrecting Golden Age myths about the worth of certain communities (Frazer and Lacey, 1993). The strong families of previous eras often treated wives as chattels with few rights.

Yet there is a concept which reaches out to environmentalism while encompassing elements of republicanism and communitarianism (see Chapter Eleven, this volume). The 'care ethic' challenges the idea that 'work' is equivalent to 'paid employment in the market'. The latter would be impossible without informal care work (most of which is performed by women) since such work is sometimes valued as contributing the equivalent of hundreds of billions to gross domestic product (GDP) (Himmelweit, 2002). If care work suddenly vanished and had to be charged for at market rates then it would be ruinously expensive. The care ethic also challenges the idea that dependency is hierarchical where some people are dependants and others are depended on. This fiction, too, maintains a sexual division between (male) breadwinning and (female) caregiving. Instead, mutual dependency is the norm and Robinson Crusoe independence a delusion. We should care about, for and with one other.

The care ethic therefore appeals to republican citizenship, whereby the public is made to encompass previously devalued and degendered notions of social participation, and to a communitarian emphasis on mutuality, reciprocity, solidarity and ontological limits. It also dovetails with an environmental ethic, as without caring for the Earth we are unlikely to conserve it. Since care and cooperation are elements of animal (and human) behaviour they provide a more secure basis for EJ than abstract rules. Sustainability has to involve a recognition of nature's intrinsic value, of something that should not be transformed into commodities to be bought and sold (Fitzpatrick, 2007a).

Yet there are potential difficulties with a care ethic. If care is treated as separate from, and perhaps superior to, an ethical politics of justice then we risk losing what is valuable about the latter. It is certainly possible to criticise some theories of justice as ignoring the intricate, everyday scale within which we actually behave justly (or otherwise) to other beings. Rawls' original position comes into criticism for 'disembodying' the actors who have to decide what justice is.

But justice is arguably universal to an extent that care is not. I care for my pet but I cannot care for all pets to an equal extent. Care, in other words, is frequently partial and partisan. Indeed, philosophical conservatives have invoked their version of a care ethic when arguing that to be human means being sectarian and patriotic (Gray, 1997: 161-70). We might try to overcome this by universalising care so that it performs all the work that the concept of justice has traditionally performed. But is this credible? Even if you *could* care for every living creature, would such care be meaningful? Doesn't the value of my care reside precisely in the fact that I care for you more than I care for that stranger over there? If we universalise care don't we then dilute it beyond meaning?

Justice without care certainly risks being hollow and inhumane, but care without justice risks being directionless, sentimental and fractional. We presumably need both to inform our views of EJ. But if that is the case then, as before, we cannot afford to toss liberalism to one side.

Summing up

It appears that each attempt to excavate a single, secure foundation for EJ flounders. And even a brief review of three contributory perspectives leaves us with an immense and complex series of questions to resolve. What would happen if we were to take account of debates surrounding egalitarianism, capabilities, recognition, reflexivity, deep ecology and many other relevant perspectives?

One option is to select and refine a particular philosophy of EJ and hope that this does most of the work. For instance, perhaps we ought to take a suitably refined Rawlsian theory of social justice and apply it to the ecological context. The danger is that we define the borders of our philosophy so narrowly, so parsimoniously, that we ignore an important range of ideas, goals and emphases.

The other option is to accept that there can be no single, all-encompassing philosophy of EJ and instead adopt a pragmatic, pluralistic approach. Here, our job is not to cook a single meal but to serve up a menu of diverse dishes from which we can select according to circumstance and judgement. If we found that one perspective (liberal, communitarian/republican, feminist) began to falter then, as Alan Carter recommends, we should recalibrate matters so that the imbalance is corrected. There would have to be some common denominator (all the dishes have to be on the same table) but lots of ways of constructing the food we consume at any one time.

What might that common denominator be? By extrapolating from the above philosophies, and relating these back to the kind of questions asked at the beginning of the chapter, we can construct *Table 6.1*.

EJ is therefore concerned with freedom, equality, community, public participation, well-being and care, but what these mean and how they interrelate is surely a matter of endless negotiation. Thus, the far right column in *Table 6.1* is not meant to supersede the others by offering the definitive, final word; nor is it likely that those favouring another column will be content with its stipulations anyway.

However, unless I am wrong, contemporary social and political philosophies require us to work out a 'core' of principles, ends and values, while acknowledging that each core is surrounded by multiple and multidimensional peripheries, all of which crisscross and shade into a diverse array of other peripheries whose cores are elsewhere. A centre configures its boundaries but is also configured *by* them and each suburb forms the outskirts of many different hubs. As such, the account given here signposts the kind of theoretical and political directions in which we must travel.

Table 6.1: Environmental justice (EJ)

	Liberalism	Republicanism and communitarianism	Feminism	Common denominators?
What are the criteria of EJ?	EJ must be consistent with the free choices and actions of individuals	EJ should be consistent with and enhance the public good and the spaces of both political and communal participation	EJ must embody a strong ethic of care	EJ should be consistent with the freedoms and rights of individuals, enabling everyone to contribute fully to the political systems and communal contexts that influence their sense of well-being, caring for those with whom we are interdependent
What are the principles and justifications underpinning the rules and practices of EJ?	Inhibiting such choice is only justified if it causes harm to others	EJ should reject and inhibit that which does not accord to the public good and/or the common good	Care denotes a relational and emotional depth that expresses our rootedness in our social and natural environments	
Who are the subjects of EJ?	Those who harm others and/or are harmed or capable of being harmed, by others	The equal and active participants of the body politic and the social community	All beings who experience, or are capable of experiencing, and thus have an interest in avoiding, harm, vulnerability and suffering	From all those who can choose either to harm or to care for others
From whom, and to whom, should EJ be rendered?	Those who are, or can reasonably be included as, members of impartial decision-making procedures	Those who belong to the eco-community, including those whose interests we recognise, and for whom we bear responsibility, even if they do not possess a means of articulating those interests	Those who deserve dignity and respect	To those who belong to the same ecological community and so therefore belong to the same *moral* community
	Such members can and should act as trustees for those (such as future generations) who are affected by our environmental practices but who cannot, realistically, possess a voice		All those who are affected by our capacity to care or not to care	All beings, wherever they are in space and time, whose lives will be significantly affected by our actions

contd

Table 6.1 (contd)

	Liberalism	Republicanism and communitarianism	Feminism	Common denominators?
Why be environmentally just? / What motives are needed for EJ to be realised?	To preserve and, if possible, enhance the agency, autonomy and well-being of those whom our socioeconomic practices affect	As a key duty of public citizenship For the good of the communities from which we derive our sense of identity and on whom we depend As obligations which we possess by virtue of being evolved parts of nature	Because all living things deserve to be treated with dignity because of who or what they are (rather than because of what they do or intend) We ought to care as a matter of respect	Because our own existence is threatened Because nature, of which we are a part, possesses intrinsic value Because we owe to future generations an equal or better quality of life Because it is right and thus the finest expression of our capacity for good
Where and when does EJ occur? / What are the socioeconomic, political and legal conditions without which EJ cannot thrive?	Across a longer, although still comprehensible, timescale than existing theories of political and social justice acknowledge In a global context, although one ultimately based on individual rights and freedoms On Rawlsian grounds, people would impartially prefer to live in whatever sustainable society is both consistent with the equal liberty of all and to the benefit of the least advantaged	Across whatever timescale relates to those with whom we share public space and communal membership Participative membership implies an equality of basic resources In a global context, although one based on a conception of both national and post-national politics, shared publics and common goods	Between all interdependent beings That which preserves and promotes relations of solidarity, mutual belonging and natural value Resources, goods and capabilities should be organised so that the well-being of all beings is enhanced	Potentially, at every present moment in time and at every location in space EJ is simultaneously global and local EJ without social justice is meaningless EJ both articulates and weaves a web of socio-natural interconnections

contd

Table 6.1 (contd)

	Liberalism	Republicanism and communitarianism	Feminism	Common denominators?
How is EJ realised? What political strategies and public policies are likely to effect those conditions?	Through democratic procedures, consent and the rule of law By lobbying political parties and other relevant agencies at local, domestic, regional and international levels	By enjoining and, if necessary, enforcing the performance of the relevant duties By encouraging and facilitating whatever public and communal practices enable sustainability	By reducing the role of those factors which prevent us from caring for one another and reforming social rules, political systems, economic distributions and cultural expectations accordingly	Through both formal and informal social, political and economic systems which enable the 'relational self' to prosper By supplying basic needs and enabling the exchange of respect By enabling the democratic control of resources so that humanitarian and sustainable goals can be realised

Practices

Of course, justice resides not only in what we think and say but also in what we do. What is the 'doing' of EJ? If we need not only to alter behaviour but also to reflect on attitudes, identities and values then how might this occur? Chapters Seven to Thirteen provide an overview of important debates within themes that are traditionally associated with social policy. But Chapter Three also offered a green critique of social policy that highlighted the importance of decentralisation and participation. Many policy reforms will fail to embody this point, for example, health and employment policies cannot simply be left to local deliberation if they are to be sustainable. This is fine. Chapter Three also argued in favour of 'gestalt governance' and Chapter Four noted the continued importance of the state. However, if the critique is correct then a green society may need to make room for ideas that currently lurk at the edge of conventional approaches to policy reform (see also Wright, 2010: Chapters 6-7). As such, the radical and the innovative should no longer be treated as after-thoughts to be addressed once 'proper' policy arenas have been examined. That is why I wish to discuss various proposals here, before we delve into the details of Chapters Seven to Thirteen.

Thus, to what extent might the following proposals allow EJ to be practised? In particular, referring back to row 5 of *Table 6.1*:

- Do they enable the 'relational self' to prosper, that is, the self which is concerned with valuing the quality of life?
- Do they permit the comprehensive distribution of basic needs and an exchange of social respect?
- Do they enable the democratic control of resources so that humanitarian and sustainable goals can be realised?

If our answer to these questions is favourable then the importance of the following ideas may grow as green politics becomes more prominent.

These proposals are, of course, selective. Initiatives in community gardening, sustainable micro-technologies and community budgets may also herald developments that bear important implications for sustainability policies in years to come. However, I will limit myself to mentioning those ideas where there has been a great deal of commentary in recent years. Appreciate, also, that while some require government action, others relate to a spirit of localised, bottom-up, civic experimentation that is incredibly diverse and so difficult to summarise (Seyfang and Smith, 2007). According to a gestalt perspective, the job of government may be to facilitate practices that are essentially non–governmental.

Basic income and assets

A basic income is the most top-down of these proposals. It would be received by everyone – on either a weekly, monthly or annual basis – as an unconditional right of citizenship, that is, without reference to marital or employment status, employment history or intention to seek employment (Fitzpatrick, 1999a; Raventós, 2007). In short, almost everyone would receive the basic income, although exemptions for certain groups, for example, prisoners, temporary residents, and so on, could be envisaged. It would replace most of the benefits, tax reliefs and tax allowances that currently exist, and could be age-related, for example with a higher basic income for older people. It therefore represents an alternative both to means testing and to the social insurance principle since the former is held to be unfair and the latter less relevant to contemporary developments than it once was. Basic income would be a national scheme, although some have proposed transnational and even global versions of the idea.

Allied to basic income is the proposal to introduce some kind of basic capital assets (BCA) scheme. For instance, Ackerman and Alstott (1999) proposed that all individuals should receive US$80,000 on reaching the age of 21, so long as they possessed a high school diploma and stayed clear of crime, the money to be distributed in four annual instalments. White (2003) has also proposed an assets scheme.

The point of both basic income and BCA is: to enhance the freedom of individuals by making them a bit less dependent on both states and markets; reduce poverty (since neither scheme is withdrawn as earnings rise); and to introduce greater gender equality into income maintenance systems since women's entitlements would be the same as men's. There is a debate on how compatible they really are but we do not need to consider that debate here (see Fitzpatrick, 2007b). Instead, there are perhaps three ways in which basic income and BCA might contribute to EJ (see also Lord, 2003; Reinikainen, 2005).

First, by guaranteeing an income to people it frees them, at least to some extent, from debilitating circumstances and relationships. If you receive one third of the average wage automatically then you can either reduce the number of hours you work in a job you hate or can depend on the guaranteed income while looking around for a better job. Rather than contributing to an economic culture of overwork many people would surely downsize, reducing their working hours to make room for personal and social activities that often get squeezed by the imperatives to constantly earn and consume. Of course, much depends on how high the basic income and BCA is set. But it can be argued that with more free time people will feel less pressured and so revive the creative, mutual, sociable habits and practices which our consumerist, competitive societies have allowed to wither.

Second, and while acknowledging that there is more to basic needs than income and wealth, basic income and BCA could provide the financial basis through which such basic needs are more comprehensively and universally realised than at present. Again, much depends on the design of such schemes but, if set at a generous enough level, then people would at least possess the monetary prerequisites for housing, healthy lifestyles, education, leisure and all other components which define our basic needs.

Finally, there are versions of basic income and BCA that tie them to the greater democratic control of the economy (see Fitzpatrick, 1999a: Chapter 7). For instance, a social dividend would in effect be a return paid to every citizen from the annual profits of socially owned industries, utilities and assets. The Alaskan Permanent Fund operates in this way. We could also imagine occasional windfall taxes, imposed on excessively powerful corporations and banks, being similarly distributed. Such democratic control could be designed to ensure that the economy supports sustainability and penalises non-sustainable forms of production and consumption.

However, environmentalists might also be wary of basic income and BCA for various reasons.

First, any transition towards an ecological society and economy is going to require a massive change in public attitudes and institutional reform, whereas basic income and BCA might do no more than consolidate existing assumptions and habits. Perhaps they place too much emphasis on individual need and consumption. Second, a basic income and BCA may encourage some people to downsize – perhaps those wealthy enough to be able to afford to do so – but there is no guarantee that these other activities will be environmentally friendly – they could be parasitic on the very productivism and materialism which greens strenuously oppose. Gorz (1992), for example, argues that although a guaranteed minimum income is a necessary condition for social participation it is not a sufficient condition. Finally, perhaps such schemes are simply too centralised and top-down to constitute real solutions to the problems we face. Either scheme would surely take many years, even decades, to fully introduce at a time when governments should be spending their energies elsewhere.

Nevertheless, as indicated above, much depends on the design of such schemes. Many Green parties around the world have supported unconditional provision as a means of encouraging us to move beyond our 'employment society'.

> ## Box 6.1: Basic income and basic capital assets (BCA)
>
> Each would provide a guaranteed level of basic income and wealth. Basic income would be unconditional. BCA might be unconditional but not necessarily.
>
> ### Advantages
> - Would free people from undesirable circumstances
> - Would offer a financial element of basic needs
> - Compatible with economic and green democracy
>
> ### Disadvantages
> - Potentially too individualistic and consumerist
> - Not a sufficient condition for sustainability
> - A distraction from more important priorities

Informal economies

Our second potential innovation involves a greater role for the informal economy. By the informal economy is meant the range of activities that contribute to social well-being but are not recognised by official measurements since they lie outside the formal economy of production, consumption and labour (Williams and Windebank, 1998). This informal economy is a 'region' of civil society which is distinct from (a) the public sector and the state, (b) commercial, market provision, (c) the not-for-profit agencies of the 'independent sector' and (d) the family. Years ago I defined such informal economies as constituting a kind of fifth sector which could help to reconfigure the other four (Fitzpatrick, 1999b).

One example of informal exchange that has attracted much attention in recent years is Local Exchange Trading Systems (LETS). LETS encourage people to exchange goods and services within their local communities (Williams, 2002; North, 2006). Each LETS is a non-profit-making network of local residents who trade goods and services with each other using a local currency. Each member advertises the skills they have to offer and/or the goods they have to sell, while being encouraged to buy skills and goods from other LETS members. When a purchase is made the relevant units of the local currency are transferred from the purchaser's account to the provider's. This local currency is issued by its members rather than by a bank and so is potentially unlimited. Economic activity need no longer be restricted by a lack of money; those whose skills and experiences are being undervalued by the formal economy can find both a 'market' for their services and an opportunity to engage in reciprocal, communal exchange with like-minded neighbours.

If we return to the questions we asked earlier, we can understand the attractions of such informal schemes when it comes to realising EJ.

First, they revive the kind of neighbourly, civic associations that many insist have been allowed to erode in an era of big government and/or hyper-capitalism. By their very nature LETS demand local interaction and face-to-face participation as people exchange goods and services. Individuals will certainly have their personal interests served but evidence suggests that they also gain by giving to others in friendly, mutualist forms of provision. Rather than simply buying in assistance from an impersonal supplier, LETS go beyond such monetary contracts to relationships that demand a greater degree of interpersonal trust and friendship. Therefore, what they stress is the qualitative or relational self that other schemes of local support, for example, credit unions, perhaps do not.

Therefore, second, they arguably allow basic needs to be provided in ways that the other (a)–(d) sectors cannot. For instance, they may constitute ways of promoting non-employment forms of work outside the formal economy. Williams (2002) has addressed the relevance of LETS to unemployment, stating that LETS can be viewed as a way of reducing social inequalities by encouraging the participation of the unemployed in informal work. The unemployed are able to trade their time to enhance their standard of living and to improve their chances of finding work in the formal economy. LETS may also provide people with the opportunity to increase their stock of 'social capital', given that they are networks which are based on, and seem to enhance, respect.

Finally, while some members of informal economies may be effectively non-active, to be a member implies having a say in how the scheme is run. This does not mean that LETS can replace centralised forms of welfare and social administration, still less that they could offer a model of political governance, but they represent one of a diverse range of civic associations in which 'democratic voice' is given much more prominence than in existing public services. The latter are sometimes statist and bureaucratic, sometimes consumerist and sometimes both. Informal economies might offer the embryo of a distinct, democratic model of bottom–up governance.

Yet there are also reasons to doubt that informal economies can do much to promote EJ. First, such schemes may always remain too small and ad hoc to constitute the kind of eco-social transformation we require. While we may in future have to stress localised forms of production and consumption (food, energy, etc), this still requires systematic, highly organised forms of government that LETS cannot supply. Second, informal economies have failed to attract significant numbers of people. No doubt this is because of the entrenchment of attitudes and habits that the advocates of informal economies wish to break.[1] But this also suggests that a green revolution will not proceed without national and global action to curb greenhouse gases (GHGs). A LETS may be environmentally friendly, by placing less stress on national and social infrastructures, but perhaps our first concern should be with reorganising the very basis of the economy. Finally, LETS may commodify activities which ought to remain separate from the cash nexus. They may bring people together but only as producers and consumers, contradicting the very value of neighbourliness and cooperation.

And yet, there are few versions of the green society that do not make some room for informal schemes of exchange and the informal economy.

Box 6.2: Informal economies

Forms of mutual, participative exchange that are distinct from, but may overlap with, elements of the other sectors of society and economy.

Advantages
- Encourage neighbourly, civic associations
- Provide goods and services that other sectors often fail to supply
- Are democratic and participative

Disadvantages
- Limitations of small-scale, bottom-up solutions given the immediate problems we face

---

Time banks

Sometimes known as 'time currencies' or 'time dollars', time banking can be regarded as another example of informal economic exchange (Cahn, 2004; Seyfang, 2005b; nef, 2010).[2] The participants deposit time in the bank which they have accumulated by assisting and supporting others; they then withdraw their time when they require assistance and support from others. This can involve a vast range of activities such as tutoring, childcare, shopping, gardening, repairs and so on.

Thus, except for the fact that time is used as a currency, the objectives of time banks are similar to those of LETS, encouraging community life, valuing currently under-valued skills, building social capital, counteracting reductions in public spending and services and providing social goods in a non-market context (Seyfang, 2009a). That said, LETS currencies tend to parallel the value of the national currency. I may need to walk Anna's dogs for two hours to earn the currency I need to pay Frank for the 30 minutes it takes him to repair my washing machine. With time banks, if you give an hour then you get an hour back. Time credits are therefore immune to inflation and less vulnerable than LETS to the problem of hoarding. This makes time banking even more of a non-monetary form of exchange, although members may need reassurance that the hour they donate will be broadly equivalent in value to the hour they receive. One solution is to allow the more highly skilled to 'charge' more for the time they donate. Hence, some schemes are hybrids of LETS and time banking.

As with LETS, then, time banks require organisation, resources and personnel to ensure that members are protected from defaulters, that the quality of work is insured and that vulnerable people are protected. Also, governments are slowly waking up to the fact that traditional income maintenance schemes (taxation, tax credits, benefits) should accommodate alternative currencies rather than penalising their members by treating such currency as just another form of earned income which ought to be taxed or means tested.

So time banks encourage communal participation and volunteering but challenge the ethos of shovelling people into the labour market on the basis that any job is better than no job. They therefore stress both needs and assets, both rights and responsibilities, but without treating the labour market as the be-all-and-end-all of social membership. In this respect, they offer a radical alternative to the welfare politics of the classic welfare state as well as to its neoliberal and third way successors.

So far as EJ is concerned, since the strengths and weaknesses of time banks resemble those of LETS I won't repeat myself – see **Box 6.2** again. Let me emphasise two important points, however. Alternative currencies are not a panacea (Seyfang, 2004). Those who, for whatever reason, imagine that informal economies can entirely replace the state and public services are either ignorant or indifferent to the inequalities in socioeconomic power that state action and the public sector go at least some of the way to ameliorating. Some needs and problems will always require the specialised, expensive, long-term or collective provision for which informal economies are simply not appropriate. Some of those who argue that the state cannot replace 'the community' are rather too quick to propose that communities can replace the state (Green, 1996).

Second, it is not the case of time banking 'delivering' sustainability since time banks may be consistent with unsustainable practices – I'll repair your car if you repair my patio heater. Instead, it is more that the principles and policies needed for sustainability are unlikely to receive support from people unless they are consistent with efforts to rebuild communities in ways that are genuinely inclusive, fair and participatory. If time banks – and other informal economies – enable this, then great, if not, then we need to envisage other mechanisms. The job of social policy activists, policy makers and researchers is to encourage and assess such social experiments, finding a place for them within a wider panoply of measures that enhance both sustainability and social justice.

Conclusion

In short, we should treat neither the philosophy nor practice of EJ as 'closed', that is, as something that can be read off from succinct, manifesto-type lists. This would be so even were it not the case that diverse cultures around the world, with their varying histories and institutions, are likely to conceive the meaning and implications of justice, well-being and care differently. The gestalt model implies a basic framework and consensus, within which a large degree of pluralism can be allowed to flourish. EJ cannot be grown in an abstract laboratory and then rolled out among a largely passive citizenry. Instead, if it is to become a meaningful point of reference in the 21st century, it needs to be an ever-evolving, dynamic concept in which philosophy and practice are mutually interactive. The long-term implications of this for social policy have yet to be worked out.

Notes

[1] Or, in a question once posed to a research assistant of mine by a junior minister, why should government be interested in LETS when few people are interested in them either?

[2] See the website of Time Banking UK (www.timebanking.org/index.htm)

Chapter summary

This chapter outlined the basic principles of EJ by exploring three established political philosophies of justice. It explained:

- the limitations of freedom and autonomy as defended by liberals;
- the drawbacks of community and public participation as defined by communitarians and republicans;
- the potential weaknesses of feminist justice.

Table 6.1 summarised the 'common denominators' of EJ but also made the point that any philosophy of justice encompassed diverse influences and multiple perspectives.

The chapter then explored three proposals that lie outside the mainstream of policy debates. It concluded that much depends on the design of such proposals. None by itself could deliver a green society and we have reason to believe that none of them fully embody the principles and desired practices of EJ.

Questions for discussion

* How is the concept of EJ different from traditional philosophies of justice?
* In addition to the perspectives outlined above, what other political philosophies might be closely related to the environmentalist case for justice?
* How important are theories of EJ to its *practice*?
* Are radical proposals, such as basic income and time banks, a distraction from more mainstream, well-established measures for realising principles of justice?

Key further reading

Dobson, A. (1998) *Justice and the environment*, Oxford: Clarendon Press.
Dobson, A. (ed) (1999) *Fairness and futurity*, Oxford: Oxford University Press.
Dobson, A. (2003) *Citizenship and the environment*, Oxford: Oxford University Press.
Hayward, T. (1998) *Political theory and ecological values*, Cambridge: Polity Press.
Scholsberg, D. (2009) *Defining environmental justice*, Oxford: Oxford University
    Press.

Useful websites

The Equality Exchange: http://mora.rente.nhh.no/projects/EqualityExchange/

Basic Income Earth Network: http://www.basicincome.org/bien/

Transaction: http://www.transaction.net/moneylets/

seven

Environmental policy

Tony Fitzpatrick

Overview

This chapter:

- categorises and describes environmental policy, looking at: (1) economic instruments; (2) regulations; and (3) education and information;
- examines the association between environmental policy and 'governance';
- outlines the meaning and implications of what I call 'greenwashing', 'piggybacking', 'mainstreaming' and 'greenstreaming';
- assesses the social effects of environmental policies through a case study of fuel poverty.

We now commence the more practical business of examining existing policies in order to understand the extent to which social and environmental agendas have begun to converge. Chapters Eight to Thirteen then take the story into analyses of specific social policy domains.

This chapter therefore asks some key questions:

- What are the main instruments available to policy makers and what are their pros and cons?
- What levels, contexts and forms of governance relate to those instruments?
- What social effects have environmental policies had to date?

This final question returns us to a theme of Chapter Three when we covered the relationship between poverty, exclusion and environmental problems.

Please note that due to lack of space we will not be covering the policy process and policy making in much detail here – for good introductions see Rosenbaum (2008: Chapter 2) and Kraft (2011: 62-74).

Varieties of environmental policy

The following sub-sections capture the main types of environmental policy that have been promoted to date. For further explorations see Jordan et al (2003), Harrington et al (2004), Rosenbaum (2008: 158-70) and Kraft (2011: 230-3).

Economic instruments

Economic instruments are concerned with financial incentives and therefore with making changes to agents' behaviour (Olmstead, 2010).

First, there is carbon trading (Stern, 2007: Chapter 15). Chapter Three discussed the principles of trading carbon permits in order to inject monetary rewards and penalties into the market system. By manipulating the price mechanism governments can make it slightly harder for the heaviest polluters to realise a profit while rewarding those who undershoot their emissions allowance. The expectation is that such green markets will drive companies towards sustainable practices, including technological innovation, by appealing to the profit motive.

To date, however, the experience has not matched the ideal. Within the European Union's (EU's) Emissions Trading Scheme, the biggest scheme to date, carbon permits were initially given away at no cost, based on a company's historic level of pollution. This was done in order to ease the transition in business practice towards carbon trading. Unfortunately, at least in its early stages, this led to 'perverse incentives' where rather than the polluter paying, the polluter was paid, effectively providing a competitive bonus to the ecologically neglectful. Even worse, the costs of something for which those companies had not even paid was then passed on to the consumer, producing massive windfall profits! Phase III of the scheme begins in 2012 and if it is to be effective then there will need to be more auctioning and less free allocation. President Obama has signalled that the US should move in a similar direction.

Critics still allege that carbon trading lets polluters off the hook. If allowances are generous, and you are a company or a nation that is highly affluent, then you can effectively purchase the right to pollute without having to change your habits. This actually impedes the shifts in ethical practices and values for which the last two chapters argued. One solution is to construct a carbon market that discourages such behaviour by auctioning few allowances at higher prices. Yet, for reasons of vested interest, the affluent may mobilise against the very implementation of such markets.

Second, governments can raise or lower taxes, and other charges, or introduce any number of subsidies, in order to steer behaviour in green directions (Stern, 2007: Chapter 14). For instance, taxing fuel-inefficient engines and pollutants can discourage their use, encourage alternatives (such as hybrid cars) and raise revenue that can be used to promote sustainable goals. Packaging and other forms of solid waste disposal can be similarly taxed. Thirty per cent of the US population has access to 'redemption', or deposit refund, programmes for beverage containers that stimulate recycling. If, through reduced bills, households are not charged for the collection of waste that is recyclable then they are provided with a cash incentive to alter their consumption habits. Subsidies can also be provided for the purchase of energy-efficient goods.

These specific measures may ultimately form part of a more ambitious strategy where the base of the economy is shifted away from labour, or payroll, taxes towards green taxes. This would make hiring workers more attractive to employers and go some way to reconciling the sometimes divergent interests of labour and environmental movements.

Ultimately, tax-based incentives and similar measures will only be effective if they are applied across the world. This leads to problems of coordination, fairness, monitoring and compliance that can be extremely difficult to resolve. International agreements are notoriously hard to effect when one country's tax breaks may appear to others as an unwarranted interference on free trade ('perverse subsidies'). Also, especially when fuelled by populist anti-tax campaigns, green taxes may not receive popular support if they are perceived as just another means of hitting consumers by revenue-hungry politicians more eager to speak than to act green. A direct and transparent line of hypothecation therefore needs to lead from green taxes to the environmental objectives they serve; for example, London's congestion charge was used to build capacity in public transport.

Furthermore, green taxes need to be fair and fairly applied. If they mainly reward those who have the time, energy and resources to take advantage of them then such instruments may effectively penalise the already disadvantaged. As Chapter Three reported, the poorest households would suffer disproportionately from higher energy bills.

At a more philosophical level, economic incentives may not appeal to, and may sometimes conflict with, the non-monetary values on which ecological justice could ultimately depend (Dobson, 2009: 126-9). We are moral agents rather than beings who respond in predictable ways to external, economic stimuli. Rather than appealing to individual self-interest, sustainability may require a more ethical sense of mutuality, collective interest and the common good. Policy makers need to be armed with something other than the blunt computerised tools of cost-benefit analysis. To its critics, the emphasis on incentives represents an unwelcome intrusion of neoliberal assumptions into environmental policy making (Bachram, 2004).

This is not to argue that economic incentives are irrelevant, but many green theorists have proposed that citizenship is something more than profit, consumerism and possessive individualism (Sagoff, 1988). Thus, in a now famous study conducted by Frey (1997: 69-77), people were *less* likely to make personal sacrifices when they were offered economic incentives to do so. Such sacrifices were more evident when people were effectively making a decision based on their membership of a social community and their contribution to a greater good. Republicans and feminists both stress the importance of appealing to non-materialistic motivations. A monetary contract may, if anything, license selfish behaviour ('I bought the right to pollute') and detract from the value commitments on which green citizenship and justice ultimately depend.

Regulation[1]

Up until the 1970s, 'command-and-control' was the dominant approach of many governments. The state would pass laws or set quality standards and targets, such as an upper limit on the amount of permissible pollution, and then penalise malefactors accordingly. Command-and-control scored some notable successes but by the 1980s this approach was being widely questioned (Mol and Buttel, 2002; Durant et al, 2004; also Press and Mazmanian, 2010).

Summary box

Command-and-control

- Establish environmental goals and objectives, taking social and economic considerations into account.
- Determine environmental quality criteria through data analysis, modelling exercises and risk assessments.
- Set environmental quality standards, that is, a level of pollution which is tolerable in terms of health and other social considerations.
- Set emissions standards, that is, the maximum amount of pollutants that can be released in quality standards are not to be exceeded.
- Enforce those standards and other requirements through negotiations, penalties and other sanctions.

Adapted from Kraft (2011: 143).

To some extent, this was due to a wider challenge to the state by those who favoured free markets. If individuals, as it was assumed, respond in rational, self-interested ways to sets of benefits and burdens, in order to maximise their wealth relative to competitors, then we need an incentives-based approach. But among environmentalists, too, command-and-control was criticised as undemocratic, adversarial and inflexible, unable to generate the levels of democratic input, popular trust and legitimacy that a politics of sustainability may ultimately require.

Nonetheless, regulation persists as a vital instrument of government action (Press and Mazmanian, 2010: 224-33; Kraft, 2011: Chapter 5); for example, by its very nature a carbon market demands some form of regulatory control and oversight. Some regulations are more 'vertical', top-down and hierarchical, corresponding to the command-and-control model. In the US, for instance, the Environmental Protection Agency is responsible for a staggering array of environmental laws and statutory programmes (Rosenbaum, 2010). But many regulations are now more 'horizontal', characterised by the need to build multidirectional partnerships and networks in order to engage the participation of numerous agencies, such as non-governmental organisations (NGOs), within civil society. Such at-a-distance governance has partly displaced older methods of direct, hands-on state management (see Chapter Four, this volume).

Horizontal governance may be concerned to incentivise the relevant actors, blurring the line between this policy instrument and that of the previous section. For instance, there are forms of voluntary, self-regulation that are incentives-based (see Chapter Eleven, this volume). Some companies have instigated private carbon markets and BP has its own internal trading scheme. These initiatives may represent examples of genuine green reform or they may be examples of 'greenwash' (see below).

Otherwise, we might identify two principal ideal-types of horizontal regulation: democratic and paternalist. First, there are regulatory frameworks in which the state engages in a genuine dialogue with civil society organisations and social movements. This is the 'active and inclusive' state that is open to negotiation throughout its policy-making processes. Sweden and Norway have gone part of the way in this direction, as Chapter Three made clear.

The second, more paternalist, type of horizontal regulation 'nudges' markets in green directions by encouraging producers to supply and consumers to demand what they might otherwise neglect. Some renewable technologies will emerge from markets without much assistance. But others may need a helping hand, with government kick-starting Research and Development (R&D) programmes in order to get the technology into the world as quickly, and as cheaply, as possible. Take the following examples (see also Knill and Liefferink, 2007: Chapter 2).

Energy efficiency standards are needed so that carbon consumption is reduced to the lowest possible level. Some regulations are already being implemented, for example, with light bulbs, refrigerators and boilers, although improvements are still required so that producers have less opportunity to game play and make extravagant claims about their product. Transparent energy labelling is therefore necessary so that consumers can know the energy efficiency of the goods they purchase. Building regulations are of particular importance. Properly designed, residential and commercial buildings can be practically self-heating, while existing stock can be made more efficient.

Another idea is to decentralise national energy grids so that power generation is located closer to the point of consumption – thus reducing energy loss – with the possibility that households will be able to make money by selling surplus energy *to* the grid. Some also envisage a real-time, internet-style form of energy interaction where commodities store surplus energy during periods of low national consumption (when prices are low) and draw on those reserves by switching themselves off during peak periods (when prices are higher).

Transport is also vital. Here, the future design of our roads and cities will be shaped by innovations relating to the efficiency of vehicles (and so the development of hydrogen and electric cars), the cleanness of fuels and by decisions over how to balance space for the private car against public mobility (walking, bicycles, rail, buses and coaches). Aviation is particularly contentious, with some arguing that it must be drastically curtailed while others insist that efficient engines and alternative fuels can make an important difference here too. The future role of power and industrial plants is also controversial. Here, regulation becomes less horizontal. With more coal-fired plants coming on line many argue the need for 'carbon capture and storage' where carbon dioxide (CO_2) is captured and sequestered underground or in reservoirs (Goodall, 2008: Chapter 8). Others argue that such technologies lack viability and divert attention from the need to develop energy renewables or, indeed, nuclear energy (Lovelock, 2007: Chapter 5). And even if renewables cannot supply 100% of our energy demands, there is considerably more scope for the development of wind, solar, tidal, biomass and geothermal power so that an eclectic system of diverse energy sources can exist (McKibben, 2007: 142-55). Additional regulatory measures are needed to halt deforestation, improve rates of reforestation and to incentivise greener agricultural practices.

Therefore, the basic argument for regulation is that it introduces a greater moral dimension into the practices of both public and private sectors than economic incentives alone can effect. However, there are several potential problems.

First, horizontal regulation might be too slow compared to the centralised planning and directives of command-and-control. If you are driving at the edge of a cliff you need to brake and reverse rather than nudge and steer. Worries about partnerships and networks might have to take a backseat when the very life of the passenger is at risk.

Second, there is the difficulty of assessing the efficacy of proposed and existing regulations. Weighing benefits against costs is a difficult exercise for governments to perform anyway, but the problem is multiplied when your assessment expands into a green timescale of decades, generations and even centuries (Rosenbaum, 2008: Chapter 5). Third, regulation faces the 'collective action problem' where, although people would benefit more from long-term cooperation, because these benefits are distant and uncertain, individuals often choose to forgo them in favour of more immediate, self-interested advantages (Potoski and Prakash, 2004). To promote cooperation, the state could prefer vertical regulation, reducing the opportunities for agents to default on their obligations. The problem here is that the heavy hand of command-and-control tends to be unpopular. Yet if government chooses a more flexible, light-touch, market-oriented approach then there is a risk of agents 'defecting' and free riding on the cooperative efforts of others. The future challenge for government is how to reconcile the flexible partnerships of horizontal regulation with the universal compliance of vertical regulation. Finally, there is the problem of ensuring international cooperation and coordination to avoid the debilitating effects of 'regulatory competition' where governments manipulate the process of making international agreements in order to gain an advantage over other nations (Knill and Liefferink, 2007: 103–15).

Education and information

The final policy instrument worth considering involves persuasion and preference formation. Since Chapter Twelve mentions education I will say little about it here, other than to add that although O'Riordan (2009) refers to schools as 'sustainability laboratories', we need not see education about green principles, problems and solutions as confined to schools and similar institutions. Some commentators also see a need to move away from a command-and-control view where scientists and teachers distribute knowledge and information that laypeople then receive uncritically. Indeed, while awareness of environmental problems is increasing, people:

• become fatigued by shock tactics and apocalyptic warnings and can adopt a 'why bother?' fatalism;

- are confused by climate science, encouraged to think that scientific evidence is undecided or unreliable;
- distrust governments (which are usually captured by business-as-usual thinking anyway) (Stern, 2007: 527).

Public education requires greater clarity and emphasis on individual empowerment and civic engagement than has been achieved to date (Guber and Bosso, 2010).

This means, first, opening up deliberative assemblies to try and ensure that public opinion is informed while expert opinion and scientific evidence is subject to democratic debate so that it flows into social narratives more effectively. Second, there is a need to use 'local knowledge' (Brown, K., 2009: 42-5). Rather than laying blanket policies over diverse communities or simply parachuting experts in, there is a need to recognise that what works in locality A won't necessarily work in locality B. Both of the above relate to the democratic forms of horizontal regulation mentioned earlier. The aim is to build a degree of social trust into environmental policy making that has often been lacking.

One kind of participative engagement that has attracted attention is 'information disclosure'. Initially, the provision of information was rather 'passive', deriving from individuals' right to know but not regarded as an important mechanism of change. Gradually, however, policy makers' attitudes towards it have shifted (Stephan, 2002; Mol, 2006).

Information disclosure is another form of horizontal regulation and intervention whereby government subtly attempts to activate opinion in desirable directions. The intent here is to improve the flow and transparency of communication between agencies (public or private) and those who have a stake in their environmental impacts. Such communication might be deliberative and consensual where the agency in question takes its environmental responsibilities seriously, or it may be conflictual and confrontational where stakeholders know, or suspect, the agency to be an environmental laggard. Stakeholders might be 'narrow' in scope, for example, confined to a small number of NGOs, or they might be extensive, for example, involving larger and broader constituencies, including the media and other relevant publics. In any event, the goal of disclosure is for government to bring other voices into policy processes and debates so that persuasion and/or force can be exerted from civil society, with government itself remaining in the background.

Imagine that a powerful supermarket has a poor environmental record. What if the company is also immensely powerful and arrogant? A government could challenge the company directly in the hope of changing its practices, but it may fear a corporate backlash and accusations of being anti-business. Policy makers might therefore prefer a subtler strategy of requiring all large companies to make information available about their record on key ecological indicators. By publishing that information in the public domain it is possible that stakeholders – suppliers, customers, employees and local residents – will demand changes that government, on its own, would be less likely to achieve. Media campaigns, lawsuits and boycotts might shame the company into changing its priorities. Through information disclosure, government potentially arms itself with additional instruments and operates with a network of civic agencies and partners.

Of course, there is the problem of ensuring that all agencies comply with the required standards. This increases the bureaucratic heaviness of the state and intensifies the burdens on agencies within a regime already weighted with audits, inspections and paperwork. There is also the problem of 'game playing' and 'greenwash' where, through public relations campaigns for instance, agencies paint themselves as more ecologically friendly than they really are and conceal information that would expose their actual record. There is also the risk that governments may use this strategy as a means of diluting their own obligations. Politicians may in effect say, 'we have equipped citizens with the tools they need to exert influence, so don't blame any failures on us'. The difficulty is obviously compounded when the agency in question is itself a state since a government has considerable power to manipulate public opinion and information in ways that supranational actors – such as the European Union (EU) or international NGOs – may struggle to prevent. For all these reasons, there may be limits to the effectiveness of information disclosure.

Summary box

Economic instruments The attempt to incentivise agents into changing their behaviour through taxes, etc	**Pros** Appeals to existing assumptions and practices **Cons** May exacerbate injustices and take the emphasis away from ethical and attitudinal changes
Regulations Vertical command-and-control and horizontal governance; setting standards and targets and nudging markets in green directions	**Pros** State action to correct negative externalities, etc **Cons** Problems of coordination, enforcement and collective action
Education and information The attempt to change preferences and therefore attitudes	**Pros** Potentially democratic **Cons** Problem of ensuring genuine participatory engagement

Governance

What forms of governance have both influenced and been influenced by these policy instruments? We have here a number of relevant categories.

Levels: global, trans-regional, regional, sub-regional, national, sub-national, local and municipal.

Actors: international organisations, nation-states, networks and alliances, philanthropic and research foundations, firms and multinational corporations (MNCs), cities, NGOs, civil society organisations, public–private partnerships, charities, communities, pressure groups and campaigns, media, social movements, administrators and practitioners.

Sectors: economy, polity, private sector, voluntary and independent sectors, public sectors, welfare systems.

These categories intersect with one another in complex, dynamic ways that are near impossible to plot. Some will be integrated horizontally (disparate actors linked together at the same level); others vertically, for example, sectors and government departments linked across levels; and obviously there can be multiple combinations of what is called 'integration' (Jordan and Lenschow, 2008).

As Chapter Four observed, 'governance' has become a popular term capturing the notion that change originates and flows across a landscape in which a simple state/society distinction no longer applies. There is a kaleidoscopic, migratory quality to governance. We might be tempted to define a municipal initiative, for example congestion charging, as 'local', but when that initiative is adopted by other cities around the world then we may be left with an interpenetrating network where things are both global *and* local. Indeed, this network may even exert a greater influence on the environmental agenda than national governments (Bulkeley and Newell, 2010: 59-62). Therefore, what follows is a highly simplified and stylised overview of a vast, byzantine reality.

How, then, can we possibly make effective interventions into this reality? Some degree of coordination and alignment between the appropriate levels, actors and sectors seems required, but we should not expect these to line up perfectly or permanently. Governance is a continuous process of reflexivity (multiple interactions which alter the medium and scale of interaction) and reflection (self-monitoring to ensure that useful re-alignments and policy developments can occur). The questions then become:

- How much alignment is necessary?
- How much is realistic?
- How can it be effected?

There are two ways we can answer these.

First, we can try and map recent 'trans-boundary' developments in order to draw conclusions about how environmental policies are currently organised (see Rosenbaum, 2008: 333-46; Kraft, 2011: 255-74). If we cross-refer our policy-making categories against the relevant levels, in order to frame various actors and sectors, we end up with **Table 7.1** (which is illustrative, not exhaustive).

Can we determine where most efforts have been concentrated to date? On the one hand, nations continue to dominate the global stage; on the other, few nations can now isolate themselves from multilateral agreements entirely. Therefore, it may well be that since 1945 de facto forms of global governance have been emerging, slowly and unsteadily, with environmental issues becoming more prominent on the agenda over the last two decades. The United Nations Environment Programme (UNEP), for

Table 7.1: Governance across boundaries

	Global	Regional	National	Local
Economic incentives	Carbon markets	EU Emissions Trading Scheme	Subsidies (such as reduced sales tax) and/or low interest loans to facilitate green choices, eg energy efficiency	Council Tax rebates
Regulation	International conferences, treaties and conventions since 1972

Millennium Development Goals (MDGs) | Polluter pays principle

EU Directives | Improved grant system to local authorities

Changes to transport and planning infrastructures | Recycling and waste management

Adaptations to buildings and energy use, eg combined heat and power |
| **Education, knowledge and information** | IPCC

Earth Days to promote public awareness | Directive on Freedom of Access to Information | Engagement with NGOs and other relevant actors within civil society | Growth of sustainable communities, eg UK eco-towns

Local Agenda 21 |

instance, is concerned with the management, monitoring and assessment of key initiatives; adjacent UN agencies deal with development issues. Also, green NGOs now account for a large proportion of the NGOs (an estimated 100,000 in 2007) which have come to occupy the world stage over the last 30-40 years and no government can afford to insulate itself from the most influential of these.

Nation-state sovereignty persists, in other words, but is not what it once was (see Chapter Four). In particular, regional unions and tactical alliances have become crucially important, both as means of binding nations together and in order to find strength in numbers when it comes to global negotiations; for example, the 'Group of 77' (which actually contains 130 countries) represents the interests of developing nations. Such alliances may themselves operate on a number of formal and informal levels and for various reasons such as geographical convenience, cultural-historical language links or political strategy. For instance, Scandinavian countries have their own distinct strategic association that cannot simply be treated as a species of European Union (EU) policy (Selin and VanDeveer, 2010: 272-5).

In short, while there is a national-regional 'spine' to existing policy developments I doubt that ***Table 7.1*** can reveal a central cluster of activity. The map has lots of busy precincts but no capital. In short, the cartography of environmental governance is a highly diverse intersection of contours and gradients. This probably makes it even harder to anticipate where current trends may lead.

The second way of addressing the alignment problem is normative. How *should* we try to align the various grids? This is an even more difficult question to answer and underpins the difficulty of achieving post-Kyoto1 agreement.

Indeed, from the 1992 Earth Summit to the 2009 Copenhagen Conference, people have struggled to answer this question. This is because, to some extent, globalisation represents a threat to sustainability. In the 1980s and 1990s, globalisation was widely seen by policy makers as the global spread of free market capitalism. Neoliberals' response to the alignment question is simple: they largely deny its salience. 'You don't need to engineer alignment', they insist, 'because the invisible hand of the free market will preserve resources and encourage technological innovation'. Regulation should be voluntary, *self*-regulation. The economy will go green when producers and consumers want to make it so. Furthermore, where pro-green agendas have appeared at the global level they have been effectively killed by the most powerful nations. Kyoto1 largely failed due to the US government's intransigence.

But with the turn of the millennium new priorities did begin to appear due to various 'global justice' campaigns and a (modest) shift in the thinking of the World Bank and International Monetary Fund (IMF). Environmentalism offers a challenge to the hegemony of neoliberalism and so may incept a new phase of globalisation. But what that 'green globalisation' should look like is a highly contested issue. For instance, the evolution of carbon markets represents a *partial* shift away from neoliberalism, but one that is still heavily indebted to profit motives and self-interest. Ecological modernisers tend to welcome such developments, while 'deep greens' are more sceptical.

Thus, environmental governance is rife with disagreements over what 'environmental governance' should even mean. To take one example, the dominant organisations – the World Trade Organization (WTO), World Bank and IMF – have not been converted to the concept of zero growth. The oft-quoted definition of sustainability proposed by the 1987 UN World Commission – meeting the needs of the present without compromising the capacity of future generations to meet their needs – could support a politics of zero growth, but just as easily upholds the prevailing wisdom whereby we need gross domestic product (GDP) growth today so that we can afford to be fully sustainable tomorrow. By contrast, green organisations are not simply concerned with the details of regulatory policy but also with affecting a fundamental paradigm shift in how we conceive ourselves and our place in nature. In other words, education is not simply about learning when to turn down the thermostat, it is about reconfiguring what it means to be a social citizen who acts with justice towards others (including animals and future generations). Yet environmentalists themselves do not form a consensus on what this post-neoliberal paradigm should resemble. Feminists will advocate an ethic of care, republicans will champion political participation within new public spaces, while liberals will argue that individual freedom has to occupy the heart of environmental politics.

Another problem concerns the appropriate distribution of responsibility, both for creating environmental problems and for taking the lead in addressing them. Sustainability is also a question of international development (see Chapter Thirteen, this volume). Developing nations argue that systems of governance should reflect the historical role the affluent West has had in creating the problem. Western governments argue that, however we got here, all nations have a responsibility to implement mitigation and adaptation policies.

Thus the normative question of policy and governance alignment is a highly contested one. We need all nations to agree to reduce carbon emissions by x% by the year y, but there are diverging views on what those targets should be and how much freedom nations can be permitted in getting from here to there. It may be, in an era of gestalt governance, that there is no simple post-neoliberal paradigm because global environmental governance is itself 'post-paradigmatic'.

Leaving the normative dimension to one side, to what extent are these current forms of environmental policies 'fit for purpose'? To what extent are they effective? In many respects, Chapters Eight to Thirteen are designed to address these questions. However, there are two, more generic, topics that we ought to explore in any chapter on environmental policy: first, the question of how environmental policies interact with established social and public policies, and, second, the principal effects which environmental policies have had on vulnerable social groups. We address these in turn.

Policy contexts

How do environmental policies intersect with the existing political and policy agenda? There are several basic possibilities.

Greenwashing
It is possible for so-called 'environmental' policies to be nothing of the sort. Policy makers might simply appeal to ecological principles and objectives, by packaging initiatives as such or even re-labelling existing measures. For instance, if a government wants to raise revenue then it may introduce or raise green taxes that conceal its real intentions. In the UK after 1992, a 'fuel duty escalator', providing above-inflation increases in fuel prices, was sold as environmental but condemned by car lobbies as another way of hitting motorists. Greenwashing might occur in order to fulfil obligations (by inappropriately counting something as green), or to court opinion or to divert attention away from unpopular realities. It might even be the case that a government is deceiving itself about its ecological credentials.

Piggybacking
A policy may be designed to fit largely into existing, non-green agendas but nevertheless have some minor environmental component. This could be intended (a means of fulfilling international obligations, perhaps) or unintended. For instance, as the UK shut down most of its coal industry in the 1980s in the 'dash for gas', one consequence was it considerably improved its record on pollution emissions. This was partly intentional (a response to a 1988 European Commission Directive, which committed member states to progressive reductions in their sulphur dioxide emissions) and partly an unintended consequence of existing policies designed to introduce privatisation, increase competition, undermine trades unions and shift the economy towards the service and financial sectors.

Mainstreaming

This is where government – often in conjunction with relevant NGOs, etc – attempts to push green reforms towards the centre of the political stage. Here, environmental objectives are woven more seriously, fully and transparently into existing social and public policies and permitted a distinct influence on future reform developments. For instance, to some extent the UK government has pushed the developments of on-shore and off-shore wind farms, partly in order to enable Britain to become a world leader in the technology – and for reasons of energy security – but also with one eye on the long-term need to 'dematerialise' and decentralise energy. Another example involves the promotion of healthy consumption as a means of evolving health services towards prevention rather than post-facto treatment. Mainstreaming may be done (1) as a matter of conviction and/or to fulfil obligations; (2) in order to pacify green campaigners; or (3) as a form of economic competitiveness (perhaps to pump-prime new industries).

Greenstreaming

This is where existing agendas are having to adapt to a thoroughgoing attempt to green the public and private sectors, due to the efforts of government, civil society actors or both. Thus, the environmental pioneers we reviewed in Chapter Three can be seen as effecting a slow paradigm shift in the structures of the economy and state, and the radical proposals we encountered in the Chapter Six have been proposed by some as a way of making substantial alterations in attitudes and behaviour.

Note that the more sincere the reform, the less likely it is to be dominated or driven by policy-making elites and opinion formers. Mainstreaming and greenstreaming are more likely to characterise environmental pioneers.

We could formulate a policy list for each of the above, although the greenstreaming list would be more prospective. And although it is too huge an exercise to perform here, we could then chart nations against these categories. So, environmental laggards would probably occupy the top of the list and pioneers would be located towards the bottom.

However, we also have to acknowledge that it could often be difficult to decide where among the above categories a particular policy and nation belongs. Take nuclear power. There has been a recent revival of interest in nuclear technology. Does this make the development of new power stations a case of greenwashing (a repackaging of what many governments have long been committed to anyway), piggybacking (a way of de-carbonising waste and pollution) or even mainstreaming (one element of a longer-term shift towards lighter, cleaner technologies)? Modernisers might be generous in their assessment whereas deep greens may well be cynical. Furthermore, it is possible that policies and nations can be located within more than one category. A policy may start out, and be designed, as greenwash, yet it may prove to have genuinely positive effects that can be developed subsequently, as a result of non-governmental campaigning for instance. And while the US is an environmental laggard overall, some states, for example, California, are better than others (Rabe, 2010: 31–42).

One key question is, does it matter? If policy *q* achieves desirable ends then should we care whether it is an example of greenwashing, piggybacking or whatever? Many liberals may deny that it matters. So long as policy makers, producers and consumers are responding to the correct set of external stimuli then they do not need to identify themselves as 'green actors' *per se*. The advantage of economic incentives and regulatory frameworks is that they affect behaviour without having to be concerned with agents' 'internal' reasons and perceptions. It is unrealistic and, in a free, pluralistic society, undesirable to expect people to internalise environmental imperatives.

Many republicans, however, will insist that it *does* matter. It is not enough for bureaucrats, firms, individuals, and so on to *act* green; they must also be motivated to do so *as* green citizens. This, first, is because a sustainable society will ultimately depend on the values and virtues of its members and, second, because external stimuli (rules, benefits/penalties, laws, targets, etc) will sometimes malfunction and, in any event, will not be applicable to every social circumstance. A moral society requires moral actors and cultures. This is precisely why education is important. Having people respond to exogenous inducements is not enough.

Chapter Six proposed that a theory of environmental justice is likely to draw on these and other perspectives. As such, green citizenship will presumably make reference to a motivational ethos where people are impelled by a sense of justice to do what is good, while allowing for the fact that, if we wait for everyone to share similar values, then global warming will probably outpace our efforts to create a sustainable society.

Where does this leave social policy? As Chapter Three proposed, social and environmental objectives will often cohere, but we cannot rule out some trade-offs remaining. Perhaps we should sometimes prefer the greenwashing and piggybacking options, even if this grades us as environmental laggards.

We are unlikely to discover a formula that specifies how to trade off. Dobson (1998) argues that political negotiations on a case-to-case basis will be vital. However, I suspect there are rules that can guide decision making (see Fitzpatrick, 2003b: 141–4).

Deferred enhancement rule:
Principle x is temporally allowed to trump principle y when, under particular circumstances, doing so allows the objectives of principle y to be met more effectively in the longer term than would otherwise be the case.

Non-futility rule:
Principle x should not be allowed to trump principle y when, under particular circumstances, doing so would be self-defeating.

We face high levels of absolute poverty across the world, particularly in sub-Saharan Africa. Alleviating such poverty means that in those areas sustainability should only be a priority if it can be demonstrated that it is consistent with poverty alleviation. If not, then sustainability objectives might have to take a back seat (that is, deferred enhancement) to anti-poverty policies (including rapid GDP growth in those regions). However, this would only be the case up to the point where such strategies become self-defeating, or futile, for example, because the timescale of effective anti-poverty policies becomes shortened due to increased ecological problems.

This is obviously very schematic, but it does capture what is at stake in current, post-Kyoto1 discussions. Developing nations advance versions of the deferred enhancement rule in arguing for continued economic development for the foreseeable future, with the obligations for fixing what they have broken falling largely on affluent nations; the latter argue for versions of the non-futility rule, in that one part of the lifeboat can only bail so much water before the other part – and eventually the entire lifeboat – sinks.

Social effects: the case of fuel poverty

The next question posed on p 155 concerned the principal effects which environmental policies have had on vulnerable social groups. Chapter Three offered a generalised analysis of poverty. Having now reviewed key aspects of environmental politics and policies there are numerous approaches we could take. We could group people within the following categories:

• Income, wealth and class
• Gender
• Ethnicity
• Age
• Dis/ability
• Geographical location.

We could then cross-refer these against any number of environmental measures, such as:

- Carbon taxes
- Congestion charges
- Health campaigns
- Home efficiency measures
- Increased reliance on renewables
- Increases in energy prices
- Recycling measures (including incentives and penalties)
- Travel subsidies.

And obviously, we could do this for many nations.

We therefore face a problem of scale and the fact that research in this field is both under-developed and widely dispersed. Rather than trying to cover everything, this chapter concludes with a case study of fuel poverty since it is arguably here that the environmental and social policy agendas have converged most closely (Bird et al, 2010). Fuel poverty obviously relates to issues of social injustice but also to levels of household carbon emissions. I will therefore relate recent UK developments to the material covered in previous sections. Fuel poverty thus stands as a proxy from which lessons for other policy reforms might be learned.

First, what is fuel poverty? In the UK, a household is defined as 'fuel poor' if it needs to spend more than 10% of its income on fuel to maintain adequate warmth (21°C degrees for the main living area, 18°C degrees for other occupied rooms). Those experiencing it habitually have to juggle heating costs against other basic needs, such as food. On this basis, *Table 7.2* provides the figures for fuel poverty since calculations began (they have not been calculated every year). 'Vulnerable households' are those that contain elderly members, children, people with disabilities or the long-term sick.

Table 7.2: UK fuel poverty levels, 1996–2007

Fuel poverty (millions of households)	1996	1998	2001	2002	2003	2004	2005	2006	2007
All UK households	6.5	4.75	2.5	2.25	2	2	2.5	3.5	4
Vulnerable households	5	3.5	2	1.75	1.5	1.5	2	2.75	3.25

Source: DECC (2009: 7)

We can see that fuel poverty had fallen considerably by 2001, bottomed out during 2003-04 and then began to rise again. This upward trend is expected to have continued so that by 2009 there were 4.6 million fuel poor households – more than one in six of the total housing stock. Fifty per cent of the fuel poor are pensioners and 10% consist of lone-parent families. In terms of income, 80% of households belonging to the poorest two deciles were fuel poor; across the poorest three deciles the figure rose to 91%. While a sizeable minority were owner-occupiers, the majority of fuel poor households rented their homes from private or social landlords.

Fuel poverty is caused by rising prices, inadequate incomes and energy-inefficient homes. The Labour government attributed the post-2004 increase mainly to rising energy prices that were only partly offset by income growth and greater energy efficiency (DECC, 2009). It should be observed, however, that New Labour's record on reducing all forms of poverty began to stall around the same time because it had mostly been helping the 'low-hanging fruit', that is, those just below the poverty line.

Official figures are therefore broadly in line with what we would expect: fuel poverty and income poverty are closely related. The lower the income the more difficult it is to provide for all basic needs and the less there is available for non-essentials and for savings, thereby affecting individuals' quality of life and sense of security. Also, a low income typically raises opportunity costs, making someone less willing and able to take risks – such as changing jobs – and more likely to be trapped in deprived circumstances. Low-income households are also more likely to use pre-payment meters that disadvantage them compared to customers paying by direct debit.

In response the UK government deployed a number of measures.

Economic instruments
- Increasing the income of the poorest, for example, through benefits (like Winter Fuel Payments) and Tax Credits (like Pension Credits).
- Reducing fuel bills through voluntary 'social tariffs' (where the government has encouraged energy companies to reduce fuel costs for vulnerable and low-income customers) and other 'social price supports' offering additional discounts.

Regulations
- Improved energy efficiencies. Some help the poorest directly, for example, the Warm Front programme provides grants and has reduced annual fuel bills by £360-£400 on average; some are more indirect, for example, the boiler scrappage scheme.
- Parallel initiatives such as the Carbon Emissions Reduction Target programme and various Public Service Agreements.

Information

- Publicity campaigns (through helplines, advertising, leaflets and consumer advice networks) to encourage greater energy efficiency, including changes to lifestyles and daily habits, and to encourage low-income households to regularly switch suppliers.
- Improved advice about benefits and welfare rights, for example, some Warm Front recipients are entitled to a subsequent benefit entitlement check, and data sharing (a recent pilot involving energy companies and the Department for Work and Pensions may be rolled out in the future).

The Labour government also set targets for itself, hoping to end fuel poverty for vulnerable households in England by 2010 and all households by 2016. Such ambitions were set in the late 1990s when energy prices had been falling. As we have seen, the 2010 target was missed.

What makes this a double blow is that New Labour wished to prioritise fuel poverty and hold off on introducing substantive carbon taxes. With fuel poverty levels falling around the turn of the millennium this may have seemed a wise strategy. But it may have hampered more radical action to combat climate change.

Therefore, with rising energy prices and renationalisation nowhere on the political agenda, the government worked 'horizontally', through a competitive and internationalised energy market. With a nationalised utility, the price of x does not necessarily have to match its cost. A government might decide to sell energy incredibly cheaply – to assist the poorest, for instance – by subsidising the industry through progressive taxes. The argument for a privatised system is that it improves efficiency by bringing costs and prices back together. Unfortunately, during the UK privatisations of the 1980s the problem of fuel poverty was ignored. New Labour therefore wanted a partial detachment of costs relative to prices for low-income households, to help them cope with rising bills, but was reluctant to challenge energy firms – still less, the ethos of privatisation and profit making – any further. One consequence was the sight of government nervousness in the face of companies quick to raise prices but less eager to lower them once market conditions improved.

As one example of such energy governance, take social tariffs. This approach dovetails with the prevailing policy makers' orthodoxy, that targeting is the most cost-efficient and effective way of assisting the poorest. Research by W. Baker (2006: 28-30) reported that suppliers, regulatory bodies and government representatives all preferred targeting in order that limited resources could reach those most in need, despite the fact that the administrative costs of targeting were high and regardless of concerns about take-up and stigma. In other words, selectivism is often less efficacious than it may appear at first (Fitzpatrick, forthcoming). Barely 25% of the money allocated to relieve fuel poverty actually goes to the fuel poor (Boardman, 2010: 53), since 'passport benefits', such as Income Support and Housing Benefits, do not necessarily identify the fuel poor accurately. And affluent households can benefit from Winter Fuel Payments, for example. By contrast, Baker's low-income participants and interest groups were more supportive of mandatory tariffs, of non-means-tested forms of eligibility, less concerned to minimise costs and less enamoured of competitive markets (see also Baker et al, 2006).

All of which suggests questions very similar to those long prevalent within social policy debates:

- How progressive and redistributive should carbon taxes be?
- How can we ensure that any targeting within the system does not further stigmatise the least well off?
- At what income level should eligibility cease?
- What help should be provided to those at risk of falling into fuel poverty but who are just above the eligibility level for benefits and Warm Front grants?
- Since the poorest 20% in society emit 60% less carbon than the richest 20%, should carbon abatement charges fall equally on everyone or is this unjustly regressive?
- If the poorest pay lower charges, how do we avoid the 'rebound effect' (where lower charges encourage more usage, so that carbon emissions do not decrease significantly)?
- What is a fair distribution of the financial burdens for housing improvements, between private landlords, social housing associations, energy companies and taxpayers?

In short, measures to address fuel poverty have been characterised by a host of arguments concerning universalism and means testing similar to those within the familiar institutions of the welfare state. Eco-social reforms are likely to offer new territories to some very old combatants.

The same conclusion applies to health-related debates. Liddell and Morris (2010) reviewed a range of literature and concluded that although reducing fuel poverty has only modest effects on the physical health of adults, there are significant impacts on the respiratory health of children and on the physical health of infants. The mental health effects on adults and adolescents are also encouraging. Macmillan Cancer Support (2010) found that people who have undergone cancer treatment in the previous year are twice as likely to be in fuel poverty as the rest of the population, and are likely to remain there because of costs associated with the disease.

Therefore, the UK's energy policies have operated within a regime of *governance* where trying to achieve a given objective depends on complex negotiations among multiple levels, actors and sectors, including those pertaining to the welfare state.

So within a genuine attempt to reconcile environmental and social priorities across a range of energy, income and other public policies, the government's freedom of movement has been restricted (sometimes because of its own timidity). The government sought to humanise competition among energy providers, largely by exhorting them to act with a social conscience. In that sense, it tried to piggyback its anti-poverty and ecological concerns onto what largely remained a neoliberal approach to the provision of energy. But there *has* also been an element of mainstreaming. The decentralisation of energy grids is being driven by the search for global warming solutions – including local, micro-generation technologies (photovoltaics, microwind and air source heat pumps). Energy efficiency measures are attractive because, ideally, they represent a one-off cost. A wall only needs to be insulated once. So by upgrading its buildings and housing stock now, the country helps to protect itself against at least some of the unforeseeable energy and climate change shocks which may hit us in decades to come.

Summary box

Examples of energy efficiency measures

- Boiler replacement and upgrade of other items, for example, refrigerators, cavity and internal wall insulation
- Double and triple glazing
- Draught proofing
- Lighting improvements
- Loft insulation
- Mechanical ventilation heat recovery

The social and environmental policy agendas, then, reveal some degree of convergence when we study fuel poverty. However, even here the UK government's record has been mixed.

First, some complain that government action remains ineffective and short-termist. Consumer Focus (2009) found that a major energy efficiency programme, costing £21 billion across seven years, would reduce fuel poverty by 83% *and* prevent the risk of fuel poverty recurring in the future. This is three times more than is currently spent but would, on average, reduce the fuel bills of the fuel poor by 52% (and 46% for all households) and their carbon emissions by 59% (55% for all). Other estimates on how much it would cost to eliminate fuel poverty range from £9.2 billion to £64 billion (Bird et al, 2010: 20–3; and see Preston et al, 2008; Jenkins, 2010).

Second, because no model of energy and building efficiency seems to eliminate fuel poverty entirely (Roberts, 2008: 4472), raising the incomes of the poorest should remain a key priority.

Finally, if the poorest are not to be victimised by global energy firms then more effective forms of transnational regulation may have to be contemplated. Even if oil is running low and the age of cheap energy is gone forever, there is a difference between a controlled landing and a crash landing which misses the low carbon runway altogether.

Conclusion

Therefore, it may well be that fuel poverty exemplifies the difficulties we face in integrating social and environmental policies. Old debates are revived and reconfigured, such as that between targeting and universalism, as we see that familiar solutions like regulation and cash transfer programmes continue to possess salience. And new ideas and innovations are needed, such as a 'carbon piggybank' which is funded through energy levies and earmarked for the poorest. It also seems clear that detailed attention to the social effects of environmental policies and the environmental effects of social policies is required if they are to work together effectively.

So, in the case of fuel poverty, because of hard-to-heat and under-occupied homes, especially in rural areas, any scheme of personalised carbon credits, although advantageous to many of the fuel poor, would be disadvantageous to others. Nor must improvements to housing stock ignore the possibility that a key problem in decades to come will be the need to keep buildings cool during increasingly hot summers. Fuel poverty may be a first step towards a wider concept of 'thermal deprivation', especially as the UK population ages.

Note
[1] See page 79 for a discussion of negative externalities as one drawback of markets which regulations are meant to address.

Chapter summary

This chapter has:

- categorised and described the main forms of environmental policy: economic instruments, regulations, education, knowledge and information;
- explored the association between environmental policy and governance, including what was called the problem of 'policy alignment';
- reviewed the contexts of policy making in order to determine whether a policy can be labelled as an example of greenwashing, piggybacking, mainstreaming or greenstreaming;
- analysed the social effects of environmental policies – through a case study of fuel poverty – in order to understand how and why social and environmental agendas are converging and to learn lessons for the future.

Questions for discussion

- What are the main goals that each environmental policy instrument is meant to realise?
- Is one type of environmental policy superior to the others?
- How effective can 'horizontal regulation' really be?
- Name, describe and assess some examples of greenwashing, piggybacking, mainstreaming and greenstreaming.
- Has the UK government done enough to address the problem of fuel poverty?
- What lessons do you think the example of fuel poverty presents for other reforms, such as congestion charging, carbon taxes and recycling?

Key further reading

Adger, N. and Jordan, A. (eds) (2009) *Governing sustainability*, Cambridge: Cambridge University Press.

Bird, J., Campbell, R. and Lawton, K. (2010) *The long cold winter: Beating fuel poverty*, London: Institute for Public Policy Research and National Energy Action.

Compston, H. and Bailey, I. (eds) (2008) *Turning down the heat*, Basingstoke: Palgrave Macmillan.

Kraft, M. (2011) *Environmental policy and politics* (5th edn), London: Longman.

Rosenbaum, W. (2008) *Environmental policy and politics* (7th edn), Washington, DC: CQ Press.

Vig, N. and Kraft, M. (eds) (2010) *Environmental policy* (7th edn), Washington, DC: CQ Press.

Useful websites

European Union: http://ec.europa.eu/environment/climat/home_en.htm

Resources for the Future: www.rff.org

UN Development Programme: www.undp.org

UN Environment Programme: www.unep.org

UN Framework Convention on Climate Change: http://unfccc.int

World Resources Institute: www.wri.org

Worldwatch Institute: www.worldwatch.org

eight

Health and environment

Glenda Verrinder

Overview

International policies have failed to arrest the widening gap of health inequalities between the most and least deprived and also failed to arrest escalating rates of environmental degradation. This chapter argues that:

- in order to address the determinants of health in a sustainable way, national and international policies need to cut across different sectors to protect and promote the health of the planet and of humans;
- despite the many policy failures, social and public policies remain a powerful lever in creating a healthy society and a healthy environment. All policy initiatives need to be examined in terms of protecting and improving the health of vulnerable groups and the most degraded environments;
- win-win solutions are possible.

Introduction

The prerequisite for human health is a healthy ecosystem. This ecosystem includes natural, built and social environments. Degradation of these environments, particularly the natural one, now threatens human health on a global scale.

This chapter discusses those measures that try to modify the effects of, and adapt to, environmental changes in order to ensure the health of humans and the environment over time. In particular, we look at international efforts that guide national governments in policy development. Some successes and failures in this endeavour are outlined.

International policies have failed to arrest the widening gap of human health inequalities between the most and least deprived and failed to arrest escalating rates of environmental degradation (Brown, L., 2009; nef, nd). The health, and perhaps the very survival, of humans is under threat.

> The toxic combination of bad policies, economics and politics is, in large measure, responsible for the fact that a majority of people in the world do not enjoy the good health that is biologically possible. (CSDH, 2008: 1)

There is now overwhelming evidence that the interaction between human biology and the natural and social environments determines health. See *Figure 8.1* for a summary of the **determinants of health**. The conditions in which people are born, live, work and age have a powerful influence on their health. There is generally no single cause or contributing factor to health or illness. Inequalities in these conditions lead to unequal health outcomes, and the majority are avoidable and also inequitable (Wilkinson and Marmot, 2003; Marmot and Wilkinson, 2006; WHO, 2009a; Wilkinson and Pickett, 2009).

We begin by reviewing some of the key literature on health, sustainability and the quality of the environment. The bulk of the chapter is then dedicated to reviewing recent policy developments, initiatives and outcomes.

Health and sustainability

Defining health

Our understanding of the interdependence of the health of the environment and the health of humans is constantly evolving. The health of humans is variously defined. The World Health Organization (WHO) (1948) defines health as 'a complete state of physical, mental and social wellbeing, and not merely the absence of disease or infirmity', highlighting that human health is about much more than the absence of disease or an individual physical state. Efforts to define health within a broader socio-ecological context have come from aboriginal health movements around the world and the environmental movement, where concern for spiritual and cultural connectedness and ecological sustainability, respectively, have moved health definitions beyond disease and the personal level; for example, Honari (1993: 23) defined health as 'a sustainable state of wellbeing, within sustainable ecosystems, within a sustainable biosphere'.

Figure 8.1: *The determinants of health and well-being in human habitation*

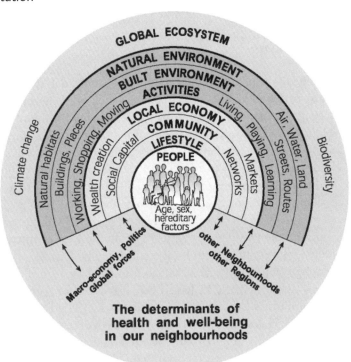

GLOBAL ECOSYSTEM

NATURAL ENVIRONMENT

BUILT ENVIRONMENT

ACTIVITIES

LOCAL ECONOMY

COMMUNITY

LIFESTYLE

PEOPLE

Age, sex, hereditary factors

Climate change

Natural habitats

Buildings, Places

Working, Shopping, Moving

Wealth creation

Social Capital

Living, Playing, Learning

Networks

Markets

Streets, Routes

Air, Water, Land

Biodiversity

Macro-economy, Politics
Global forces

other Neighbourhoods
other Regions

The determinants of health and well-being in our neighbourhoods

Source: Barton and Grant (2006).

Defining sustainability

Concern for the sustainable use of resources has seen expression in societal rules and rituals from ancient times. The concept of sustainability is embedded in human consciousness and our understanding changes as our relationship with our environment changes. In the English language the concept has been expressed by the use of the word 'sustenable', traced by the *Oxford English Dictionary* to around 1400 and 'sustainability' to 1611 (Wheeler, 2004: 19). In the 1970s the term **sustainable development** was coined in Meadows et al (1972) and defined later as: 'Sustainable development is development that meets the needs of the present without compromising the ability of future generations to meet their own needs' (WCED, 1987: 43). Wheeler's (2004: 24) process–oriented definition – 'sustainable development is development that improves the long-term health of humans and ecological systems' – allows debates about the carrying capacity of the Earth and about human needs to converge.

Concerns about living sustainably re-emerged, of necessity, in response to rampant industrialisation in the 19th century in Britain, Europe and the US. This period in history still influences societal responses today.

Historical dimensions

While the value of the natural environment was celebrated in the poetry of Keats, Wordsworth and Shelley, urban planners such as Ebenezer Howard raised the awareness of unsustainable urban development. Environmentalists such as Henry David Thoreau, social commentators such as Frederick Engels and novelists such as Charles Dickens commented on various aspects of the conditions emerging in towns and the social and environmental impacts of the industrial transition (Wheeler and Beatley, 2004). The writing of the appalling conditions in Britain by social reformers such as Edwin Chadwick eventually led to the Public Health Act in 1848. Industrialising countries around the world passed similar laws in the 19th century. These laws protected communities from local environmental hazards.

The links between ecological sustainability and human health at the global as well as the local level have been discussed for some time in scientific communities (see, for example, Hancock, 1985; Boyden, 1987; Brown et al, 2005; Hales and Corvalan, 2006; WHO, 2009a). The 'three e's' of sustainable development (environment, equity, and economy) (Wheeler and Beatley, 2004: 8) have been recurrent concerns for public health and sustainability activists for more than a century. Within the healthcare sector there have been two major insights in relatively recent times.

First, it has been acknowledged that the unprecedented environmental changes of the last half of the 20th century, such as global warming, reduction in atmospheric ozone, loss of biodiversity and the pervasiveness of toxic environmental contaminants, have affected global population health. Second, it has been recognised that vulnerable populations such as children and those who are poor are most at risk and inadequately protected from these environmental changes (CAPE, nd; Brown, L., 2009; WHO, 2009a).

There have been attempts internationally to guide governments in policy development in order to address major concerns about the environment and human health. For example see the summary box on international declarations, conventions and agreements on page 193 for important milestones in this respect. These will be discussed later in the chapter.

Societal responses

Thus, the relationship between humans and their environment has undergone major changes in human history. Mitigation and adaptation to the effects of the human–environment relationship through policy is not new. Arguably, there have been four major phases in human history and the next phase has now emerged (see **Table 8.1**).

About one million years ago we began the process of adapting biologically to the environment. We were hunter-gatherers and moved in small groups

Table 8.1: Responses to the human–environment interrelationship

Phase	Illness	Technical/ practical action	Policy response
Hunter-gatherers – tested sustainable development (40,000 years of survival)	Occasional zoonosis. Well nourished from variety in diet and activity	Nomadic, fire-stick farming. The group was more important than the individual	Community rules, eg mutual avoidance in interpersonal strife
Agricultural revolution and early urban development	Zoonosis, human variants of animal diseases especially measles and smallpox and plague in the early urban phase; injuries; malnutrition	Land clearing, irrigation systems, machinery, food storage, hierarchical society	Religious rules, eg about type of food consumed; government legislation, eg land closures; quarantine acts
Industrial revolution	Infectious disease from overcrowding, especially cholera and tuberculosis; malnutrition and starvation	Sewerage to separate clean water from waste; urban design; environmental monitoring, social action	Public health acts; poor laws; housing regulation; environmental protection acts
Globalisation – unsustainable development	Cumulative effects of pollution of air, water, soil and food in a carbon-based economy; increased incidence of cancer, lung diseases, cardiovascular disease, developmental disorders; inequity fuelling social disease	Renewable energy sources such as solar and wind, slow food movement, social and environmental movements	Transport planning; *Our common future, Agenda 21, Declaration of Alma-Ata, Ottawa Charter for Health Promotion;* Millennium Development Goals; *The diplomatic road to Copenhagen*

Source: Adapted from Brown et al (2002); Verrinder (2003)

for procreation and protection, and in those social groups the beginnings of rules for living in society emerged. In the next phase, about 12,000 years ago, we started farming and this phase is associated with an explosion of the population, land degradation and the rise of infectious disease due to our increasing contact with each other and with animals – all risks that needed to be thought about and reduced to protect human health. Very early rules were developed by hunter–gatherer groups and then religious organisations to protect resources such as food supply and the health of the community.

Government policies to protect the environment and human health began to proliferate as humans began living in towns and cities. Records of pollution control in England, for example, date from 1388 and quarantine laws began in 1300 in response to the plague in Europe (Wheeler and Beatley, 2004). Communicable diseases led governments to develop policies around quarantine but economics rather than the welfare of the population was often the impetus for quarantine to protect trade.

Industrialisation and the burgeoning of towns and cities meant that the human hierarchy that emerged during the previous phase strengthened governmental responses to keep the well-oiled machinery of the new industrial societies functioning. Engineers separated waste from clean water, and governments became increasingly aware of the delivery of fresh food to city dwellers, standards of housing and so on because social reformers noticed that people, particularly poor people, were falling ill due to communicable diseases and starvation. The 'factory fodder' were dying too early, leaving their dependants behind. The average life expectancy in England in the mid–1800s ranged from 25 years for labourers to 55 years for the gentry (McMichael, 2001).

The emergence of the scientific method and a few social reformers provided much needed understanding on the possible causes of communicable diseases and the health inequalities between rich and poor that resulted in social reform through legislation, such as the Public Health Acts of the 20th century (Shelton, 2002). This social reform and local action improved the lives of many people in industrialising countries. However, by then,

> ... much of the planet had been substantially restructured by the visions, inventions, engineering skills and ignorance of human beings. The way nature used to organise itself had been severely compromised by ploughs, houses, towns, cities, roads, railways, canals, sewers, locks, weirs, irrigation schemes, [and later], herbicides, fungicides, pesticides, insecticides, chemical fertilisers, and by burning fossil fuels.... (Verrinder, 2003: 4)

Now, there is recognition between the inextricable links of inequality, wars, climate change and other man-made disasters. Each of these phases still exist somewhere in the world today, but the next phase of human history is upon us and is bringing its own set of responses. We now go on to explore this in more detail.

Global degradation of the environment leads to disease

Clean water, air and soil are prerequisites for human health, and pollution of these threatens human health on a global scale. Human health effects from environmental degradation of any sort are often cumulative, long term and complex (Kickbusch, 1989; McMichael and Woodruff, 2002; WHO, 2009a). Environmental degradation of water, land and air leads to cancer, respiratory, cardiovascular, neuropsychiatric and communicable diseases (OECD, 2008).

Despite international efforts to mitigate major emissions it is projected that there will be a six-fold increase in deaths attributable to ozone by 2030. Infant mortality from respiratory disorders such as asthma is on the rise. Millions are dying from polluted water. Some countries and populations are affected more than others. Deaths from unsafe water are 40.5 times higher in countries such as Brazil, Russia, India, China and South Africa than in OECD (Organisation for Economic Co-operation and Development) countries (OECD, 2008).

Vulnerable populations

Vulnerability at the individual level is influenced by biological aspects (such as age and sex), social aspects (such as social connectedness and social policy) and environmental aspects (such as geographical location). Children, older people and people who are poor are most vulnerable. Children, for example, have a higher metabolic rate than adults and are exposed to different risks because of their activities. Asthma resulting from air pollution, leukaemia resulting from exposure to pesticides *in utero*, neurodevelopmental disorders resulting from lead poisoning and birth defects resulting from drinking contaminated water still occur because children's vulnerability is often not factored into policies (OECD, 2008).

Vulnerability at the population level means access to resources to adapt to changing conditions. Some countries and groups do not have the resources for adequate responses to environmental determinants:

> It is no coincidence that the poor live downwind, downstream and downhill (unless the hillsides are dangerous, in which case

they live uphill!). Nor is it a coincidence that it is the citizens of the poorest countries, and the poorest residents of any country, who live on the most environmentally unsustainable and marginalised land, and who out of poverty are often forced to use their land and resources in environmentally unsustainable ways. (Hancock, 1994: 38)

In the coming years, vulnerable populations such as children, those who are poor, those who are already frail and indigenous communities will bear the brunt of further environmental degradation. It is fair to say that those who already suffer social and environmental injustice will continue to do so unless policy decisions are made to address inequality in general, and poverty, discrimination, pollution and natural resource depletion in particular.

Climate change

Climate change is arguably the single biggest global health threat today (WHO, 2003; *The Lancet*, 2009). Pollution of air, water and land, and water stress will reduce agricultural production in many regions and exacerbate food security problems. Famines due to climatic influences are well recognised. Temperature changes and rising sea levels will give rise to changing patterns of disease. Traditional ways of life are already threatened in every nation. Displacement, loss of means to work and psychological stress due to climate change are all part of the new fabric of the social determinants of health. All regions are affected.

The global burden of disease due to anthropogenic climate change was estimated at 150,000 deaths and five million disability adjusted life years (DALYs) per year, between the mid-1970s and 2000, through increased incidences of diarrhoea, malaria and malnutrition. These occurred primarily in developing countries (WHO, 2002).

The estimated 22,000 to 45,000 deaths due to the heatwave in Europe in 2003 is a clear example of risks associated with temperature change (Patz et al, 2005). Variations in the climate also have profound impacts on infectious disease. There have been studies on changing patterns of vector-borne disease in Australia (Woodruff et al, 2003; Tong et al, 2004), plague in the US (Parmenter et al, 1999) and bluetongue in Europe (Purse, 2005). These changes parallel trends in global warming (Patz et al, 2005). It is estimated that by 2030 the annual death rate from global warming will be 500,000, with another 660 million people seriously affected (Cole, 2009).

In 2008 the World Health Organization (WHO) declared World Health Day as 'protecting your health from climate change' in recognition that 'wherever you live, climate change threatens your health'. The WHO summarises the concern as:

> Our increasing understanding of climate change is transforming how we view the boundaries and determinants of health. While our personal health may seem to relate mostly to prudent behaviour, hereditary, occupation, local environmental exposures, and health-care access, sustained population health requires the life-supporting 'services' of the biosphere. Populations of all animal species depend on supplies of food and water, freedom from excess infectious disease, and the physical safety and comfort conferred by climate stability. The climate system is fundamental to this life-support. (McMichael et al, 2003: 2)

The health sector is already responsible for many protective measures such as health education, preventive programmes such as mosquito control and food hygiene, surveillance of disease, disaster preparedness and forecasting future health risks. These responsibilities and policy development extend beyond the sector and include early warning systems of extreme weather events, neighbourhood watch for vulnerable people, involvement in urban planning for green spaces and cool spaces, climate-proof housing and work spaces. As we have said, human health is determined by many factors and will be promoted and protected in many sectors. This introduces us to the idea of 'health in all policies', an idea that was first developed by the WHO and refined in 1988 at the Second International Conference on Health Promotion.

Health in *all* policies

Health and social policy reforms in the 19th century improved the health of populations by improving living and working conditions and, in doing so, reduced mortality and morbidity from infectious disease in the industrialised nations. Policy reforms promoted health and prevented illness. The focus of health sector policy then moved over time to the delivery of healthcare services for sick people and this focus remains today. This focus of treating illness still dominates budgets within health sectors in most countries, despite the evidence and understanding that has accrued about the determinants of health and the means available to tackle them. There is still a persistent assumption that health sector policy and policies that promote and protect health are one and the same thing. However, within health sectors, promoting and protecting health remains on the margins of policy development.

There have been attempts to change this focus. At the Second Global Conference on Health Promotion in 1988 it was recognised that 'healthy public policy' makes the social and physical environments health-enhancing, which makes health choices possible and easier for citizens. The conference delegates made plain their belief that all sectors should pay as much attention to health as to economic considerations and be accountable for the health consequences of their policy decisions. They called on government sectors concerned with agriculture, trade, education, industry and communications to take health into account as an essential factor when formulating policy (WHO, 1988).

Similarly, eight central issues were selected by the World Commission on Environment and Development (WCED): population, energy, industry, food, settlement, economics, environmental management and international relations. There was an acknowledgement that these issues were 'all about health' (WCED, 1987). And at the Earth Summit in 1992 the focus was ostensibly on environmental issues; however, there were debates about over-population, consumption rates and the global economy.

'Health is created where people live, love, work and play and where they shop, Google and travel' (Kickbusch, 2008). Given that health is determined by many things, it is reasonable to think that most policies that promote health and protect humans from risks of disease are subsumed in sectors other than health. In 2008 there was a renewed call for all sectors to engage with the development of health policy, including education, agriculture, transport, industry, consumer affairs and sports (Kickbusch, 2008).

Developing policy

The importance of global governance, regulation and government cooperation in providing political security was emphasised in the 2009 global financial crisis (Costello, 2009). Security extends to social and environmental security and the security of essential elements for human health such as clean air, water and land to produce food.

There are numerous ways to look at the aim and process of policy development. Take that of Johnson (2007: 2-3), for instance. This schema makes reference to various policy dimensions. Some focus on human health, such as regulation of air pollutants and water contaminants. Then there are those policies that focus on environment protection which indirectly impact on human health, such as the protection of biodiversity in a region. Then there are policies that focus on neither humans nor environment but which have an impact on the health of both, such as national energy policies. The primary strategy of policy makers may be 'prospective', for example, air pollution regulations, or 'retrospective', such as clean-ups of hazardous wastes. Some policies are developed to provide information about these. International organisations, governments, the private sector and professional and citizen groups are also potential actors in the development of such policies. Interest groups lobby governments for policy change. Professional bodies such as the Union of Concerned Scientists and public health associations develop policies on a range of issues to protect human health. They also provide advice to government. There are also hazards that do not get regulated. One of the issues hotly debated across the globe at present is the emission of carbon dioxide (CO_2).

Brown et al (2002) argue that there is an underlying 'social contract' in health policy development. Different approaches reflect a view of health, and each is negotiated and must operate within the social context of the time:

> Policies for health are the outcomes of a synthesis of power relationships, demographic trends, institutional agendas, community ideologies, and economic resources. (Brown, 1992: 104)

There are arguably four major approaches to policy development (see *Table 8.2*):

- the minimalist approach to protect human health by providing a safety-net;
- the equality approach where everyone is given an equal chance of achieving an optimal level of health;
- the equity approach where fairness is taken into consideration and vulnerable groups are provided with extra resources to achieve health;
- the ecological approach where the planet and all it encompasses is taken into account.

The safety-net protects those in the community who are most vulnerable. The equality approach is broader in that governments take responsibility for services for the whole community, but do not necessarily differentiate between groups other than the most vulnerable. Social justice is the expression of equity and understanding the social determinants of health forms the basis of this approach. The ecological approach is broader again. Here, health is viewed as the interrelationship between humans and their environment, which can be social or physical, natural or built (Brown, 1992). The most vulnerable are provided with extra resources, governments

Table 8.2: Policy development

	Safety-net	Equality	Equity	Ecological
Primary aim	Damage control	Equal chance	Bridging the health status gap	Sustainable development
Policy goals	Economic growth	Level playing field	Social justice	Equity, environment, economy
Resource base	Productivity	Natural resources	Social and environmental potential	Ecological and social balance
Community action	Consultation	Democratic elections	Participation	Community ownership
Services goal	Treatment	Prevention	Development	Sustainability

Source: Adapted from Brown et al (2002)

take responsibility for services to the whole community and social and environmental justice is expressed through the principle of equity. The social contract for policy development in the future will need to incorporate the ecological approach to achieve social and environmental justice and to bring sustainable development to fruition.

Having established the importance not just of health policies but also of wider social policies we now go on to review some of the key international initiatives in this field.

International policy responses

In ancient times when a place became uninhabitable because of climate change, pollution or other forms of degradation it was abandoned. This is still the case but population pressures are making this more difficult (Diamond, 2005).

During the 20th century there was a massive rise in national activities to protect the environment. Governments responded to old problems such as drought, pestilence and local pollution, and newer problems caused by new pollutants, to address ozone depletion and persistent organic pollutants (POPs) (Brown, 2000; Frank et al, 2000; Nicholson, 2000).

The protection of national parks, the emergence of non-governmental organisations (NGOs) such as the World Wildlife Fund (WWF), increased membership of intergovernmental organisations such as the International Whaling Commission, environmental impact assessment laws and environmental ministries are indicators of this increase (Brown, 2000; Frank et al, 2000: 436; Nicholson, 2000). Internationally, there were fewer than 40 national parks before 1900; however, by 1990 there were 7,000 listed by the International Union for the Conservation of Nature (Frank et al, 2000). Similarly, the growth of intergovernmental organisations, developing policies for the protection of the global commons such as oceans, rivers and the atmosphere, proliferated. The Intergovernmental Panel on Climate Change (IPCC) is a welcome addition to such organisations.

There have been many drivers of change. The advocacy of international environmental organisations and scientists and the development of global blueprints for national environmental activities have all played a part (Frank et al, 2000; Newbold, 2000). Public opinion has also driven change. It is possible that in industrialised countries basic human needs have been met and consideration of quality of life issues through the lens of environmentalism is becoming more widespread.

Summary box

International declarations, Conventions and agreements

* *Our common future* (WCED, 1987)
* The Rio Declaration on Environment and Development
* Agenda 21
* The Convention on Biological Diversity
* Framework Convention on Climate Change
* Principles of Forest Management
* *Declaration of Alma-Ata* (WHO, 1978)
* *The Ottawa Charter for Health Promotion* (WHO, 1986)
* Millennium Development Goals (MDGs)
* *Closing the gap in a generation: Health equity through action on the social determinants of health* (CSDH, 2008)
* International Covenant on Economic, Social and Cultural Rights

Cross-sector policies

At the international level there have been two arms of the United Nations (UN) that have provided direct leadership on global matters concerning the health of humans and the health of the environment. These can be taken as examples of **cross–sector policies**.

First, there have been a number of attempts internationally to raise awareness about, and support action for, the protection of the environment and thus human health. In 1972, the Declaration of the UN Conference on the Human Environment acknowledged that '… both aspects of man's environment, the natural and the man–made, are essential to his well-being and to the enjoyment of basic human rights: the right to life itself' (UNEP, 1972). Second, the WCED was created to address growing concern about the accelerating deterioration of the human environment and natural resources and the consequences of that deterioration for economic and social development. One major contribution of the WCED was the recognition that the many crises facing the planet are interlocking crises and of the vital need for the active participation of all sectors of society in working towards sustainable development. In 1992 The UN Conference on Environment and Development (UNCED) in Rio de Janeiro reaffirmed the 1972 Declaration and sought to build on it. The first principal of the Rio Declaration states:

> Human beings are at the centre of concerns for sustainable development. They are entitled to a healthy and productive life in harmony with nature. (UNCED, 1992)

In 1992 many countries signed five agreements on global environmental issues. Two of these, the Framework Convention on Climate Change and the Convention on Biological Diversity, were formal treaties. The other three were non-binding statements on the relationship between sustainable environmental practices and the pursuit of social and socioeconomic development. The intent of Agenda 21 from the conference in Rio de Janeiro was to improve social and environmental conditions. The Statement on Principles of Forest Management pledged parties to more sustainable use of forest resources. The Rio Declaration is still held up as a consensus document outlining the principles of sustainable development.

Sustainable development

As stated above, environment, equity and economy are the 'three e's' of sustainable development. These are the targets for the principles of sustainable development as they were laid down in the Rio de Janeiro Declaration on Environment and Development. There are five overarching principles to guide policy development (see below).

Summary box

Targets for the principles of sustainable development as they were laid down in the Rio de Janeiro Declaration on Environment and Development:

- The *precautionary principle*, where lack of full scientific certainty should not be used as a reason for postponing measures to prevent environmental degradation (see Chapter Two).
- *Biodiversity conservation* to protect ecosystems, natural habitats and to maintain viable populations of species in natural surroundings.
- *Environmental resource accounting* is a means of benchmarking the current usage against ideal usage and then for the future, reporting on the progress.
- *Community participation* acknowledges that the practice of sustainable development is dependent on the involvement of communities at the local level.
- *Intergenerational equity* that extends the principle of fairness and justice to future generations (see Chapter Five).

Unfortunately, the 2009 global economic crisis focused the minds of world leaders on only one element of sustainable development. The crisis apparently gave climate change sceptics a lever to say that we cannot afford to move from a carbon-based economy to one that is sustainable. The IPCC among others disagree. A carbon-based economy is making people, particularly poor people, and the planet sick and the health benefits of reducing carbon emissions are not widely understood. The road to a new international agreement on carbon in Copenhagen proved to be a bumpy one.

Millennium Development Goals

The Millennium Development Goals (MDGs) emerged from the world summits in the 1990s. They are ostensibly supported by the international community through the UN Development Programme (UNDP). The aim is to reduce poverty, disease and child mortality in particular, and to promote education, maternal health and gender equality (UN, 2005). Goal seven is concerned with sustainability and has several main targets:

- Integrate the principles of sustainable development into country policies and programmes and reverse the loss of environmental resources.
- Reduce biodiversity loss, achieving, by 2010, a significant reduction in the rate of loss.

- Halve, by 2015, the proportion of the population without sustainable access to safe drinking water and basic sanitation.
- By 2020, to have achieved a significant improvement in the lives of at least 100 million slum dwellers.

Unfortunately the UN reports that progress towards MDGs is further threatened by the global financial crisis and diminishing resources, which does not bode well for poor nations. A great deal of enthusiasm remains in the UN in achieving the goals but in war-torn countries the conflict is as much about pressure on resources as it is about the politics of the countries involved (Jay and Marmot, 2009).

World Health Organization (WHO)

In the health division of the UN the WHO is responsible for shaping the health research agenda, setting norms and standards, articulating evidence-based policy options, providing technical support to countries and monitoring and assessing health trends.

Two landmark documents of the WHO acknowledge the interrelationship between human health and the environment. The *Declaration of Alma-Ata* includes in its preamble that methods of preventing and controlling health problems include involving 'all related sectors and aspects of national and community development, in particular agriculture, animal husbandry, food, industry, education, housing, public works, communication and other sectors; and demands the coordinated efforts of all those sectors…' (WHO, 1978). *The Ottawa Charter for Health Promotion* (WHO, 1986) supported the intent of the *Declaration of Alma-Ata* (see below).

Summary box

Excerpts from the Ottawa Charter for Health Promotion

Health promotion goes beyond health care. It puts health on the agenda of policy makers in all sectors and at all levels, directing them to be aware of the health consequences of their decisions and to accept their responsibilities for health.... Health promotion policy requires the identification of obstacles to the adoption of healthy public policies in non-health sectors, and ways of removing them. The aim must be to make the healthier choice the easier choice for policy makers as well....

Our societies are complex and interrelated. Health cannot be separated from other goals. The inextricable links between people and their environment constitutes the basis for a socio-ecological approach to health. The overall guiding principle for the world, nations, regions and communities alike, is the need to encourage reciprocal maintenance – to take care of each other, our communities and our natural environment. The conservation of natural resources throughout the world should be emphasized as a global responsibility....

Systematic assessment of the health impact of a rapidly changing environment – particularly in areas of technology, work, energy production and urbanization – is essential and must be followed by action to ensure positive benefit to the health of the public. The protection of the natural and built environments and the conservation of natural resources must be addressed in any health promotion strategy.

Source: WHO (1986)

The Ottawa Charter for Health Promotion, with its emphasis on building healthy public policy as an integral component of promoting health, marked a formal recognition in the health sector of the role that all public policy plays in influencing health and the role of the environment in shaping opportunities for health. All public policies, mandated activities or regulated activities not just those labelled as 'health' policies, have health consequences. Policies are the foundation for action and perpetuate the effects of programmes (Talbot and Verrinder, 2009).

Policy outcomes

There have been some successes and many failures in attempting to achieve the noble ideals of international policies to prevent pollution, to restore the natural environment to a healthy state and to improve human health. On the one hand, some endangered species have been brought back from the brink of extinction, some rivers have been unlocked and allowed to flow to restore balance and the air is cleaner in some cities. On the other hand, degradation is widespread and on the increase globally. The air quality in some cities such as Beijing is generally poor and this impacts on the planet as a whole. Rules appear to be flouted routinely and penalties for transgressions may or may not be enforced (Frank et al, 2000). There has been 'no significant effort to reverse' the trend of environmental decline (Brown, L., 2009: 38).

Reducing the release of chlorofluorocarbons (CFCs) and related compounds is an international success story. These compounds have been found to reduce the ozone layer of the upper atmosphere, which shields the surface of the earth from ultraviolet radiation (UV) from the sun. If the ozone layer continues to thin, then the intensity of UV will continue to rise. *The Montreal Protocol* (UNEP, 2000) shows what can be done with enough political will. It is hoped that the ozone layer will be back to normal by 2015. The increased intensity of UV has impacts starting from the destruction of phytoplankton which is the base of the oceanic food chain right through to an increase in skin cancer and cataracts, and depressing the immune system in humans.

The Stockholm Convention on Persistent Organic Pollutants came into force in 2004 with the aim of ridding the world of POPs (UNEP, 2005). POPs are compounds that have been used in numerous technological processes. They enter the food chain and accumulate in the tissues of living organisms. POPs such as dioxins are released during paper pulp processing, coal combustion and waste incineration; and polychlorinated biphenyls are used for a range of electrical, insulation, lubrication, and other industrial purposes and pesticides (Boyden, 2005). This Convention is a good example of global recognition of the impact of human activity on the environment and the consequences for human health. The short- and long-term effects of POPs continue to be a concern for health professionals. Animals living in polluted waters have been seen to be more affected by several kinds of cancer, twisted spines and other skeletal disorders, ulcers, pneumonia, bacterial and viral infections, thyroid abnormalities and reproductive disorders than those in unpolluted waters (UNEP, 2005). These disorders have not been proven conclusively to contribute to poor health in humans but the precautionary principle is an important mechanism to prevent further damage to other species and perhaps humans.

Evidence shows that environmental, social and economic benefits are achieved through the implementation of environmental policies. Air pollution abatement measures have been evaluated in many countries including Canada, the US, Mexico and also in Europe. In all cases, interventions were found to induce significant health benefits, which were largely greater than their costs. Policies that targeted several pollutants at once were found to be more effective (OECD, 2008). The policies varied greatly; however, the OECD (2008) report that even less stringent policies can be effective. For example, the benefits of the EU Thematic Strategy on Air Pollution delivered a cost–benefit ratio of more than three to one, and the ratio was 10 to 19 in Mexico's fuel policy that requires ultra-low sulphur. Similar success was found in evaluation of measures to improve water quality and sanitation.

'Joined-up' policy

There have been successful attempts to develop policy for cross-cutting issues in national governments due to the recognition that traditional departmental structures are unsuited to address some of the more complex policy issues (Jones and Lucas, 2000). This is sometimes called 'joined-up policy' development. The Healthy Cities programme is one example that has been taken up globally for more than 20 years. The aim of this WHO programme is comprehensive and systematic in terms of both policy and planning. There is an emphasis on health inequalities and urban poverty, the needs of vulnerable groups, participatory governance and the social, economic and environmental determinants of health. There have been five phases in this programme. The overarching goal of the current phase, Phase V (2009–13), is health and health equity in all local policies. Cities are focusing on three core themes: caring and supportive environments, healthy living and healthy urban design.

Health sector policy and planning continues to play an important role in programmes such as Healthy Cities and it is that to which we now turn.

Health sector responses: primary, secondary and tertiary disease prevention

There is a role for the health sector in primary, secondary or tertiary disease prevention strategies in the face of unprecedented environmental changes. In the health sector, primary prevention is understood as inhibiting the development of disease. Broad issues that have an impact on the health of a population, such as poverty, discrimination, polluted environments and the depletion of natural resources, need primary prevention strategies. Furthermore, social and environmental *injustice* is felt most by the most vulnerable in each society. As we have said, the conditions in which people are born, live, work and age have a powerful influence on their health. Resource-rich communities can adapt to adverse environmental pressures much more than resource-poor communities; however, vulnerable groups such as indigenous communities, children, older people and frail groups within all communities are much more exposed to environmental threats than others in the community. There is a great deal of evidence that reveals that the more unequal the society, the worse the health status of the population is overall. That is, inequality is bad for everyone (Wilkinson and Pickett 2009). A primary prevention strategy would reduce inequalities using equity as an underpinning principle, thus achieving social and environmental justice. Mitigation means the same as primary prevention: taking action to reduce the extent of a problem such as global warming.

In this instance primary prevention or mitigation includes reducing greenhouse gas (GHG) emissions and sequestering GHGs already emitted.

There are health benefits to be gained by reducing carbon emissions. Policies that reduce GHG emissions are predicted to bring about immediate reductions in many diseases, for example, heart disease, cancer, obesity, diabetes, mental illness, and also road deaths and injuries, through promoting substantially increased physical activity, for example, walking and cycling (Costello, 2009; *The Lancet*, 2009). Not only will overall health be improved but there is also good evidence that such action will contribute to minimising the gap in health between rich and poor (Wilkinson and Pickett 2009), promoting more biodiversity and a more sustainable food system – both important additional determinants of a just and sustainable society. To reverse environmental decline there must be a cut of carbon emissions by 80% from 2006 levels by 2020, a stabilisation of the population at eight billion by 2040, the eradication of poverty and the restoration of forests, soils and aquifers (Brown, L., 2009). Hardly a small task, then.

Secondary prevention or adaptation is understood as strategies that enable populations to deal with risks and threats. In the health sector, policies that enable communities to adapt to the social and mental impact of drought or cope with higher than normal temperatures, wild fires, water scarcity and other problems of climate change are examples.

In tertiary prevention, the aim is to prevent long-term impairment and disability. This may be too late in some areas given that the impact of toxins on the fertility of animals and the pollution of the food chain is already upon us and irreversible.

Health sector differences between countries

Raphael and Bryant (2006) provide a useful analysis of the considerable differences between jurisdictions in public policy development to address the determinants of health. They conclude from their examination of the UK, the US, Canada and Sweden, that ideological commitments to health equity in the UK and Sweden provided a solid platform on which policy was developed from empirical findings concerning broader determinants of health. The US policy environment was resistant to a broad-based 'determinants of health' approach, and in Canada the public health community profoundly influenced the public policy environment:

> The selection of a dominant model by which the origins of health are understood is itself influenced by the political, economic and social environments within which public policy

and public health activities operate. (Raphael and Bryant, 2006: 40)

What their cross-national analysis highlights is that, if the dominant model in the health system is highly individualised and focused on biological dispositions and the effects of risk behaviours, the efforts in the health sector will be directed to sickness care and managing risk factors for chronic disease such as hypertension, elevated cholesterol, weight issues and tobacco use. These approaches are known as the medical and behavioural models of health and they dominate health sector policy and financing globally.

If, alternatively, the model is a socio-ecological model, then preventative efforts will be directed towards social justice in areas such as income maintenance, education and the built and natural environment. Healthcare is a balanced approach including health promotion, disease prevention, sickness care and rehabilitation. Primary care services such as community health centres are well supported in this model. Access to all services is based on need, not the ability to pay. This model provides an opportunity for governments to consider health in all policies, and within the health sector, to consider the environmental determinants of health.

Win-win policies: the example of public transport

Globally we have the human and financial resources to mitigate and adapt to environmental changes and to protect human health. Our role in the sustainability transition is clear. Primarily, it is a matter of political will. And such will has frequently been lacking. For instance, car use is increasing across the globe (see Chapter Ten, this volume). In the UK, for example, the use of cars has risen 10 times since 1952, and in the US, the average person drives twice as much as they did 25 years ago (Wheeler, 2004).

There appears be a correlation between GHG efficiency and the health of the public (Bloomberg and Aggarwala, 2008). Currently, environment policies tend to focus on mitigation policies such as reducing GHG emissions whereas health policies focus on adaptation policies to reduce the impact of climate change on humans. Policies to improve or protect the environment have direct health benefits for humans. There are environmental and human health benefits to be derived from increased use of public transport. Reducing the use of cars and therefore fossil fuels globally lessens the impact of GHGs while at the same time reducing air pollution, and increasing physical activity at the local level. A reduction in air pollution and an increase in physical activity reduces mortality and morbidity in respiratory conditions, cardiovascular disease, diabetes and road traffic accidents.

Governments are becoming increasingly aware of the social, environmental and health benefits of supporting the use of 'active' transport. Public transport needs to be clean, safe, secure and easier to use than private cars; non-car users need to be able to access employment, services, recreation and family. Policies need to ensure this. Getting to and using public transport of itself promotes exercise (people walk or cycle to transport stops). Even if driving to a transport node, people walk about the transport system. There are many direct and indirect benefits.

> ## Summary box
>
> **Health benefits of public transport**
>
> - Thirty minutes of exercise daily helps to promote weight loss and improve physical fitness. Weight loss and fitness help prevent obesity and chronic diseases such as diabetes and coronary heart disease.
> - Exercise promotes psychological well-being via endorphin release.
> - Exercise reduces osteoporosis later in life.
> - Reduced use of motor cars reduces exposure for drivers, residents and workers along traffic corridors, and users of public spaces to particulate, chemical and noise pollution.
> - More use of public transport will result in reduced GHGs and so will help to mitigate global warming.

Conclusion

The prerequisite for human health is a healthy ecosystem. This ecosystem includes natural, built and social environments. Degradation of these environments, particularly the natural environment, now threatens human health on a global scale.

The conclusion is that social policy has the potential to be a powerful lever in creating a healthy society and a healthy environment. In order to address the determinants of human health in an equitable and sustainable way, national and international policies need to cut across different sectors to protect and promote the health of the planet and so humans.

Chapter summary

This chapter has:

- discussed some societal responses to modify the effects of, and adapt to, environmental changes in order to improve the health of humans and of the environment;
- focused on international efforts that guide national governments in such policy developments;
- concluded that international policies have failed to arrest the widening gap of health inequalities between the most and least deprived and failed to arrest escalating rates of environmental degradation;
- acknowledged some successes, including what can be called win-win policies.

Questions for discussion

- What kind of healthcare policies might promote the goal of sustainable development?
- What policies and reform strategies proposed by international agreements might assist those goals?
- To reverse environmental decline there must be (Brown, L., 2009):
  - a cut of carbon emissions by 80% from 2006 levels by 2020;
  - stabilisation of the population at eight billion by 2040;
  - eradication of poverty.
- Taking one of these 'targets', discuss some of the policy initiatives the government in your country has developed to achieve ecological sustainable development.

Key further reading

Brown, V.A., Grootjans, J., Ritchie, J., Townsend, M. and Verrinder, G. (eds) (2005) *Sustainability and health*, London: Earthscan.

Johnson, B. (2007) *Environmental policy and public health*, Boca Raton, FL: Taylor and Francis.

McMichael, A., Campbell-Lendrum, H., Corvalen, C., Ebi, K., Githeko, A.K., Schwraga, J.D. and Woodward, A. (eds) (2003) *Climate change and human health*, Geneva: World Health Organization.

Talbot, L. and Verrinder, G. (2009) *Promoting health,* Marrickville, Australia: Elsevier.

Verrinder, A. (2003) *Human ecology and health*, Bendigo: LaTrobe University.

Useful websites

World Health Organisation: www.who.int/en/

Institute for Sustainability, Health and Environment: www.uwe.ac.uk/ishe/

United Nations Development Programme: www.undp.org/

nine

Planning and the urban environment

Stephen M. Wheeler

Overview

It often falls to the field of urban and regional planning to implement broad environmental policy goals. Planning staff at different levels of government and within the private sector work with many different constituencies to analyse trends and impacts, produce planning documents, develop regulations and involve the public in decision making. Specific topic areas that planners work with include land use, housing, transportation, energy, urban design, environmental protection and economic development. Although it draws at times on many types of theory, including radical environmental perspectives, planning can be seen as a pragmatic effort to guide society towards a better future.

This chapter:

- explores the role of the planning profession;
- considers the planning process;
- examines a range of specific issues.

Introduction

Planning staff within local, regional and national governments have the task of regulating development and preparing plans, policies and programmes to help society move towards a better future (Duerksen et al, 2009). Most cities and towns of any size have a professional staff that develops and administers land use regulations and issues permits for land development. Working in conjunction with engineering, public works, parks, housing and social welfare departments, planning staff also frequently plan infrastructure systems, develop housing policy, undertake economic development initiatives and create strategies to protect local environmental quality. Since most of these areas of work affect the environment in one way or another, planning can be seen as a principal means for the implementation of environmental policy.

This chapter discusses the role of the planning profession in relation to environmental policy (see also Frey, 1999) and after general consideration of the planning process examines the specific planning topics of: sustainability planning; land use and urban design; transport and infrastructure; energy efficiency and resource use; parks, public spaces and ecosystems; environmental justice; and urban planning in the developing world.

The planning process

Typically, planners work with elected officials and members of the public to create planning documents laying out an overall vision for the place in question. These documents guide future growth and initiatives within the relevant jurisdiction over many years. Several levels to these plans may be created: an overall plan for the entire jurisdiction; area plans for particular neighbourhoods or districts; and sometimes very detailed specific plans for development sites. Issue-specific plans for topics such as energy, transportation and climate change may also be created. Ideally such documents are linked to regulatory codes or standards, although the degree to which this actually happens in communities around the globe varies greatly.

At broader scales of government more general types of plans or planning guidance are often developed. Counties, regions, states, provinces and nations may establish planning frameworks in areas such as transportation, housing, energy, land use and environmental policy. Sometimes these guidelines are optional for local governments (Hack et al, 2009). However, in other cases these higher-level plans mandate specific actions, and ideally also provide funding for the lower-level agencies that are required to act. In the US, for example, although there is little specific national planning guidance, federal legislation over the years has required regional planning related to air pollution, water pollution and transportation systems. In the UK, the national government has long provided much more specific planning guidance, and indeed has the power to institute new forms of regional government, which it has done from time to time. In particular, the national Communities and Local Government (CLG) department has issued Planning Policy Statements on topics such as climate change, biodiversity, renewable energy, coastal change and sustainable development in rural areas. Local governments are required to take their contents into account when preparing plans.

Summary box

Planning versus policy

Urban planning – or 'town and country planning' as it has been called historically in the UK (Nadin and Cullingworth, 2010) – overlaps with public policy in some ways, but also involves different functions. Both set goals for the future and develop strategies to meet those goals. But planning often takes place at a staff level within government, and deals with pragmatic questions about regulating land development, improving transportation systems, protecting environmental quality and organising social programmes. Planning creates specific documents ('plans') that establish a vision for the future, and has established regulatory mechanisms, urban design procedures and public involvement processes to implement overall goals.

The planning process is often highly political, and elected officials, landowners, businesses, labour unions and other interests express strong points of view during public workshops, through written comments or in meetings with planning staff. Increasingly, environmental advocacy groups and other non-governmental organisations (NGOs) participate in the planning process, either as invited workshop participants and members of advisory committees, or as organisers and lobbyists seeking to get certain points of view into the process. Groups such as Friends of the Earth and Greenpeace are active in many countries, and may propose detailed policies or planning solutions. Other environmentally minded organisations work at a smaller scale within particular regions and localities.

Planning processes are often slow and receive little public attention. But creating or revising plans and codes is a very practical step that can be taken towards improving both environmental and social well-being in a given place. Not surprisingly, the process of developing and revising plans is highly political. Although government staff may develop a range of alternative strategies and recommend one set of actions, the final decisions on broad policy in any given topic area are made by elected officials, and are subject to extensive input from residents, landowners, advocacy organisations, businesses, labour unions and other stakeholders.

Planning and development approval processes are, in fact, often the main opportunity for the public to participate in shaping the development of their community. Many nations now have requirements for public consultation, and planning staff or appointed commissions often receive public comment, host public workshops or coordinate design charrettes (intensive workshops focusing on the configuration of public spaces and neighbourhoods). Planning staff typically oversee environmental impact analysis of proposed projects as well, which may involve additional public consultation.

Forms of planning and ways that these relate to environmental policy are constantly evolving. For example, only in recent years have governments begun developing climate change plans in response to the realisation that these are needed to reduce emissions and help communities adapt to a changing climate. Recently, many governments have also become more sensitive to environmental justice concerns – the disproportionate impacts of environmental problems on low-income and minority communities.

The process of planning is inherently interdisciplinary and holistic. It requires meshing goals in diverse areas such as social policy, economic development and environmental protection. As such, planning is at the forefront of sustainable development and environmental policy, but requires an ability to think broadly, to work with many different constituencies, to facilitate consensus and to figure out creative strategies to achieve results within complicated bureaucracies and political systems.

Cities and sustainability

At the broadest levels, many local governments have attempted to address environmental policy concerns by creating overall sustainability plans (Hall, 2002; Hardy, 2008; Newman and Jennings, 2008); in Europe these are often known as Local Agenda 21 plans after a document adopted by 178 nations at the 1992 United Nations (UN) Rio Conference on Environment and Development. These plans seek to establish an overall environmental policy framework that includes attention to social and economic concerns as well as ecological ones. London, for example, produced a Sustainability Plan geared towards greening the city for the 2012 Olympics. In 2007 New York City adopted an ambitious PlaNYC focusing on 10 sustainability goals for 2030 in areas such as housing, transportation, energy and greenhouse gas (GHG) reductions. In the mid-2000s Taipei developed a Sustainable Taipei Eco-City Plan that called for 'creating a sustainable city encompassing cyclic symbiosis of environment and resources' (City of Taipei, 2004). Many smaller cities and other governmental jurisdictions have created similar comprehensive documents that set environmental policy in many areas and link it to social and economic development issues.

A big question, of course, is how well these plans will bring about actual change. The results are certainly mixed. Sometimes planning documents consist mainly of well-meaning rhetoric, created to make places or elected leaders look 'green', but yielding few practical results. At other times, however, elected leaders and government staff do take planning visions seriously, and develop the detailed programmes, regulatory revisions, staffing changes and funding allocations necessary to make them work. Pressure from NGOs and the news media can help ensure that this happens.

To evaluate progress towards sustainability goals, governments often establish indicators to measure change. In some cases these are tied to legal mandates from the courts or higher levels of government, for example, to improve local air quality or to reduce GHG emissions. At other times agencies may voluntarily use them to refine policy and programmes in succeeding years. Or such indicators may be primarily educational in nature, created to help the public understand the degree of change needed to progress towards a more sustainable society.

One of the most famous examples internationally has been the Sustainable Seattle indicators, originally created in the early 1990s by a citizen organisation that brought hundreds of representatives of different Seattle constituencies together to brainstorm indicators that would help show the community's overall progress towards sustainability. Some of these indicators focused on symbols that everyone in the region could relate to, such as the number of wild salmon returning to spawn in rivers. Salmon has historically been an extremely important food for Native Americans as well as more recent settlers, and helps indicate the overall health of the region's waterways. Sustainable Seattle also included many non-environmental indicators in its list, such as children living in poverty, distribution of personal income and voter participation. The belief was that these social and economic indicators were linked to the overall goal of a healthy and sustainable community. However, in practice social equity and sustainable economy concerns are often overlooked by decision makers and the public.

In recent years, comprehensive sustainability planning has taken on a new impetus as the public has come to realise the need to combat climate change. Since GHG emissions are affected by virtually every area of human activity, and since a wide range of actions is needed for society to adapt to climate change, climate change planning virtually requires a broad-based sustainability approach. As the climate change threat grows, the need for more radical comprehensive planning is likely to increase in the coming years.

We now go on to explore some of the key issues that will affect, for better or worse, future progress, beginning with **land use** and **urban design**.

> **Summary box**
>
> **Planning and climate change**
>
> Urban planning will have many roles to play in implementing climate change policies developed through national or international agreements. Detailed plans will be needed for renewable energy facilities and transmission grids, as well as for programmes to improve energy efficiency within existing homes and factories. Action will be needed as well in virtually every other topic area listed in this chapter. In particular, more compact, mixed-use land development can help reduce transportation emissions, and a range of urban greening strategies can help make communities comfortable in the hotter years ahead. Detailed plans will also be needed to prepare for flooding dangers and sea level rise.

Land use, housing and urban design

The core of the planning profession historically lies in the regulation of land and housing. As cities expanded in the late 19th century, architects and landscape architects turned their attention to the design of urban growth, seeking to improve housing conditions and create new suburban districts, park systems and urban renovations. Local governments began establishing planning departments in the early 1900s, and governments adopted mechanisms such as zoning codes (in the US) and design codes (in Britain) to regulate development.

Such regulatory codes have very large environmental implications (Randolph, 2004). They help determine which land is going to be built on and which areas will be preserved for agriculture, parks or wilderness. They establish basic forms and densities of development, and so determine how much a metropolitan area will sprawl outwards. They may specifically protect streams, wetlands, hilltops, shorelines and other ecologically sensitive areas. And by specifying the location and mixtures of land use (residential, commercial, industrial and so forth), they help determine how far people need to travel to get to daily destinations, and whether the community will be car-dependent or pedestrian-friendly.

Although regulatory frameworks vary from country to country, several different types of codes are often used to govern development. Subdivision regulation determines how and when large parcels of land can be divided into many small lots with different owners, an essential process in order for urbanisation to occur. Land use codes (called '**zoning**' in the US and 'design codes' in Britain) specify the types of development permitted on each parcel, the form of allowable buildings, parking requirements and many other development details. Building codes, increasingly standardised internationally but usually tailored to local conditions by local governments, regulate the structures themselves, including aspects such as fire and earthquake safety, and water and energy efficiency.

Increasingly, public or private organisations are creating additional green development guidelines that give special awards to development that is very environment-friendly. The Leadership in Energy and Environmental Design (LEED) system in the US, the Building Research Establishment (BRE) Environmental Assessment Method (BREEAM) system headquartered in Britain, and the Green Globes system in Canada are examples of such green building rating systems. These frameworks are expanding to include other aspects of development such as site design and neighbourhood design. From an environmental point of view the problem is that such rating systems are voluntary; developers only seek certification if they are highly motivated to do so. This situation is slowly changing, as many governments increasingly require that public buildings and even some private buildings be certified green. Also, mainstream building and development codes are slowly becoming greener. But the process is slow and speeding it up is a priority for many environmentally minded planners.

A priority of land use planning in many countries is to manage urban growth and preserve undeveloped land from the seemingly inexorable process of urbanisation (Wheeler, 2004; Wheeler and Beatley, 2008). One option is for government simply to purchase land for parks or open space, but this is expensive. Another approach has been to establish greenbelts around cities in which building construction and/or land subdivision are prohibited, as is common in Britain. Historically France has established large 'deferred development zones' to protect its countryside. Switzerland and some West Coast US cities such as Portland use urban growth boundaries to control development (see *Figure 9.1*). Some European cities such as Stockholm use 'land banking' programmes to manage growth, in which public agencies hold land and lease or resell it for development only at appropriate times and places.

Growth management has been weakest historically in the US, which gives local governments the main authority over land development and values private property rights highly. Some US communities have a limited urban infrastructure (roads, sewers, water systems), which in effect limits growth, and many others have established agricultural zoning to protect farmland, although this is a relatively weak mechanism easily overturned through political votes. Increasingly in the US, NGOs purchase development rights from landowners in an attempt to ensure that rural usage continues on the land, establishing 'conservation easements'. Each of these methods of growth management has strengths and weaknesses, and in nations such as the US and Australia the battle against urban sprawl has generally been a losing one.

Figure 9.1: *Portland Urban Growth Boundary (detail)*

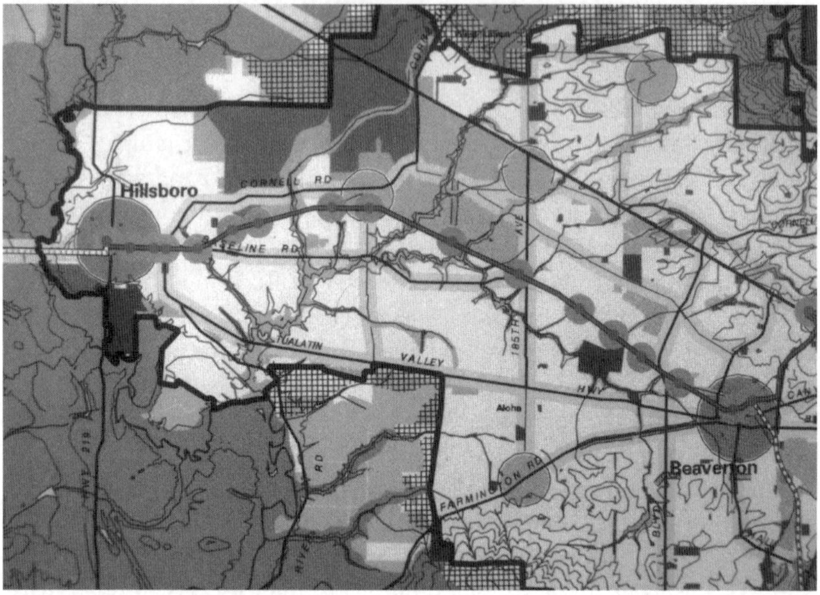

Note: The dark line is the Urban Growth Boundary, established in 1980. Lighter circles inside the boundary represent transit-oriented development along a light rail line.

Portland, OR, is a good US example of regional planning.

Source: Portland Metro.

To limit sprawl and encourage urban revitalisation, many cities worldwide encourage development on previously used land, a process known by terms such as 'infill', 'intensification', 'redevelopment' or 'reurbanisation'. These initiatives often require preparation of detailed design plans for new districts or neighbourhoods, environmental analysis, public subsidy to clear land and add infrastructure and revisions to development codes for those areas. Contaminated sites formerly used by industry, the military or other polluting users are often called 'brownfield' sites, and cleaning them up through public or private sector initiative is often a major challenge.

Planners also typically seek to coordinate land use with public transit systems, a process called **transit-oriented development**. Such building can result in new **transit villages**, that is, clusters of dense, mixed-use development around stations. These projects can help reduce driving and encourage more people to use public transport.

Exactly how compact or dense to make communities in the future is a topic of some debate. The one-storey, large-lot housing model of many North American and Australian cities is widely seen as unsustainable in that it consumes large amounts of land and requires lots of driving. But is a two- to three-storey city with relatively small lots, as in many British or East Coast US communities, dense enough? Should a three- to five-storey built landscape be sought instead, one that implies more apartment living, but provides densities adequate to support high levels of public transit service? The centre of Paris and many other European cities were built on this model. Or is a true high-rise model, as seen in New York, Vancouver, Hong Kong, Tokyo or the Brazilian city of Curitiba, more ecological in the long run? Such densities support fast, frequent subway services and a very rich, vibrant local economy at street level. Large apartment buildings can be made very energy efficient, and can take advantage of neighbourhood-scale heating and cooling systems that further reduce energy use. But a key challenge then is to provide urban residents with an attractive public realm and adequate green space – perhaps using building roofs as well as park systems.

An extensive academic debate has taken place over the extent to which compact cities should be a goal of environmental planning. Michael Breheny, for example, points out that past ideals of compact urban redevelopment and garden cities have often proved less than sustainable in practice (Breheny, 1996). High-rise buildings also tend to have high levels of embodied energy due to their concrete-and-steel construction when compared to one- to three-storey buildings. However, if well built their operating energy consumption is often lower, and a US study led by Reid Ewing has found that compact development can reduce driving (and hence GHG emissions) by 20% to 40% over conventional development (Ewing et al, 2008). There are some, in fact, who argue that one of the greenest North American communities is Manhattan, with its extremely high densities (Owen, 2009). Overall, the relation between sustainability and urban compactness is complex. Dense or high-rise environments are not necessarily the most ecological or liveable. But given all the environmental problems connected with low-density, car-dependent development in many parts of the world, the consensus of many observers is that new models of dense but green urban development are desirable (for example, Frey, 1999). A relatively dense urban environment with varied housing forms and sizes is also likely to accommodate the most diverse variety of residents, including low-income individuals and families, and so thus may be important on social equity grounds.

There are no easy answers to questions about ecological urban form and land use. Much depends on the ways that particular forms are designed, and the ways that social policy interacts with the planning of the physical landscape to raise overall quality of life. However, it does seem clear that many communities worldwide must move in the direction of greater compactness, to reduce car and resource use and preserve agricultural land, and that creative new types of urban environments must be planned and built.

Housing

Housing policy and development affects the environment in many ways, for example, in terms of energy use, and affects us personally because the dwellings we live in are shaped by housing regulations and development practices. City land use codes determine what types of housing can go where, often establishing entire neighbourhoods with particular forms such as single-family detached homes, duplexes or semi-attached units, rowhouses, low-rise garden apartments or various types of mid- and high-rise residential structures. In recent years cities have often made efforts to increase the mixture of housing types within a given neighbourhood, since a greater mix generally means a wider range of prices, increased affordability and a more diverse community. Explicit rent subsidies, public housing construction or grants to non-profit builders enabling them to build affordable units can also help ensure that everyone in the community is housed.

Contrary to what many people think, the most important ecological feature of a home is not its construction but its location. It is counterproductive to build green homes out in the country, where residents will need to drive long distances and the home site itself may be disrupting agriculture or local ecosystems. A smaller unit within an existing city will have far fewer requirements for car use and new infrastructure, and can help support public transportation, small local businesses and urban vitality in general. Smaller, attached housing forms also tend to consume less energy than detached 'McMansions'. For these reasons 'site selection' is an important category in the LEED green building rating system.

That being said, improving the energy efficiency of housing is crucial, especially as societies try to reduce their GHG emissions. A starting point has been to revise housing codes – the basic construction regulations for housing – to require high levels of wall and roof insulation, double- or triple-paned windows, more efficient heating, cooling and ventilation systems, and similar other measures. But a more radical effort is also under way to move towards carbon-neutral dwellings, or the 'passivehaus', as it is known in Germany. These homes have an extremely well-insulated building envelope – the set of walls, roofs, doors and windows that enclose interior space – so their heating and cooling needs are very low. And they actively generate enough power through photovoltaics or other means to offset their low level of energy use. Some jurisdictions are beginning to integrate carbon-neutral housing goals into their building codes. Austin, Texas, for example, is planning to require that all new single-family homes be zero net-energy capable by 2015. To attain the top (six-star) rating in the 2006 British Code for Sustainable Homes, new buildings must be carbon-neutral. Although this code is voluntary, the government intends that all new housing meet this goal by 2016. Both the US (through Obama administration programmes) and Britain (through the Warm Front programme) have also emphasised improving the efficiency of existing homes belonging to low-income individuals, for social equity as well as environmental reasons.

The highest level of energy efficiency is likely to be gained from thinking systematically about energy use across a whole neighbourhood or community. Ideally this is done when neighbourhoods are first designed, so that buildings can share systems for heating, cooling and electricity. Structures can also be oriented so as to take maximum advantage of the sun's energy for winter heat and local breezes for summer cooling. Drainage systems can preserve rainfall onsite to irrigate landscaping, and greywater systems within buildings can reuse shower and sink water for toilets. Community energy plans can also take steps to reduce motor vehicle use and water consumption, and to facilitate recycling of many materials. The Hammarby neighbourhood in Stockholm is one example of this sort of thinking.

Another related initiative to reduce energy consumption is to provide far better information to residents and workers about real-time building energy use. Panels can show people how much energy the building is using or generating, and help them understand the easiest ways to reduce consumption. 'Smart meters' can also be linked electronically to utilities so that energy consumption and generation can be more efficiently managed, helping to create a 'smart grid' on either a decentralised or centralised basis.

Virtually every building material within buildings can be 'greened' in some way that has far-ranging benefits for the environment. Lumber can be reused or come from sustainably harvested forests. Concrete can be recycled and lower-emission forms of it can be employed. Floors and countertops can be made from recycled or sustainably grown materials. Paints, wallboard and carpets can have greatly reduced emissions of volatile organic compounds, chemicals that degrade indoor air quality. Year by year companies are creating new green products for home construction.

The orientation of the building on the lot makes a big difference in terms of passive solar design – the use of the sun's energy and natural wind patterns to warm the house in the winter and cool it in the summer. Having the long face of the building oriented south with plentiful windows allows low-angle winter sunlight to warm the interior. Having sun shades above windows and having trees shading the roof helps prevent summer sun from overheating the structure. And having windows oriented towards the prevailing summer breezes, as well as whole-house fans or ventilation towers to move hot air out of the building, can reduce cooling needs during hot summer months.

How the site is treated outside the building also greatly determines environmental impacts. Instead of scraping off all vegetation and culverting waterways during the site preparation process, developers can preserve wildlife habitat and the landscape's existing hydrology. Instead of channelling stormwater run-off into pipes, use of permeable paving and swales (linear depressions where water can settle) can allow stormwater to infiltrate the ground locally, recharging water tables and reducing downstream flooding and erosion that might otherwise occur. Instead of planting large areas of water-intensive lawn that typically is treated with high levels of synthetic fertilisers and herbicides, developers can install native or drought-tolerant landscaping using water-saving drip irrigation, and recreate wildlife habitat onsite. Planners are increasingly seeking to require such practices within local development.

Figure 9.2: Ecolonia Passive Solar Home

Note: This home in the Dutch community of Ecolonia is constructed facing south, with large windows so that the sun's energy will warm the home in the winter, a strategy known as passive solar design. The wetland in front treats stormwater run-off.

Source: Stephen M. Wheeler.

Transport and infrastructure

The ever-growing use of cars is one of the most unsustainable trends in current cities and towns (see Chapter Ten, this volume). Large-scale transport policy, including most funding for long-distance road and rail systems, is handled at the national level in Britain, the US and many other countries. However, regional and local governments are responsible for planning smaller-scale facilities and programmes. Planning strategies in three complementary areas can help reduce driving. One step is to make a wide range of transportation alternatives available to people, including public transit systems, bicycle facilities and pedestrian-friendly paths and streets. Such an approach has important social justice as well as environmental benefits. Another is to revise land use planning so that over time people do not need to travel as far to get to daily destinations. This means creating more balanced, mixed-use towns in which shops, workplaces, recreational facilities and public transit stations are within easy walking distance of homes. Lastly, incentive structures must be changed to encourage less driving. This means higher prices for parking, car ownership and use, financial incentives from employers for not driving alone to work and better information about alternatives such as lift-sharing and telecommuting programmes.

To put things another way, the 20th-century approach of trying to deal with traffic congestion by building more and wider roads – increasing the supply of automobile infrastructure – has been replaced in many places by a new strategy of managing the demand for car use, through the means outlined above.

Another key challenge facing the planning of transportation is the design of streets and parking lots. Many older roads worldwide were created with only the car in mind. Too often, overly wide arterial streets are lined by expansive parking lots, fast food outlets and other suburban strip-style buildings. These street environments are profoundly unfriendly to pedestrians and public transit. They also contribute to other ecological problems such as excessive stormwater run-off and 'urban heat island' effects, through which asphalt and other hardscape materials soak up the sun's energy and raise urban temperatures by many degrees compared with the surrounding countryside.

Cities have begun to green these car-oriented environments. Roadways can be narrowed and street trees added within new medians or planting strips. Drainage from roads, parking lots and building roofs can be absorbed locally through planted swales. New pavements and bicycle paths can be created. Car speeds can be reduced, usually to 30mph (50kph) or less, speeds that are more energy efficient, less noisy and vastly safer for pedestrians and cyclists. Meanwhile, land use planning can seek to place new buildings along the streetscape, turning asphalt-dominated strips into vibrant, people-oriented urban environments.

Other forms of infrastructure also have significant environmental impacts (Wheeler, 2004; Wheeler and Beatley, 2008). Stormwater systems created during the 20th century usually tried to move rainwater off the land, eventually dumping it into distant rivers, lakes or oceans. Nowadays more and more urban designers are trying to keep run-off onsite, as mentioned above. The federal Clean Water Act in the US requires all large and medium-sized cities to take steps to reduce surface run-off, since such 'non-point source' pollution is the largest cause of water quality problems. Rainwater from roofs and paved surfaces can also be stored for later use in irrigation. New building systems to reuse greywater – used water from sinks and showers – are also becoming popular.

Infrastructure to provide drinking water is also being rethought. Traditionally, cities and towns obtained potable water from wells or reservoirs behind large dams. But the destructiveness of dam building to flora and fauna along rivers is now widely recognised, as is the problem of depleting local aquifers through excessive pumping from wells. Planning and policy responses typically emphasise water conservation, to reduce the overall need for potable water, as well as reuse of greywater and well-treated sewage, which is indistinguishable from fresh water. New strategies for water management, such as in-ground storage, are also being investigated.

Energy efficiency and resource use

Energy infrastructure has many impacts on urban and rural environments. Large power plants release pollution that affects both local air quality and the global climate. Nuclear plants require large amounts of water for cooling, in addition to producing radioactive waste. Mining and drilling operations for coal, oil, uranium and natural gas create pollution and endanger miners, often disproportionately affecting disadvantaged or minority communities. Transmission lines cut across the landscape, spoiling views and creating electromagnetic fields that may be unhealthy.

Moving to more efficient, non-fossil fuel energy systems, is one of the largest planning challenges we face, one that has moved centre stage in the 21st century with increasing concern about climate change. Big picture energy and climate change initiatives happen at state, national or international levels, since they involve large questions of public investment and policy. Energy agencies and regulatory commissions play a large role in overseeing utility operations, issuing permits for power plants using both renewable and non-renewable energy and developing power grids and pipelines. Planning is under way for large-scale wind farms, solar thermal power plants, geothermal plants and other forms of alternative energy.

Much energy planning is also done at a local level. Municipal governments develop programmes to help homeowners retrofit their homes for greater energy efficiency, to improve the energy performance of schools and other public buildings and to encourage consumers to move towards more energy-efficient appliances and lifestyles. One example of the latter is the 'low-carbon diet' programme adopted by US cities such as Portland, Oregon and Davis, California, through which the city works with households to help them reduce their GHG emissions by $5,000 a year. As mentioned previously, local planning staff can also collaborate with developers to create entire new neighbourhoods that are more energy efficient, often through the creation of community energy plans and the use of district heating and cooling systems.

One of the most visible environmental planning initiatives involves the use of everyday materials, since many of us sort our newspapers, drink containers, cans and plastic bags into containers for pick-up by municipal recycling programmes. Widespread city-run recycling programmes date back to the 1970s and 1980s, and are often seen as a symbol of local commitment to the environment. Yet recycling programmes only capture around 30% of the municipal waste stream in the US, Canada and Britain, with the rest still being dumped in landfill or burned in incinerators. Other nations do somewhat better: Switzerland, Belgium, Germany, Sweden and the Netherlands have material recovery rates of at least 50%, and Austria has reported a rate of 64% (Friends of the Earth, 2007). New programmes can be planned to increase recycling rates, for example by offering prizes for the highest levels of household recycling, or by increasing fees for rubbish collection and charging different monthly rates for bins depending on their size.

However, recycling is only the tip of the iceberg when it comes to such usage. Before the widespread use of plastic containers for beverages began in the 1960s and 1970s, virtually all drink containers were reusable. This is still the case in a number of European nations that require such reuse, but has vanished in North America and many other parts of the world, where containers are made to be thrown away. Reuse represents a 'deeper green' materials strategy than recycling, since far less energy is used in washing and recirculating a container than in crushing it, melting it down and reforming it into a new unit.

An even deeper green strategy is to reduce the consumption of such materials in the first place. In many cases a particular function – building a car, for example – can be accomplished with reduced use of metals or energy. Consumers can also decide to make do with one vehicle (or none!) per household instead of two. Such reductions represent even greater levels of material savings. 'Reduce, reuse, recycle' is thus both a mantra of ecological materials use and a declaration of priorities. Local governments, unfortunately, still mostly emphasise the last of these through their programmes, and reducing consumption overall may mean rethinking economies in fundamental ways.

In many parts of the world, national, state or provincial governments could do what many European nations have done and require that drinks and other products be sold in reusable containers. And they could establish disincentives for excessive consumption in general, for example by taxing purchases of large cars, houses, boats or other items. Other policies might apply to industry and business. For example, large numbers of wooden pallets used to ship goods that were often discarded in the past are now recycled, preventing the waste of enormous quantities of wood.

Parks, public spaces and ecosystems

One of the most pressing planning needs in many cities and towns is for additional green space (Wheeler, 2004; Wheeler and Beatley, 2008). What green spaces do exist are often passed-over lots, cemeteries or private yards and golf courses, and have little recreational or ecological function. Many of the urban parks that have been created historically are rectangles of lawn and large trees which, although pleasant, offer nearby residents little experience of nature, and have little value as habitat for non-human species or as drainage for the local watershed.

In recent decades park design has changed so that now the focus is on creating interconnected networks of parks and greenways throughout an urban region. Such a regional park system offers many benefits to both people and the ecosystem. For people, it creates a network of linear trails useful for walking, running, cycling or rollerblading, and can also offer a variety of different types of places to experience. For ecosystems, such a park system creates or preserves a variety of habitat patches and wildlife corridors that can accommodate a far greater range of species than the typical urban park. A greenway system can also preserve or restore the natural waterways and wetlands of the watershed, an immense environmental value.

Many quite urban green spaces – plazas, boulevards, playgrounds and waterfront promenades – can be created within cities. Almost all can contain some natural elements, such as trees, grasses, planters, local stone and wood and water features, and serve as a way for residents to get out of doors for recreation or socialising. Indeed, a public environment that promotes extensive outdoor activity is increasingly seen as essential for public health, in an era in which obesity rates are increasing across many societies.

Within existing urban and suburban areas all traces of original ecosystems have often been lost. But many ecosystem elements can be restored, and 'restoration' has become a principal goal of environmental planning. This term encompasses many types of efforts to clean up abandoned industrial sites, to remove unneeded infrastructure, to dig out invasive, non-native vegetation, to replant native species, restore streams and recreate naturalistic landscapes that have both human and ecological value.

Planners often deal with one further dimension of urban greening – the support of **urban agriculture** and the development of more sustainable food systems in general. It is now widely recognised that existing food systems involve excessive inputs of artificial fertilisers, pesticides and herbicides, too much long-distant transportation of food products and frequently unhealthy food choices, especially for lower-income populations. As a result, a variety of initiatives are under way worldwide to reintegrate food production into cities and to improve **food security** – access for all to healthy food. The creation of community, allotment and rooftop gardens is one common focus. Planning staff may need to work with citizen groups or builders to help them secure space for such facilities or to amend building codes so as to allow green roofs and walls. Promotion of farmers' markets, community-supported agriculture (in which urban residents sign up with local farmers for weekly produce shipments) and full-service grocery stores within low-income neighbourhoods are other common areas of emphasis. Simply preserving agricultural land near cities is important for food security, as is an effort to ensure that schools and other public institutions serve healthy food.

Environmental justice

Beginning in the 1980s, a sizeable movement arose in the US and other nations demanding that disproportionate environmental impacts falling on low-income communities and communities of colour be addressed (Faber, 1998; see also Chapters Three and Six, this volume). Findings that asthma caused by freeway pollution most often affects minority inner-city neighbourhoods, that landfills and incinerators are most often sited in low-income communities and that electronic waste from computers often harms the health of impoverished people in places like China, fuelled the new movement. Evidence that most environmental activists and policy makers were white males also led to protests from underrepresented demographic groups.

Although such environmental justice problems still persist, changes to planning processes have helped address them to some extent. The US government now requires environmental justice analysis and outreach to underrepresented communities within most major federally funded projects. Some governmental decision-making processes have become more transparent as a result of such mandates. In the UK, the environmental justice movement has focused more on environmental risks related to poverty than 'race'. Although government documents such as the 2003 Sustainable Communities Plan tend not to address the topic of environmental justice by name, they do emphasise tackling environmental quality, housing affordability and public health in the country's least affluent communities, and stress effective engagement and participation in decision making by local people. NGOs such as the London Sustainability Exchange and the Environmental Justice Foundation (which is based in London but works internationally) have also emphasised environmental justice in their work (London Sustainability Exchange, 2004).

On a practical level, environmental and social justice movements have helped to diversify planning staff and advisory boards in many communities, and have given the interests of minority communities new weight in public discussions (for an example, see *Figure 9.3*). The process still has a long way to go, and it is impossible to incorporate some underrepresented environmental constituencies into official processes, such as non-human species and future human generations. But steps to increase the diversity of public participation in planning hold the promise of producing policies and programmes that are more appropriate to local contexts.

Urban planning in the developing world

Urban and environmental planning issues in the developing world are often somewhat different than in wealthy countries such as in North America, Europe and parts of Asia. Large problems often exist with basic water and sanitation infrastructure, as well as roads and public transport systems. Air and water pollution are less regulated, toxic chemical contamination of soils and aquifers may occur unnoticed and regulation of land use and development is often weak. Governmental corruption and lack of openness are major impediments to effective action.

That being said, there are a number of environmental planning successes in the developing world, some of which put more developed countries to shame. The Brazilian city of Curitiba embraced dozens of innovative urban planning policies under former Mayor Jaime Lerner beginning in the 1960s, and as a result has one of the world's most efficient public transport systems, a regional park system that also serves as a flood prevention facility, vibrant pedestrian districts and effective public housing programmes. Bogata, Columbia has become known for its bicycle and pedestrian planning. The Indian state of Kerala is known for policies that have increased social and

Figure 9.3: *Arbolera de Vida Neighbourhood Plan*

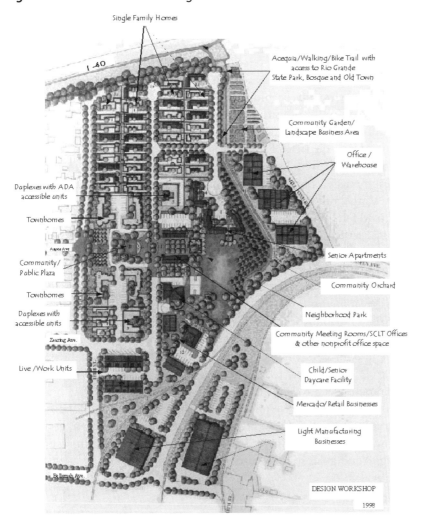

Note: A community-based organisation planned this new infill neighbourhood on a brownfield site in Albuquerque, New Mexico. A number of different housing and workplace types were created and the land is collectively owned to keep housing affordable.

Source: Sawmill Community Land Trust.

ecological welfare compared with other parts of that country. And China has planned large-scale alternative energy systems likely to make it the world's largest producer of wind power.

The developing world has some unique characteristics that present particular planning challenges. One main trend has been the growth of megacities – cities of more than 10 million inhabitants. In 1950 there was only one such city in the world: New York. By 2005 there were 25, mostly in Asia, Africa and Latin America. And by 2015 there are projected to be 33 megacities, with virtually all the new additions in the developing world. This enormous urban expansion has outstripped the abilities of local governments to regulate development and ensure basic services. As a result, environmental protection has frequently gone by the wayside. Stabilising population sizes and cleaning up damaged environments in the world's megacities is now a pressing task.

Another main characteristic of developing world cities is 'informal' housing. Large districts of self-built housing spring up virtually overnight without official building permits, city services or title to the land. Informal developments invade private land, municipal watersheds or even parkland. Homes are built from whatever materials are at hand, ranging from cardboard to reinforced concrete. Once established, it is difficult to remove informal settlements, although some municipalities have bulldozed them, creating great suffering for the residents. Generally they are slowly upgraded over time, and residents eventually gain title to the land, although the process is often not easy. How to service and upgrade informal settlements is one of the great environmental planning challenges of the developing world.

Finally, enormous social and environmental questions exist concerning the balance between the developed and developing world (see Chapters Five and Thirteen, this volume). Should the residents of less affluent countries be entitled to the current western lifestyle? Should their governments seek to replicate western-style infrastructure, with all of its dependency on intensive resource and car use? Conversely, should a less materialistic society be sought within affluent nations, with governments planning accordingly? Answers to such questions will determine planning strategies and goals in the decades ahead.

Conclusion

Every day planning staff within various levels of government work on urban development topics that relate directly to environmental policy goals. They are joined in these activities by other professionals working for environmental organisations, community development organisations, non-profit organisations, developers, unions, banks, utilities and many other agencies. This planning activity helps develop long-range vision for cities, towns and entire countries, and also puts in place the detailed regulatory codes, incentives, financial mechanisms and decision-making processes to implement big picture policy. At times planning activities are highly creative and exciting; at other times they are slow and require great patience, especially in terms of dealing with many public constituencies with different needs and opinions. Particular skills of facilitating group consensus and working out creative ways through bureaucratic mazes are sometimes required. But overall, planning and urban development represents an important and often under–appreciated adjunct to the field of environmental policy.

Chapter summary

This chapter has:

- reviewed the key questions and problems facing cities when it comes to long-term planning to ensure ecological sustainability;
- looked specifically at land use, housing policy, housing design, transport and infrastructure;
- explored the issue of public spaces and public consultation;
- outlined some key developments around the world and summarised the planning difficulties faced by the developing world.

Questions for discussion

- What planning strategies might lead to a carbon-neutral society?
- How can political support be developed for sustainable city or carbon-neutral development programmes?
- What planning, public policy and urban design steps could be taken to make more compact and denser cities more livable?
- Will people ever be willing to live without driving on a regular basis, and what steps might best help reduce car use?
- What are the possibilities for ecosystem restoration in the community where you live? How might such restoration come about?

Key further reading

Duerksen, C.J., Gregory Dale, C. and Elliott, D.L. (2009) *The citizen's guide to planning* (4th edn), Chicago, IL: APA Planners Press.

Hack, G., Birch, E., Sedway, P. and Silver, M. (eds) (2009) *Local planning: Contemporary principles and practice*, Washington, DC: The International City/ County Management Association.

Hall, P. (2002) *Cities of tomorrow* (3rd edn), London: Blackwell.

Nadin, V. and Cullingworth, B. (2010) *Town and country planning in the UK*, London: Routledge.

Owen, D. (2009) *Green metropolis: What the city can teach the country about true sustainability*, New York, NY: Riverhead Books.

Wheeler, S.M. (2004) *Planning for sustainability: Creating livable, equitable, and ecological communities*, London: Routledge.

Wheeler, S.M. and Beatley, T. (eds) (2008) *The sustainable urban development reader* (2nd edn), London: Routledge.

Useful websites

Congress for the New Urbanism (CNU): www.cnu.org/

Planners Network: The Organization of Progressive Planning: www.plannersnetwork. org/publications/magazine.html

Sustainable Communities Network (SCN) (US): www.sustainable.org

United Nations Habitat Programme's database of international best practices in sustainable development: www.bestpractices.org

ICLEI (Local Governments for Sustainability [International]): www.iclei.org

Transport

Michael Cahill

Overview

This chapter outlines:

- the environmental impact of transport, focusing on the car;
- the links between transport and health;
- the social inequalities produced by a car-dependent society;
- the impact of car dependence on children, people with disabilities and older people;
- government policy on transport;
- the possibilities for sustainable transport policy.

Introduction

As governments confront the climate change crisis, how we travel has become a pressing ethical, environmental and social issue in the 21st century (Cahill, 2007). Carbon emissions from transport are a significant and growing global problem and transport policy is being forced to confront the fact that a transport system based on the fast diminishing supply of oil needs fundamental rethinking.

The industrial revolution that transformed human life and aspirations has, in its successive phases, utilised different means of transportation, from the canals of the 18th century to the jet engines of today. Transport modes are vital for the functioning and development of both the economy and society. Globalisation is predicated on transport and speed of movement, making transportation an integral part of the world economy. This is vividly illustrated from time to time when dissident groups resort to direct action, whether French fishermen blockading cross-Channel ports, French farmers halting motorway traffic or British lorry drivers protesting against the price of fuel by blockading oil refineries.

In the 20th century motor cars progressed from their early days as a hobby for the rich to become the transport of choice for the majority in rich societies, thus weakening and eroding the ethos and practices of public transport. The people's car offering 'mobility for all', whether that be the Model T Ford or the Volkswagen or most recently the Indian Nano, became emblematic of consumer capitalism, enabling an identification of man/woman with machine, a vehicle which told the world about oneself in much the same way as one's choice of clothes did. Some sociologists argue that this identification of humans with cars goes further, resulting in a hybrid 'car-driver' part human, part machine (Dant, 2004: 75). The car has achieved a psychic hold on large sections of the population in rich societies while many people in poor and developing countries are keen to become motorists.

The transformative power of the car is enormous and its environmental impact is clear, thousands of hectares of agricultural land and beautiful countryside have disappeared as roads, parking lots, petrol stations and motorway service stations cater to its ever increasing demands. In rich societies the 20th century was 'the century of the car' and this process of social and spatial transformation is now under way in developing and poorer societies. China attained the top position in the global car sales chart in 2009 – helped no doubt by the downturn in car purchases in the US and Europe following the 2008/09 recession – and car manufacturers see China and India as lucrative markets in the 21st century (Waldmeir, 2009). The car is a transformative technology that has changed the face of cities, towns and the countryside. To say that the car is transformative is not just to list the countless ways in which it has changed landscapes, however, for it is a technology which has changed our notions of distance, speed, time and convenience. The availability of the car means that centralisation of services in city centres becomes difficult, for car journeys to city centre locations become tiresome when there are so many traffic jams and, with the press of congestion, parking becomes expensive. The response has been to provide out-of-town retail and office parks with free parking. These land usage decisions tend to increase the length of journeys and hence carbon emissions. Out-of-town locations, whether for shopping or working, are difficult to reach by public transport, hence making access for the carless that bit more difficult. The car's promise of individual mobility has been seductive in the rich world and with more than 750 million cars on the world's roads it looks set to transform poor and developing countries as well. In the last decade the Chinese and Indian governments have turned their back on the bicycle and opted for the car as the default mode of transport.

It took social scientists some time to appreciate the extent of the transformation wrought by mass car ownership, with serious engagement not emerging until the end of the 20th century (Urry, 2000). The car system – automobility – has been characterised as 'political institutions and practices that seek to organize, accelerate and shape the spatial movements and impacts of automobiles' (Bohm et al, 2006: 3). Mainstream political parties are united in their support for this system. The car is the ultimate consumer good, lusted after and worshipped, the object of 'automotive emotions' (Sheller, 2004). Automobility is central to consumer capitalism and has redefined our concept of the 'good life' (Urry, 2008: 115-19). The car affords the privacy that many desire when travelling, which is not available on public transport. Given the hegemony of the car in contemporary transport the environmental challenge is to create a system of personal mobility that does not produce carbon emissions and further deplete dwindling oil stocks. Auto(nomous) mobility via cycling and walking could offer a real alternative for many short journeys.

After a brief outline of the environmental problems produced by a car-based transport system this chapter focuses on the carless, their problems and some possible solutions. The chapter cannot discuss all elements of the transport infrastructure (for rail and bus, shipping and airports, see Headicar, 2009) and, instead, focuses on the car, because it is the most pervasive personal technology producing environmental and social consequences that cannot be overestimated.

Pollution and other health impacts

The consequences of pollution from transport are seen in the damage to human health and the natural environment (see Chapter Eight, this volume). The environmental impact of the production and destruction of cars can be summarised under five headings (see below).

Summary box

- The use of natural resources – metals, rubber, oil and water
- Energy used in vehicle manufacture
- Waste products from the manufacturing process
- The transport of materials for car production
- The scrappage of vehicles

Source: Cleaner Vehicles Task Force (2000: 2)

Eighty to ninety per cent of a car's lifetime energy consumption occurs when it is in use. Road traffic is a major cause of poor air quality and certain urban areas that are heavily trafficked have very high concentrations. The UK government's Air Quality Expert Group estimated that poor air quality reduces life expectancy by an average of seven to eight months (AQEG, 2007: 7). There is an especial risk from particulates – the tiny particles often known as PM10s – which inflame the lungs and can cause debilitating symptoms for those with heart and lung conditions, coronary heart disease and lung cancer. The last official estimate was that these particulates were responsible in the UK for up to 24,000 premature deaths. Children are especially susceptible to traffic fumes as their lungs are immature, and children living close to busy roads are more likely to suffer from respiratory conditions (WHO, 2004a). There is also some evidence that cancers are more prevalent in children who live close to a major source of pollution such as a bus or a petrol station. To their credit, car manufacturers have made successful efforts to reduce the pollution from their vehicles. The problem is that the reduction in pollution from each vehicle is outweighed by the increasing numbers of cars on the roads. Transport-related noise pollution is also a growing problem. As the Royal Commission on Environmental Pollution report on transport remarked, 'For the majority of people in the UK, transport is the most pervasive source of noise in the environment' (Royal Commission on Environmental Pollution, 1994: 46). The impact of transport-related noise on health is seen in raised blood pressure and sleep disturbance. Nor is this purely an urban phenomenon: mass car ownership has meant that increased traffic noise is a rural problem spoiling the ambience of the countryside (Taylor et al, 2008):

> Fifty-five per cent of those living in urban areas with more than 250,000 inhabitants in the EU–27 – almost 67 million people – endure daily road noise levels above the lower EU benchmark … for excess exposure. (EEA, 2009b: 22)

Exposure of children to both high aircraft noise and road traffic noise has also been shown to result in cognitive impairment.

The environmental damage from automobility is extensive and multifaceted. Roads demand space and this has led to the destruction of thousands of hectares of countryside. In 1989 the Conservative government announced the 'biggest road building programme since the Romans', to quote the then Transport Secretary, but by the mid–1990s this was curtailed because of widespread opposition from environmental campaigners in league with traditional Tory voters in the shires. The Labour government restored many of the axed road schemes so that after 10 years of New

Labour, the road building programme was at a higher level than in the late 1990s. Studies revealed that new road schemes actually generate more traffic as distances become shorter and quicker (Matson et al, 2006). The before-and-after pictures of beautiful landscapes fractured by major highways are shocking. The damage to urban areas from major road schemes is less remarked on but nonetheless real. The noise, air pollution and community severance generated by these roads is a high price that has to be paid by the local environment and the community. That price is not only direct but also indirect, in that a less attractive physical environment can contribute to stress, alienation and other factors that carry adverse consequences for health, social interaction and the general quality of life.

Transport can make us healthier or it can exacerbate unhealthy habits. Active travel – walking or cycling – has the potential to increase physical fitness while too much sedentary travel can be harmful for the body (Mindell et al, 2010). The UK has the highest level of obesity in the European Union (EU) and the changing nature of the way we travel has played some part in this. With the decline of physically active modes of walking and cycling the sedentary mode of car driving has become the norm for adults. Furthermore, the decline in public transport use has contributed to these sedentary habits since almost all public transport journeys involve some walking (and therefore exercise). Extensive car use is only one part of a modern trend to make life more convenient that has involved a reduction in physical activity. Davis et al (2007: 3) point out that:

> Main car drivers walk only half the distance and for half the time of adults in non-car owning households. This equates to a deficit of 56 minutes of walking every week for those drivers relative to adults in non-car households and over a decade this could lead to a weight gain of more than 2 stones.

Motorisation has created many 'obesogenic environments', that is to say, areas where it is difficult to walk or cycle or too dangerous to do so and where little physical energy needs to be expended. Generally these obesogenic environments will be built around access by car on the presupposition that everyone will have such access. Increasing physical activity is now one of the priorities of the Department of Health as the decline of physical activity has been identified as one of the individual risk factors that can lead to the onset of chronic disease.

The carless

Among adults there tend to be three groups of non-drivers: those who cannot pass the driving test because of a disability, those who cannot afford to run a car and those who choose not to drive a car. Being unable to drive does not preclude a person enjoying the benefits of the car, for they may be able to rely on family or friends to drive them. Disadvantage occurs when people do not have access to a car. In a sense they are second-class citizens and this captures the often restricted lives of carless people in an economy and society built around the presupposition that all adults have cars (Paterson, 2008).

Children

Children's lives have been circumscribed by the car. The prohibitions which parents issue to their children on not playing in the street, not crossing the road without an adult and so forth are born of fear, the fear of a road crash involving their child. This is justified as road crashes are the major cause of death and serious injury for children, with car accidents accounting for nearly half of all accidental injury fatalities in children (Towner and Dodswell, 2001, cited in Millward et al, 2003: 2.3.1). Yet the consequences for children's health are also serious. The Department of Health's current recommendation is that children should engage in an hour of physical activity a day, yet 30% of boys and 40% of girls in the UK are not achieving this (Mackett, 2001). Play is a natural way for children to be physically active and the obvious place for them to play is in their immediate neighbourhood but heavy and speeding traffic has led to more and more children leading an indoors childhood. Often this is not playing with other children but time spent in front of a screen, be that a games machine, a computer or a television. On average a British child today will spend five hours a day in front of a screen. According to the *National Travel Survey* 2005 only 15% of children aged 5 to 15 played outside on the street (DfT, 2006). Because of our car-saturated environments, children have lost independence: play is independent activity, what children choose to do when they are not being told what to do by an adult. There is far less play by children outside their homes than 40 or 50 years ago. Children's independent mobility has also suffered, that is, those journeys which children make of their own volition whether on foot or by bicycle. This is a particular loss for children after the age of 11 when they would want to be independently mobile. So we have the paradox of over 80% of children owning bicycles but very few of these being used for transport (Gill, 2005: 12). Worse, in comparison with earlier generations, children tend to have more sophisticated bicycles but use them a lot less. For children walking and cycling should be important forms of exercise.

The *National Travel Survey* reveals that during the 1990s the average distance walked by children declined by 20% (ONS, 2005: 1). There has been a 40% decline in the distance cycled by boys under 16 and over 50% for girls (Gill, 2005: 4). The growth in childhood obesity is not a direct result of this decline in physical activity, but it is related. In 2007, 17% of boys and 16% of girls aged 2 to 15 were obese (NHS Health and Social Care Information Centre, 2009).

Children have been the major losers in the last 50 years as cars have come to dominate public spaces. This is not an inevitable outcome as some other European countries, notably the Netherlands, Germany and the Nordic countries, have demonstrated that urban areas can be traffic calmed and pedestrianised so that children regain the freedom to play on the streets.

Autodisability

Currently each year almost 1.3 million people die on the world's roads. Over 90% of these deaths occur in low- and middle-income countries although they have only 48% of the world's vehicles (WHO, 2009b). In the European Union (EU) more than 50,000 people a year are killed on the roads and more than 150,000 are disabled for life (WHO, 2004b: 50). In the UK, road crashes are the leading cause of disability for those under 40 years of age.

By 2030 WHO predicts that deaths from car crashes will be the fifth leading cause of death worldwide (WHO/UNICEF, 2008: 31). This is because poor countries are now being motorised in the same way that rich societies were in the first half of the 20th century. The car asserts its dominance by killing and injuring those who use other forms of transport. In the early 1930s, in the UK annual deaths from road crashes were running at over 8,000 a year with a car population of only 2.5 million (Dean, 1947). By way of contrast, in 2007 there were just over 2,500 deaths with a car population of around 28 million (Milmo, 2009). Between ages 5 and 35 a large – often the largest – cause of death is transport related, most commonly road traffic accidents (Shaw et al, 2008: xiii; see also Monbiot, 2007b).

Road deaths make car driving a dangerous form of travel, not only for the motorists but also for other road users, particularly children. Since the car became the hegemonic form of transport, speed has been a problem. For pedestrians the road environment is particularly hazardous for those with a disability as Freund has remarked, the organisation of space-time 'favours the quick and the spry and disables those who are not' (Freund, 2001: 697). The most vulnerable are those from the lower social classes who are five times more likely to be killed by a car than children from social class I. It is only comparatively recently that there has been an acknowledgement that death rates from roads are far too high. Leading the way in rethinking has been Sweden, which has adopted Vision Zero, with the objective of ensuring that by 2020 there will be no road deaths or serious injuries at all in that country. It assumes a holistic approach where responsibility for a road crash is seen as lying with a broad range of people and structures, those who designed the road as well as the driver (Whitelegg and Haq, 2006)

Medical advances mean that some road crashes which, in the past, would have resulted in death now enable the victim to survive, but this can mean that they are severely disabled and hence require considerable care from health services and from their family. Some road crashes can result in brain injury where the person's body survives but their personality has changed, which can obviously be difficult for their loved ones having to get to know and to care for a changed person – see the website of Headway, the brain injury association, at www.headway.org.uk. Traumatic brain injury is the most frequent form resulting from road crashes (WHO, 2002).

Social exclusion

Those adults who do not drive are denied access to a range of facilities that have been created to be convenient for the car driver. The difficulties are compounded by the assumption of planners that most people have access to a car so that often facilities – shops, doctors' surgeries, hospitals, post offices – are accessible by car but difficult or impossible to reach without one. This can mean that non-drivers have a reduced quality of life compared with drivers. In the UK if one does not possess a driving licence then, outside urban areas with good public transport, social life and employment can be quite difficult. The Social Exclusion Unit found that for people living in deprived areas there was a clear association between the ability to drive and the chances of finding work (SEU, 2003). Sixty per cent of people with disabilities in the UK did not have household car access in 2002, while for people who were wheelchair users this figure increased to 62% and for those with a visual impairment the figure was 88% (DPTAC, 2002; Campion et al, 2003).

In the UK, two thirds of people with disabilities are elderly and in a car-dependent society they are at an obvious disadvantage if increasing infirmity and the onset of disability has meant they have had to stop driving. Given that a great deal of housing has been built on the assumption that residents will be car owners, older people without a car can find themselves isolated if they are not within walking distance of a decent bus service. If unable to walk to the bus stop then, for some older people, taxis may be the only way to get the shopping or reach the doctor's surgery (see Cahill, 2010).

Sustainable transport

The most environmentally benign forms of transport are walking and cycling and it has been official government policy since 1997 that these are to be given priority by local transport planners (Shaw and Docherty, 2008). In practice this has not happened and the reasons why this should have been the case illustrates the difficulty of moving from a car-dependent society to a sustainable transport system. Walking and cycling have been in decline for several decades and despite the growing evidence on the health benefits from both modes it is proving difficult to arrest this trend. Fear of traffic is a major reason why more people do not cycle and why parents are reluctant to allow their children to cycle any distance. Congested roads do not make for a pleasant experience when cycling. There is no inevitability about this as the Netherlands, Germany and Nordic countries have shown it is possible to increase cycling rates without lowering speed limits too severely, for example, 20mph as the default speed in urban areas, traffic calming and segregated cycle ways. The modal share of cycling trips, of all trips, is 27% in the Netherlands and 18% in Denmark (European Conference of Ministers of Transport, 2004: 9). Most car journeys are under five miles in the UK, making them ideal for cycling if roads were safer and slower. The health benefits of regular cycling are considerable when set against the sedentary form of car driving.

Walking, like cycling, is an excellent form of aerobic exercise and is useful for journeys under two miles. Walking, however, does require safe infrastructure and in many towns and cities this is no longer the case given the widespread incursions of cars onto pavements; broken paving stones, cracked pavements and parked cars all present hazards, particularly for those who are frail or have difficulty walking for whatever reason. Falls are a major cause of accidents among older people, a leading cause of disability in people aged 65 plus and a major reason for the deaths of people who are over the age of 75 (Millward et al, 2003: 31).

UK government and EU transport policy

Summary box

UK transport policy time chart

1989	Roads for Prosperity programme launched. High point of 'predict and provide' strategy
1992	Fuel duty escalator introduced designed to increase fuel duties by 5% a year above inflation. First big direct action protest against road building at Twyford Down, near Winchester
1993	Policy Planning Guidance 13 issued to local authorities recommends an end to planning permission for out-of-town shopping centres and other traffic-generating developments
1994	Royal Commission on Environmental Pollution report on transport says that policy must change
1994	Report of government expert committee – Standing Advisory Committee on Trunk Road Assessment (SACTRA) – concludes that road building generates traffic
1996	Transport Green Paper announces end of 'predict and provide' in road building. National Cycling Strategy launched with a target to quadruple cycling by 2010
1997	New Labour government merges Department of the Environment and Department of Transport
1998	Publication of *A New Deal for transport*, which announces government's integrated transport policy, including local transport plans, Bus Quality Partnerships, Strategic Rail Authority, maximum half-price fares for older people
2000	Publication of Ten-year Transport Plan
2000	Transport Act gives permissive powers to local authorities to introduce road-charging schemes
2003	London congestion charge introduced
2003	Aviation White Paper predicts major growth in UK air travel
2004	*The future of transport* White Paper announces no national road pricing measures until at least 2014
2007	National free bus travel for over-60s and people with disabilities introduced
2008	Climate Change Act commits UK to 80% reduction in carbon emissions by 2050
2009	Department for Transport publishes *Low carbon transport: A greener future*
2010	Department of Health and Department for Transport publish *Active Travel Strategy* to promote walking and cycling

For decades governments in the UK have pursued a transport policy that sees good transport links as vital to a successful modern economy. The policy of estimating transport demand and future growth and then building the roads to meet this demand was dubbed 'predict and provide'. By the 1990s it was becoming obvious that this was not going to cope with the problem of congestion without incurring unacceptable social and environmental damage. The Labour government elected in 1997 produced a major White Paper, *A New Deal for transport* (DfT, 1998). This was a programme for sustainable transport making the connections between the economic, environmental and social implications of the transport system.

John Prescott MP, then Secretary of State for Environment and Transport, made this pledge in June 1997: 'I will have failed if in five years' time there are not many more people using public transport and far fewer journeys by car. It's a tall order, but I urge you to hold me to it …' (quoted in Shaw and Docherty, 2008: 9-10). Five years later the number of car journeys was still increasing and 10 years after New Labour came to power the car population of the UK had increased by six million while the government had restored many of the road building schemes that had been abandoned by the previous Conservative government. Between 1994 and 2009 road traffic increased by nearly 25% (Vidal, 2009). There are various explanations as to why this U-turn on transport policy should have occurred (Cahill, 2007). Some would argue that the Labour government, despite its good intentions, did not realise the power of the car lobby; not just motor manufacturers and lobbyists, but millions of motorists, members of the AA or RAC, who baulk at the idea of not being able to use their car as much as they do now. The government was alerted to how powerful this lobby can be in the autumn of 2000 when the fuel protests led to a Conservative lead in the opinion polls for the first time in the life of the Blair government. Whatever the reasons for the change of heart, the fact remains that since 2000 the Labour government sought to reassure motorists and sanctioned a programme of road building. The strength of public opinion on this issue was revealed in 2007 when a petition on the Number 10 website against a national road pricing scheme attracted over 1.8 million signatures. In modern political life, public opinion is endlessly monitored by governments and political parties, and this would apparently show that voters do not mind greatly if politicians break their environmental promises. It is argued that the public are not consistent in their environmental attitudes so that when asked by pollsters they will agree to a proposition such as 'For the sake of the environment we should all drive less, walk and cycle more' but when it comes down to their own behaviour few people are prepared to change. Is this a manifestation of insincerity on the part of the electorate?

Certainly, some of the reported views of the public give environmentalists food for thought. For example, in 2004 the Energy Saving Trust reported that 85% of UK residents believed the effects of climate change would not be seen for decades (Lorenzoni et al, 2007). Stradling et al (2008: 148-9) found that fully 23% of drivers agreed with the statement that 'People should be allowed to use their cars as much as they like, even if it causes damage to the environment'. The same survey also found that only 21% of respondents supported the idea of motorists paying higher taxes for the sake of the environment. There has been a great deal of effort directed to informing public opinion about the benefits to human health and the environment of reducing car use, which makes these figures disappointing. From the late 1990s there was a growing consensus that road building would not be the answer to the increasing car population and that there should be some management of the demand for more road space. There are various forms of demand management. The London congestion charge, a fixed charge levied on all vehicles entering central London, is the best known and the powers were there for other local authorities to introduce a similar measure using the Transport Act 2000. Using the same Act local councils can levy a tax on employers who provide free parking for their staff, giving them the option to pass on the charge or to absorb it. Until now only Nottingham City Council has seriously considered this, where the levy would provide some of the funding for an extension to the city's

Figure 10.1: Greater Manchester Transport Referendum

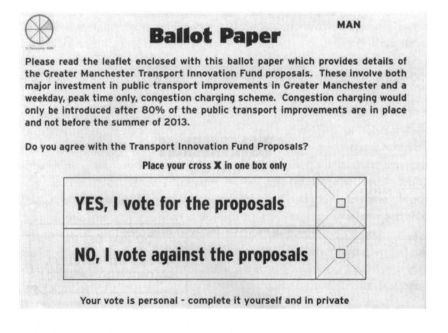

tram service (Chapman, 2009). The technology exists for a national road pricing scheme which would allow charges to be made for driving on certain routes at certain times of the day. Yet there is considerable reserve on the part of government to the implementation of such a scheme, and the Labour government gave repeated assurances that its arrival was some years away. The London congestion charge has been successful not only in reducing the amount of traffic entering central London – reducing congestion by 30% – but also in increasing cycling and bus use. Nonetheless at the end of 2008 Manchester residents rejected by a large majority the council's proposal for Greater Manchester to have a congestion charging scheme to be accompanied by a substantial increase in public transport, including an extension of the Manchester tram system. This vote highlights the difficulty for governments in seeking support for measures designed to improve public transport and to reduce congestion if they involve extra costs for motorists.

There is a tension in EU transport policy between the imperatives which flow from the creation of a single market – good road, rail and air links promoting economic development – and the desire of some, but not all, member states to reduce carbon emissions and move their populations away from car dependence. Another division is that between those countries which have their own car industry – principally France, Germany, Italy and the UK – and those which do not. One controversial result of EU policy was the Renewable Transport Fuel obligation introduced in 2008 that stipulated that by 2010 at least 5% of a fuel supplier's sales had to come from biofuels. The measure that was introduced in order to reduce carbon emissions has been a policy fiasco, however.

Biofuels such as ethanol were an apparently attractive alternative to fossil fuels because even though carbon would be needed for the production and distribution of the relevant crops, the savings in emissions once they were used as an alternative to fossil fuels would be significant. Looking ahead, they were seen as particularly attractive as greater use of biofuels would enable the car economy and society to continue its growth, while reducing carbon emissions. But biofuels have a dangerous downside, for as farmers saw the profits that could be made from them, many, particularly in the US, switched to production of biofuels and away from crops grown for food. This resulted in a significant increase in food prices worldwide and was also accompanied by a rise in oil prices, adding to food production costs. The production of biofuels in Brazil and Indonesia often means using land that was once rainforest.

Climate change and transport

An analysis of the first 10 years of the Labour government's transport policy concluded that it exhibited 'pragmatic multimodalism', that is to say, more road building was pursued alongside extra spending on public transport and encouragement of walking and cycling (Docherty and Shaw, 2008). This might well be electorally acceptable but it fails to engage with the problem of climate change and raises questions as to the ability of modern democracies to respond adequately to the challenge of low carbon lifestyles.

Because of the carbon emissions produced by motor vehicles it could be said that there is a direct link between climate change and individual travel behaviour. Indeed, personal car travel accounts for 29% of the average person's carbon emissions (Parkhurst, 2009). In the aggregate, government has been pushing for years for motorists to reduce their driving and backed various campaigns to reduce car use and increase walking, cycling and public transport. There is some evidence that these measures can influence people to change their travel behaviour and the UK government has backed a series of campaigns that go under the heading of 'smarter choices' (Sloman, 2006). The range of activities that come under this heading includes: car sharing, teleworking, teleconferencing, home shopping, school travel plans and public transport information and marketing (Cairns et al, 2004). But changing how we travel also extends to flying, and here the reduction of carbon emissions poses a series of challenges for governments and individuals.

Aviation

Airports have recently become the site of major environmental protests, just as new roads were in the 1990s. Airports have always found it hard to be good environmental neighbours as they generate excessive amounts of noise and pollution. Governments have seen air traffic as vital to the economic success of the country and operate with a 'predict and provide' approach to air demand, arguing that the UK has to make sure that the projected increase in air travel will be routed through UK airports. This sits uneasily, to say the least, with the UK government's commitment to reduce carbon emissions by 80% by 2050. If further controls are not placed on carbon emissions from aviation then by 2030 aviation will account for around 80% of the UK's carbon emissions (Bows and Anderson, 2007).

Carbon emissions from aircraft are over twice as damaging to the environment given that they are released at such high altitudes. There are those who argue that short haul flights should be prohibited in favour of rail because of the carbon cost.

In reality short flights have much higher emissions per km flown as a greater proportion of the emissions arise from the take off section of flight. (Jardine, 2009: 4)

This point is reinforced by Hillman and Fawcett (2004: 150):

Each kilometer covered by air within Europe accounts for around two and a half times the equivalent carbon dioxide emissions of the same distance by car (and around five times those by train).

There are major pressures pushing aviation towards becoming a mass transit system that would have huge environmental implications. The government's White Paper on aviation, published in 2003, forecast as many as 400 million people passing through UK airports by 2020 and 500 million by 2030 (DfT, 2003).

The deregulation of airlines gave the opportunity for the growth of low-cost carriers in Europe and the US that has led to an increased demand for flights. There is a belief that this expansion of airlines and proliferation of flights has attracted a significant new source of passengers, that is, those people on modest incomes. The available data on use of airlines does not bear this out, however. Survey evidence shows people from the top three social classes take on average more than four times as many flights in a year as those in the bottom three social classes (Bishop and Grayling, 2003: 64). The *National Travel Survey* reported that, in 2007, 25% of those in the lowest income households had made an international flight in the last 12 months, compared with 71% of those in the highest income households.

Peak oil and transport futures

In the 20th century oil was cheap, enabling the car to become a mass transport option with road freight replacing rail as the premier way to transport goods. This era of cheap oil is at an end. Peak oil – that point at which maximum production is reached – may be only a few years away (Leggett, 2005). The prospects for new oil supplies are limited as they include the exploitation of tar sands and deep oil drilling, which is not only extremely expensive but potentially harmful to the environment, as was demonstrated by the worst oil spill in US history in the Gulf of Mexico in April 2010. While the UK government believes that any peak in oil production is some decades away it is perhaps significant that two UK transport companies, Virgin and Stagecoach, were among a task force on peak oil that issued a report warning of an 'oil crunch' by 2013 (UK ITPOES, 2008).

Transport is extremely oil dependent so that any crisis in supply will have an immediate and severe impact. Hence the search for a fuel source which can replace oil. Electricity is the most favoured option, whether that is generated by renewables or by nuclear power. Yet there remain serious doubts as to whether sufficient generating capacity would be possible to fuel the present rate of mobility and transport. In the second half of the 20th century, in common with other rich countries, the UK saw its population travel further each year and make more journeys. A sustainable transport policy would need to pay attention not only to how we travel but *where* we travel. This means that high-density living would have to become the preferred form of settlement, in contrast to the post-1945 suburbanisation of the UK that saw a movement from the cities to the suburbs. This is a tall order but the exigencies of carbon emissions reduction could make it appear more attractive, indeed imperative. For distances less than two miles, walking and cycling are feasible options and will provide much needed physical activity.

The Labour government's decision to commit the country to an 80% cut in carbon emissions by 2050 sets the context for thinking about transport futures. There are many possible scenarios (see Dennis and Urry, 2009) and one crucial decision will be whether we continue with a car system or opt for a post-car society. If cars are to survive as a mass mode of transport they will need to be powered by hydrogen, electricity or biofuels. A post-car – or sustainable transport – future would be one in which there had been a switch from mass car use to walking, cycling and public transport. To support this, high-density living would become the norm and distances between home and work and home and shopping would be greatly reduced. Both scenarios are beset with difficulties. The UK has built substantial areas of low-density housing premised on the assumption of mass car ownership and it will take some considerable time before this can be replaced. At present, densities in many areas are too low to support bus services and it would take a national emergency, for example, a severe reduction in petrol supplies with a consequent price rise before many people would use – or more accurately, be forced to use – the buses.

Conclusion

Whatever the form that personal transport takes in the future the state will need to devise ways to achieve a fair and equitable transition to a low carbon economy. Carbon credits allocated every year to each person are an attractive option (see Chapter Three, this volume). Those who needed more than their allowance – because they drive or fly a lot – would be able to purchase them from people who did not use all their credits. The latter would tend to be people on low incomes so that there would be an element of redistribution built into the scheme (Prescott, 2008). How we travel in the 21st century will be determined by environmental considerations and there will be a continuing need to ensure that social inequalities are not exacerbated by the transport system.

Chapter summary

This chapter has explored how:

- the car has transformed economy, space, society and social relations;
- transport pollution is a significant health hazard and carbon emissions from transport are a major environmental problem;
- opportunities to participate in the economy and society are restricted for those without access to a car;
- road deaths and injuries remain a serious health problem while walking and cycling offer the physical exercise which a sedentary lifestyle lacks;
- the growth of aviation poses major environmental problem for governments;
- peak oil and climate change will produce difficult decisions for transport policy.

Questions for discussion

- Why has car ownership and use become so common?
- Why have walking and cycling declined as transport modes?
- Is Vision Zero a realistic policy goal for the UK?
- Are personal carbon allowances the best and fairest way to reduce carbon emissions from transport?

Key further reading

Cahill, M. (2010) *Transport, environment and society*, Maidenhead: Open University Press.

Dennis, K. and Urry, J. (2009) *After the car*, Cambridge: Polity Press.

Headicar, P. (2009) *Transport planning and policy in Great Britain*, London: Routledge.

Mindell, J., Watkins, S. and Cohen, J. (eds) (2010) *Health on the move 2: Policies for healthy transport*, Stockport: Transport and Health Study Group.

Urry, J. (2008) *Mobilities*, Cambridge: Polity Press.

Useful websites

ACT Travelwise: www.acttravelwise.org/

Campaign for Better Transport: www.bettertransport.org.uk/

Carfree UK: www.carfree.org.uk/

Carbon Limited: http://carbonlimited.org

Department for Transport: www.dft.gov.uk/

Living Streets: www.livingstreets.org.uk/

RoadPeace: www.roadpeace.org/

eleven

Green jobs

Nikolay Angelov and Maria Vredin Johansson

Overview

This chapter examines 'green jobs' and the relationship between environmental policies and employment. We critically study this subject from three different angles:

- *Structural change:* we find that the net impact of environmental policies on employment is either zero or slightly positive and we indicate that green jobs have a fairly polarised skills profile, that is, they can be either low skilled and low paid or high skilled and high paid.
- *Policy issues:* we emphasise the importance of being able to classify studies correctly before drawing policy conclusions regarding the prospects for green jobs.
- *The future:* we examine some of the available forecasts on the future number of green jobs and discuss the difficulties involved in making long-term forecasts.

In the final section we round off the analysis and discuss future directions for research.

All over the world, endowments of natural resources shape the size and structure of national economies. Saudi Arabia's economy is, for instance, petroleum-based, whereas the Maldives' is tourism-based. Economic activities, on the other hand, affect the environment through the use of natural resources, emission of pollution and generation of waste. The existence of a strong and reciprocal link between the economy and the environment means that millions of people, directly or indirectly, depend on the environment for their livelihoods.

Defining green jobs

There is no universal definition of what constitutes a green, or an environmental, job. The literature offers several definitions (OECD/ Eurostat, 1999; Bezdek et al, 2008; UNEP, 2008). Many of these are relative rather than absolute (OECD, 1997). Bezdek et al (2008), for example, define green jobs as *all jobs that are performed more pro-environmentally today than before*. Their definition consequently encompasses a continuum of industries and jobs which all, due to environmental policies, aim at minimising the environmental impact of products, processes and services. A more pragmatic definition could originate in a definition of the 'environmental' sectors of the economy. Yet because many different industrial activities are engaged in producing green goods and services, identification of the environmental sectors is not straightforward. Finding an all-purpose definition of green jobs with clear boundaries is difficult. Instead, the definition employed needs to be appropriate for the specific context in which it is used. Green jobs simply come in different shades, meaning that some jobs generate greater environmental benefits than others.

The Organisation for Economic Co-operation and Development (OECD) and Eurostat have agreed on a definition of the environment industry and give recommendations for data collection so that comprehensive and comparable data can be produced (OECD/Eurostat, 1999). According to their definition, the environmental goods and services industry:

> ... consists of activities which produce goods and services to measure, prevent, limit, minimise or correct environmental damage to water, air and soil, as well as problems related to waste, noise and eco-systems. (OECD/Eurostat, 1999: 9)

The classification of environmental goods and services is done in three levels where the highest level distinguishes between three main groups of activities: pollution management, cleaner technologies and products, and resource management.

Pollution management consists of products and services that have a clear environmental purpose, for example, activities that significantly reduce pollution (OECD/Eurostat, 1999). Cleaner technologies, or 'clean tech', are defined as technologies with three main characteristics (Goodstein, 1996). They provide goods and services:

- of comparable quality to existing technologies;
- at a cost that is comparable to existing technologies;
- in a more environmentally benign fashion than existing technologies.

Resource management activities are products and services that may have an environmental purpose, although their main aim, for example, energy efficiency measures, is not necessarily environmental protection (OECD/ Eurostat, 1999).

The OECD/Eurostat's definition has clear statistical boundaries but does not include all jobs for which the environment is an essential input into the production process, for example, agriculture and traditional tourism (GHK Consulting, 2007). The United Nations Environment Programme (UNEP) (2008: 3), on the other hand, defines green jobs as:

> ... work in agricultural, manufacturing, research and development [R&D], administrative, and service activities that contribute substantially to preserving or restoring environmental quality. Specifically, but not exclusively, this includes jobs that help to protect ecosystems and biodiversity; reduce energy, materials, and water consumption through high-efficiency strategies; de-carbonize the economy; and minimize or altogether avoid generation of all forms of waste and pollution.

The UNEP's definition is more specific than the OECD/Eurostat one, since it also focuses on industries and jobs that aim at mitigating a specific environmental problem, like de-carbonising the economy.

Depending on the operational definition of green jobs, the share of green employment to total employment can vary. If green jobs are defined as jobs in the 'environmental-related activities' of the economy, three forms of economic activities are included: (i) activities where the environment is a resource input (for example, mining and fishing); (ii) activities related to the management of the environment (for example, waste and water management); and (iii) activities that are dependent on environmental quality (for example, tourism and recreation) (GHK Consulting, 2007). Using this typology and a rather narrow definition of the activities included, GHK Consulting (2007) estimates the total green employment[1] in the European Union (EU) member countries. Employing their figures and a measure of the total employment from the European Commission (2007), we calculate the share of green employment in relation to total employment (see *Figure 11.1*). The largest share of green employment, exceeding 7%,

Figure 11.1: *Green employment as percentage of total employment in EU countries, 2000*

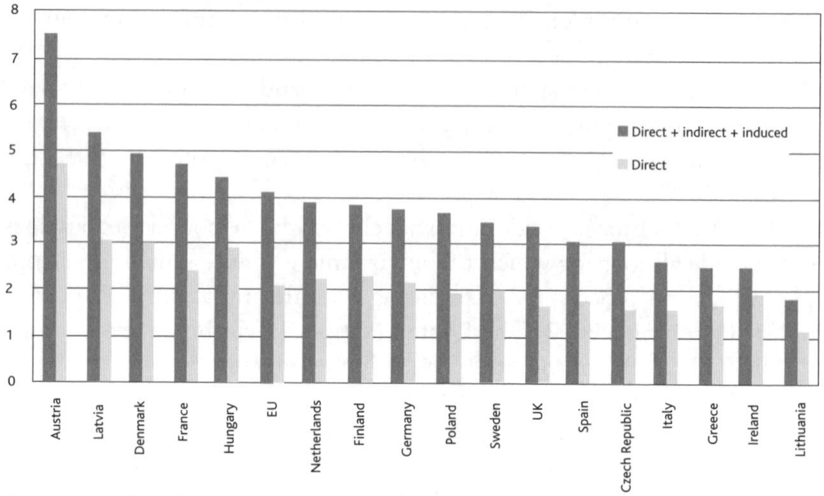

Sources: GHK (2007); European Commission (2007)

can be found in Austria, whereas the smallest share, less than 2%, can be found in Lithuania.

Structural change

Summary box

In addition to structural unemployment there are two other forms of unemployment:

- cyclical unemployment, which occurs at recessions, that is, when the gross domestic product (GDP) growth rate declines;
- frictional unemployment, that is, short-term transitional unemployment that results from people moving between jobs, careers and locations.

The last type of unemployment, which is the consequence of labour mobility and new entries to the labour market, is generally not considered to be a societal problem – at least not if it occurs at reasonable levels.

The question of whether environmental policies generate or eliminate jobs was first raised in the 1970s when environmental policies aimed at reducing emissions to water and air were introduced. In the US, the

Clean Air Act 1970 and the Clean Water Act 1972 induced changes in production technologies and investments in abatement technologies. In 1990 the Clean Air Act Amendment launched a US national programme in tradeable sulphur dioxide emission permits in the electricity sector. About the same time, in 1990 and 1991, Sweden introduced taxes on emissions of carbon dioxide and sulphur dioxide. Thus, a shift from regulatory to economic instruments in environmental policy occurred (see also Chapter Seven, this volume).

Economic instruments are incentive-based instruments that work through the price system, for example, emissions taxes, deposit–refund schemes, tradeable emission permits and subsidies. The main advantage of these instruments is that they, at least in theory, minimise the aggregate cost of achieving a given level of environmental protection. The literature on economic instruments and their efficiency is abundant; see Hanley et al (1997) and Stavins (2003) for overviews. In spite of the cost-minimising character of economic instruments, their choice also depends on, for instance, interest group pressures, political negotiations, considerations about administration and enforcement costs, distributional issues and the presence (or absence) of incentives for development and diffusion of better and cheaper emission control technologies. Thus, the choice of policy instrument depends both on the environmental problem addressed and the social, political and economic context in which the instrument is to be implemented. Other frequently employed environmental policy instruments are regulations, information and voluntary agreements.

Regulations are quantity-focused instruments, such as emission limits and specifications of the prescribed or prohibited technology. Regulations are preferable when the welfare loss from not attaining the environmental target is high, for example, when dealing with extremely hazardous substances. The main advantage of regulations is that they, at least in countries with high regulation enforcement compliance, achieve the environmental target. The associated cost may be very high, however. On the other hand, with economic instruments, the environmental target may not be achieved although the emissions are reduced at least cost.

For information campaigns to be a useful policy instrument there must, of course, be an information gap to alleviate. Currently, there is little available knowledge of the conditions of success for information. Comparative studies of different communication strategies are rare, and there does not seem to be any evidence available that compares the effects of communication to those of regulation and economic instruments (Hansson et al, 2010).

Presently, voluntary agreements are gaining interest as an environmental policy instrument. The term 'voluntary agreement' is commonly used to denote an agreement between the government and one or more private actors that involves a commitment by the private actor(s) to improve environmental performance beyond legal requirements. The agreement can relate to general issues, such as energy efficiency or reporting on emissions, but it can also relate to specific environmental targets. According to the European Commission (1996), voluntary agreements have several advantages: they can promote a pro-active attitude on the part of the industry, they can provide cost-effective solutions to environmental problems and they can allow for a faster and smoother achievement of environmental objectives. Many industries prefer voluntary agreements because they provide an opportunity to cope with environmental issues in a cheaper and more flexible way (Dijkstra, 1998). Still, very little is known about the efficiency of voluntary agreements (IPCC TAR, 2001). The major reason is that it cannot be ascertained what measures would have been taken in absence of the agreement.

All environmental policies, as well as changes therein, constitute a ground for *structural change*, that is, an alteration of the economy's fundamental structure, (ILO, 2009). For instance, changes in relative prices can lead to changes in both production and trade patterns. Even though structural change often brings necessary alterations of, for example, production technology, a drawback is the structural unemployment that may follow. Structural unemployment occurs when there is no demand for the type of workers that are available on the market.

Summary box

In general, structural change has three effects on employment within a country. Jobs will be:

- created
- substituted
- eliminated.

As an example, consider an increase in carbon taxes.

First, this might result in an increased demand for biofuels, creating new jobs in the forest industry, for instance in the refinement of forest raw materials into pellets or briquettes.

Second, if the demand for biofuels increases, the traditional use of forest raw material may be driven out of competition, implying that people in the traditional forest industry may switch to jobs in the new biofuel industry.

Third, if the increased demand for biofuels leads to a decrease in the demand for fossil fuels, jobs in the fossil fuel industry will be lost.

Note that a government subsidy to biofuels will result in the same end-effect, that is, jobs will be gained, substituted and eliminated. Using public funds to stimulate one sector of the economy means, at least in the long run, that funds must be taken from some other sector, implying that there can be no large net gain in employment. Furthermore, with a subsidy there are less public funds to compensate the victims of a policy change.

Although some regions, sectors and individuals may suffer seriously from structural change – at least in the short run – the long-run net employment effect appears to be zero or slightly positive (OECD, 1997; Lundmark and Söderholm, 2004; SOU, 2007: 36; GHK Consulting, 2007; ECORYS, 2008). Thus, on the aggregate level, environmental policies neither generate nor destroy employment opportunities. Instead, the European Commission (2005) argues that the biggest impact of environmental policies is on the *composition* of the labour market rather than on its *size*.

A common concern in this respect is the 'pollution haven effect' (Copeland and Taylor, 1994, 2004; Antweiler et al, 2001)[2] according to which pollution-intensive industries relocate from high-income countries to low-income countries when environmental policies are tightened in the high-income countries. The presumption is that low-income countries' low wages, lax environmental and occupational safety policies are decisive in the high-income countries' plant locations, while the increased financial resources and industrial development are pivotal for the low-income countries (ignoring additional pollution even if not fully internalised). According to the pollution haven effect, low-income countries provide pollution havens for dirty industries, and employment therefore relocates from high- to low-income countries whereby total world pollution is also increased. Until recently, there was empirical consensus that differences in environmental policy intensities had little or no effect on plant locations (Jaffe et al, 1995). Even though several studies (Lucas et al, 1992; Birdsall and Wheeler, 1993; Mani and Wheeler, 1998) have found evidence in support of the pollution haven effect, these studies often suffer from the difficulty of isolating the environmental regulations' effects from *other* effects – for example, of factor endowments and differences in technology – on plant location (Copeland and Taylor, 2004). However, support for the pollution haven effect has been found in the US (Becker and Henderson, 2000; Greenstone, 2002; Keller and Levinson, 2002; List et al, 2003).

Although not confirmed on a global scale, stricter environmental policies seem to encourage plant relocations, and therefore employment transfer, from countries with stringent environmental policies to countries with laxer environmental policies. If lax environmental policy is positively correlated with lax occupational safety regulations, stricter environmental policy in wealthy countries may generate more indecent jobs in less prosperous countries. Therefore, when considering the environmental sector's potential for job growth, not only the *number* of green jobs should be of interest but also the *quality* of the jobs generated.

The 'decency' of green jobs

At present, far more is known about the numbers of jobs than about their quality (Renner et al, 2008). But, of course, jobs in the environmental sector of the economy should be no less 'decent' than jobs in other sectors of the economy, meaning that green jobs should satisfy national and international demands on acceptable wages, working conditions and worker rights.

Green jobs can encompass a wide array of skills, educational backgrounds and occupational characteristics. However, not all green jobs are 'decent'. There are, in fact, several types of green jobs that are dirty and dangerous – especially in the developing countries of the world. Jobs in sugarcane and palm oil plantations, for example, do not in general entail decent working conditions (Amre et al, 1999; Down to Earth, 2004; Friends of the Earth et al, 2008). Recycling and waste picking can also involve undesirable and unhealthy jobs (Medina, 2005; Cointreau, 2006).

A French study cited in OECD (1997) shows that jobs in the environmental sector are not, in general, very advanced. Because most employment can be found in the waste collection, disposal and recycling businesses, as well as in the operation of pollution abatement equipment, more than a third of the jobs are, in fact, low skilled and low paid. As a consequence of technical progress, jobs in the clean tech industries are naturally often more high skilled and high paid (World Bank, 2008).

A later OECD (2004) report compiles data on environment-related employment collected partly through surveys and partly from other sources, such as Eurostat, the European Commission, individual consultants and research institutes. Even if the information is not completely comparable over the different countries, some findings show that the highest share of foreign workers is found in waste management and that the share of female employees is smaller in the environmental sector than in other sectors of the economy.

When the largest impact of environmental policies is on the *composition* of the labour market, not on its *size*, it is somewhat alarming that there is so little known about the skills profile of green jobs in general (European Commission, 2005). It is important to know what types of jobs are being lost or created in order to determine what sort of retraining one would need to assure that jobs remain in the region.

Issues for policy: methods and models

Analysing the connection between environmental policies and employment requires choosing a particular methodology. In this chapter, we discuss methods and models used in the current literature, and point out some of the problems associated with them. Towards the end of the chapter we summarise how and why future research needs to address those problems in order to improve decision making.

Causal versus descriptive analysis

There are two broad approaches to the analysis of green jobs:

* descriptive analyses of green sectors;
* causal analyses of the effects of environmental policies on the number and quality of created jobs.

A further distinction can be made by considering micro (individual-level) or macro effects/differences. It might also be useful to distinguish between gross effects, for example, the effect of environmental policies on the number of green jobs in the economy, and net effects, for example, the effect of environmental policies on the number of green jobs in the economy minus the effect of environmental policies on the number of jobs in other sectors.

The importance of identifying causal effects of environmental policies on economic variables cannot be overstated. To cite a recent example, the Ministry of Environmental Protection in China announced that the country is planning to more than double its spending on environmental protection, reaching US$454 billion between 2011 and 2015.[3] Needless to say, decision makers spending large amounts of money on environmental policies are interested in the effects these policies have on economic variables like employment and economic growth, even if the main purpose of environmental spending is to protect the environment.

The identification of causal effects of environmental policies on various economic variables has very important policy implications. To see this, first consider the extreme case where a certain environmental effect is needed so desperately that an environmental measure has to be performed irrespective of its direct economic effects. If there is only one way of achieving the environmental goal, economic effects are of subordinate importance and would not affect policy choice. Then consider the more realistic case where there are several different policy options of achieving the same environmental goal, but where the options differ in their effects on economic variables. For instance, a reduction in carbon dioxide emissions can be achieved either through a carbon tax or through emissions trading. Clearly, rational decision makers should choose the policy that is most favourable for the economic variables.

Green jobs can also be analysed in a descriptive setting. Notwithstanding the merits of causal analysis, many causal questions are very difficult to answer. In such circumstances, descriptive analysis is important since it creates hypotheses and suggestive evidence of potential effects. These hypotheses can then be more thoroughly studied and tested in order to improve the policy. Compared to causal analysis, description requires far fewer modelling assumptions, while data requirements are roughly the same. Descriptive analysis could, for instance, include the following:

- changes over time in the number of jobs in the green sector;
- the level of education of people employed in the green sector, as compared to other sectors of the economy;
- changes over time in the risk of unemployment among people employed in the green sector, compared to the same individuals when they were employed in other sectors;
- differences in the share of part-time workers and so on.

Descriptive analysis gives answers to different types of questions than causal analysis, although both can have clear policy implications.

Consider, for instance, the following two questions:

A What is the effect of a specific environmental policy on part-time employment?
B What is the share of part-time employees in the growing environmental sectors?

Question A is about a causal relation, whereas B is of a descriptive nature. Given sufficient data, question B can be answered relatively easily. Retrieving causal relations from non-experimental data is much more difficult, especially at the macro level (see below).

An interesting question is the following. Provided one has the correct answers to questions A and B above, what is their respective importance for policy analysis? The short answer is that *policy evaluation* requires causal studies while both causal and descriptive analyses can be used to draw conclusions about *policy implications.* This is best seen through an example. Assume that the effect in A is positive, that is, implementing the policy leads to an increase in the share of employees working part time. If full-time is preferred to part-time employment, this finding has clear policy implications. It could for instance lead to:

(1) a reduction in the likelihood of similar policies in the future; and/or
(2) an adjustment of labour legislation so that it better fits employees working part time.

Note that (1) cannot (or should not) follow from a purely descriptive analysis. On the other hand, (2) is possible as a consequence of descriptive analysis. To see why, suppose that a descriptive analysis of the green sector concludes that the share of part-time workers is higher than in traditional sectors. Regardless of the reason behind this difference, provided the share of green sectors in the economy is increasing, it might be a good idea to adjust labour legislation so that it better fits employees working part time.

This discussion highlights the importance of classifying empirical results before drawing policy conclusions. In the available literature on the effect of environmental policy on employment, few studies attempt to estimate causal effects from data; Berman and Bui (2001) and Greenstone (2002) are recent exceptions. Causal interpretation of results is nonetheless very popular. A typical approach is to perform policy evaluations within an economic model, rather than by estimating effects from data. One of the benefits is that not only the effect, but also the theoretical mechanisms causing the effect, can be specified and assessed (see below). An obvious drawback is the relative lack of empirical content; after all, the effect of a certain environmental policy is not based on actual data.

The next two sections discuss two different approaches currently used for policy evaluation.

Policy evaluation in the labour literature

When attempting to estimate the causal effect of a policy on an economic variable such as employment, the first step is to define the intervention and outcome variables. In the labour economics literature, the 'intervention variable' is usually denoted as 'treatment'. Although treatment can be broadly described as any intervention that changes incentives for the population of interest, labour economists have mostly focused on active labour market programmes. Below are some examples of programmes that are often targeted at specific groups (see Heckman et al, 1999):

- education, either vocational or general;
- wage subsidies consisting of payments to firms, either as a lump-sum per employee, or as a fraction of wages, for hiring new workers;
- temporary work experience or employment in the public sector; and
- job search assistance.

Empirical labour economists and econometricians have developed tools for analysing the effects of such programmes on economic outcome variables such as unemployment risk and duration, future income, and so on. Modern programme evaluation techniques provide tools for considering the following broad types of questions:

- evaluating the impact of historical interventions on outcomes;
- forecasting the effect of interventions implemented in one environment on outcomes in other environments; and
- forecasting the impacts of interventions never historically experienced on various environments.

Various evaluation techniques aimed at performing the above analyses are discussed in Heckman and Vytlacil (2007).

A central issue when evaluating programmes is how to construct counterfactual states. A counterfactual is a hypothetical, that is, not observed, state for an outcome variable relevant for the evaluation in question. A typical example is the following. Assume that a labour market training programme is targeted at long-term unemployed workers. The economic question of interest is to evaluate the causal effect of training on, say, unemployment duration. Typically, a researcher has access to a sample of individuals, some of whom have taken part in the training programme, while others have not. But to evaluate the effect of training on unemployment duration, one would ultimately need to compare the outcome variable of interest observed in the following two situations:

A: for individuals that have taken part in a training programme of interest, and
B: for the *same* individuals as in A that have *not* taken part in the training programme.

Either A or B is, of course, never observed and can therefore be referred to as the counterfactual. Much of the evaluation literature focuses on how to construct counterfactuals and, under various assumptions, to approximate the value of the outcome variable under the counterfactual state.

When evaluating the effect of environmental policies on economic variables such as the number of jobs in an economy, a researcher is faced with essentially the same type of considerations as the economist evaluating an active labour market programme: a counterfactual needs to be constructed (what can we say about the number of jobs in the economy should the policy not have been implemented?) and then the actual outcome needs to be compared with the estimated number of jobs under that counterfactual state.

Figure 11.2 provides an illustration. Assuming that a green policy is implemented at time 0 and the evaluation is made at time *t*, a readily available estimate of employment change is given by A+B in the figure. But to evaluate the effect of the policy, one would need an estimate of A alone. This is because in the counterfactual state (that is, assuming no intervention), employment changes with B. Estimating employment under the counterfactual, or in other words, estimating B, is therefore crucial for evaluation of the green policy.

Figure 11.2: Evaluating policy interventions

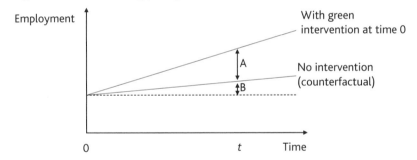

Attempts to provide direct estimates of causal effects of environmental policies on economic variables are not abundant in the literature. Berman and Bui (2001) study the effect of local air quality regulation on employment without finding any substantial effects. On the other hand, Greenstone (2002) uses variation in the implementation of the Clean Air Act over different countries to conclude that 590,000 jobs were lost in 'non-attainment' countries (those that were regulated to a greater extent), relative to attainment countries during the period 1972–87.

Policy evaluation in the literature on green jobs

With some exceptions, environmental policies are generally not primarily designed to affect economic variables such as unemployment, wages or working hours. Nevertheless, environmental policies often affect economic incentives, and thus, important economic variables. Consequently, researchers have tried to estimate these effects using various methods.

Generally, the green jobs literature has focused on the effect of environmental policy on macro variables such as employment and gross domestic product (GDP) growth (see also Jorgensen and Wilcoxen, 1990). But because it is difficult to estimate causal effects on macro variables using direct empirical methods, much of the available results rely on applications of economic theory rather than on direct empirical estimates. Typically, analyses of the effects of environmental policies on employment are performed by specifying an economic model, estimating parameters entering the model, and finally, changing a policy variable of interest within the model (for example, a tax) in order to estimate the policy effect of the change (for example, on the number of jobs in the economy). Parameters entering the model are estimated when the economy is in one state (without the tax) and the counterfactual state is when the economy is in another, unobserved state (when the tax is present). The main difference between this approach and the traditional policy evaluation discussed in the previous section is that the latter attempts to estimate the counterfactual *directly using empirical data*, while the former constructs and evaluates the counterfactual *within an economic model*.[4]

The main economic tools that are currently used to analyse the effect of environmental policies on employment are the following:[5]

(1) Supply and demand analysis of the affected sector
(2) Supply and demand analysis of multiple markets
(3) Fixed-price, general equilibrium simulations (input–output [I–O] and social accounting matrix [SAM] multiplier models)
(4) Non-linear, general equilibrium simulations (computable general equilibrium [CGE] models).

The various methods are useful in different situations. The first two partial-equilibrium methods are only useful when the effects of a policy are limited to a single sector or to just a few sectors. Consider for instance the economic impact of a ban on the toxic chemical tributyltin (TBT) in anti-fouling paint, used for painting the hull of a boat. TBT in anti-fouling paint was banned on all boats in Sweden in 1993 and on all boats entering European Union (EU) ports in 2008. A TBT ban could of course affect employment in the paint industry. Assuming that it implies higher prices, the economic effect could be estimated by using estimated supply and demand functions for the paint market (method 1 above). But a ban on TBT could also affect the whole shipping industry: if the new types of anti-fouling paint are less efficient against the growth of barnacles and weed on the hull, the maximum speed and fuel efficiency of ships would be reduced, resulting in lower profits. In this case there might be need to perform an analysis of the paint as well as the shipping industry (method 2 above).

An example of a partial-equilibrium approach is given in Morgenstern et al (2002), who look at four industries: pulp and paper mills, plastic manufacturers, petroleum refiners and iron and steel mills. The effect of regulation on employment is divided into three distinct components: factor shifts to more or less labour intensity; changes in total expenditures; and changes in the quantity of output demanded. Plant level data are used to estimate the key parameters describing factor shifts and changes in total expenditures. Aggregate time-series data are used to estimate the demand effect. The main finding is that environmental spending does not generally cause a significant change in industry-level employment; the estimated net gain is 1.5 jobs per US$1 million, with a standard error of 2.2 jobs. However, in the plastics and petroleum industries, there are small but significant positive effects: 6.9 and 2.2 jobs, respectively, per US$1 million in additional environmental expenses.

Although the TBT ban from the example above could have effects in more than one market, it is not likely to affect employment in the economy as a whole by a significant amount. But often, interest lies in examining the effects of environmental policies that can be expected to affect the whole economy. One such example is a carbon tax, whose economic impact clearly deserves a general-equilibrium approach. It is useful to make a distinction between linear I-O or SAM models on the one hand, and non-linear CGE models on the other. Both approaches imply setting up a model of the macro economy and, within the model, changing variables of interest and comparing different outcomes. The Appendix to this chapter provides a short description of these methods for the interested reader.

Examples of I-O models that provide assessments of employment effects of environmental policies are given in Scott et al (2008) and Wade et al (2000), where the latter also sets up a CGE model (see below). Both studies analyse the effect of energy efficiency regulation on employment and find substantial positive effects in the EU (Wade et al, 2000) as well as in the US (Scott et al, 2008).

Because I-O and SAM models rest on the assumption of exogenous prices, using them to study the effects of large, widespread policies such as carbon taxes can result in significant inaccuracy. For such situations, endogenously set relative prices are an essential part of any model. This feature is offered by a commonly used class of models called CGE models. A CGE is a multi-sector model of one or several national economies, used as a tool for analysis of resource allocation and income distribution issues, described in the Appendix to this chapter.[6]

Jorgenson and Wilcoxen (1990) study the relationship between pollution abatement costs and economic growth using a CGE model of the US economy. The costs of environmental regulation are quantified and compared with those of governmentally mandated activities financed directly through the government budget. The benefits resulting from a cleaner environment are not included in the analysis. The conclusion of the study is that environmental regulation reduces the growth of the gross national product (GNP) with on average 0.2% annually over the period 1973–85. In another study, Hazilla and Kopp (1990) estimate the effect of the Clean Air Act and the Clean Water Act on employment in the US and find substantial negative effects in most sectors of the economy.

A concern when using CGE models for evaluating employment effects is the assumption of full employment (Arnold, 1999; Morgenstern et al, 2002). In other words, the real-wage adjusts such that labour demand equals supply. As regulation is assumed to lead to real-wage decreases (due to lower labour or capital productivity), it also leads to lower employment because the relative price of leisure becomes lower. Therefore, environmental policies leading to real-wage decreases are likely to lead to a drop in employment. Note that this is not the notion of unemployment that the general public and politicians find important, namely involuntary, regulation-induced layoffs. In a standard CGE, unemployment is rather a question of individuals choosing to consume more leisure when the real-wage decreases. Some attempts have been made to provide a more realistic model of unemployment in CGEs. A recent study by Küster et al (2007) incorporates wage rigidities in the form of minimum wages for unskilled labour and wage curves for skilled labour as ways to model involuntary unemployment.[7]

The future

Summary box

According to the European Environment Agency *Glossary* (EEA, 2009a) the 'eco-industry' includes companies that provide:

- clean technologies;
- renewable energy;
- waste recycling, nature and landscape protection;
- ecological renovation of urban areas.

In the EU, the 'eco-industry' accounts for 1.7% of the total paid employment, corresponding to 3.4 million full-time equivalents (European Commission, 2007). The eco-industry, thus, employs more people than, for example, the European car industry (2.7 million full-time equivalents). In the US, ASES and MISI (2008) found that the renewable energy and energy efficiency industries created more than nine million jobs in 2007. That same year, the revenues from these industries exceeded the combined sales from the three largest US corporations: Wal-Mart, ExxonMobil and GM.

The core of the environmental sector's activities is the pursuit of cleaner technologies and products. Consequently, policies aiming at reducing the end-of-pipe impact of industries and human activities on the environment can be expected to create jobs in cleaning up, treating soil and water and controlling air pollution. In the long run, cleaner technologies will reduce the need for end-of-pipe and clean-up solutions. Logically, the stringency of environmental policies affects the number of *direct and indirect jobs* both immediately and over time.

The long-term effect of a cleaner environment and a more sparing use of resources, including energy, on economic growth, and hence on employment, is very difficult to assess. This illustrates the difficulties of making forecasts for the (net) number of jobs to which environmental policies give rise. In the long run, it might therefore be more useful to discuss different scenarios, rather than only providing point estimates of the number of jobs resulting from environmental policies.

Using scenarios where the share of renewable power in the total power generation mix increases over time, US Metro Economies (2008) estimates through extrapolation from existing data that, by 2038, approximately 4.2 million new green jobs can be generated in three sectors (renewable power generation, residential and commercial retrofitting, and renewable transportation fuels) of the US economy. This figure includes both direct jobs (two thirds) and indirect jobs (one third).

Roland-Holst (2008) uses a CGE model of the Californian economy to simulate the employment effect of existing and proposed policies to reduce the emissions of greenhouse gases (GHGs) by 30% below a business-as-usual scenario. Allowing for technological innovation, he estimates that more than 400,000 new jobs can be created in California by 2020. The main reason for the increase in employment is re-direction of money saved from energy efficiency measures.

ASES and MISI (2008) use I-O techniques (see the Appendix to this chapter) and three different scenarios (base case, moderate and advanced) to forecast the number of jobs in the renewable energy and energy efficiency industries to 2030. In the base case scenario (business-as-usual), the number of jobs increases by 80%, that is, from 9 million to 16.3 million. In the moderate scenario, the job increase is 117% (to 19.5 million jobs) and, in the advanced scenario, the increase is 314% (to 37.3 million jobs). Under all scenarios the employment effect is orders of magnitude larger in the energy efficiency industry than in the renewable energy industry.

The aforementioned studies are, by no means, a full account of all existing forecast studies – for an extensive compilation of European and US studies see GHK Consulting (2009). But, given the inherent difficulty in assessing environmental policies' effects on employment, it is not surprising that a wide range of numbers is found in the literature. A major problem with many of the forecasts for green jobs is that the analyses are not transparent and they often build on unclear assumptions and appear to be non-reproducible. For example, little is known about the foundations for the following employment projections made by, for example, China and South Korea. It is possible that these projections are exaggerated, due to their political impetus. Nevertheless, even after discounting for exaggerations due to wishful thinking, there seems to be a bright future for green jobs.

Employment and the 2008 financial crisis

As one example of this, consider the following (see also the Introduction, this volume).

In 2008 the world faced triple crises: financial, environmental and humanitarian. The financial crisis led to the worst economic recession since the Great Depression. Consequences on the global scale have been slumping, or negative, growth rates and increased unemployment. The reduced economic activity following the financial crisis has, on the other hand, somewhat eased the environmental crisis. Still, climate change and resource scarcities, such as shortages of food and fresh water, are urgent, aggravating the humanitarian crisis. As a solution to the triple crises, the United Nations (UN) proposed a Global Green New Deal (GGND) (UN-DESA, 2009). The GGND should be a counter-cyclical measure with three main objectives (UNEP, 2009): (1) to revive the world economy and create employment opportunities; (2) to reduce carbon dependency, ecosystem degradation and water scarcity; and (3) to support the Millennium Development Goals (MDGs) of eradicating extreme poverty and hunger by 2015.

In response to the financial crisis several countries, for example, the US, Japan, China, Australia and EU countries, launched recovery packages influenced by the GGND. In the US, for example, the recovery package amounts to US$787 billion (US Government, 2009). China's recovery plan consists of US$218 billion and South Korea's of US$38.1 billion (UNEP, 2009). The greenness of the stimulus packages varies across countries. In

South Korea the share of green measures is 79%, in the US 12% and in Italy only 1% (UNEP, 2009). There are also differences between the countries in terms of expenditures per capita. For example, South Korea spends more than US$1,200 per capita on green stimulus whereas the US spends less (US$365 per capita). Among EU countries, France's recovery package amounts to US$6.1 billion (18% green) and Germany's to US$105 billion (13% green). *Figure 11.3* gives the green stimulus as a percentage of the total stimulus as well as the green stimulus in US$ billions.

Figure 11.3: Green stimulus as a percentage of total economic stimulus, 2009

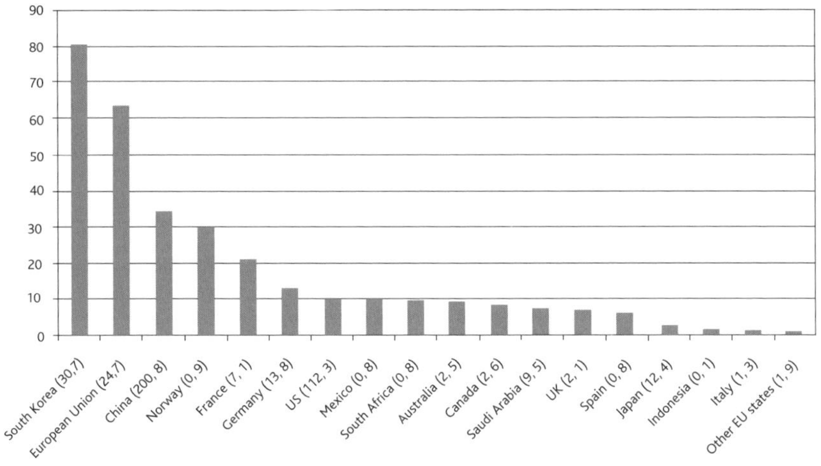

Source: HSBC (2009)

In China, every US$100 million stimulus to green investments is estimated to create 600 new jobs (UNEP, 2009). In South Korea, the national plan for green growth is expected to generate between 1.56 million and 1.81 million new jobs in green industries in the first five years (UNEP, 2009) and in the US the American Recovery and Reinvestment Act (ARRA) plus an Act on clean energy (ACESA) are expected to create 1.7 million new jobs (UNEP, 2009).

These are just a few examples of the national recovery plans' expected effects on employment. By greening the economy, the leaders of the world envision a simultaneous solution of the world's financial, environmental and humanitarian crises.

Conclusion

Greening the economy will unequivocally have three effects on employment: jobs will be created, substituted and eliminated. It is important to know, therefore, what types of jobs will be lost and created in order to help people to adapt and to determine what sort of (re)training is necessary. Based on the arguments of this chapter we can conclude that a substantial amount of future research needs to be directed towards both descriptive and causal analyses of green jobs.

First, we need to increase our knowledge about the historic and present green job profiles and compare it with the 'brown' job profile. Comparisons can be made both at the industry level and at the individual level. In the past, lack of sufficient data has been one of the obstacles for performing such analyses. Presently, the industry classification of, for instance, firms in the relevant Swedish databases includes the environmental sector.[8] It is thereby possible to link firms to individuals, and the databases include all firms and the whole Swedish working population. This high-quality data can be used to provide unique comparisons between employees (although for privacy reasons, it is not possible to identify specific individuals in the database) in the green and brown sectors, such as:

- educational levels and fields of specialisation;
- incomes and wages;
- immigrant status;
- part-time work and unemployment duration, and so on.

Such analyses will most certainly generate interesting hypotheses that could result in an even better data collection in order to test the hypotheses empirically.

There is also, secondly, a need for more empirical studies of the causal effects of environmental policies on economic variables. Although there is a vast literature on labour market programme evaluation, these types of causal analyses are seldom performed on environmental policies' effect on employment and other non-environmental variables. Without doubt, one of the reasons for this is the relative lack of qualitative micro-data related to environmental policy. Labour economists have long had access to rich datasets on individuals' decisions on education, labour supply, and so on, combined with comprehensive information on socioeconomic background. With increased availability and quality of environmental and labour data, the possibilities for empirically testing policy relevant hypotheses are greatly improved.

Unfortunately, using empirical data for direct estimation of causal effects of environmental policies on economic variables is difficult to perform at the macro level. Therefore, CGEs have their given place in the analyses of the effects of environmental policies (see the Appendix at the end of this chapter). As discussed in Bergman (2005), CGE models provide a bridge between economic theory and policy analysis, and they are very important in that they enable estimation of general equilibrium effects, without the restriction of linear functional forms.

Although CGE models are necessary for capturing *all* effects of environmental policies, empirical studies of the causal effects of environmental policies on economic variables are important to provide the CGE models with realistic expectations about the effects of environmental policies on employment in specific sectors of the economy. If the results from CGE modelling and causal micro evaluation significantly diverge on commonalities, exploring the causes for the divergence could improve the CGE models. Such cross-fertilisation between both approaches seems promising.

Notes

[1] Employment is defined as *direct*, *indirect* and *induced* employment in full-time equivalents. Direct employment is employment in the core environmental activity, for example, fishing. Indirect employment is employment in activities supporting the core activity, for example, production of boats and fishing gear. Induced employment is employment resulting from the spending of those employed in the core and supporting activities.

[2] Copeland and Taylor (2004) make a distinction between the 'pollution haven effect', defined as the environmental regulations' effect on plant location and trade flows, and the 'pollution haven hypothesis', defined as trade liberalisation's effects on the very same. In general, there are three prerequisites for a pollution haven to emerge: environmental regulations must differ between countries; capital needs to be mobile; and trade rules need to allow firms to relocate but still sell their goods to its old customers (Fullerton, 2006).

[3] Published in the Chinese newspaper *People's Daily* online. The statement was made by Liu Zhiquan, Deputy Director General of Department of Technology Standards, Ministry of Environmental Protection, at a forum on 24 November 2009. Information retrieved on 10 May 2010 from: http://english.people.com.cn/90001/90778/90862/6823402.html

[4] For instance, Bergman (2005: 1274) writes about one of the available methods that '[...] CGE modeling is a way of *using* rather than *testing* economic theory [...]' (emphasis added).

[5] The following description draws heavily on Berck and Hoffman (2002).

[6] For more detail, see Bergman (2005) for an overview of environmental applications, and Dixon and Parmenter (1996) for a discussion of computer algorithms for solving CGEs. Rose (1995) discusses the extent to which I-O analysis serves as a foundation to CGE models.

[7] Minimum wages imply less flexibility on the labour market. With decreasing productivity, the market clearing real wage falls, but if the minimum wage is higher than the market clearing wage, labour supply is not equal to labour demand at the minimum wage, resulting in involuntary unemployment. The wage curve hypothesis states that wages are negatively correlated with local unemployment rates, that is, high unemployment leads to lower wages. Just as in the case of wage rigidity through a lower real-wage bound, a wage curve modelling implies substituting the flexible wage by a wage equation, only that the price of labour is not linked to a minimum level, such as a consumption price index, but to the level of unemployment (Küster et al, 2007).

[8] Environmental firms are defined according to OECD/Eurostat standards (OECD, 1997), which facilitates international comparisons.

Chapter summary

At present, the eco-industry employs more people than the European car industry and, in the US in 2007, the revenues from the renewable energy and energy efficiency industries exceeded the combined sales from the three largest US corporations. The green sector of the economy thus seems to be a sector with both a high employment potential *and* a high revenue generating potential.

This chapter has:

- found that the net impact of environmental policies on employment is either zero or slightly positive;
- emphasised the importance of economic methods and modelling to discussions of policy evaluation and the implications for reform;
- presented some of the principal forecasts on the future number of green job;
- explained the factors which make forecasting difficult and made recommendations for future research.

Questions for discussion

- How should we understand the relationship between employment and environmental policies?
- What are the main factors influencing the growth in green jobs?
- Why are accurate forecasts of employment trends difficult to make in relation to green jobs?

Key further reading

Berck, P. and Hoffman, S. (2002) 'Assessing the employment impacts of environmental and natural resource policy', *Environmental and Resource Economics*, vol 22, pp 133-56.

Bergman, L. (2005) 'CGE modelling of environmental policy', in K-G. Mäler and J.R. Vincent (eds) *Handbook of environmental economics*, Amsterdam: Elsevier.

Bezdek, R.H., Wendling, R.M. and DiPerna, P. (2008) 'Environmental protection, the economy, and jobs: national and regional analyses', *Journal of Environmental Management*, vol 86, pp 63-79.

Copeland, B.R. and Taylor, M.S. (2004) 'Trade, growth and the environment', *Journal of Economic Literature*, vol XLII, pp 7-71.

GHK Consulting (2009) *The impacts of climate change on European employment and skills in the short to medium-term: A review of the literature. Final report, Volume 2* (http://ec.europa.eu/social/main.jsp?catId=88&langId=en&events Id=172).

Heckman, J.J. and Vytlacil, E.J. (2007) 'Econometric evaluation of social programs, part I: causal models, structural models, and econometric policy evaluation', in J.J. Heckman and E. Leamer (eds) *Handbook of econometrics*, Amsterdam: Elsevier.

Renner, M., Sweeney, S. and Kubit, J. (2008) *Green jobs*, Worldwatch Report no 177.

Useful websites

Eurostat: http://epp.eurostat.ec.europa.eu/portal/page/portal/eurostat/home/

International Labour Organization (ILO): www.ilo.org/global/lang--en/index.htm

European Commission: http://ec.europa.eu/index_en.htm

United Nations Environment Programme: www.unep.org/

Appendix

Input-output (I-O) and social accounting matrix (SAM) models

I-O analysis was pioneered by Leontief (1970), who was also the first to propose using the I-O model in an environmental policy context. At the basis of a SAM or an I-O model is a simple demand-driven economic base model. Economic activity is primarily driven by exogenously determined exports or investment. Domestic production is allocated to domestic consumption, export and investment. Consumption is a linear function of production and, in equilibrium, income must equal regional expenditure, which is the sum of domestic consumption, export and investment. A more complete model would, for instance, include import. This is a demand-driven economic system, where an exogenous change in export sales implies increased demand for domestic labour and consequently, higher domestic income. To the extent that this income increase is spent on domestically produced rather than imported goods, demand for domestic production increases. In turn, this demand increase generates further domestic labour demand. The *economic base multiplier* is the factor by which regional income will change in response to a change to exogenous demand.[*]

Provided export sales are exogenous and the domestic consumption multiplier can be estimated from empirical data, this simple model could be very useful for analysing short-run effects of a certain policy that has an effect on exogenous demand. This describes the basic mechanism behind I-O models and SAM, but because interest often lies in the multiplier of a single industry or a small number of industries, there is need to further disaggregate the economy. SAMs and I-O models do that by representing transactions between different sectors of the national economy and household consumption. Compared to I-O models, SAMs include a greater number of flows in the economy, and in addition, provide a more detailed disaggregation of households (by income or demographic characteristics) and institutions (such as levels of government).

A SAM is a table representing all transactions that occur in an economy at a particular time. These transactions occur among various agents of the economy: producers, owners of primary production factors, households, government and the rest of the world. The effect on output of a change in exogenous demand for a certain good is calculated by using the multiplier for the specific good in question, rather than by using a multiplier for the whole economy as in the economic base model described above. As a last step, one would convert the change in output to a change in jobs by dividing by the average number of output per job.

Computable general equilibrium (CGE) models

The basic ingredients of a CGE are a number of equations that describe producer and household optimising behaviour. For instance, the model might include factor demand by producers, product demand by households. In addition, there is an income constraint on behalf of households, and a number of macro constraints, such as total savings equal to investment. Parameter values are either estimated from real-world data, calibrated[**] or set exogenously. One of the merits of CGE as compared to I-O analysis is that the former allows non-linear relationships. But this greater flexibility comes at a cost: due to the complexity of the model, finding an analytical solution is not feasible and therefore, numerical methods are used. In environmental applications, the main purpose of a CGE analysis is usually to analyse the effects of environmental policies on economic variables of interest.

Notes

* Solving this model for domestic income results in the simple expression $Y=(1/(1-c))(X+I)$, where Y is income, c is the share of income that is used for consumption of domestically produced goods, and X and I are exogenously determined export sales and investment, respectively. The economic base multiplier is given by $(1/(1-c))$.

** Loosely speaking, a calibration means that parameters are set so that the equilibrium of the CGE reproduces the transactions observed in the data.

twelve

Citizenship and care

Sherilyn MacGregor

Overview

The voluntary participation of citizens in environmental protection is a key piece of the sustainability puzzle. Examining the values and actions of individuals is therefore important to an understanding of the impetus for, and impacts of, environmental policy making. This chapter looks at the role of individuals as citizens and carers in the public and private spheres. The following themes and debates are explored:

- the traditional division of care and citizenship into separate spheres;
- definitions of environmental citizenship;
- caring for and about the environment;
- why connecting citizenship and care is important for environmental sustainability;
- examples of policies that enable a more sustainable balance of care and citizenship.

Introduction

This chapter is concerned with social membership and participation. Citizenship and care are contested terms that have different meanings for different political theorists as well as for the individuals who put them into practice. Here citizenship is defined as:

- membership in a political community;
- a legal status carrying rights and entitlements;
- a practice involving responsibilities to the wider community (see Kymlicka and Norman, 1994).

There are many theoretical perspectives on citizenship – liberal, communitarian, civic republican, feminist and green – each bringing different assumptions and goals to the discussion. Care can be viewed as an ethical orientation and as a practice of providing support (protection and sustenance) for something or someone. Most scholarly work on care is done by feminist theorists who look at the gender aspects of care and women's socially ascribed role as caregivers in families. There is also a vast literature on social care, which looks at the delivery of caring services like childcare, education and health in welfare states.

It is significant that care and citizenship are being considered together in this chapter because in traditional western approaches to politics they belong to two separate spheres: citizenship to the public sphere of politics and care to the private or domestic sphere. In the dominant political traditions citizenship is celebrated as the means by which humans can fulfil their true nature, while care is constructed as a 'necessary evil' that must be provided so that citizens may get on with the real business of politics. Some argue that the relegation of care to the household has fostered a belief that citizens are autonomous individuals who do not depend on others. As Sevenhuijsen (1998: 130-1) puts it, '… care is associated with immanence, necessity and the private sphere, while politics is constructed as a social activity that enhances the freedom of the human subject, by freeing him from the burdens of necessity'.

In recent decades it has become common to question any rigid division of public and private spheres and to challenge the archetype of the 'citizen' as independent, asocial and disembodied. From feminists arguing that 'the personal is political' to green theorists claiming consumer choices to be acts of citizenship, there is a growing movement to recognise the relevance of the private sphere – and activities and relationships that take place therein – to political life. As we will see, the concept of environmental citizenship presents fundamental challenges to longstanding conceptions of what it means to be a citizen. However, the connections between citizenship and care have been under-theorised in both the environmental citizenship and broader environmental policy literature. It is this gap that later sections of the chapter aim to fill.

Defining environmental citizenship

Until the 1960s few acknowledged the relevance of the natural environment to the sphere of politics or the concept of citizenship. Today, most contemporary texts on citizenship cite trans-boundary environmental problems, like biodiversity loss and climate change, as reasons why traditional liberal understandings of citizenship have become outdated. There is now a need to rethink both the spatial and temporal construction of citizenship as being confined to people living in bounded, sovereign territories, for example, nation-states, in the here and now. Green political theorists have gone further than this to develop a literature on environmental citizenship, drawing on but also reinterpreting civic republican, communitarian, feminist and liberal understanding of citizenship to accommodate green concerns. These perspectives will not be discussed in detail here, having been reviewed in relation to 'justice' in Chapter Six (this volume). The aim of this section is to summarise some of the key themes that are relevant to environmental policy making, with environmental rights and responsibilities coming top of the list.

   The reason why citizenship is such an important issue in environmental politics is that moving towards a 'sustainable society' (or a less unsustainable one) will require fundamental changes in how people live together and distribute resources to meet their needs. These are ultimately political questions. Unless we want a Leviathan-style authoritarian ruler to come along and 'save us' (which most people agree is an undesirable prospect) it will be necessary to involve citizens democratically in the process of change. The argument is that citizen involvement will not only enable good policies, but also ensure the consent of all concerned. People with environmental values must have their interests represented if there is to be a democratic transition to a sustainable society. But when considering the idea of representation, two important questions are commonly raised. First, how might we take the interests of future generations into account in decision making? And second, should citizenship be limited to humans? How will the interests of non-human animals and the rest of nature be taken into account? These are challenging questions that follow from the green commitment to expanding the circle of moral consideration beyond humans to the larger biotic community (see Chapter Five, this volume).

   In addition to becoming a topic of debate among green theorists, since around the mid-1990s the concept of environmental citizenship has been deployed by governments and environmental non-governmental organisations (NGOs), particularly in affluent countries, as part of an institutional environmental agenda.

> ## Summary box
>
> A common definition of environmental citizenship includes:
>
> (i) *rights*, both to participate in environmental decision making and to a clean and liveable environment, and
> (ii) a set of *responsibilities*, for example to protect the interests of future generations and non-humans, by actively participating in democratic debate about sustainability and by engaging in environmentally sound practices.

We shall now look more closely at how theorists and policy makers understand environmental rights and responsibilities.

Environmental rights

Governments are ahead of green theorists in considering the practical implementation of environmental rights as an entitlement of green citizenship. Many countries have officially recognised the rights of citizens in environmental matters. *Environmental rights are generally defined as the rights to a clean and liveable natural environment.* It is possible to expand this definition beyond a human-centred focus by considering the rights of nature itself, but this move is controversial and not directly relevant to a discussion of the inherently humanist concept of citizenship.

Prompted by Agenda 21, the most common manifestation of environmental rights comes in the form of *procedural rights*, meaning rights to participate in environmental decision making. The most important example is the Aarhus Convention, which came into force in the European Community in 2001 to give citizens a right of access to information, to participation in decision making and access to justice on local, national and transnational environmental issues. Civil society organisations and individual citizens can invoke their Aarhus rights in order to challenge government decisions and plans when it is suspected that they have not followed fair and transparent procedures. For example, in the Czech Republic in 2006 a group of 170 citizens, opposing a proposed new runway at the Prague-Ruzyne airport, successfully used the Aarhus Convention to contest a land use plan on the grounds that they had not been properly consulted, nor had an environmental impact assessment been carried out. The Czech Supreme Administrative Court agreed with their motion and effectively cancelled the runway plan, sending it back to the planners to redraft. Significantly, the Court's judgment states that the Aarhus Convention has preference over Czech law (Justice and Environment, 2006).

The theoretical case for environmental rights is made by Hayward (2005), who argues that they should be included in the constitutions of all modern democracies. Potentially more radical than procedural rights are the *substantive rights* to a clean and liveable environment. Substantive environmental rights may, to some extent, be understood as being similar to Marshall's (1992) argument for social rights: the state has a duty to provide citizens with the conditions for exercising their political and civil rights. In a similar way, it is argued that adequate environmental quality is a necessary condition for human functioning and therefore should be protected by law. This issue is of particular concern to environmental justice scholars, who have argued that politically and economically marginalised populations (that is, people disadvantaged by class, 'race', gender and disability) need to be able to claim environmental rights as human rights in order to be protected from the harm caused by capitalist development. Hayward (2005: 5), however, goes further still, arguing that treating environmental rights as social rights (and lumping them in with social policy) and/or restricting them to procedural rights is not good enough. In his view, for environmental rights to 'have teeth' they need to be binding rights on a par with human rights and they need to be included in constitutions.

There is currently a long way to go and much work to be done to bring this vision to fruition. Hayward (2005: 3) estimates there are approximately 50 states in the world with constitutional environmental rights, but these tend not to be the wealthiest and most powerful countries. South Africa, Hungary and Bolivia have enshrined the substantive right to a healthy environment in their constitutions. For example, Article 24 of South Africa's Bill of Rights states that:

> Everyone has the right to an environment that is not harmful to their health or well-being ... and to have the environment protected, for the benefit of present and future generations, through reasonable legislative and other measures that prevent pollution and ecological degradation; promote conservation; and secure ecologically sustainable development and use of natural resources while promoting justifiable economic and social development. (www.deat.gov.za)

Although these words appear very robust from an environmental perspective, it should be noted that there is not a very good track record of enforcement or delivering on these rights in any country in which they are in place.

Environmental rights as part of green citizenship tend to equate only to the entitlements of *human citizens* to a clean and liveable environment. The debate over whether non-humans can be citizens has not yet been resolved. Since only human citizens can claim their rights through existing political and legal processes, it is difficult to imagine a practical way of extending environmental rights to animals or the rest of the biotic community. Although it has received considerable attention (see Chapter Five, this volume), the debate over animal rights has thus far not been central to the literature on environmental citizenship. However, there has been some movement towards granting rights to non-human great apes. The Great Ape Project has been advocating the extension of legal rights (to life, to individual liberty and freedom from torture) since 1993. In 2008 Spain became the first country to give rights to these animals on the grounds that humans share approximately 99% of their active genetic material with non-human primates.

> ## Summary box
>
> ### Environmental rights
>
> - *Procedural rights:* rights to information pertaining to environmental developments, the right to participate in environmental policy making, access to justice in the event of disputes.
> - *Substantive rights:* rights to a clean and liveable environment, for example, Article 24 of South Africa's Bill of Rights.
> - *Environmental rights as human rights:* some argue that there ought to be a binding guarantee of fundamental environmental rights in all national constitutions (see Hayward, 2005).
> - *Animal rights:* should non-human animals have environmental rights?

Environmental responsibilities

Environmental citizenship belongs within the frame of 'a new generation of citizenship that takes the politics of obligation seriously' (Smith and Pangsapa, 2008: 9). Central to the idea of environmental citizenship is the normative claim that citizens have duties to the environment, future generations and those with whom they share the planet. This may be seen as a response to the dominance of rights in theories of citizenship over the past two centuries in the West. In recent years, some have argued that too many rights and entitlements have led to a breakdown in community bonds as well as a crisis of ecological unsustainability. Because people in affluent countries have been socialised into prioritising their own material interests and claiming their 'just deserts' from the state, they are less inclined to consider how their own actions contribute to or detract from the common good. If we are to move towards a more sustainable society, there needs to be dramatic change in the way people understand their relationship to the state and with fellow inhabitants of the environment. In short, ask not what the state can do for its citizens, but what citizens can do for the planet.

Many environmental theorists are sceptical of the idea that the state should take the lead in bringing about environmental change. Although there is ample evidence to suggest that environmental regulation can lead, and has led, to important incremental changes (such as laws banning aerosol use or making recycling mandatory), most theorists of green citizenship place greater emphasis on the adoption of environmental values. For example, Dobson and Bell (2006) suggest that environmental citizenship is a preferable alternative to government policies that use 'carrots and sticks' (such as subsidies and taxes) to actively influence or control people's behaviour. Instead, they insist it should be about individual citizens voluntarily making choices to adopt more sustainable practices *because they believe it to be the right thing to do.* If people do things because they are compelled by the state, then the prospects for long-term, fundamental social change are rather dim. What is needed is a change in attitude, a 'change of mind'.

This approach makes a discussion of green values, virtues and attitudes fundamental to any vision of environmental citizenship. Proponents of environmental citizenship debate what these should be, but they share the view that people need to adopt the kinds of pro-environmental values, virtues and attitudes that make the exploitation of nature unacceptable. The key virtues listed include 'resourcefulness' (Hayward, 2006), 'self-reliance' and 'self-restraint' (Barry, 1999: 228) and 'justice' (Dobson, 2003). For Dobson (2003), justice is the primary virtue: when a citizen recognises that she has taken more than her fair share of 'ecological space', justice demands that she reduces and redistributes resources so that others have a chance of a decent quality of life. Signalling a radical break with traditional approaches to citizenship, Dobson (2003) suggests that an ethic of care should inform environmental citizenship. Public and private virtues come together, and abstract notions of justice should be complemented by a concrete sense of caring and compassion about nature and the well-being of distant others (including future generations).

> **Summary box**
>
> **Environmental responsibilities**
>
> - *Change your mind:* adopting the values, virtues and attitudes that lead citizens to behave more sustainably.
> - *Have your say:* the duty to participate actively in environmental decision making as well as in one's own community, thereby putting forward the arguments in favour of sustainability.
> - *Do your bit:* the responsibility to put one's pro-environmental attitudes into practice in everyday life.

Smith (2005: 281) defines 'the green citizen' as 'an individual who recognises their duties in relation to the environment and takes responsibility to act in line with those duties'. Clearly changing one's mind is not enough: citizens must adopt a range of pro-environmental behaviours and practices. One type of pro-environmental behaviour is citizens 'having their say' through civic participation. Coming from a civic republican perspective, Barry (2006: 33) advocates the cultivation of active environmental citizenship in civil society rather than compelling people to follow the rules devised by the state. He argues that environmental citizens have the duty to participate so that they might challenge environmentally destructive development and demand the kinds of changes that would bring about sustainability. So not only do they have the right to participate (enshrined in the Aarhus Conversion), they also have a civic duty to participate in the political process, as environmental citizens and activists. This participation ranges from getting involved in public consultations on environmentally risky proposals to engaging in non-violent direct action to try to stop development from going ahead. Barry (2006: 28–9) goes so far as to suggest that environmental citizenship might include a form of 'compulsory sustainability service', similar to national service. This proposal stems from his view that civic participation is good not only because it ensures that the path to sustainability is democratic but also because, consistent with republicanism, it is an end in itself.

Good environmental citizens do not simply hold green values and take action to demand policy change; perhaps even more importantly they also 'do their bit' for their environment in everyday life. The kinds of responsibilities that are commonly listed under the banner of environmental citizenship include a range of practices that reduce environmental impact and improve the quality of degraded ecosystems, such as reducing energy consumption and growing one's own food. Breaking with the traditional understanding of politics, many theorists of green citizenship believe that it is in the private sphere that the most meaningful changes can take place. As Dobson and Bell (2006: 7) note,

> ... one key environmental point has always been that "private" actions can have important public consequences. Decisions ... as to how we hear or cool our homes, or how and what we choose to consume in them, are decisions that have public consequences in terms of [their] environmental impact.

Consumption, once not seen as an act of citizenship but of an exchange between buyer and seller in the marketplace, is now central to visions of environmental citizenship. Sustainable consumption is a growing field of research that examines why people make choices to buy certain products and not others and how these decisions might be influenced by particular values (Seyfang, 2009b). While most greens want people in the affluent world to reduce their consumption, the past decade has also seen the emergence of a trend towards ethical and green consumerism where people decide to purchase goods that are fair trade, organic and low on carbon emissions.

It is worth debating whether citizen-consumer demand is bringing about the greening of capitalism or whether businesses are simply capitalising on a fashionable trend. As will be discussed in the next section, with a disproportionate emphasis on individual choice in the realm of consumption there are further questions to be asked about the extent to which environmental citizenship obscures key questions of fairness, power and social inequality. Many people regard 'going green' as a lifestyle choice accessible only to those with middle-class incomes and post-materialist values. Without taking these issues into account, the concept of environmental citizenship as private duty will not be possible for all and therefore may be limited as a means to the goal of sustainability.

Caring for and about the environment

Care can be defined as a feeling or ethical orientation ('I *care about* how that lab rat is being treated') and as a practice of doing things to support others ('I am *caring for* my ageing father'). We saw above that caring about the well-being of the environment, non-human animals, distant others and future generations can be an important motivation for acting responsibly as environmental citizens. It is fair to say that this affective meaning of care is the one more often invoked in the literature on environmental citizenship. It is also increasingly common to see it used in public relations campaigns of corporations who wish to announce their green and ethical intentions. A

Google search of the phrase 'environmental care' brings up the websites of large manufacturers like Volvo, Fujitsu and Canon, who all claim to follow environmentally responsible business practices. In policy circles, the concept of a 'duty of care', traditionally used to protect individuals and their property from harm, is being extended into the environmental arena. In the UK, for example, there is 'duty of care' legislation to ensure that all businesses and households take responsibility for their waste (DEFRA, 2009). Clearly the concept of care and its relation to environmental sustainability is open to different interpretations.

Beyond hoping that citizens will care about the environment, few people make explicit connections between citizenship and the practice of 'caring for' in the context of environmental policy. Those who have made connections tend to work from a feminist environmental (or **ecofeminist**) perspective to analyse the exclusion of care from the realm of politics and the gender roles and assumptions that shape social constructions of care (MacGregor, 2006). Feminists are interested in care because it is performed disproportionately by women, an association that has contributed to the devaluation of women throughout history. Cross-national data show that even with cultural changes in laws and cultural norms, women still do the lion's share of unpaid caring: serving the needs of children and dependent adults as well as the domestic work involved in managing households (Bittman and Wajcman, 2000). Meanwhile, in most countries 'men are not culturally expected to make a productive contribution to the social product by fulfilling a reasonable share of care duties' (Kershaw, 2005: 161).

Most feminists see care as a feminised form of labour that is made up of a range of practices that together are called **social reproduction** (di Chiro, 2008). Social reproduction involves the provision of services on which the economy, the state and individual citizens depend for survival. Moreover, those who deliver 'sustaining services' (O'Hara, 1997, quoted in Perkins, 2007) or do 'provisioning work' (Langley and Mellor, 2002) make it possible for people to act as citizens. Provisioning work in the private sphere is also deeply implicated in visions of a more environmentally sustainable society. There is a long list of ways that people might green their households (for example, recycling, pre-cycling, self-provisioning, etc). These green practices can be rewarding, giving people who care about the environment a tangible sense of doing their bit to 'save it'. However, they can also be time-consuming and inconvenient in societies where the physical infrastructure, services, education and dominant norms have not yet caught up with the green vision.

Private sphere activities ensure the ongoing reproduction and maintenance of life and yet, traditionally, have been 'ignored or trivialised in mainstream political, economic and environmental analyses' (di Chiro,

2008: 281). We saw above that they are now becoming central to the definition of environmental citizenship. However non-feminist green theorists tend to work with a one-dimensional understanding of the private sphere, describing it as primarily a place of consumption and giving little or no consideration to the division of labour within it. This is worrying for feminists because when household activities are seen in gender–neutral terms, environmental policies that address them are usually aimed at people in general with no specific recognition of the gender-specific roles they play (Vinz, 2009). The emphasis on individual lifestyle change as central to environmental citizenship has prompted feminist critics to warn against the privatisation and feminisation of environmental responsibility (Littig, 2001; MacGregor, 2006; Vinz, 2009). In other words, gender-blind policies and strategies carry the risk of perpetuating existing inequalities.

As Littig (2001: 23) writes, for example, the

> ... end–of–the pipeline strategy [separating the waste instead of reducing packaging] of environmental politics usually represents more work for women since they are responsible for reproductive labour....The feminist critique is mainly aimed at the fact that contemporary environmental policy preserves ... the traditional gendered division of labour and responsibilities.

Recognising this risk, the United Nations Environment Programme (UNEP) has made it clear that 'mainstreaming' gender roles into the policy process at an early stage – by specifically taking into consideration the needs and perspectives of different groups of men and women – makes for more effective policies (UNEP, nd).

Care–citizenship–environment connections

In short, the connections between citizenship and care, and their relevance to sustainability, have been under-theorised in both the environmental citizenship and broader environmental policy literatures. In order to begin to redress this lack of attention, the following three forms of connection are now considered.

Summary box

Connecting citizenship and care

- Environmental degradation increases the demand for care.
- People who do the work of caring tend to care more about environmental quality.
- More caring requires more time, which may reduce time available for civic participation.

Environmental degradation increases the demand for care

The amount of care needed in a society is determined by a range of factors such as demographic patterns, income levels, access to basic subsistence needs and political and economic stability. Environmental quality also plays a part in the demand for caring services. Environmental degradation and pollution can cause ill health (such as asthma, various forms of cancer, miscarriages and birth defects) that increases vulnerability and thus dependency on care. Droughts, floods and other extreme weather conditions increase the need to care for people as well as to restore damaged ecosystems. Caring for people and animals is made more difficult in conditions of environmental scarcity. Feminist research has shown that women are more dramatically affected by environmental degradation than men due to their social roles as carers and 'provisioners'. In developing countries, in particular, women's everyday provisioning work is made more difficult due to environmental impacts. Women must walk further for clean water and firewood and struggle to gather and grow food for families when conditions are poor (Terry, 2009).

People who do the work of caring tend to care more about environmental quality

Although a subject of debate, there is evidence to suggest that the work of caring and the ethic of care are interconnected. Feminist moral philosophers have long argued that because women are closely involved in caring for others they have a different moral orientation than men (Robinson, 1999). The same argument tends to be made with respect to environmental care. Just as women's socially ascribed roles as carers and provisioners make them more vulnerable to the impacts of environmental degradation, women tend to feel more responsible for, and more concerned about, the quality of the environment. Social psychological research into environmental attitudes has found that, generally, women are more concerned about environmental issues than men (Dietz et al, 2007). In the UK, a survey conducted in 2007 by the Women's Environmental Network and the Women's Institute found that women are more concerned about climate change than men and feel that women are in a unique position to address it by making changes in household practices.

There is a debate about whether it is useful to celebrate women's greater environmental concern, when this is rooted in traditional gender norms that sustain inequality. However, if we accept the logic that the closer people are to life-sustaining practices in everyday life, the more concerned about environmental quality they become, then it stands to reason that the more people who are involved in caring work, the better it will be for the planet.

More caring requires more time, which may reduce time available for civic participation

Similar to the idea that more people need to be involved in the work of care is the argument that it is important for as many people as possible to participate as citizens in democratic environmental decision making. There is a problem, however, in that these two activities can be very time-consuming and difficult for individuals living in capitalist societies to juggle. This juggling act is more difficult for some than for others. Research has shown that 'the activity involved in maintaining an ecologically conscious household usually represents extra work for women' (Littig, 2001:64).Vinz (2009: 163) uses the term '*eco*-stress' to describe the increased pressure on women to juggle competing roles with duties to incorporate pro-environmental practices at home. Significant for environmental citizenship is that even though women may 'care more' about sustainability, they actually tend to participate less in public environmental action because of their heavy load of work in the private sphere (MacGregor, 2006).

This problem illustrates the continued existence of the public–private dichotomy that has resulted in gender inequality and the devaluation of care in most societies. There may be a new interest in making care relevant to environmental politics and citizenship, but so far there have been few changes in the way we live that enable people to do both.

Policy implications and promising examples

Langley and Mellor (2002: 49) define sustainability as

> ... combining conditions of existence where human beings achieve their potential without exploiting the labour and resources of other individuals, groups or societies with a level of ecological replenishment necessary not only for human

futurity but for the continued existence of other species and their ecosystems.

The key policy question that emerges from this definition, and from the foregoing discussion, concerns how caring work can be distributed in ways that avoid exploitation and give people time for pro-environmental citizenly pursuits. This question cannot be addressed unless caring is regarded as a social responsibility on the same par with employment, paying taxes and other forms of active citizenship (Kershaw, 2005: 155). This may seem like a tall order, but for ecofeminists and others who are committed to making sustainability socially just, the search for innovative policy solutions is of vital importance. For example, Vinz (2009: 165) calls for

> ... the development of sustainability strategies that no longer assume that unpaid care work provides the basis for an economy by serving as a "natural resource". Instead, economic and welfare models should be developed that organize care work in an ecologically sustainable manner consistent with gender justice.

The development of such policies requires different ways of thinking about work and the value of people's time. But there might be a win–win situation here: what are some ways of acknowledging and simplifying valuable caring work that, at the same time, strengthen the social bonds of citizenship and reduce environmental impact? In this final section, we briefly review some policy approaches and innovations for how care and citizenship might be integrated.

Mainstreaming care in socio-environmental policy

The lobbying efforts of women's organisations at the United Nations Conference on Environment and Development (UNCED) in 1992 resulted in a long list of recommendations for making environmental policies more sensitive to gender roles, specifically to the social value of caring work. The lasting result has been an acceptance by UN policy makers of the need to mainstream these concerns in policy rather than to add them in as an afterthought (known as **gender mainstreaming**). Feminist activists have argued that if women are to participate equally as experts and citizens in sustainable development, then there is a clear need to reduce and redistribute their burden of unpaid work.

Agenda 21, chapter 24.3(d), calls for

... programmes to promote the reduction of the heavy workload of women and girls at home and outside through the establishment of more affordable nurseries ... and the sharing of household tasks by men and women on an equal basis....

Concrete examples of how this idea is making its way through the environmental movement can be found in green party platforms in many countries. Many green parties advocate child and elder care on the grounds that they can serve a dual social and environmental purpose. For example, the main policy document of Canada's Green Party, *Vision Green* (nd), includes state-funded workplace childcare, not only because it is good for children and their parents but also because it enables more sustainable transport.

Collectivising care in the community

There are ways in which collectivising basic aspects of daily life can reduce the burden on individual carers as well as reducing impacts on the environment. These efforts can also foster the social bonds of citizenship. Collectivisation can happen through voluntary organisation and is ideally supported through government policy. Examples include designs for communal living, as is common in Scandinavian co-housing, where variously defined family units live together and share common tasks like childcare and building maintenance. Cooperative house keeping in small units is also advocated by some feminist environmental researchers in Germany (Littig, 2001: 101) as a way to encourage the equal sharing of care and housework. More modest types of collectivisation can be seen at community level, such as 'walking school buses', neighbourhood laundries and ride-sharing schemes.

In this respect, the best examples around food provisioning include the collective kitchens and milk programmes in Latin America and the growing transnational Slow Food movement that celebrates collective preparation and enjoyment of food. Local fruit and veg box schemes reduce the amount of time and travel needed to acquire food for households at the same time as supporting local producers. Vinz (2009: 172) argues that the state should facilitate these kinds of projects and move to increase the provision of food by mandating cafeterias in workplaces, childcare facilities and schools. Organised with social and environmental factors in mind, these measures can tick all three boxes: care, citizenship and sustainability.

Valuing time as a scarce resource

Greens often embrace alternatives to the capitalist market that operate at the community level as being good for citizenship and for the project of sustainability. Feminists are in favour of such measures because they acknowledge the contribution of unpaid work to local economies and value time as a scarce resource. Local Exchange Trading Systems (LETS) and community time banks are examples of projects that combine a blend of social, community, economic and environmental objectives. As Chapter Six made clear, these projects reward people (with time dollars) for the time they spend performing voluntary activities in the community; the credits earned can be used to purchase services from others. They are designed to build social capital, promote civic participation and reduce social exclusion (Seyfang, 2003). They can also have environmental benefits. Perkins (2007: 232) observes that 'community currencies provide one way of acknowledging the value of unpaid work while minimizing throughput growth'. While there is some evidence of government support for these projects in those places where they have been developed (for example, the US, the UK and Canada), there is need for a supportive policy framework to allow them to grow and widen the range of services they can offer.

Enabling work-care-citizenship life balance

Kershaw (2005) argues that for caring to be shared fairly, there must be a better work–life balance than is currently possible in capitalist societies. Beyond welfare state provision and organised mutual aid, a more radical policy for fostering the greater integration of care and citizenship, for the sake of sustainability, is work time reduction (WTR). This has been a popular idea with environmentalists for several decades. European green parties have led the way in advocating WTR as a way to integrate economic, social and environmental policy goals. French political economist and former green party leader Alain Lipietz (1992), for example, has made the case for shorter working weeks as a way to reduce unemployment, increase productivity without increasing resource use and to create more time for citizens to engage in voluntary, non-consumptive activities that are good for (or at least not harmful to) the environment.

France's Aubry Law, passed in the late 1990s by the left–green government of Lionel Jospin, is perhaps the most successful example of state-led WTR policy; it made the 35-hour working week a national standard (Paehlke, 2003). Other European and several Scandinavian countries have similar kinds of policies that enable citizens to live more balanced lives. Feminist theorists generally agree that these are a positive move towards gender equality because they allow women to juggle their multiple roles more easily and therefore provide opportunities for public involvement – as well as providing the time for men to play a bigger part in the private sphere (MacGregor, 2006).

Of course, as Paehlke (2003: 253) writes, 'reduced work time does not ensure virtuous environmental behaviour, but it may render it a more likely choice'. It is also true that reducing the amount of hours people spend in paid work does not necessarily mean that they will spend more time caring for their families and communities, a point which leads us to consider our final policy area.

Education for eco-social sustainability

People might be given opportunities to spend time doing pro-environmental work in their homes and communities but, unless they are motivated out of a sense of commitment, there is no guarantee that they will do so. People might choose to spend their 'free time' going on long-haul vacations, shopping or playing video games. Research has shown that when workers are given extra time off from paid work, men tend to use it for leisure and women use it to catch up on the housework (Bittman and Wajcman, 2000). Governments can give fathers a legal right to paid paternity leave, but they may choose not to take it. It is therefore necessary to consider how policy can be used to foster the kind of cultural change that would make a balancing of social reproduction and environmental citizenship both possible and *normal*.

Dobson (2003) highlights the vital importance of education for the cultivation of environmental citizenship. Making sustainability part of the educational curriculum is an important environmental policy recommendation to which many governments have responded. Arguably the most effective approaches seem to be 'activity-based' learning where students develop environmental values, knowledge and skills while interacting in the environment. Innovative projects often allow students to model the collective work that needs to be done to live sustainably. Eco-schools projects bring children, teachers, parents and community members together to engage in collective projects like growing vegetables and cleaning up parks. The informal education that community groups and parents provide also has a role to play. By giving children the responsibility for green chores in the household and neighbourhoods, they may grow up to see these as normal everyday practices that have no gender associations. It should also be recognised that children do a lot of 'eco-consciousness raising' in their families; this is how formal education can have impacts far beyond the classroom.

Keeping in mind the goal of integrating care and citizenship, the most important result of educational projects and policies is to promote a belief that responsibility for sustaining human life and the planet on which it depends should be shared equally. By cultivating active environmental citizens, the added result – ideally – will be that they will demand the kinds of policy and structural changes that are needed to make sustainability a reality rather than a distant goal.

Chapter summary

This chapter has considered how citizenship and care are connected in ways relevant to environmental policy. The aim has been to consider how policies might enable people to combine caring and citizenship in ways that make the collective search for a more sustainable way of living more possible. The key points are as follows:

- Whereas traditional definitions of citizenship rested on a rigid separation of public and private spheres and excluded care, environmental and feminist reinterpretations now consider care to be of vital importance to the search for a sustainable society.
- Citizens can be motivated to adopt pro-environmental behaviours by feelings of care about the well-being of loved ones, distant others, future generations and the biotic community.
- Individuals who do the caring work in the private sphere tend to carry out a disproportionate amount of existing pro-environmental practices.
- Care and citizenship are time-consuming activities that can clash when structures are not in place to facilitate their integration.
- When the provision of care is taken for granted it can be exploited in ways that are ultimately neither just nor sustainable.
- Finding ways to make it easier for people to combine caring and citizenship can also be good for the environment.

Questions for discussion

- In what ways has environmentalism changed the meaning of citizenship?
- Which will be more effective in the long term: (1) citizens making behavioural changes voluntarily, or (2) the state compelling and coercing people to change their behaviour?
- What changes in your own everyday life and activities would make it more possible to combine caring with environmental citizenship?

Key further reading

Dobson, A. (2003) *Citizenship and the environment,* Oxford: Oxford University Press.

Dobson, A. and Bell, D. (2006) *Environmental citizenship*, Cambridge, MA: The MIT Press.

Hayward, T. (2005) *Constitutional environmental rights,* Oxford: Oxford University Press.

Kershaw, P. (2005) *Carefair: Rethinking the responsibilities and rights of citizenship*, Vancouver: University of British Columbia Press.

MacGregor, S. (2006) *Beyond mothering earth: Ecological citizenship and the politics of care*, Vancouver: University of British Columbia Press.

Smith, M.J. and Pangsapa, P. (2008) *Environment and citizenship: grating justice, responsibility and civic engagement*, London: Zed Books.

Useful websites

Aarhus Convention: www.unece.org/env/pp/documents/cep43e.pdf

Article 24 of South Africa's Bill of Rights: www.info.gov.za/documents/constitution/1996/96cons2.htm#24

Eco-schools: www.eco-schools.org.uk/

Great Apes Project: www.greatapeproject.org/

thirteen

International development and global poverty

Carolyn Snell and Claire Quinn

Overview

This chapter:

- introduces four key issues associated with developing countries and the environment: poverty and environmental degradation; development and environmental degradation; structural inequalities, development and the environment; and the unequal effects of environmental degradation;
- outlines the key challenges for sustainable development, illustrated using the 'environmental Kuznets curve';
- plots key developments in international decision making, highlighting the shift over the last three decades from 'global environmental politics' to 'global sustainable development';
- describes two international-level environment-related programmes situated within developing countries and reflects on their effectiveness.

Understanding the issues

The causes and effects of environmental degradation and pollution are complex and multifaceted within a developing world context. There are four main issues: first, poverty and environmental degradation; second, development and environmental degradation; third, structural inequalities, development and the environment; and fourth, the unequal effects of environmental degradation. We start by looking at each of these in turn.

Poverty and environmental degradation

The dominant view has been that environmental degradation is caused by poverty (WCED, 1987; Duraiappah, 1998; Gray and Moseley, 2005). It has been argued that poverty causes people, by necessity, to act in a selfish manner when it comes to the environment, putting short-term needs above the long-term sustainable use of resources. The Brundtland Report states this most clearly when it says, '[m]any parts of the world are caught in a vicious downward spiral: poor people are forced to overuse environmental resources to survive from day to day, and their impoverishment of their environment further impoverishes them, making their survival ever more uncertain and difficult' (WCED, 1987: 27). The outcome is a vicious downward spiral of poverty and environmental degradation. Rising populations push agriculture onto marginal land, and weak state institutions fail to prevent clearance and the use of protected areas. At the same time, low agricultural production from impoverished soils and increased exposure to climate variability, that is, drought, limits the opportunities of people to improve their livelihoods (Lufumpa, 2005).

However, this dominant view is disputed as simplistic and the relationship between poverty and the environment is considered to be more complex (Leach and Mearns, 1995; Duraiappah, 1998). Often it is government intervention in terms of local resource management, elite capture of development projects and the influence of the external economy that drives environmental degradation, rather than poverty alone (Gray and Moseley, 2005). At the same time, there is evidence from across Africa that shows that the poor do think of the longer term and will hold on to assets such as ploughs, as well as limiting their present food intake, to ensure their ability to plant crops and sustain food production in the future (de Waal, 1989; Devereux, 1993). Environmental degradation need not be, and is not always, the consequence of poverty. Instead it may be wealth and economic development that are 'more likely culprits' (Gray and Moseley, 2005: 19).

Development and environmental degradation

As an economy grows, the impact on the environment increases rapidly as industrialisation and the demand for natural resources drive increasing levels of pollution and environmental degradation (Dinda, 2004). Most industrialised countries can trace a history of deforestation, species loss, soil degradation and water and air pollution from the late 19th and early 20th centuries as economic development and industrialisation saw a rise in new industries and demands for energy. For example, the UK became the fourth largest emitter of sulphur dioxide (a major constituent of acid rain) in Europe in the 1970s and 1980s because of the use of coal and oil in power generation and industrial processes (Barnaby, 1988). The acid rain produced damaged forests and acidified soils and water courses not only in the UK but also in other countries in Europe.

Case study

The case of Latin America

Economic development in Latin America has been built on its natural resources (Barton, 2006). In the 1980s over 80% of the total exports from the region were primary products and in 2003 they still represented nearly 50% of all exports. International trade agreements and private investments from multinational companies have both encouraged countries to capitalise on their natural resource base and restricted the development of secondary or tertiary industry. This dependence on natural resources has had significant consequences for the environment. Between 1990 and 1997 around 2.2 million hectares of forests were lost to logging and clearance for agriculture (Achard et al, 2002). Evidence for soil degradation, biodiversity loss and overgrazing can be found across the region as both poor and non-poor alike exploit natural resources for their livelihoods (Swinton et al, 2003). At the same time nearly 215 million people in Latin America are believed to live in poverty (Markowitz, 2007) and some 84 million people lack access to clean drinking water (Garcia, 1998). Although many countries have environmental legislation, most commonly based on the legislation of the US Environmental Protection Agency, most lack the capacity to adequately monitor or enforce the legislation (Rincon et al, 2007).

The perceived failure of capitalist forms of governance, particularly in their ability to reduce poverty, has led to the rise in socialism across Latin America (Markowitz, 2007). Many Latin American leaders, such as Hugo Chavez, are openly critical of the Washington Consensus, a cornerstone of capitalist politics, which seeks deregulation, trade liberalisation and privatisation of state-owned companies. Instead he and others look towards developing mixed economies involving the state and private sectors as a way of overcoming poverty. What this means for the environment and sustainable development is unclear. While it might be argued that socialism and sustainable development share the core value of social justice, recent research has shown that democracy may be more important in determining levels of sustainability (Whitford and Wong, 2009).

If, as sometimes argued, current global consumption levels are unsustainable, then there may be dire consequences for the environment if developing countries follow a similar development path. The problem is that for most developing countries the priority is to develop first to reduce levels of poverty, and then treat pollution and environmental degradation later (Zhang, 2008). However, for some environmental problems like climate change, it may not be possible to deal with the consequences later. The cartographic map in *Figure 13.1* shows the increase in carbon emissions globally between 1980 and 2000. Jarraud (2005: 1) finds that 'the biggest increases in carbon dioxide emissions over this period were in China, the US, and India', suggesting that at least some developing countries are already following the traditional, environmentally degrading, development path taken by industrialised countries over the last century.

Figure 13.1: Increased carbon dioxide emissions, 1980–2000

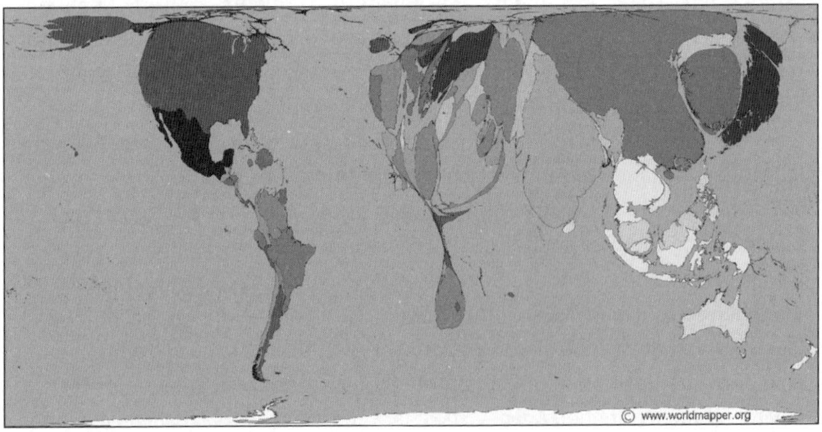

Note: Territory size shows the proportion of all territory level carbon dioxide emissions that occurred there (Jarraud, 2005).

Source: WorldMapper.org

© Copyright 2006 SASI Group (University of Sheffield) and Mark Newman (University of Michigan).

As developing countries have adopted, or been coerced into adopting, 'catch-up' development policies, there have been significant social, economic and environmental costs (Baker, S., 2006). Since the 1980s commodity prices, debt and barriers to free trade have shaped the economies of developing countries (Chasek et al, 2006). In the early 1970s there was a switch from aid and foreign direct investment to sovereign borrowing as the main form of capital inflow to developing countries (Avery, 1990: 503). Funds were borrowed for numerous development purposes including the creation and improvement of infrastructure. However, some were also linked to arms imports and political corruption (Avery, 1990: 511). Avery finds that between 1970 and 1982 medium and long-term indebtedness from the least developed countries increased by 20% annually. The 'developing country debt crisis' was triggered in 1982 by the Mexican default, and the following five years were witness to numerous plans to restructure debts (Arslanalp and Henry, 2005: 1021). By 1989:

> 16 developing countries reached debt relief agreements with their private creditors under the Brady Plan [one of a number of debt restructuring plans]. (Arslanalp and Henry, 2005: 1018)

At the end of 1997, outstanding debts on loans guaranteed by the UK government, through the Export Credit Guarantee Department to the 41 poorest countries, amounted to £4,685 million (Hillyard, 1998: 3). Indeed, Chasek et al (2006: 234) suggest that 'in 1995 total external debt of least developed countries was $136 billion, which represented 112.7 per cent of their GNP for that year'. Historically, when countries have struggled with external debts, involvement from the International Monetary Fund (IMF) is sought. The IMF had an increasingly frequent role in the 1970s and 1980s as more countries struggled with debts (Avery, 1990: 517). During this period the prescriptions of the IMF typically included:

(1) removal of price controls and subsidies
(2) abolition of foreign exchange and import controls
(3) currency devaluation
(4) greater openness towards foreign investment
(5) anti-inflationary measures such as reduction in public sector spending and the restriction of the money supply.

However, these prescriptions have had quite significant effects on the countries involved. Despite the liberalisation of markets within developing countries, numerous trade barriers have been erected by industrialised countries against imports of processed goods from developing countries (Chasek et al, 2006: 234). Protectionist measures taken include both tariff and non-tariff measures – such as import restrictions, sanitary measures and subsidies to protect against cheap imports. Equally, the liberalisation of developing countries' agricultural markets has also met with policies within the developed world that dissuade exports – especially those of manufactured/processed goods (Chasek et al, 2006: 236). As a result there have been significant implications for the environment. Baker suggests that the liberalisation of agriculture has undermined subsistence agriculture, placing a greater emphasis on cash crops rather than food crops (Baker, S., 2006: 159). High demand for certain goods such as cotton has disrupted traditional practices, displacing farmers, and encouraging environmentally damaging practices such as high levels of pesticide use in order to maximise yield (Chasek et al, 2006: 236). The combination of industrialised countries' protectionist policies, debt burdens and a fall in commodity prices encourages greater production of certain goods, with little regard to the resulting rapid depletion of land and natural resources. As a consequence of the factors described above, some suggest that former colonial relationships are now played out in trade conflicts between the industrialised countries and developing countries (Baker, S., 2006: 159).

Unequal effects of environmental degradation

In the distant past human activities tended to be localised in scale and impact. However, developments in industry, communications and technology over the last 200 years mean that we are now entering an era of unprecedented influence on the global environment. Globalisation acts as a driver of environmental degradation because global markets and the demand for goods and services mean that what we do in one country has implications for the environments in other countries. Environmental impacts have also become globalised in the sense that human activities are affecting the global environment. The use of fossil fuels in developed countries – in transport, manufacturing and energy generation – is contributing substantially towards the widespread and sustained problem of climate change. In contrast, developing countries have contributed virtually nothing towards the problem, as demonstrated by *Figure 13.2*, which indicates the global distribution of carbon emissions in 2000 (with high levels of emissions clearly visible in western Europe and the US, and notably low levels in African countries).

At the same time, developing countries will be disproportionately affected by the consequences of climate change such as rising sea levels, reduced crop yields and increased disease burden. They are more vulnerable because of their geographical locations and because their ecological systems are often more sensitive to climate change. Their social systems also make them less likely to be able to adapt and defend themselves against the effects of climate change because they lack capital assets (for example, physical, social or financial) that provide the capacity for adaptation, or political and institutional frameworks that are necessary to support adaptation (Frazer et al, 2010). Particularly vulnerable to sea level rise caused by climate change are low-lying countries such as Bangladesh and Mozambique – rated 13th and 15th worst affected by floods between 1975 and 2000 (see *Figure 13.3*). While low-lying countries such as the Netherlands are also vulnerable, they are far more likely to be able to adapt and respond to climate-related threats because of their capital assets (particularly physical and financial) and their strong institutions for managing flood defences.

Figure 13.2: *Carbon dioxide emissions, 2000*

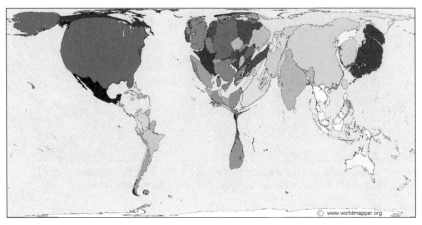

Note: Territory size shows the proportion of all territory level emissions of carbon dioxide emissions in 2000 that occurred there.

Source: WorldMapper.org

© Copyright 2006 SASI Group (University of Sheffield) and Mark Newman (University of Michigan)

The unequal effects of environmental degradation occur not only at an international scale between countries, but also within countries between men and women, between different ethnic groups and between the poor and the better off. Exposure is often unequal because of social injustice and the uneven distribution of power (Maples, 2003). The low social status of individuals and communities can expose them to the problems of environmental degradation through location (polluting industries are often located in poorer areas) or through their activities. For example, the traditional roles of women in poorer households mean that they are often more exposed to the impact of deforestation, which can add as much as 11 hours a day to fuel collection activities (Fleuret and Fleuret, 1978). Their use of wood fuels for cooking and heating also exposes many women to indoor air pollution. As a result, an estimated 59% of the 1.6 million deaths globally that are attributed to indoor air pollution are of women (WHO, 2005). In addition to low social status, a lack of power to affect decision making often means that these individuals or communities offer a 'path of least resistance' for distributing environmental risks (Maples, 2003: 236). Women, the poor and minority ethnic groups usually have less access

Figure 13.3: People killed by floods, 1975–2000

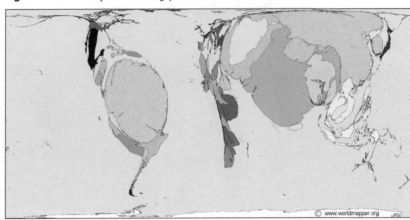

Note: Territory size shows the proportion of all people who have died in disasters due to flood, 1975–2000. A disaster, here, is an event that overwhelms local resources.

Source: WorldMapper.org

© Copyright 2006 SASI Group (University of Sheffield) and Mark Newman (University of Michigan).

to and influence on political structures meaning that their interests can be marginalised for the sake of other, more powerful, interests (Adeola, 2000; Maples, 2003). The consequences of this can be profound, with communities facing extreme environmental degradation with little or no compensation. This was the case for the Ogoni people in Nigeria who have had to deal with the devastating environmental and social consequences of oil extraction in the Niger Delta caused by a history of discrimination against minority ethnic groups in Nigeria and their lack of political power to prevent government-sanctioned oil exploration (see Boele et al, 2001).

The development challenge

Clearly there are consequences if developing countries follow the traditional path of economic development in order to increase welfare and overcome poverty. This path was first described by Selden and Song (1994) and termed the **environmental Kuznets curve** (EKC) after the economist who first described an inverted U-shaped relationship between income inequality and economic development (Kuznets and Simon, 1955). *Figure 13.4* shows a simplified version of the EKC.

The curve represents the relationship between economic growth and environmental impact. Following initially high levels of pollution, two important changes occur as the economy grows and incomes rise. First,

Figure 13.4: *Environmental Kuznets curve*

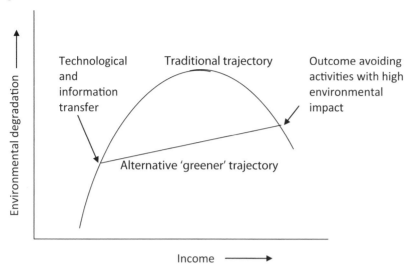

Source: Adapted from Dinda (2004)

higher incomes mean that most people are able to meet their immediate needs and are able to start valuing their environment more. As a result, environmental legislation becomes more effective and people are able and willing to pay abatement costs. Second, as economies develop they tend to move towards less polluting service industries and develop technologies to reduce the impact of polluting ones, which in turn reduces the pressure on the environment (Tisdell, 2001). The result is that the environmental impacts reduce even as the economy continues to grow.

Some studies, particularly using water and air pollution data, have found evidence for the EKC (Dinda, 2004). However, Dinda (2004) suggests that the presence of the curve for some pollutants may be the result of displacement of polluting industries to poorer countries with weaker regulations. For other sources of environmental degradation, particularly those with global and long-term impacts, research suggests that the curve may not exist at all. It is also argued that while globalisation might stimulate economic growth in already developed countries it exacerbates levels of poverty, population increase and urbanisation in developing countries (Galatchi, 2007). Benvenisti (2008) suggests that we should be looking for local solutions to local problems based on bottom-up approaches and co-management with local communities. In contrast, Zhang (2008) suggests that globalisation could provide part of the solution. The straight line on *Figure 13.4* illustrates an alternative path that developing countries could take to avoid some of the environmental impacts of economic growth, referred to as 'green growth' by the United Nations (UN) (UN ESCAP, 2005). To achieve this path of economic growth and limited environmental damage, developing countries would require support to develop the right policy mix of legislation and market-based instruments accompanied by technology and knowledge transfer from developed countries.

Global policy responses

The policy challenge

As indicated above, there is a clear preference in international policy discourse for 'green growth' among developing countries; however, perceived negative impacts of environmental policy solutions can often act as a barrier to policy development (Carter, 2007). Using climate change as an example, Roberts and Parks (2007: 7) highlight the potential of a 'triple inequality of responsibility, vulnerability and mitigation' associated with both the effects of climate change and mitigation policies. They argue that while developing countries have contributed least to greenhouse gas (GHG) emissions and are likely to suffer negative effects disproportionately compared to developed countries, they are often unfairly asked to act in a way that will negatively affect their development.

As also identified above, particular socioeconomic and demographic groupings are often more vulnerable to the effects of environmental problems than others, and this is often also the case for policy solutions. For example, policies that seek to change patterns of energy use may have negative effects on those least able to pay for alternative forms of energy, or increased costs associated with existing forms. Within this policy area, the Global Network on Energy for Sustainable Development (GNESD) makes a clear case for the protection of the poorest communities within developing countries, ensuring their protection from policy measures that may negatively affect progression towards the eight Millennium Development Goals (MDGs). GNESD indicate the importance of matching 'clean' forms of energy with anti-poverty measures, citing a case study from South Africa's National Electrification Programme (NEP):

> Though NEP provided electricity to many poor households, it did not ensure that the poor households could afford to buy it. Thus, the Government of South Africa introduced a policy in 2003 on electricity subsidy to reduce the worst effects of poverty on communities. The policy provides a 'poverty tariff' targeted at the poor. (GNESD, 2007: 6)

Summary box

Key treaties and protocols

1946   International Convention for the Regulation of Whaling

1973   CITES Convention on International Trade in Endangered Species of Flora and Fauna comes into effect (international treaty with more than 150 signatories); came into effect in 1975

1979   Convention on Long Range Transboundary Air Pollution (LRTAP) adopted

1982   UN Convention on the Law of the Sea adopted over fishing

1985   Vienna Convention for the Protection of the Ozone Layer

1987   Following the Vienna Convention, the Montreal Protocol on Substances Depleting the Ozone Layer is adopted

1989   Basle Convention on the Control of Transboundary Movements of Hazardous Wastes and their Disposal

1992   Rio Earth Summit – outputs include:

       Agenda 21

       Convention on Biology Diversity

       Framework Convention on Climate Change

       Rio Declaration

       Non-binding Forest Principles

1994   UN Convention to Combat Desertification

1997   Signing of Kyoto Protocol (Climate Change); agreed legally binding targets

1998   Aarhus Convention on Access to Information, Public Participation in Decision-making and Access to Justice in Environmental Matters signed (largely European Union [EU] states, but also central Asian states)

2000   Cartagena Protocol on Bio-safety

2005   Kyoto Protocol comes into force

Source: Adapted from iisd.org 2002 (sustainability timeline)

Bearing in mind the factors discussed above, this chapter now discusses key conferences and protocols, and outlines attempts to integrate environment, poverty and development concerns within these.

Key conferences and protocols

Historically the developing world has been suspicious that the environmental regimes proposed by developed countries were a way of controlling resources (especially oil), and generally preventing economic development (see Najam, 2005 or Chasek et al, 2006). However, some progress was made in 1972 with the Founex Report suggesting the following:

> ... the developing countries would clearly wish to avoid
> ... the environmental mistakes and distortions that have
> characterised the patterns of development of the industrialised
> societies ... however, the major environmental problems of the
> developing countries are essentially of a different kind – they
> are predominantly problems that reflect the poverty and very
> lack of development in their societies. (Founex, 1972: 5-6)

It became clear during this period – culminating with the 1972 UN
Conference on Human Environment in Stockholm – that '... environment
and development could not for long be in conflict' (Trzyna, 1995: 7). The
Founex Report fed into the Stockholm Conference in 1972, bringing
together issues of development, the environment and poverty for the
first time. As a result, terminology evolved over the following 10 years,
from vague terms such as 'environmentally sound development' and 'eco-
development', to 'environmental management' and similarly broad holistic
concepts. Shortly after, 'The World Conservation Strategy' was derived from
the World Conservation Union in 1980, working closely with the World
Wildlife Fund (WWF) and the UN Environment Programme (UNEP).
This was a major attempt to integrate environmental and developmental
concerns into an umbrella concept of conservation. While the term
'sustainable development' was not used in the body of the text, it was used
in the subtitle and this highlighted the term. The strategy provided a more
concrete focus than the more diffuse attempts prior to it, and made space
for issues concerning efficiency, distribution and equity, conservation and
resource management, and intergenerational responsibility (Trzyna, 1995:
8). This represented a global shift in perspective. The view of nature shifted
from 'a treasure to be preserved into a resource whose yield had to be
sustained' (Sachs, 1997: 72).

As discussed in previous chapters, the approach was continued and
developed by the Brundtland Report, *Our common future* (WCED, 1987),
which is thought to be the most groundbreaking in terms of sustainable
development (Voisey and O'Riordan, 1997: 26). The report argued that
sustainable development should include social, economic and environmental
elements and that it should be 'Development that meets the needs of the
present without compromising the ability of future generations to meet
their own needs' (WCED, 1987: 8). The issues raised by *Our common future*
were then discussed at the UN General Assembly in 1989 and Resolution
44/228 – a call for a UN Conference on Environment and Development
(UNCED) – was passed. The Conference was held in 1992 in Rio, and
Agenda 21 was the main outcome. Agenda 21 utilised the themes outlined
by Brundtland, and was the result of an international consensus that was

reached over four meetings of the UNCED Preparatory Committee. The Rio Earth Summit in 1992 placed a much greater emphasis on development, and was viewed by many developing countries as an extremely positive event.

Since Rio, there have been three further milestones. First, the Kyoto Protocol was negotiated in 1997, recognising the importance of a global reduction in GHG emissions in order to slow down the effects of climate change. While this was rejected by President Bush in 2001, it came into force in 2004 after it was ratified by Russia. Second, the Millennium Summit and **Millennium Development Goals** (MDGs) (to be discussed in detail below). Third, in 2002 the Johannesburg Earth Summit was held and looked back at the progress of Agenda 21, and also set targets for sanitation, energy use, health, agriculture and biodiversity. The key difference between this summit and previous ones was the increased focus on countries outside the European Union (EU) and the US; indeed, Najam (2005: 312) suggests that the post-Rio period saw developing countries becoming more engaged in environmental discourses, leading up to the 2002 World Summit on Sustainable Development in Johannesburg, with developing countries moving to a new phase of 'active engagement' (Najam, 2005: 313). Yet without a strong presence from the US the outputs were criticised by many as limited.

However, there are still very different priorities between developed and developing countries. Within developed countries there tends to be a focus on ecological issues, whereas developing countries 'do not view these to be sufficient in and of themselves unless due attention is also paid to developmental and equity concerns' (Najam 2005: 318). Chasek et al (2006) argue that there has been a shift from global environmental politics towards global sustainable development. Despite widening development gaps within developing countries, they still often act as a collective when it comes to issues around environmental politics:

> ... the insistent choice to use the term 'South' is more than a matter of semantics and reflects a central aspect of their [developing countries] collective identity and their desire to negotiate as a collective ... the dominant presence of developing countries in global environmental politics has come through the collective voice of the South, articulated through the Group of 77. (Najam 2005: 304-5)

(This is not to say that states do not pursue their own interests as well, and the division between oil-producing and non-oil producing countries can become more apparent during particular types of negotiation.)

As perspectives on the environment changed at the international level, a number of treaties and **protocols** were developed. A reason for the rise in international agreements lies in the changing nature of environmental issues. When concerns were local in their extent, nation-states could take their own steps to deal with the causes and consequences of environmental problems. However, environmental issues have become increasingly trans-boundary and global. The scale of these environmental problems means that they cannot be solved by individual states working alone and international cooperation is required if they are to be dealt with effectively.

In addition to the meetings, reports and treaties discussed above, the Millennium Declaration and MDGs are of great significance to global environmental policy. These were built on a number of UN global conferences during the 1990s. The UN Millennium Declaration

> ... marked a strong commitment to the right to development, to peace and security, to gender equality, to the eradication of the many dimensions of poverty and to sustainable human development. (UN, 2005: v)

Within the Declaration were the eight MDGs, and 18 time-bound targets. The Declaration was adopted by 157 heads of state and 189 states. The Millennium Summit and resulting MDGs are thought to have furthered the shift in focus from environmental policy to sustainable development, as most

> ... environmental regimes have been struggling to place their priorities in line with the MDGs so that they will continue to receive attention within the larger development agenda that has overtaken the international community since the millennium summit. (Chasek et al, 2006: 271)

Case study

Comparing Africa and Asia

The African continent poses a significant challenge to achieving the goals of poverty reduction and sustainable development. Although foreign aid has been increasing, from an average of almost US$26 billion a year between 1986 and 2002 to more than US$42 billion by 2006 (Youell, 2008), the number of poor people in Africa is still increasing (Lufumpa, 2005) and even the UN recognises that many of the MDGs will not be met in Africa by 2015 if current trends continue (UN, 2005). The reasons posited for this failure are various. Collier (2007) cites corrupt governments and continued conflict as important 'traps' that prevent foreign aid investment from working to reduce poverty. Hyden (2007) suggests that the problem is much more fundamental: the transfer of western styles of governance and economics does not work in countries where the informal sector and social networks are more important to livelihoods. Instead he suggests a bottom-up approach that is matched to the particular socioeconomic conditions of countries in Africa. However, the international aid community is still focused on transforming formal structures to facilitate poverty reduction.

On the other hand Asia has achieved considerable success in reducing levels of poverty (Farrington and Clarke, 2006; Humphrey, 2006). Countries such as China, Indonesia and Vietnam had already achieved the MDG of reducing poverty by half in 2003, with some 204 million people in China alone raised above the US$1 a day poverty line (Humphrey, 2006). This poverty reduction has been driven by high levels of economic growth in the region, with most countries seeing per capita growth rates above 4%. However, environmental resources such as fertile soils, water and forests have made a significant contribution to this growth, with the result that development has come at a substantial environmental cost, through pollution, water scarcity and deforestation, which tends to be disproportionately felt by the poor (Bass and Steele, 2006). The 'develop now and deal with pollution later' approach has been fundamental to the economic growth of Asia but for growth to continue in the longer term, and to overcome the inequities that have developed as a result, a more balanced approach underpinned by sustainable development will be necessary. Humphrey (2006) suggests that the evidence for this shift in thinking is already apparent with eco-efficiency programmes in Thailand, energy efficiency promotion in China and the regional Asia Forest Programme and Asian Forest Law Enforcement and Governance programme.

The MDGs echo the themes within Agenda 21 and the Brundtland Report. Many of the problems highlighted by the MDGs are likely to cause environmental degradation, and environmental degradation is also likely to perpetuate a number of the issues underlying the MDGs. The similarities in these documents indicate the close-knit relationship between international development and sustainable development, and the likelihood that sustainable development will be limited without a balance of these different dimensions. The similarities also demonstrate the shift from global environmental politics to global sustainable development.

Table 13.1 outlines the main components of the Brundtland Report, Agenda 21 and the MDGs. The similarities between these are striking.

Table 13.1: Brundtland Report, Agenda 21 and the MDGs

Brundtland Report (1987)	Agenda 21 (1992)	MDGs (2000)
Common challenges	Key social and economic	Eradicate extreme poverty
Population and human	dimensions	and hunger
resources	International cooperation	Primary universal
Food security: sustaining	Combating poverty	education
the potential	Changing consumption	Promote gender equality
Species and ecosystems:	patterns	and empower women
resources for	Demographic dynamics	Reduce child mortality
development	Human health	Improve maternal health
Energy: choices for	Human settlements	Combat HIV/AIDS, malaria
environment and	Strengthening the role of	and other diseases
development	major groups	Ensure environmental
Industry: producing more	Women	sustainability
with less	Children and youth	A global partnership for
The urban challenge	Indigenous people	development
Common endeavours	Farmers	
Managing the commons	Implementation	
Peace, security,	Education and awareness	
development and the	Capacity building in	
environment	developing countries	
Towards common action:	International institutions	
proposals for institutional		
and legal change		

Resulting projects

A number of key initiatives have come out of the conferences and agreements outlined above. The most significant two are the Global Environment Facility (GEF) and the Clean Development Mechanism (CDM). GEF is the largest funder of projects to improve the global environment (GEF, 2007: 2), and is the only multi-donor funding mechanism specifically designed to tackle global environmental issues (Mee et al, 2008: 800). GEF is a joint programme between the UN Development Programme (UNDP), UNEP and the World Bank, and since 1991 US$4.4 billion in grants and US$28 billion in co-financing has been provided to more than 1,900 projects in over 160 countries (GEF, 2007: 2). Discussions held at the Rio Earth Summit around the structure of GEF raised a number of concerns. First, questions were raised over the legitimacy of the governance structure of the World Bank and, second, many developing countries wanted a broader developmental focus rather than a narrow ecological one (Najam, 2005: 310). GEF has evolved considerably since 1991, and following the most recent funding agreement in 2006, a set of reforms were introduced to improve the efficiency and effectiveness of the institution with the aim of 'ensuring that countries are in the driver's seat when it comes to setting programming priorities' (GEF, 2007: 5).

Mee et al (2008) suggest that there are four main challenges to GEF at present. First, as described previously, the spatial distribution of pollution sources and pollution effects can be highly variable, with a problem caused by one country being felt in another (for example, acid rain in Sweden as a result of activities in the UK). However, this is a major challenge for the GEF, as a global problem such as this is difficult to resolve at the local or regional scale (because the polluting countries have a limited incentive to act, and those affected by pollution are unable to prevent the problem). Mee et al (2008: 802) comment that 'many GEF projects are ... inappropriate for dealing with these drivers and could only ever result in partial solutions'. Second, there is a temporal challenge: where projects do not have immediate gains or outcomes they can be less popular – Mee et al (2008: 802) suggest that 'the typical response times present a huge practical challenge as well as a political one'. As a result it is difficult to assess project success, but also to ensure long-term stakeholder buy-in. Third, and closely related to that point, assessing the effectiveness of GEF is also a challenge. While GHGs are used as marketable currency, other environmental issues are far harder to quantify. Mee et al (2008) suggest that pressure to demonstrate positive outcomes within the conservation community can lead to the use of output performance indicators that are potentially of limited value. Clearly, this makes it harder to assess the overall impact of the GEF. Fourth, and typically associated with issues of sustainable development, many institutions struggle to deal with the multisectoral response needed to make meaningful policies of sustainable development.

Case study

Africa Community Outreach Programme (COP) for Conservation and Sustainable Use of Biological Resources – A GEF project

The project was designed to assist Botswana, Malawi, Mozambique, Namibia, South Africa, Zambia and Zimbabwe (all parties to the Convention on Biological Diversity) to conserve biological resources of global significance through a public education and awareness programme using local and traditional means of communication to promote incentives for local community participation in implementing the objectives of the Convention. Fourteen actors, two from each of the participating countries, were selected as actor-facilitators for the programme. They underwent theatrical skills training in South Africa and facilitation training in Namibia. The project spent up to six weeks in each country, holding theatrical workshops and creating local productions with the input of communities, the local COP Partners and the two-person teams. The 'regional roadshow' was successfully staged in 16 cities of the seven countries between October and December 2000.

Source: http://gefonline.org/projectDetailsSQL.cfm?projID=24

Clean Development Mechanism (CDM)

The Kyoto Protocol introduced three mechanisms that would allow developed countries to reduce their GHG emissions abroad: joint implementation, international emissions trading and the CDM. Of most relevance to developing countries is the CDM, which allows developed countries to 'reduce' their GHG emissions in part through the financing of emission reduction projects in developing countries. CDM has been successful in some respects, with Woerdman (2000) arguing that it is more effective, efficient and politically acceptable than other mechanisms within the Kyoto Protocol.

Summary box

Clean Development Mechanism (CDM)

Defined in Article 12 of the Protocol [the CDM] allows a country with an emission-reduction or emission-limitation commitment under the Kyoto Protocol to implement an emission-reduction project in developing countries. Such projects can earn saleable 'certified emission reduction' credits, each equivalent to one tonne of carbon dioxide (CO_2), which can be counted towards meeting Kyoto targets. A CDM project activity might involve, for example, a rural electrification project using solar panels or the installation of more energy-efficient boilers.

The mechanism stimulates sustainable development and emission reductions, while giving industrialised countries some flexibility in how they meet their emission reduction or limitation targets.

Source: UNFCC (2009)

Boyd et al (2007) suggest that there are four main challenges associated with the CDM. First, the actual impact of projects is very difficult to measure. A baseline must be established to assess what would happen along a 'business as usual' scenario. However, by nature such a scenario is hypothetical and will not take into account other changes that might have occurred without the CDM project. Second, CDM projects must take 'additionality' into consideration; this means that projects must contribute in a way that would have not occurred without the intervention – for example, they should help to overcome technical, financial or institutional barriers. Third, 'leakage' is a challenge within CDM projects – this generally refers to the effects of a project on GHGs elsewhere. This could mean that a problem is displaced to another country, and emissions increase there, or that other factors such as changes in market conditions then lead to increased emissions within the project country. Fourth, there are issues around the scientific validity of projects. Reforestation and afforestation are currently fundable activities within the CDM; however, there is a push to include more modern technologies such as carbon capture and storage from 2012 onwards; some argue that these are questionable in effect.

Criticisms of GEF and CDM

In addition to the challenges presented by both GEF and CDM, there are several criticisms about their effectiveness. Both GEF and CDM are criticised for their inability to deal with complex problems – Mee et al (2008: 806-7) suggest that within GEF there is a temptation to go for short-term 'easy wins'; this often means that projects that may have a greater, more long-term impact on both the environment and development are less common. Likewise, Boyd et al (2007) find that the CDM is effective when it comes to achieving cost-effective emission reductions through the carbon market, meaning that the other main aim, to achieve sustainable development in developing countries, has been sidelined. Critics suggest that because CDM is a market-based mechanism, aspects that are less 'marketable' are marginalised, and while CDM may be effective as means of producing the lowest-cost emission reductions, what is left out of the market are the sustainable development benefits (see Boyd et al, 2007; Olson, 2007; Pearson, 2007). Olson (2007: 67) concludes that 'left to market forces, the CDM does not significantly contribute to sustainable development in developing countries'. Likewise, Pearson (2007: 249) suggests:

> ... the CDM is a market, not a development fund.... Its aim is to provide tradable emission credits at the lowest cost in a limited timeframe, primarily up to 2012. Its aim is not to direct funding to projects that provide the greatest environmental and social benefit or that help direct a developing country down a sustainable development path in the long term.

There are criticisms levelled at both GEF and the CDM; for instance, that the projects funded are not those that will be of greatest value to the recipient country. Likewise, projects with broad social and environmental benefits are often overlooked – Pearson (2007: 252) suggests 'the market will seek out the cheapest [carbon] credits, not the best environmental outcomes'.

Conclusion

Industrialisation and development has come at a substantial environmental cost – the developed world has already contributed substantially towards widespread and sustained environmental problems such as climate change. Developing countries, while contributing virtually nothing to these global environmental problems, are likely to be disproportionately affected by them and are least able to adapt or respond effectively. While the poor often remain reliant on natural resources for subsistence livelihoods, and can be trapped in a cycle of poverty and environmental degradation, wealth and development are just as likely to contribute to environmental degradation.

As developing countries have adopted, or been coerced into adopting, 'catch-up' development policies, there have been significant social, economic, and environmental costs. Despite the liberalisation of markets within developing countries, numerous trade barriers have been erected by industrialised countries against imports of processed goods from developing countries. The combination of industrialised countries' protectionist policies, debt burdens and a fall in commodity prices has encouraged greater production of certain goods, with little regard to the resulting rapid depletion of land and natural resources.

If developing countries follow the traditional path of economic development there are likely to be serious environmental and social implications. This path was termed the EKC. To achieve an alternative path of economic growth and limited environmental damage, developing countries require support to develop the right policy mix of legislation and market-based instruments accompanied by technology and knowledge transfer from developed countries.

The key challenges faced by developing countries are embodied by the MDGs: economic development (including the eradication of absolute poverty), social development (including overcoming illiteracy and disease), ecological sustainability and overcoming social and political barriers (including corruption, conflict, drugs trafficking and gender discrimination). Sustainable development will be limited without these elements being appropriately balanced.

The scale of global-level environmental problems means that they cannot be solved by individual states working alone and international cooperation is required if they are to be dealt with effectively. Developing countries have been suspicious that the environmental regimes proposed by developed countries were a way of controlling resources. However, the nature of international treaties and protocols has changed since the 1970s with many arguing that there has been a shift from global environmental politics towards global sustainable development. However, there is still concern that international-level projects such as the GEF and CDM will not be of greatest value to developing countries, and may not have the longevity or scope required for sustainable development.

Chapter summary

The chapter:

- introduced four key issues associated with developing countries and the environment and explained the meaning and problems of 'catch-up' development policies;
- outlined the key challenges for sustainable development and critiqued the relevance of the EKC to these challenges;
- investigated key developments in international decision making over recent decades, highlighting a gradual shift from 'global environmental politics' to 'global sustainable development';
- described two international-level environment-related programmes (GEF and CDM) and offered a critique of their effectiveness.

Questions for discussion

- Is poverty solely responsible for environmental degradation?
- What barriers to sustainable development exist in developing countries and how might they be overcome?
- Account for the shift from 'global environmental governance' to 'global sustainable development'.
- How successful have international interventions been in reducing poverty and increasing environmental protection?

Key further reading

Baker, S. (2006) *Sustainable development*, London: Routledge.

Chasek, P., Downie, D.L. and Brown, J.W. (2006) *Global environmental politics* (4th edn), Boulder, CO: Westview Press.

Roberts, J.T. and Parks, B.C. (2007) *A climate of injustice, global inequality, North-South politics, and climate policy*, Cambridge, MA: The MIT Press.

Useful websites

Brady Plan: www.emta.org/template.aspx?id=35

UN Millennium Development Goals: www.un.org/millenniumgoals/

UK Department for International Development: www.dfid.gov.uk/

World Bank: www.worldbank.org/ (see the programme dealing with sustainable development)

Conclusion

Tony Fitzpatrick

Before leaving the house you check that the interactive energy grid is on. This means that the few appliances you need to leave active during the day – like the fridge – will store what they need and only draw energy from the local network when required. Besides, you checked your eco-account yesterday and you've been selling more energy *to* the network recently than you've been taking from it. Your new microgeneration plant started paying for itself last year.

You wait at the end of the road for your regular personalised transit cart (PTC). You climb aboard and insert your 3C (carbon credit card) into the reader. It deducts 20 credits from your monthly allowance and automatically deducts a 3% contribution from your eco-account. That percentage was dropping year on year as levels of global poverty reduced. You are joined by seven other neighbours who also work in the Shelton borough and off you go. The PTC is driverless and follows a series of dioptric lights set into the road.

Other carts follow the same lights before and behind you, but because they have been programmed to aim for different sectors they will ultimately divert onto alternative routes. You are surprised to see one or two private vehicles on the road this morning. Normally, even top-of-the-range hydros are curfewed until the hours of 9.30am–3.30pm. But then you remember that the country is ahead of meeting its annual emissions targets and things have been relaxed slightly. This won't make you late for work, however. There are few traffic jams these days and public vehicles always have right of way.

You walk the last half mile to school, through one of the thousands of Lifeparks now scattered throughout the city, scanning the news headlines as they scroll down the inside screen of your neuro–glasses. Yes, that confirms it. Having become carbon neutral 10 years earlier the country was steadily becoming a carbon *absorber*, more than counteracting the emissions of those few countries still allowed to pursue old-fashioned economic growth because of the awful deprivation which centuries of underdevelopment had left them with.

You smile at another story. The Futurist Movement was again complaining that sustainable growth had prevented humans from achieving the marvels which might have been expected by now: space tourism, 4D channels, 90-minute flights to Australia, etc, etc. You shrug. If those things were worth having they'd happen eventually, and with much less cost to the ecosystem.

You quicken your step. The day is a bit chilly but, of course, the world was continuing to heat anyway because of the reckless decisions and lifestyles of previous generations. Still, the rate of warming was slowing and promised to halt entirely within the next half–century. Your generation would be remembered for bequeathing a better legacy than any before it.

A morning's work means that you will have fulfilled your 25–hour quota for the week. However, the head had asked for a little bit of flexibility due to a colleague's illness and you remind yourself to visit her later today. In any event, some overtime wouldn't hurt. You've already got several hours saved up and should be able to reduce your working week to 20 hours for the next fortnight. You look forward to the day when the required average for everyone could be reduced to that level automatically.

Your class slowly assembles and receives their assignment marks. You'd asked them to imagine how life had been like 50 years ago and to write a story about a typical school day. Some stories had been hopelessly optimistic, portraying schools that were earlier versions of the reality the children were used to. Others had been overly dramatic. One girl had imagined a school that kept everything switched on permanently (computers, lights, furnaces, air conditioning), where everyone drove cars everywhere and which concentrated on swimming lessons because of the rising sea levels! The children then enjoy their daily trip to the school's solar fields and to its microfarm.

Later, you visit your colleague, riding to the hospital using one of the free bicycles provided by the municipality. You travel past a factory that converts old consumables (such as clothing and furniture) into new goods. There is now less obsession with waste and obsolescence but people still want novelty. Recycling doesn't have to mean stagnation and uniformity.

Your colleague suffered from a condition that some doctors were still sceptical about: Lawson's Syndrome. After centuries of breathing in atmospheric pollutants medical researchers thought that the human body had adapted until it treated pollution as normal! Some people therefore struggled to adapt to the cleaner air of recent decades. But other doctors thought that Lawson's Syndrome was a nonsense diagnosis. Previous generations had also been addicted to stress, aggression, inequality, status competition, acquisition of possessions and market dependency. Should they invent syndromes for the disappearance of those stupidities too?!

Still, it was nice sitting beneath the smart windows – which regulated the atrium's temperature automatically – feeling the grass beneath your feet, the natural ventilation and hearing about your colleague's new wellness plan. On one side, the vertical gardens reach from the very bottom to the very top of the building; the rainwater loops providing soothing, relaxing sounds. On the other side, the space was flooded with daylight, as were all the corridors and most of the interiors due to extensive light shelves.

It was difficult to tell a patient from a visitor from a medic. Many people were young, here for their Healthy Living consultations no doubt. You are aware that this small hospital lacks any mental health specialists. However, there are far fewer psychological ailments to deal with these days anyway.

That afternoon, you put some time into a local project, helping to upgrade its cooling panels and the recyclable irrigation system on its agricultural plot. That repays the community for the repair to your greywater system that a neighbour provided last week. You stay for a meal at the communal gardens, where much of the neighbourhood's local produce was grown, and return home before dark and plan what you are going to do tomorrow, on your 30th birthday: 1 June 2061. You are most likely to get presents of free time. It didn't matter. You'd end up giving most of them back for others' birthdays anyway! What mattered these days wasn't 'how much?'. Enjoyment, progress and development were more important than ever because the price that used to be paid for them was so high. There was still a long way to go, but at least the world had slowed down to the point where it could breathe again.

Okay, so it probably won't look anything like that. Nonetheless, it will have to look like something and, in getting from here to ... wherever, social policy has two basic tasks.

The first is to do what it already does, only better. Hospitals, schools, houses, employment and income maintenance schemes will all still be needed in some form or another. They have many roles to perform, many principles to embody and many dangers to avoid. Yet, as stated in the Introduction to this volume, unless they are consistent with the demands of a sustainable society then they won't get to do very much of anything.

Second, social policy has to establish new connections as the world around it changes, hopefully for the better (but see below). This means both attending to and influencing the polity, the economy, the values and the wider array of sociocultural relations into which social policies are woven. The above story does not draw neat, inflexible boundaries between what social policies are and are not, nor does this book and nor should you either. Categories are indispensible but they become impediments to thinking when the lines distinguishing one from the other are allowed to become impermeable.

What we face, in other words, are circumstances that challenge us to revise our social administrations and our social imaginations. The former is crucial and we always need social policy engineers to build, maintain, repair and tell us how things work within their specialities. But without vision, idealism, ambition and utopianism, social policy can be a very dull affair, dedicated to intervening in people's lives without much idea of why or with what purpose in mind.

The questions that were posed on page 1 thus stand but are far from being complete or conclusive. Furthermore, other chapters have had many additional questions to ask, both in terms of what we are doing and what we should be doing. Some readers will be unhappy with this. When thinking about the practicalities of policy, isn't it futile for the questions to outnumber the answers? But eco-social policy debates are new and still far from the centre of both governmental and academic debates. It is easy to push your way into the centre of a crowd by constructing a manifesto for change, one promising magical solutions to all our problems. But you are likely to drown in a cacophony of other voices and other manifestoes – recall the taxonomy on page 10. If the eco-social agenda is to advance there will have to be some harmonisation of these voices, one that needs to happen sooner rather than later. But environmentalism also has to evolve our politics beyond an era in which simple answers have been proposed to complex questions, most recently, the notion that markets are the answer to everything. Since we are all helping to create ecological crises, if they are to be effective we are going to have to take collective ownership of and responsibility for the solutions too.

Both I and the contributors to this book have taken things as far as we can. For now. Much of what we have said will be out of date within a decade. But whether it will date for good reasons or for bad ones is as much up to you as it is up to us.

Having given you the optimistic scenario here is its evil impostor. The week before this book went to press two major reports revised down the more alarming predictions of the 2007 Intergovernmental Panel on Climate Change (IPCC) report (Jowit and Ottery, 2010). But, they concluded, existing trends are still taking us towards warming above pre-industrial levels of 3.5°–4°C by the end of the century. This would bring major extinctions, threats to the food supply, severe droughts, floods, soil erosion, water pollution, biodiversity loss, sea level rises, heatwaves and health problems. It surely goes without saying that this would hit the poorest hardest.

If these trends continue then another policy dimension is likely to become more and more important: survivalism. This refers to the need for disaster management and emergency relief for those in distressful and life-threatening situations. At the moment fairly small international sums are readily available for this purpose and, in truth, need not occupy a large slice of expenditure at present. But if the world warms beyond 2°C, then we can expect the above effects to magnify. As this happens the need for survival funds will surely grow. If we recall the IPCC categories given in **Table 3.2** (Chapter Three) then we end up with something like the following scenario in **Figure c.1**.

Figure c.1: *The evolving priorities of eco-social policies*

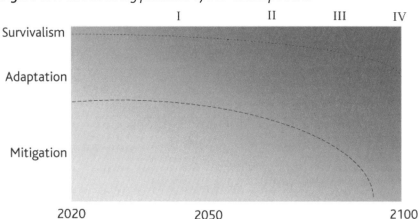

Looking down the Category I column in **Table 13.2**, mitigation and adaptation are our main priorities. If we could be confident of having done enough to stabilise emissions at Category I levels – approximately 2°C – then those distributions would presumably remain. If not, if we overshoot 2°C, then we would shift towards Categories II and III where survivalism becomes more prominent. If stabilisation at these levels also failed then, as Category IV becomes more likely towards the latter part of the century, mitigation as we currently define it begins to fade, adaptation and survivalism occupy the bulk of spending and activity as efforts are concentrated on coping with warming of 4°C. If we overshoot even this then, in the 22nd century, we have to contemplate the nightmare scenario of Categories V and VI. Here, mitigation and adaptation as we currently define them are gradually superseded. Humans cling to an ever more hostile planet, migrating *en masse* towards the warming poles. Efforts to avoid warming beyond 4°C involves shutting down as much high–carbon activity as possible, whatever the economic consequences.

At this point, we abandon social policies as we understand them today and enter a state of crisis management, one a long way from Lovelock's (2007: 200) sedate conception:

> One thing we can do to lessen the consequences of catastrophe is to write a guidebook for our survivors to help them rebuild civilisation without repeating too many of our mistakes.

We can do better than this, can't we?

Glossary

Adaptation	Measures to ensure that organisms (not limited to humans) can adapt to the global warming that is already unavoidable
Anthropocentrism	The view that only humans possess intrinsic value
Agenda 21	Principle output of the Rio Earth Summit in 1992; 178 countries signed up to the plan of action for sustainable development
Biocentrism	The view that all living beings possess intrinsic value
Brundtland Report	Officially titled *Our common future*, the Brundtland Report is the main publication of the 1987 World Commission on Environment and Development (WCED) and is credited with placing the issue of sustainable development on the global agenda
Cap-and-trade	A mixture of carbon taxes and carbon quotas that many believe is essential if we are to achieve a green economy. Taxes and quotas discourage unsustainable practices in terms of both supply and demand, production and consumption
Communitarianism	Opposed to extreme forms of individualism and advocates that individual liberties have to be contextualised by, and balanced against, what is good for the social community since our values and identities are derived substantially from the latter
Contraction and convergence	By contraction we mean the shrinking of carbon emissions over time; by convergence we mean that the amount of carbon emitted by developed nations falls as, for a time, that of developing nations continues to rise so that crucial social issues, for example, poverty, can be addressed
Cross-sector policies	Policies that cut across sectors such as the health sector and the environment sector for equal benefits, for example, policies to reduce air pollution improve the health of the environment and humans

Determinants of health	These are factors that influence health positively or negatively, including: income, education level, living environment, personal behaviour, healthcare access, genetics and social/cultural issues
Direct and indirect jobs	Direct jobs are jobs that are generated directly by an environmental policy. For instance, production of wind turbines could be a direct job, whereas intermediate production of inputs, such as steel production for wind turbines, is an indirect job. Other indirect jobs are generated by the economic multiplier effects
Discounting	Relating the well-being of future generations to that of present generations. A high discount rate means prioritising the interests of the present generation; a low rate means treating the needs and interests of present and future generations on a more equal basis
Ecocentrism	The view that species and ecosystems possess intrinsic value. Some ecocentrists hold that we should extend moral concern to include species and ecosystems within our moral deliberations while others hold that only ecosystems possess intrinsic value, and that their parts (including human beings) only possess instrumental value and, what is more, only possess it insofar as they contribute to the value of ecosystems
Ecofeminism	A branch of feminist theory that has as its central concern the connections and intersections between the historic domination/exploitation of the environment by humans and the oppression/ exploitation of women and their labour by patriarchal capitalism. Feminist political ecology and feminist ecological economics also fall within this branch
Ecological modernisation	A perspective that argues that economic growth and environmental damage can be decoupled, using new technologies and reforming institutions
Environmental citizenship	Part of a general trend towards reinventing the concept of citizenship to be more suited to 21st-century conditions, environmental citizenship includes *rights* to a clean environment and a set of *responsibilities*: to protect the interests of future generations and non-humans by actively participating in democratic political debate about sustainability and engaging in environmentally sound practices in daily life

Environmental justice	Originally referring to the fact that ecological burdens are most often borne by the socially disadvantaged, it has more recently referred to additional debates regarding the relevance of both social and environmental factors to the concept of justice, for example, in terms of non-human animals and future generations
Environmental Kuznets curve	Graphical representation of a theoretical U-shaped relationship between economic development and environmental degradation
Feminism	Concerned with gender and the extent to which women tend to be socially, politically and culturally disadvantaged, to varying degrees, across all societies
Food miles	The distance food travels to the consumer from the point of production. Excessive food miles make a major contribution to global warming and have increased with the globalisation of trade
Food security	Access to safe, healthy food for urban residents
GDP and GNP	Gross domestic product measures what is produced *within* national borders. Gross national product measures what is produced by the citizens of a nation no matter where in the world that production takes place
Gender mainstreaming	The process of including gender as a cross-cutting dimension in all policy fields; ensuring that policies do not impact negatively on people as a result of their gender roles or perpetuate gender inequality; ensuring that men and women have equal access to resources and equal participation in decision making
Gini coefficient	A statistical measure of dispersion, typically used to map inequalities in income and wealth. The closer a country is to 0 then the more equal it is; the closer to 100 the more unequal it is
Governance	A descriptive label that seeks to capture the fragmentation of the policy process and the rescaling of states
Instrumental value	The value that something has in virtue of its being a means to an end
Intrinsic value	The value that something has in its own right
I=PAT model	An iconic equation mathematically depicting the measurable effects of population size, resource consumption, and technology on the Earth. Environmental impact (I) is determined by the combined effects of population size (P), affluence (A), and technological development (T)

Justice	That which is fair, good and right. Acting justly involves recognising what others are entitled to or what they deserve and behaving accordingly. It may refer to the principles that impel acts, the consequences of those acts or to the virtuous disposition of the agent. Justice may also relate to social conditions and so to the distribution of social and public goods
Land use	The character and form of development, for example residential, commercial and industrial types
Liberal democracy	A form of democracy where elected representatives control the policy process but where constitutional provisions protect individual liberties (for example, freedom of speech, private property rights, and so on) and the rights of minorities
Liberalism	Concerned to define and defend individual freedom as the most important social, moral and legal value
Millennium Development Goals (MDGs)	Eight goals set out in the Millennium Declaration, which was adopted by 157 heads of state and 189 states
Mitigation	To slow the rate at which global warming increases so that the rate of growth can eventually be halted and reversed
Neoliberalism	An ideology and political movement that privileges free markets over state intervention
Planning	A variety of public or private processes intended to help prepare for the future, usually producing documents setting forth particular goals and policies
Post-industrialism	Denotes a society that has experienced a transition from a manufacturing-based economy to a service-based economy. It is characterised by much smaller units of production, often requiring a high level of technical education. This economic transition leads to a restructuring in society as a whole, including its values and norms
Post-materialism	A theory which argues that younger and more affluent people in western democracies are moving away from material concerns for income and security to post-material concerns such as a concern for civil liberties or for the environment
Precautionary principle	The notion that, faced with uncertainty, it is better to be overcautious and plan for the worst-case scenario so long as this does not make us too risk-averse
Protocol	A treaty under international law
Republicanism	Traditionally referring to a system where the head of state is elected, as a philosophical concept it advocates the importance of public participation, active citizenship and civic belonging to a free, democratic and solidaristic society

Social justice	The application of the concept of justice to society; often a prescriptive term advocated by those who believe in some form of socioeconomic and cultural egalitarianism, such as (1) equality of opportunity, or (2) the redistribution of wealth
Social reproduction	The provision of life-sustaining services on which the economy, the state and the lives of individual citizens depend. Feminists argue that women have been largely responsible for social reproduction and that it has been devalued or invisible in mainstream political and economic perspectives
Sustainability	This means ensuring that we do not deprive future generations of the environmental resources they need. Sustainability therefore implies some form of equity. It also implies that we should avoid overloading the earth's ability to absorb the consequences of human activities, that is, in terms of the atmosphere's pollution content and species extinction
Sustainable consumption	Refers to the conscious choice to purchase goods and services that meet basic needs and improve the quality of life while minimising the use of natural resources, toxic materials and the emission of waste and pollutants over their life cycle. Decisions are guided by an ethical commitment not to jeopardise the needs and choices of future generations
Sustainable development	Development that improves the long-term health of humans and ecological systems. According to the famous definition of the Brundtland Report, it means 'development that meets the needs of the present without compromising the ability of future generations to meet their own needs'
Transit-oriented development	New homes, shops, workplaces and other facilities near public transportation
Transit villages	Dense, mixed-use development at a transit station, intended to create a vibrant, walkable place
Urban agriculture	The growing of food crops in and near cities, usually through intensive production, and sometimes using unconventional sites such as rooftops
Urban design	The process of creatively determining the form and character of new development, usually at scales above that of the individual building
Zoning	A mechanism for regulation of land use through the creation of multiple 'zones' within a community subject to different regulations
Zoocentrism	The view that sentient animals possess intrinsic value

References

Achard, F., Eva, H.D., Stibig, H.J., Mayaux, P., Gallego, J., Richards, T. and Malingreau, J.P. (2002) 'Determination of deforestation rates of the world's humid tropical forests', *Science*, vol 297, no 5583, pp 999-1002.

Ackerman, B. and Alstott, A. (1999) *The stakeholder society*, Yale, CT: Yale University Press.

Adam, D. (2009) 'Grassroots groups move to fight global warming', *The Guardian Weekly*, 4 September, pp 1-2.

Adebowale, M. (2008) 'Understanding environmental justice', in G. Craig, T. Burchardt and D. Gordon (eds) *Social justice and public policy*, Bristol: The Policy Press.

Adeola, F.O. *(2000)* 'Endangered community, enduring people: toxic contamination, health, and adaptive responses in a local context', *Environment and Behavior*, vol 32, no 2, pp 209-49.

Altheide, D. (1976) *Creating reality: How TV news distorts events*, Beverly Hills, CA: Sage Publications.

Amre, D.K., Infante-Rivarde, C., Dufresne, A., Durgawale, P.M. and Ernst, P. (1999) 'Case-control study of lung cancer among sugar cane farmers in India', *Occupational Environmental Medicine*, vol 56, no 8, pp 548-52.

Anand, S. and Sen, A. (2000) 'Human development and economic sustainability', *World Development*, vol 28, no 12, pp 2029-49.

Anderson, E. (1999) 'What is the point of equality?', *Ethics*, vol 109, pp 287-337.

Anderson, J., Bowyer, C., Fergusson, M., Pallemaerts, M. and Valsecchi, C. (2007) *T-Page background paper on European actions on climate change and energy*, London: Institute for European Environmental Policy, Transatlantic Platform for Action on the Global Environment.

Anderson, K. (2009) *Climate change in a myopic world*, Tyndall Briefing Note No 36, Norwich: Tyndall Centre for Climate Change Research (www.tyndall.ac.uk/publications/briefing_notes/bn36.pdf).

Anderson, T. and Leal, D. (2001) *Free market environmentalism* (2nd edn), Boulder, CO and Basingstoke: Westview Press and Palgrave Macmillan.

Antweiler, W., Copeland, B.R. and Taylor, M.S. (2001) 'Is free trade good for the environment?', *The American Economic Review*, vol 91, no 4, pp 877-908.

AQEG (Air Quality Expert Group) (2007) *The Air Quality Strategy for England, Scotland, Wales and Northern Ireland*, London: AQEG.

Arnold, F.S. (1999) 'Environmental protection: is it bad for the economy? A non-technical summary of the literature', Washington, DC: US Environmental Protection Agency (http://yosemite.epa.gov/ee/epa/eerm.nsf/vwDFUS/212979DC5448DEAD8525683000732F35).

Arslanalp, S. and Henry, P.B. (2005) 'Is debt relief efficient?' *Journal of Finance*, vol 60, no 2, pp 1021-55.

ASES (American Solar Energy Society) and MISI (Management Information Services, Inc) (2008) *Defining, estimating, and forecasting the renewable energy and energy efficiency industries in the US and in Colorado*, Boulder, CO and Washington, DC: ASES and MISI (www.greenbiz.com/sites/default/files/document/CO_Jobs_Final_Report_December2008.pdf).

Attfield, R. (1995) *Value, obligation and meta-ethics*, Amsterdam: Rodopi.

Avery, W. (1990) 'The origins of debt accumulation among LDCs in the world political economy', *The Journal of Developing Areas*, vol 24, no 4, pp 503-22.

Bachram, H. (2004) 'Climate fraud and carbon colonialism', *Capitalism, Nature, Socialism*, vol 15, pp 5-20.

Baker, S. (2006) *Sustainable development*, London: Routledge.

Baker, W. (2006) *Social tariffs – A solution to fuel poverty?*, Bristol: Centre for Sustainable Energy.

Baker, W., Hyldon, V. and Templar, G. (2006) *Integrating welfare rights and fuel poverty services*, Bristol: Centre for Sustainable Energy.

Barnaby, F. (1988) 'Acid rain: UK policies', *Ambio*, vol 17, no 2, pp 160-2.

Barry, B. (1995) *Justice as impartiality*, Oxford: Oxford University Press.

Barry, J. (1999) *Rethinking green politics*, London: Sage Publications.

Barry, J. (2006) 'Resistance is fertile: from environmental to sustainability citizenship', in A. Dobson and D. Bell (eds) *Environmental citizenship*, Cambridge, MA: The MIT Press.

Barry, J. and Eckersley, R. (eds) (2005) *The state and the global ecological crisis*, Cambridge, MA: The MIT Press.

Barry, J. and Paterson, M. (2004) 'Globalisation, ecological modernisation and New Labour', *Political Studies*, vol 52, pp 767-84.

Barry, J. and Smith, K. (2008) 'Civic republicanism and green politics', in S. White and D. Leighton (eds) *Building a citizen society*, London: Lawrence & Wishart.

Barton, J.R. (2006) 'Eco-dependency in Latin America', *Singapore Journal of Tropical Geography*, vol 27, no 2, pp 134-49.

Barton, H. and Grant, M. (2006) 'A health map for the local human habitat', Journal for the Royal Society for the Promotion of Health, vol 126, no 6, pp 252-61.

Bass, S. and Steele, S. (2006) 'Managing the environment for development and to sustain pro-poor growth', *IDS Bulletin-Institute of Development Studies*, vol 37, no 3, pp 7-16.

Bauman, Z. (2005) *Work, consumerism and the new poor* (2nd edn), Maidenhead: Open University Press.

Becker, R. and Henderson, V. (2000) 'Effects of air quality regulations on polluting industries', *Journal of Political Economy*, vol 108, no 2, pp 379-421.

Bell, D. (1993) *Communitarianism and its critics*, Oxford: Clarendon Press.

Benvenisti, E. (2008) 'Asian traditions and contemporary international law on the management of natural resources', *Chinese Journal of International Law*, vol 7, pp 273-83.

Berck, P. and Hoffman, S. (2002) 'Assessing the employment impacts of environmental and natural resource policy', *Environmental and Resource Economics*, vol 22, pp 133-56.

Bergman, L. (2005) 'CGE modeling of environmental policy', in K.-G. Mäler and J.R. Vincent (eds) *Handbook of environmental economics*, Amsterdam: Elsevier.

Berman, E. and Bui, L.T.M. (2001) 'Environmental regulation and labor demand: evidence from the South Coast Air Basin', *Journal of Public Economics*, vol 79, pp 265-95.

Bezdek, R.H., Wendling, R.M. and DiPerna, P. (2008) 'Environmental protection, the economy, and jobs: national and regional analyses', *Journal of Environmental Management*, vol 86, pp 63-79.

Bird, J., Campbell, R. and Lawton, K. (2010) *The long cold winter: Beating fuel poverty*, London: Institute for Public Policy Research and National Energy Action.

Birdsall, N. and Wheeler, D. (1993) 'Trade policy and industrial pollution in Latin America: where are the pollution havens?', *Journal of Environment and Development*, vol 2, no 1, pp 137-49.

Bishop, S. and Grayling, T. (2003) *The sky's the limit: Policies for sustainable aviation*, London: Institute for Public Policy Research.

Bittman, M. and Wajcman, J. (2000) 'The rush hour: the character of leisure time and gender equity', *Social* Forces, vol 79, no 1, pp 165-89.

Bloomberg, M. and Aggarwala, R. (2008) 'Think locally, act globally. How curbing global warming emissions can improve local public health', *American Journal of Preventive Medicine*, vol 35, no 5, pp 414-23.

Boardman, B. (2010) Memorandum submitted to the Energy and Climate Change Committee on Fuel Poverty, *Fifth Report of Session 2009-10: Volume II*, London: House of Commons.

Boele, R., Fabig, H. and Wheeler, D. (2001) 'Shell, Nigeria and the Ogoni. A study in unsustainable development: I. The story of Shell, Nigeria and the Ogoni people – environment, economy, relationships: conflict and prospects for resolution', *Sustainable Development*, vol 9, pp 74-86.

Bohm, M., Jones, C., Land, C. and Paterson, M. (eds) (2006) *Against automobility*, Oxford: Blackwell.

Bookchin, M. (2005) *The ecology of freedom*, Edinburgh: AK Press.

Bows, A. and Anderson, K. (2007) 'Policy clash: can projected aviation growth be reconciled with the UK government's 60% carbon reduction target?', *Transport Policy*, vol 14, no 2, pp 103-10.

Boyd, E., Hultman, N.E., Roberts, T., Corbera, E., Ebeling, J., Liverman, D.M., Brown, K., Tipperman, R., Cole, J., Mann, P., Kaiser, M., Robbins, M., Bumpus, A., Shaw, A., Ferreira, E., Bozmoski, A., Villiers, C. and Avis, J. (2007) *The Clean Development Mechanism: An assessment of current practice and future approaches for policy*, Working Paper 114, Norwich: Tyndall Centre for Climate Change Research.

Boyden, S. (1987) *Western civilization in biological perspective*, Oxford: Clarendon Press.

Boyden, S. (2005) *People and nature*, Canberra, Australia: Nature and Society Forum.

Breheny, M. (1996) 'Centrists, decentrists, and compromisers: views on the future of urban form', in M. Jenks, E. Burton and K. Williams (eds) *The compact city: A sustainable urban form?*, London: E & FN Spon.

Brown, K. (2009) 'Human development and environmental governance: a reality check', in W. Adger and A. Jordan (eds) *Governing sustainability*, Cambridge: Cambridge University Press.

Brown, L. (2000) 'Worldwatch', in H. Newbold (ed) *Life stories*, Berkeley, CA: University of California Press.

Brown, L. (2009) 'Could food shortages bring down civilization?', *Scientific American*, May.

Brown, V.A. (1992) 'Health care policies, health policies or policies for health?', in H. Gardner (ed) *Health policy*, Melbourne: Churchill Livingstone.

Brown, V.A., Nicholson, R. and Stephenson, P. (2002) 'Environmental health policy in a time of change', in H. Gardner and S. Barraclough (eds) *Health policy in Australia* (2nd edn), Melbourne: Oxford University Press.

Brown, V.A., Grootjans, J., Ritchie, J., Townsend, M. and Verrinder, G. (eds) (2005) *Sustainability and health*, London: Earthscan.

Brulle, R.J. and Young, L.E. (2007) 'Advertising, individual consumption levels, and the natural environment, 1900-2000', *Sociological Inquiry*, vol 77, no 4, pp 522-42.

Bulkeley, H. and Newell, P. (2010) *Governing climate change*, London: Routledge.

Burchell, K. (1998) 'Fractured environments: diversity and conflict in perceptions of environmental risk', *Research Papers in Environmental and Spatial Analysis*, no 52, London: Department of Geography and Environment, London School of Economics and Political Science.

Burningham, K. and Thrush, D. (2001) *'Rainforests are a long way from here'*, York: Joseph Rowntree Foundation.

Butler, J. (1990) *Gender trouble*, London: Routledge.

Buttel, F.H. (2003) 'Social institutions and environmental change', in C. Humphrey, T. Lewis and F. Buttel (eds) *Environment, energy and society: Exemplary works*, Stamford, CT: Thomson–Wadsworth.

Cahill, M. (2001) *Social policy and the environment*, London: Routledge.

Cahill, M. (2002) 'The implications of consumerism for the transition to a sustainable society', in M. Cahill and T. Fitzpatrick (eds) *Environmental issues and social welfare*, Oxford and Malden, MA: Blackwell.

Cahill, M. (2007) 'Why the U-turn on sustainable transport?', *Capitalism, Nature and Socialism*, vol 18, no 4, pp 90-103.

Cahill, M. (2010) *Transport, environment and society*, Maidenhead: Open University Press.

Cahill, M. and Fitzpatrick, T. (eds) (2002) *Environmental issues and social policy welfare*, Oxford: Blackwell.

Cahn, E. (2004) *No more throw away people*, Washington, DC: Essential Books.

Cairns, S., Sloman, L., Newson, C., Anable, J., Kirkbride, A. and Goodwin, P. (2004) *Smarter choices: Changing the way we travel*, London: Department for Transport.

Caldwell, L.K. (1970 [1963]) *Environment: A challenge for modern society*, Garden City, NY: The Natural History Press.

Caldwell, L.K. (1997) 'Environment as a problem for policy', in L.K. Caldwell and R.V. Bartlett (eds) *Environmental policy: Transnational issues and national trends*, Westport, CT: Quorum Books.

Callicott, J.B. (1995) 'Animal liberation: a triangular affair', in R. Elliot (ed) *Environmental ethics*, Oxford: Oxford University Press.

Campion, J., Greenhalgh, C. and Knight, J. (2003) *Mind the gap: Leonard Cheshire's Social exclusion report 2003*, London: Leonard Cheshire.

CAPE (Canadian Association of Physicians for the Environment) (nd) *Children's Environmental Health Project*, Toronto (www.cape.ca/children/).

Capstick, S. and Lewis, A. (2008) 'Personal carbon trading: perspectives from psychology and behavioural economics', Paper commissioned for the Institute for Public Policy Research.

Carter, A. (2001) 'Can we harm future people?', *Environmental Values*, vol 10, no 4, pp 429-54.

Carter, A. (2004) 'Saving nature and feeding people', *Environmental Ethics*, vol 26, no 4, pp 339-60.

Carter, N. (2007) *The politics of the environment*, Cambridge: Cambridge University Press.

CEC (Commission of the European Communities) (2009a) *Adapting to climate change: Towards a European framework for action*, White Paper, Brussels, 1 April, COM (2009) 147 final.

CEC (2009b) *Summary of the Impact Assessment*, Commission Staff Working Document accompanying the White Paper *Adapting to climate change: Towards a European framework for action*, Brussels, 1 April, SEC (2009) 388.

Chapin, M. (2004) 'A challenge to conservationists', *World Watch*, November/December, pp 17-31.

Chapman, G. (2009) 'Car park charges: why Nottingham needs the Workplace Parking Levy', *Daily Telegraph*, 4 August.

Chasek, P., Downie, D.L. and Brown, J.W. (2006) *Global environmental politics* (4th edn), Boulder, CO: Westview Press.

Christie, M. (2001) *The ozone layer*, Cambridge: Cambridge University Press.

Christoff, P. (1996) 'Ecological modernisation, ecological modernities', *Environmental Politics*, vol 5, no 3, pp 476-500.

Church, J.A. and White, N.J. (2006) 'A 20th century acceleration in global sea-level rise', *Geophysics Research Letters*, vol 33, LO1602, d.o.i. 10.1029/2006GLo27513

City of Taipei (2004) 'Sustainable Taipei Eco-City: declarations and commitments' (www.tcgdep.taipei.gov.tw/tsd/english/declaration.htm).

Cleaner Vehicles Task Force (2000) *The environmental impacts of motor manufacturing and disposal of end of life vehicles*, London: Department of Trade and Industry.

Climate Institute (2009) *Oceans and sea level rise: Consequences of climate change on the oceans*, Washington, DC: Climate Institute (www.climate.org/topics/sea-level/index.html#sealevelrise).

Cointreau, S. (2006) *Occupational and environmental health issues of solid waste management. Special emphasis on middle- and lower-income countries*, Washington, DC: The World Bank.

Cole, A. (2009) 'Climate change could cause half a million deaths a year by 2030, warns report', *British Medical Journal*, vol 338, p 2227.

Collier, P. (2007) *The bottom billion*, New York, NY: Oxford University Press.

Consumer Focus (2009) *Raising the SAP: Tackling fuel poverty by investing in energy efficiency*, London: Consumer Focus.

Coote, A. and Franklin, J. (2009) *Green Well Fair: Three economics for social justice*, London: New Economics Foundation.

Coote, A., Franklin, J. and Simms, A. (2010) *21 hours*, London: New Economics Foundation.

Copeland, B.R. and Taylor, M.S. (1994) 'North-south trade and the environment', *Quarterly Journal of Economics*, vol 109, no 3, pp 755-87.

Copeland, B.R. and Taylor, M.S. (2004) 'Trade, growth and the environment', *Journal of Economic Literature*, vol XLII, pp 7-71.

Costello, A. (2009) 'Making climate change part of global health', *The Lancet*, vol 373, p 1669.

CSDH (Commission of the Social Determinants of Health) (2008) *Closing the gap in a generation: Health equity through action on the social determinants of health, Final Report of the CSDH*, Geneva: World Health Organization.

Dale, A. (in collaboration with S.B. Hill) (2001) *At the edge: Sustainable development in the 21st century*, Vancouver: University of British Columbia Press.

Daly, H. (1996) *Beyond growth*, New York: Beacon Press.

Dant, T. (2004) 'The driver-car', *Theory, Culture and Society*, vol 21, nos 4-5, pp 61-79.

Davis, A., Valsecchi, C. and Fergusson, M. (2007) *Unfit for purpose: How car use fuels climate change and obesity*, London: Institute for European Environmental Policy.

de Waal, A. (1989) *Famine that kills*, Oxford: Clarendon Press.

Dean, J.S. (1947 [reprinted 2007]) *Murder most foul: A study of the road deaths problem*, London: George Allen & Unwin.

DECC (Department of Energy and Climate Change) (2009) *Annual report on fuel poverty statistics*, London: DECC.

DEFRA (2009) *Waste: Duty of care*, summary leaflet and code of practice. Available at: http://www.defra.gov.uk/environment/waste/controls/duty. htm#code. Accessed 15 October, 2010.

Dennis, K. and Urry, J. (2009) *After the car*, Cambridge: Polity Press.

Devereux, S. (1993) 'Goats before ploughs: dilemmas of household response sequencing during food shortages', *IDS Bulletin*, vol 24, pp 52-9.

DfT (Department for Transport) (1998) *A New Deal for transport*, London: DfT.

DfT (2003) *The future of air transport*, London: DfT.

DfT, Mobility and Inclusion Unit (2006) *Young people and transport: Understanding their needs and requirements*, London: Mobility and Inclusion Unit, DfT.

Di Chiro, G. (2008) 'Living environmentalisms: coalition politics, social reproduction and environmental justice', *Environmental Politics*, vol 17, no 2, pp 276-98.

Diamond, J. (2005) *Collapse*, New York, NY: Viking Press.

Dickens, P. (2004) *Society and nature*, Cambridge: Polity Press.

Dietz, T., Dan, A. and Shwom, R. (2007) 'Support for climate change policy: social psychological and social structural influences', *Rural Sociology*, vol 72, no 2, pp 185-214.

Dijkstra, B.R. (1998) *The political economy of instrument choice in environmental policy*, Groningen: Groningen University.

Dinda, S. (2004) 'Environmental Kuznets curve hypothesis: a survey', *Ecological Economics*, vol 49, pp 431-55.

Dixon, P.B. and Parmenter, B.R. (1996) 'Computable general equilibrium modeling for policy analysis and forecasting', in H.M. Amman, D.A. Kendrick and J. Rust (eds) *Handbook of computational economics*, Amsterdam: North-Holland.

Dobson, A. (1998) *Justice and the environment*, Oxford: Clarendon Press.

Dobson, A. (ed) (1999) *Fairness and futurity*, Oxford: Oxford University Press.

Dobson, A. (2003) *Citizenship and the environment*, Oxford: Oxford University Press.

Dobson, A. (2006) 'Citizenship', in A. Dobson and R. Eckersley (eds) *Political theory and the ecological challenge*, Cambridge: Cambridge University Press.

Dobson, A. (2009) 'Citizens, citizenship and governance for sustainability', in W. Adger and A. Jordan (eds) *Governing sustainability*, Cambridge: Cambridge University Press.

Dobson A. and Bell, D. (2006) *Environmental citizenship*, Cambridge, MA: The MIT Press.

Docherty, I. and Shaw, J. (2008) *Traffic jam: Ten years of 'sustainable' transport in the UK*, Bristol: The Policy Press.

Dorling, D., Rigby, J., Wheeler, B., Ballas, D., Thomas, B., Fahmy, E., Gordon, D. and Lupton, R. (2007) *Poverty, wealth and place in Britain, 1968 to 2005*, York: Joseph Rowntree Foundation.

Down to Earth (2004) *Sustainable palm oil: Mission impossible?*, Down to Earth No 63, November (www.rspo.org/?q=page/866).

Downs, A. (1972) 'Up and down with ecology: the issue-attention cycle', *The Public Interest*, vol 28, pp 38-50.

Doyle, T. (1998) 'Sustainable development and Agenda 21: the secular bible of environmental management', *Third World Quarterly*, vol 19, no 4, pp 771-86.

Doyle, T. (2008) 'The politics of hope', in T. Doyle and M. Risely (eds) *Crucible for survival: Environmental security and justice in the Indian Ocean region*, New Brunswick, NJ and London: Rutgers University Press.

Doyle, T. and Doherty, B. (2006) 'Green public spheres and the green governance state: the politics of emancipation and ecological conditionality', *Environmental Politics*, vol 15, no 5, pp 881-92.

Doyle, T. and Risely, M. (eds) (2008) *Crucible for survival: Environmental security and justice in the Indian Ocean region*, New Brunswick, NJ and London: Rutgers University Press.

DPTAC (Disabled Persons Transport Advisory Committee) (2002) *Attitudes of disabled people to public transport: Research study conducted for Disabled Persons Transport Advisory Committee*, London: DPTAC.

Dryzek, J. (2005) *The politics of the earth* (2nd edn), Oxford: Oxford University Press.

Dryzek, J. (2008) 'The ecological crisis of the welfare state', *Journal of European Social Policy*, vol 18, no 4, pp 334-7.

Dryzek, J., Downes, D., Hunold, C. and Schlosberg, D. with Hernes, H.-K. (2003) *Green states and social movements: Environmentalism in the United States, United Kingdom, Germany, and Norway*, Oxford: Oxford University Press.

Duerksen, C.J., Gregory Dale, C. and Elliott, D.L. (2009) *The citizen's guide to planning* (4th edn), Chicago, IL: APA Planners Press.

Duffy, R. (2006) 'Non-governmental organisations and governance states: the impact of transnational environmental management networks in Madagascar', *Environmental Politics*, vol 15, no 5, pp 731-49.

Duraiappah, A.K. (1998) 'Poverty and environmental degradation: a review and analysis of the nexus', *World Development*, vol 26, no 2, pp 2169-79.

Durant, R., Fiorino, D. and O'Leary, R. (eds) (2004) *Environmental governance reconsidered*, Cambridge, MA: The MIT Press.

Durham, W.H. (1995) 'Political ecology and environmental destruction in Latin America', in M. Painter and W.H. Durham (eds) *The social causes of environmental destruction in Latin America*, Ann Arbor, MI: The University of Michigan Press.

Eckersley, R. (2004) *The green state*, Cambridge, MA: The MIT Press.

ECORYS (2008) Environment and labour force skills. Overview of the links between the skills profile of the labour force and environmental factors (http://ec.europa.eu/environment/enveco/industry_employment/pdf/labor_force.pdf).

EEA (European Environment Agency) (2009a) *Glossary*, Copenhagen, EEA (http://glossary.eea.europa.eu/).

EEA (2009b) *Turn down the noise: Softening the impact of excess transport noise*, Copenhagen: EEA.

Ehrlich, P. and Ehrlich, A. (1968) *The population bomb*, New York: Ballantine Books.

Ehrlich, P. and Ehrlich, A. (1970) *Population resources environment: Issues in human ecology*, San Francisco, CA: W.H. Freeman & Company.

European Commission (1996) *Communication from the Commission to the Council and the European Parliament on Environmental Agreements*, 27 November, COM (96) 561 final, Brussels.

European Commission (2005) *Commission staff working document on the links between employment policies and environment policies*, Commission of the European Communities, SEC (2005) 1530 (http://ec.europa.eu/environment/integration/pdf/sec_2005_1530_en.pdf).

European Commission (2007) *Facts and figures. The link between EU's economy and the environment*, European Commission.

European Conference of Ministers of Transport (2004) *Implementing sustainable urban travel policies: National policies to promote cycling*, Paris: Organisation for Economic Co-operation and Development.

Ewing, R., Bartholomew, K., Winkelman, S., Walters, J. and Chen, D. (2008) *Growing cooler: The evidence on urban development and climate change*, Washington, DC: Urban Land Institute.

Faber, D. (ed) (1998) *The struggle for ecological democracy*, New York, NY: Guilford Press.

Fagan, A. (2008) 'Global–local linkage in the Western Balkans: the politics of environmental capacity building in Bosnia-Herzegovina', *Political Studies*, vol 56, pp 629-52.

Farrington, J. and Clarke, J. (2006) 'Growth, poverty reduction and development assistance in Asia: options and prospects', *Development Policy Review*, vol 24, no s1, s13-28.

Fitzpatrick, T. (1999a) *Freedom and security*, Basingstoke: Macmillan.

Fitzpatrick, T. (1999b) 'New welfare associations', in T. Jordan and A. Lent (eds) *Storming the millennium*, London: Lawrence & Wishart.

Fitzpatrick, T. (2001) 'Making welfare for future generations', *Social Policy and Administration*, vol 35, no 5, pp 506-20.

Fitzpatrick, T. (2003a) 'Environmentalism and social policy', in N. Ellison and C. Pierson (eds) *New developments in British social policy*, Basingstoke: Palgrave.

Fitzpatrick, T. (2003b) *After the new Social Democracy*, Manchester: Manchester University Press.

Fitzpatrick, T. (2004) 'Time and social policy', *Time and Society*, vol 13, nos 2/3, pp 197-219.

Fitzpatrick, T. (2005) *New theories of welfare*, London: Palgrave.

Fitzpatrick, T. (2007a) 'Social Democracy beyond productivism', *Renewal*, vol 15, nos 2/3, pp 74-82.

Fitzpatrick, T. (2007b) 'Streams, grants and pools: stakeholding, asset-based welfare and convertibility', *Basic Income Studies*, vol 2, no 1.

Fitzpatrick, T. (2008a) *Applied ethics and social problems*, Bristol: The Policy Press.

Fitzpatrick, T. (2008b) 'From contracts to capabilities and back again', *Res Publica*, vol 14, no 2, pp 83–100.

Fitzpatrick, T. (2009) 'Deliberative democracy, critical rationality and social memory', *Studies in Philosophy and Education*, vol 28, no 4, pp 313–27.

Fitzpatrick, T. (2010) 'Post-productivism, sustainability and liberalism', *Basic Income Studies*, vol 4, no 2.

Fitzpatrick, T. (2011) *Welfare theory* (2nd edn), Basingstoke: Palgrave.

Fitzpatrick, T. (forthcoming) 'Cash transfers', in J. Baldock and N. Manning (eds) *Social policy* (4th edn), Oxford: Oxford University Press.

Fitzpatrick, T. and Cahill, M. (eds) (2002a) *Environment and welfare*, Basingstoke: Palgrave.

Fitzpatrick, T. and Cahill, M. (2002b) 'The new environment of welfare', in T. Fitzpatrick and M. Cahill (eds) *Environment and welfare*, Basingstoke: Palgrave.

Flaherty, J., Veit-Wilson, J. and Dornan, P. (2004) *Poverty: The facts* (5th edn), London: Child Poverty Action Group.

Fleuret, P.C. and Fleuret, A.K. (1978) 'Fuelwood use in a peasant community: Tanzanian case study', *Journal of Developing Areas*, vol 123, pp 315–22.

Foley, J., Grayling, T. and Dixon, M. (2005) 'Sustainability and social justice', in N. Pearce and W. Paxton (eds) *Social justice*, London: Politico's.

Foster, J.B. (1999) *The vulnerable planet: A short economic history of the environment* (new edn), New York: Monthly Review Press.

Founex (1972) *Development and environment*, Report and Working Papers of Experts Convened by the Secretary General of the United Nations Conference on the Human Environment, Founex, Switzerland, 4–12 June 1971, Paris: Mouton.

Frank, D.J., Hironaka, A. and Schofer, E. (2000) 'The nation-state and the natural environment over the twentieth century', *American Sociological Review*, vol 65, pp 96–116.

Fraser, E.D.G., Dougill, A.J., Hubacek, K., Quinn, C.H., Sendzimir, J. and Termansen, M. (2010) 'Assessing vulnerability to climate change in dryland livelihood systems: conceptual challenges and interdisciplinary solutions', *Ecology and Society*, vol 15, no 2.

Frazer, E. and Lacey, N. (1993) *The politics of community*, Hemel Hempstead: Harvester Wheatsheaf.

Freeman, S. (2007) *Rawls*, London: Routledge.

Freund, P. (2001) 'Bodies, disability and spaces: the social model and disabling spatial organisations', *Disability and Society*, vol 16, no 5, pp 689–706.

Frey, B. (1997) *Not just for the money*, Aldershot: Edward Elgar.

Frey, H. (1999) *Designing the city: Towards a more sustainable urban form*, London: E & FN Spon.

Friberg, L. (2008) 'Conflict and consensus: the Swedish model of climate politics', in H. Compston and I. Bailey (eds) *Turning down the heat*, Basingstoke: Palgrave Macmillan.

Friends of the Earth Europe (2007) *Stopping the waste*, Policy briefing (www.foeeurope.org/publications/2007/FoEE_EEB_WasteBrief_Sep07.pdf).

Friends of the Earth, LifeMosaic and Sawit Watch (2008) *Losing ground: The human impacts of oil palm plantation expansion in Indonesia*, February (www.internal-displacement.org/8025708F004CE90B/(httpDocuments)/FA8 9FA0523761115C12574FE00480313/$file/losingground.pdf).

Fullerton, D. (ed) (2006) *The economics of pollution havens*, Aldershot: Edward Elgar.

Furedi, F. (2002) *Culture of fear: Risk taking and morality of low expectation*, London: Continuum.

Galatchi, L.D. (2008) 'Global environmental change and the international efforts concerning environmental conservation', in P. Liotta, D. Mouat, W. Kepner and J. Lancaster (eds) *NATO Advanced Research Workshop on environmental change and human security*, Newport: RI.

Gannon, Z. and Lawson, N. (nd) *Co-production*, London: Compass.

Garcia, L.E. (1998) *Integrated water resources management in Latin America and the Caribbean*, Technical Study No ENV-123, Washington, DC: Inter-America Development Bank.

Garnaut, R. (2008) *Garnaut climate change review, Final report*, Cambridge: Cambridge University Press.

Gavin, N.T. (2009) 'Addressing climate change: a media perspective', *Environmental Politics*, vol 18, no 5, pp 765-80.

GEF (Global Environment Facility) (2007) *Investing in our planet: GEF Annual Report 2006–07*, Washington, DC: GEF.

George, V. and Wilding, P. (1994) *Welfare and ideology*, Hemel Hempstead: Harvester Wheatsheaf.

Germanwatch (2008) *The Climate Change Performance Index: Results 2009*, Bonn/Brussels: Germanwatch/Climate Action Network Europe (www.germanwatch.org/klima/ccpi09.pdf).

GHK Consulting (2007) *Links between the environment, economy and jobs* (http://ec.europa.eu/environment/enveco/industry_employment/pdf/ghk_study_wider_links_report.pdf).

GHK Consulting (2009) *The impacts of climate change on European employment and skills in the short to medium-term: A review of the literature, Final report, Volume 2* (http://ec.europa.eu/social/main.jsp?catId=88&langId=en&eventsId=172).

Giddens, T. (2009) *The politics of climate change*, Cambridge: Polity Press.

Gill, T. (2005) *Cycling and children and young people*, London: National Children's Bureau.

Gitlin, T. (1980) *The whole world is watching: Mass media in the making or unmaking of the New Left*, Berkeley, CA: University of California Press.

GNESD (Global Network on Energy for Sustainable Development) (2007) *Reaching the Millennium Development Goals and beyond: Access to modern forms of energy as a prerequisite* (www.gnesd.org/Downloadables/MDG_energy.pdf).

Goodall, C. (2008) *Ten technologies to save the planet*, London: Profile.

Goodstein, E. (1996) 'Jobs and the environment: an overview', *Environmental Management*, vol 20, no 3, pp 313-21.

Gordon, D. and Townsend, P. (eds) (2000) *Breadline Europe*, Bristol: The Policy Press.

Gore, A. (2007) *An inconvenient truth*, London: Bloomsbury.

Gorz, A. (1992) *Critique of economic reason*, London: Verso.

Gough, I. (2008) 'Introduction', *Journal of European Social Policy*, vol 18, no 4, pp 325-31.

Gould, K., Pellow, D.N. and Schnaiberg, A. (2004) 'Interrogating the treadmill of production: everything you wanted to know about the treadmill but were afraid to ask', *Organization & Environment*, vol 17, no 3, pp 296-316.

Gould, K., Schnaiberg, A. and Weinberg, A.S. (eds) (1996) *Local environmental struggles: Citizen activism in the treadmill of production*, Cambridge, UK and New York: Cambridge University Press.

Gray, J. (1997) *Endgames*, Cambridge: Polity Press.

Gray, L.C. and Moseley, W.G. (2005) 'A geographical perspective on poverty and environmental interactions', *The Geographical Journal*, vol 171, no 1, pp 9-23.

Green, D. (1996) *Community without politics*, London: Institute of Economic Affairs.

Green Party of Canada (nd) *Vision Green* (www.greenparty.ca/issues/vision-green).

Greenstone, M. (2002) 'The impacts of environmental regulations on industrial activity: evidence from the 1970 and 1977 Clean Air Act Amendments and the census of manufacturesr', *Journal of Political Economy*, vol 110, no 6, pp 1175-219.

Grendstad, G., Selle, P., Strømsnes, K. and Bortne, Ø. (2006) *Unique environmentalism*, London: Springer.

Guber, D. and Bosso, C. (2010) 'Past the tipping point? Public discourse and the role of the environmental movement in the post-Bush era', in N. Vig and M. Kraft (eds) *Environmental policy* (7th edn), Washington, DC: CQ Press.

Hack, G., Birch, E., Sedway, P. and Silver, M. (eds) (2009) *Local planning: Contemporary principles and practice*, Washington, DC: The International City/County Management Association.

Hales, S. and Corvalan, C. (2006) 'Public health emergency on planet earth: insights from the Millennium Ecosystem Assessment', *EcoHealth*, vol 3, pp 130-5.

Hall, P. (2002) *Cities of tomorrow* (3rd edn), London: Blackwell.

Hancock, T. (1985) 'The mandala of health: a model of human ecosystem', *Family and Community Health*, November, pp 1-10.

Hancock, T. (1994) 'Sustainability, equity, peace and the (green) politics of health', in C. Chu and R. Simpson (eds) *Ecological public health*, Nathan, Australia: Griffith University.

Hanley, N., Shogren, J.F. and White, B. (1997) *Environmental economics*, Oxford: Oxford University Press.

Hannigan, J. (2006) *Environmental sociology* (2nd revised edn), London and New York: Routledge.

Hansen, J., Sato, M., Kharecha, P., Beerling, D., Berner, R., Masson-Delmotte, V., Pagani, M., Raymo, M., Royer, D. and Zachos, J. (2008) 'Target atmospheric CO_2: where should humanity aim?', *The Open Atmospheric Science Journal*, vol 2, pp 217-31.

Hansson, S.O., Edvardsson Björnberg, K. and Vredin Johansson, M. (2010) 'Making climate policy efficient. Implementing a model for environmental efficiency', Manuscript available from Maria Vredin Johansson.

Hardin, G. (1982) 'Living on a lifeboat', in J. Narveson (ed) *Moral issues*, Toronto: Oxford University Press.

Hardin, G. (1998) 'The tragedy of the commons', in J. Baden and D. Noonan (eds) *Managing the commons*, Indiana, IN: Indiana University Press.

Hardy, D. (2008) *Cities that don't cost the earth*, London: Town and Country Planning Association.

Harper, C.L. (2001) *Environment and society: Human perspectives on environmental issues*, Upper Saddle River, NJ: Prentice Hall.

Harrington, W., Morgenstern, R. and Sterner, T. (eds) (2004) *Choosing environmental policy*, Washington, DC: Resources for the Future.

Harrison, G. (2004) *The World Bank and Africa: The construction of governance states*, London: Routledge.

Hay, C. (1994) 'Environmental security and state legitimacy', *Capitalism, Nature, Socialism*, vol 5, no 1, pp 83-97.

Hay, P. (2004) *Main currents in Western environmental thought*, Sydney: University of New South Wales Press.

Hayward, T. (1998) *Political theory and ecological values*, Cambridge: Polity Press.

Hayward, T. (2005) *Constitutional environmental rights*, Oxford: Oxford University Press.

Hayward, T. (2006) 'Ecological citizenship: justice, rights and the virtue of resourcefulness', *Environmental Politics*, vol 15, no 3, pp 435-46.

Hazilla, M. and Kopp, R.J. (1990) 'Social cost of environmental quality: a general equilibrium analysis', *Journal of Political Economy*, vol 98, no 4, pp 853-73.

Headicar, P. (2009) *Transport planning and policy in Great Britain*, London: Routledge.

Heckman, J.J. and Vytlacil, E.J. (2007) 'Econometric evaluation of social programs, part I: causal models, structural models, and econometric policy evaluation', in J.J. Heckman and E. Leamer (eds) *Handbook of econometrics*, Amsterdam: Elsevier.

Heckman, J.J., LaLonde, R.J. and Smith, J.A. (1999) 'The economics and econometrics of active labor market programs', in A. Aschenfelter and D. Card (eds) *Handbook of labor economics*, Amsterdam: Elsevier.

Heltberg, R., Siegel, P. and Jorgensen, S. (2010) 'Social policies for adaptation to climate change', in R. Mearns and A. Norton (eds) *Social dimensions of climate change*, Washington, DC: The World Bank.

Henson, R. (2008) *The Rough Guide to climate change*, London: Penguin.

Hilgartner, S. and Bosk, C. (1988) 'The rise and fall of social problems: a public arenas model', *American Journal of Sociology*, vol 94, pp 53-78.

Hillman, M. and Fawcett, T. (2004) *How we can save the planet?*, London: Penguin.

Hills, J. (2009) 'Future pressures, intergenerational links, wealth, demography and sustainability', in J. Hills, T. Sefton and K. Stewart (eds) *Towards a more equal society?*, Bristol: The Policy Press.

Hills, J. and Stewart, K. (2005) *A more equal society?*, Bristol: The Policy Press.

Hillyard, M. (1998) *Cancellation of Third World debt*, Research Paper 98/81, London: House of Commons.

Himmelweit, S. (2002) 'Making visible the hidden economy: the case for gender-impact analysis of economic policy', *Feminist Economics*, vol 8, no 1, pp 49-70.

Hirst, P. (2001) *War and power in the 21st century*, Cambridge: Polity Press.

Hirst, P. and Thompson, G. (1999) *Globalization in question* (2nd edn), Cambridge: Polity Press.

Hodgson, S.M. and Irving, Z.M. (2007) 'Studying policy: a way forward', in S.M. Hodgson and Z.M. Irving (eds) *Policy reconsidered*, Bristol: The Policy Press.

Hodgson, S.M., Maltby, L., Paetzold, A. and Phillips, D. (2007) 'Getting the measure of nature: ecosystem services as a way to understand environment and society', *Interdisciplinary Science Reviews*, vol 32, no 3, pp 249-62.

Honari, M. (1993) 'Advancing health ecology: where to from here?', in N. Newman (ed) *Health and ecology*, Proceedings of the 'Nursing the Environment Conference', Australian Nursing Federation, Melbourne.

Hood, C. (1991) 'A public management for all seasons?', *Public Administration*, vol 69, no 1, pp 3-19.

Houghton, J. (2009) *Global warming: The complete briefing* (4th edn), Cambridge: Cambridge University Press.

House of Commons (2008) *Personal carbon trading*, Environmental Audit Committee, Fifth Report of Session 2007–08, London: The Stationery Office.

Huby, M. (1998) *Social policy and the environment*, Milton Keynes: Open University Press.

Hulme, M., Neufeldt, H. and Colyer, H. (eds) (2009) *Adaptation and mitigation strategies: Supporting European climate policy*, The Final Report from the ADAM Project, Norwich: Tyndall Centre for Climate Change Research, University of East Anglia (http://adamproject.info/index. php/Download-document/454-Adam-Final-Report-May-2009.html).

Humphrey, C., Lewis, T. and Buttel, F.H. (eds) (2002) *Environment, energy and society: A new synthesis*, Belmont, CA: Wadsworth.

Humphrey, J. (2006) 'Prospects and challenges for growth and poverty reduction in Asia', *Development Policy Review*, vol 24, no s1, pp s29-s49.

Husain, Z. and Bhattacharya, R. (2004) 'Privatising the commons: a critical review of the property rights paradigm', *International Journal of Environment and Development*, vol 1, no 1, pp 83-100.

Hyden, G. (2007) 'Governance and poverty reduction in Africa', *Proceedings of the National Academy of Science*, vol 104, no 43, pp 16751-6.

ILO (International Labour Organization) (2009) *Global employment trends January 2009*, Geneva: ILO (www.ilocarib.org.tt/portal/images/stories/ contenido/pdf/LabourMarketInformation/get09.pdf).

Inglehart, R. (1977) *The silent revolution: Changing values and political styles among western publics*, Princeton, NJ: Princeton University Press.

Inglehart, R. (1990) *Culture shift in advanced society*, Princeton, NJ: Princeton University Press.

IPCC (Intergovernmental Panel on Climate Change) (2007) *Climate change 2007: Synthesis report*, Geneva: IPCC.

IPPCC TAR (Third Assessment Report) (2001) 'Climate change 2001: mitigation', Contribution of Working Group III to the Third Assessment Report of the Intergovernmental Panel on Climate Change, Geneva: IPCC.

ISHE (Institute for Sustainability, Health and Environment) (2008) *The health map* (www.uwe.ac.uk/ishe/).

Jackson, T. (2002) 'Quality of life, sustainability and economic growth', in T. Fitzpatrick and M. Cahill (eds) *Environment and welfare*, London: Palgrave.

Jackson, T. (2009) *Prosperity without growth*, London: Sustainable Development Commission.

Jaffe A.B., Peterson, S.R. and Portney, P.R. (1995) 'Environmental regulation and the competitiveness of US manufacturing: what does the evidence tell us', *Journal of Economic Literature*, vol XXXIII, pp 132-63.

Jardine, C. (2009) *Calculating the carbon dioxide emissions of flights*, Oxford: Environmental Change Institute.

Jarraud, M. (2005) *Carbon emissions increase* (www.worldmapper.org/display.php?selected=297).

Jay, M. and Marmot, M. (2009) 'Health and climate change: will global commitment be made at the UN climate change conference in December?', *British Medical Journal*, vol 339, pp 645-46.

Jefferson, T. (2006) *The essential Jefferson*, edited by J. Yarbrough, Indianapolis, IN: Hackett Publishing.

Jenkins, D. (2010) 'The value of retrofitting carbon-saving measures into fuel poor social housing', *Energy Policy*, vol 38, no 2, pp 832-9.

Johnson, B. (2007) *Environmental policy and public health*, Boca Raton, FL: Taylor and Francis.

Johnson, V. and Simms, A. (2007) *Taking the temperature: Towards an NHS response to global warming*, London: New Economics Foundation.

Johnson, V., Simms, A. and Cochrane, C. (2008) *Tackling climate change, reducing poverty*, London: New Economics Foundation.

Jones, P. and Lucas, K. (2000) 'Integrating transport into "joined-up policy appraisal"', *Transport Policy*, vol 7, pp 185-93.

Jordan, A. and Lenschow, A. (eds) (2008) *Innovation in environmental policy?*, Cheltenham: Edward Elgar.

Jordan, A., Wurzel, R. and Zito, A. (eds) (2003) *'New' instruments of economic governance*, London: Frank Cass.

Jordan, B. (2010) *What's wrong with social policy and how to fix it*, Cambridge: Polity Press.

Jorgenson, D.W. and Wilcoxen, P.J. (1990) 'Environmental regulation and US economic growth', *RAND Journal of Economics*, vol 21, no 2, pp 314-39.

Jowit, J. and Ottery, C. (2010) 'World faces 4C rise in temperature', *The Guardian*, 6 July.

Justice and Environment (2006) *Implementation of the Aarhus Convention in EU member states: Case study collection*, European Network of European Law Organisations (www.justiceandenvironment.org/wp-content/wp-upload/JE2006Aarhuscasestudy.pdf).

Keller, W. and Levinson, A. (2002) 'Pollution abatement costs and foreign direct investment. Inflows to US states', *The Review of Economics and Statistics*, vol 84, no 4, pp 691–703.

Kershaw, P. (2005) *Carefair: Rethinking the responsibilities and rights of citizenship*, Vancouver: University of British Columbia Press.

Khakee, A., Elander, I. and Sunesson, S. (eds) (1995) *Remaking the welfare state*, Aldershot: Avebury.

Kickbusch, I. (1989) *Good planets are hard to find*, WHO EURO Healthy Cities Papers, No 5, Copenhagen: FADL Publishers.

Kickbusch, I. (2008) 'Healthy societies: addressing 21st century health challenges', Adelaide Thinker in Residence, Department of the Premier and Cabinet, Adelaide: State of South Australia, May.

Kingdon, J. (1995) *Agendas, alternatives and public policies* (2nd edn), New York: Longman.

Knill, C. and Lieferink, D. (2007) *Environmental politics in the European Union*, Manchester: Manchester University Press.

Kooiman, J. (ed) (1993) *Modern governance*, London: Sage.

Kooiman, J. (2003) *Governing and governance*, London: Sage.

Kraft, M. (2011) *Environmental policy and politics* (5th edn), London: Longman.

Küster, R., Ellersdorfer, I. and Fahl, U. (2007) *A CGE-analysis of energy policies considering labor market imperfections and technology specifications*, Fondazione Eni Enrico Mattei, Working Paper 73.

Kuznets, P. and Simon, P. (1955) 'Economic growth and income inequality', *American Economic Review*, vol 45, pp 1–28.

Kymlicka, W. and Norman, W. (1994) 'Return of the citizen: a survey of recent work on citizenship theory', *Ethics*, vol 10, no 4, pp 257–89.

Kyoto Protocol Status of Ratification (2006) *United Nations Framework Convention on Climate Change* (http://unfccc.int/kyoto-protocol/status-of-ratification/items/2613.php).

Lafferty, W.M. and Meadowcroft, J. (eds) (2000) *Implementing sustainable development: Strategies and initiatives in high consumption societies*, Oxford: Oxford University Press.

Lancet, The (2009) 'Editorial', 16 May, vol 373, p 1659.

Langley, P. and Mellor, M. (2002) '"Economy", sustainability and sites of transformative space', *New Political Economy*, vol 7, no 1, pp 49–65.

Leach, M. and Mearns, R. (1995) *Poverty and environment in developing countries*, Brighton: Institute for Development Studies.

Leggett, J.K. (2005) *Half gone: Oil, gas, hot air and the global energy crisis*, London: Portobello.

Leontief, W. (1970) 'Environmental repercussions and the economic structure: an input-output approach', *The Review of Economics and Statistics*, vol 52, no 3, pp 262-71.

Leopold, A. (1970) *A Sand County Almanac, with essays on conservation from Round River*, New York: Ballantine Books.

Lewis, S. (2006) 'Climate change: in my view', *Royal Society: Science Issues – Climate Change* (http://royalsociety.org/page.asp?id=4689&tip=1).

Liddell, C. and Morris, C. (2010) 'Fuel poverty and human health: a review of recent evidence', *Energy Policy*, vol 38, pp 2987-97.

Lipietz, A. (1992) *Towards a new economic order: Post-Fordism, ecology and democracy*, Oxford: Oxford University Press.

List, J.A., Millimet, D.L., Fredriksson, P.G. and McHone, W.W. (2003) 'Effects of environmental regulations on manufacturing plant births: evidence from a propensity score matching estimator', *The Review of Economics and Statistics*, vol 85, no 4, pp 944-52.

Littig, B. (2001) *Feminist perspectives on environment and society*, Harlow: Pearson Education Ltd.

Little, A. (2002) 'Working-time reductions', in T. Fitzpatrick and M. Cahill (eds) *Environment and welfare*, London: Palgrave.

Lock, I.C. and Ikeda, S. (2005) 'Clothes encounters: consumption, culture and economy', in D. Davidson and K. Hatt (eds) *Consuming sustainability: Critical social analyses of ecological change*, Halifax, NS: Fernwood Publishing.

Lomborg, B. (2007) *Cool it*, New York: Knopf.

London Sustainability Exchange (2004) *Environmental justice in London: Linking the equalities and environment policy agendas* (www.lsx.org.uk).

Lord, C. (2003) *A citizen's income*, Oxford: Jon Carpenter Books.

Lorenzoni, I., Nicholson-Cole, S. and Whitmarsh, L. (2007) 'Barriers perceived to engaging with climate change among the UK public and their policy implications', *Global Environmental Change*, vol 17, nos 3-4, pp 445-59.

Lovelock, J. (2007) *The revenge of Gaia*, London: Penguin.

Lucas, R.E.B., Wheeler, D. and Hettige, H. (1992) *Economic development, environmental regulation and the international migration of toxic industrial pollution 1960–88*, Background paper for the *World Development Report 1992*.

Lufumpa, C.L. (2005) 'The poverty-environment nexus in Africa', *African Development Review/Revue Africaine de développement*, vol 17, pp 366-81.

Lundmark, R. and Söderholm, P. (2004) *Brännhett om svensk skog – en studie om råvarukonkurrensens ekonomi*, Stockholm: SNS Förlag.

Lundqvist, L. (2001) 'A green fist in a velvet glove: the ecological state and sustainable development', *Environmental Values*, vol 10, pp 455-72.

Lundqvist, L. (2004) *Sweden and ecological governance*, Manchester: Manchester University Press.

Lynas, M. (2008) *Six degrees*, London: Harper.

MacGregor, S. (2006) *Beyond mothering earth: Ecological citizenship and the politics of care*, Vancouver: University of British Columbia Press.

MacIntyre, A. (1999) *Dependent rational animals*, London: Duckworth.

McCormack, J. (2002) 'Environmental policy in Britain', in U. Desai (ed) *Environmental politics and policy in industrialized countries*, Cambridge, MA: The MIT Press.

McHale, J. (1970) *The ecological context*, New York: George Braziller.

McKibben, B. (2007) *Deep economy*, Oxford: Oneworld.

McKie, R. and Helmore, E. (2009) 'America's green guru sparks anger over climate change U-turns', *The Observer*, 24 May.

McMichael, A.J. (2001) *Human frontiers, environments and disease*, Cambridge: Cambridge University Press.

McMichael A.J. and Woodruff, R. (2002) 'Climate change and human health: what do we know?', *Medical Journal of Australia*, vol 325, no 7378, pp 1461-6.

McMichael, A.J., Campbell-Lendrum, H., Corvalen, C., Ebi, K., Githeko, A.K., Schwraga, J.D. and Woodward, A. (eds) (2003) *Climate change and human health*, Geneva: World Health Organization.

Mackett, R.L. (2001) 'Are we making our children car dependent?', Lecture at Trinity College, Dublin, 17 May.

Macmillan Cancer Support (2010), Memorandum submitted to the Energy and Climate Change Committee on Fuel Poverty, *Fifth Report of Session 2009-10: Volume II*, London: House of Commons.

Mani, M. and Wheeler, D. (1998) 'In search of pollution havens? Dirty industry in the world economy, 1960-1995', *Journal of Environment and Development*, vol 7, no 3, pp 215-47.

Maples, W. (2003) 'Environmental justice and the environmental justice movement', in N. Bingham, A. Blowers and C. Belshaw (eds) *Contested environments*, Milton Keynes: Open University Press.

Markowitz, N. (2007) 'Socialism and Latin America today' (www.politicalaffairs.net/article/articleview/5026/).

Marmot, M. and Wilkinson, R.G. (2006) *Social determinants of health* (2nd edn), Oxford: Oxford University Press.

Marshall, T.H. (1992) *Citizenship and social class*, London: Pluto.

Martell, L. (1994) *Ecology and society: An introduction*, Cambridge: Polity Press.

Maslin, M. (2004) *Global warming*, Oxford: Oxford University Press.

Maslow, A.M. (1954) *Motivation and personality*, New York: Harper.

Matson, L., Taylor, I., Sloman, L. and Elliott, J. (2006) *Beyond transport infrastructure: Lessons for the future from recent road projects*, London: Campaign for the Protection of Rural England.

Meadowcroft, J. (1999) 'Planning for sustainable development: what can be learned from the critics?', in M. Kenny and J. Meadowcroft (eds) *Planning sustainability*, London: Routledge.

Meadowcroft, J. (2005) 'From welfare state to ecostate', in J. Barry and R. Eckersley (eds) *The state and the global ecological crisis*, Cambridge, MA: The MIT Press.

Meadowcroft, J. (2007) 'Who is in charge here? Governance for sustainable development in a complex world', *Journal of Environmental Policy and Planning*, vol 9, pp 299-314.

Meadowcroft, J. (2008) 'From welfare state to environmental state?', *Journal of European Social Policy*, vol 18, no 4, pp 331-4.

Meadows, D.H., Meadows, D.L., Randers, J. and Behrens, W.W. (1972) *The limits to growth*, London: Earth Island.

Meadows, D.L. (1973) 'Introduction to the project', in D.L. Meadows and D.H. Meadows (eds) *Toward a global equilibrium: Collected papers*, Cambridge, MA: Wright-Allen Press, Inc.

Meadows, D.L. and Meadows, D.H. (1973) 'Preface', in D.L. Meadows and D.H. Meadows (eds) *Toward a global equilibrium: Collected papers*, Cambridge, MA: Wright-Allen Press, Inc.

Medina, M. (2005) 'Serving the unserved: informal refuse collection in Mexico', *Waste Management and Research*, vol 23, no 5, pp 390-7.

Mee, L.D., Dublin, H.T. and Eberhard, A.A. (2008) 'Evaluating the global environment facility: a goodwill gesture or a serious attempt to deliver global benefits?', *Global Environmental Change*, vol 18, pp 800-10.

Miliband, D. (2007) 'A greener shade of red', in N. Pearce and J. Margo (eds) *Politics for a new generation*, Basingstoke: Palgrave Macmillan.

Millward, L.M., Morgan, A. and Kelly, M.P. (2003) *Prevention and reduction of accidental injury in children and young people*, London: Health Development Agency.

Milmo, D. (2009) 'UK road deaths fall to record low', *The Guardian*, 25 June.

Mindell, J., Watkins, S. and Cohen, J. (eds) (2010) *Health on the move 2: Policies for healthy transport*, Stockport: Transport and Health Study Group.

Mol, A. (2006) 'Environmental governance in the Information Age: the emergence of informational governance', *Environment and Planning C: Government and Policy*, vol 24, pp 497-514.

Mol, A. and Buttel, F. (eds) (2002) *The environmental state under pressure*, London: Elsevier.

Monbiot, G. (2007a) *Heat*, London: Penguin.

Monbiot, G. (2007b) 'A million road deaths every year? It's just the price of doing business', *The Guardian*, 15 May.

Monbiot, G. (2009) 'The poor will not destroy the planet', *The Guardian Weekly*, 9 October, p 19.

Morgenstern, R.D., Pizer, W.A. and Shih, J.-S. (2002) 'Jobs versus the environment: an industry-level perspective', *Journal of Environmental Economics and Management*, vol 43, pp 412-36.

Nadin, V. and Cullingworth, B. (2010) *Town and country planning in the UK*, London: Routledge.

Najam, A. (2005) 'Developing countries and global environmental governance: from contestation to participation to engagement', *International Environmental Agreements*, vol 5, pp 303-21.

nef (New Economics Foundation) (2008) *A Green New Deal*, London: nef.

nef (2010) *The new wealth of time*, London: nef.

nef (nd) *The unHappy Planet Index 2.0* (www.happyplanetindex.org/public-data/files/happy-planet-index-2-0.pdf).

Newbold, H. (ed) (2000) *Life stories*, Berkeley, CA: University of California Press.

Newman, P. and Jennings, I. (2008) *Cities as sustainable ecosystems: Principles and practices*, Washington, DC: Island Press.

NHS Health and Social Care Information Centre (2009) *Statistics on obesity, physical activity and diet: England, February 2009*.

Nicholson, M. (2000) 'Nature conservancy', in H. Newbold (ed) *Life stories*, Berkeley, CA: University of California Press.

Nordhaus, W. (2008) *A question of balance*, New Haven, CT: Yale University Press.

North, P. (2006) *Alternative currency movements as a challenge to globalization?*, Aldershot: Ashgate.

Nozick, R. (1974) *Anarchy, state and utopia*, New York: Basic Books.

O'Riordan, T. (2009) 'Reflections on the pathways to sustainability', in W. Adger and A. Jordan (eds) *Governing sustainability*, Cambridge: Cambridge University Press.

O'Sullivan, P. (2008) 'The collapse of civilizations: what palaeoenvironmental reconstruction cannot tell us, but anthropology can', *The Holocene*, vol 18, no 1, pp 45-55.

OECD (Organisation for Economic Co-operation and Development) (1997) *Environmental policies and employment*, Paris: OECD.

OECD (2004) *Environment and employment: An assessment*, Paris: OECD.

OECD (2008) *Policy brief* (February), Paris: OECD.

OECD/Eurostat (1999) *The environmental goods and services industry. Manual for data collection and analysis*, Paris: OECD.

Offe, C. (1996) *Modernity and the state*, Cambridge: Polity Press.

Offer, A. (2006) *The challenge of affluence*, Oxford: Oxford University Press.

Okin, S.M. (1991) *Justice, gender, and the family*, New York: Basic Books.

Olmstead, S. (2010) 'Applying market principles to environmental policy', in N. Vig and M. Kraft (eds) *Environmental policy* (7th edn), Washington, DC: CQ Press.

Olson, K.H. (2007) 'The Clean Development Mechanism's contribution to sustainable development: a review of the literature', *Climatic Change*, vol 84, no 1, pp 59-73.

Olson, S. (2009) 'The political scientist', *SEED*, no 22, pp 56-64.

ONS (Office for National Statistics) (2005) *National Travel Survey*, London: ONS.

Owen, D. (2009) *Green metropolis: What the city can teach the country about true sustainability*, New York, NY: Riverhead Books.

Paehlke, R. (2003) *Democracy's dilemma: Environment, social equity and the global economy*, Cambridge, MA: The MIT Press.

Paehlke, R. (2010) 'Sustainable development and urban life in North America', in N. Vig and M. Kraft (eds) *Environmental policy* (7th edn), Washington, DC: CQ Press.

Pantazis, C., Gordon, D. and Levitas, R. (eds) (2006) *Poverty and social exclusion in Britain*, Bristol: The Policy Press.

Parfit, D. (1984) *Reasons and persons*, Oxford: Oxford University Press.

Parkhurst, G. (2009) 'Tackling transport issues', Sustainable Communities Conference, Exeter, July.

Parmenter, R.R., Yadav, E.P., Parmenter, C.A., Ettestad, P. and Gage, K.L. (1999) 'Incidence of plague associated with increased-spring precipitation in New Mexico', *American Journal of Tropical Medicine*, vol 61, pp 814-21.

Paske, G.H. (1989) 'The life principle: a (metaethical) rejection', *Journal of Applied Philosophy*, vol 6, no 2, pp 219-25.

Pateman, C. (2008) 'Why republicanism?', *Basic Income Studies*, vol 2, no 2.

Paterson, M. (1996) *Global warming and global politics*, London: Routledge.

Paterson, M. (2008) *Automobile politics: Ecology and cultural political economy*, Cambridge: Cambridge University Press.

Paterson, M., Doran, P. and Barry, J. (2006) 'Green theory', in C. Hay, M. Lister and D. Marsh (eds) *The state: Theories and issues*, Basingstoke: Palgrave.

Patz, J., Campbell-Lendrum, D., Holloway, T. and Foley, J.S. (2005) 'Impact of regional climate change on human health', *Nature*, vol 438, no 17, pp 310-17.

Pearson, B. (2007) 'Market failure: why the Clean Development Mechanism won't promote clean development', *Journal of Cleaner Production*, vol 15, pp 247-52.

Pepper, D. (2005) 'Utopianism and environmentalism', *Environmental Politics*, vol 14, no 1, pp 3-22.

Pepper, D. (2007) 'Tensions and dilemmas of ecotopianism', *Environmental Values*, vol 16, pp 289-312.

Perkins, P.E. (2007) 'Feminist ecological economics and sustainability', *Journal of Bioeconomics*, vol 9, pp 227-44.

Pettit, P. (1999) *Republicanism*, Oxford: Oxford University Press.

Phillips, D. (2006) 'Quality of life and sustainability', *International Journal of Environmental, Cultural, Economic and Social Sustainability*, vol 2, pp 103-12.

Pickvance, C. (2009) 'The construction of UK sustainable housing policy and the role of pressure groups', *Local Environment*, vol 14, no 4, pp 329-45.

Pierre, J. and Stoker, G. (2000) 'Towards multi-level Ggovernance', in P. Dunleavy, A. Gamble, I. Holliday and G. Peele (eds) *Developments in British Politics 6*, Basingstoke: Palgrave.

Pierson, C. (2006) *Beyond the welfare state? The new political economy of welfare* (3rd edn), Cambridge: Polity Press.

Pierson, P. (2001) 'Post-industrial pressures on the mature welfare states', in P. Pierson (ed) *The new politics of the welfare state*, Oxford: Oxford University Press.

Pirages, D.C. and DeGeest, T.M. (2004) *Ecological security: An evolutionary perspective on globalization*, Oxford: Rowman & Littlefield.

Pogge, T. (2008) *World poverty and human rights* (2nd edn), Cambridge: Polity Press.

Poncelet, E.C. (2001) '"A kiss here and a kiss there": conflict and collaboration in environmental partnerships', *Environmental Management*, vol 27, no 1, pp 13-25.

Porritt, J. (1984) *Seeing green*, Oxford: Blackwell.

Potoski, M. and Prakash, A. (2004) 'The regulation dilemma: cooperation and conflict in environmental governance', *Public Administration Review*, vol 64, pp 137-48.

Pralle, S.B. (2009) 'Agenda-setting and climate change', *Environmental Politics*, vol 18, no 5, pp 781-99.

Prescott, M. (2008) *A persuasive climate*, London: Royal Society of the Arts.

Press, D. and Mazmanian, D. (2010) 'Toward sustainable production: finding workable solutions for government and industry', in N.Vig and M. Kraft (eds) *Environmental policy* (7th edn), Washington, DC: CQ Press.

Preston, I., Moore, R. and Guertler, P. (2008) *How much? The cost of alleviating fuel poverty in England*, Bristol: Centre for Sustainable Energy Research.

Preuss, P. (2008) 'IMPACTS: on the threshold of abrupt climate change', Lawrence Berkeley National Laboratory/US Department of Energy (http://newscenter.lbl.gov/feature-stories/2008/09/17/impacts-on-the-threshold-of-abrupt-climate-changes/).

Purse, B.V. (2005) 'Climate change and the recent emergence of bluetongue in Europe', *Nature Review: Microbiology*, vol 3, pp 171-81.

Rabe, B. (2010) 'Racing to the top, the bottom, or the middle of the pack? The evolving state government role in environmental protection', in N. Vig and M. Kraft (eds) *Environmental policy* (7th edn), Washington, DC: CQ Press.

Rachels, J. (1982) 'Killing and starving to death', in J. Narveson (ed) *Moral issues*, Toronto: Oxford University Press.

Randolph, J. (2004) *Environmental land use planning and management*, Washington, DC: Island Press.

Raphael, D. and Bryant, T. (2006) 'The state's role in promoting population health: public health concerns in Canada, USA, UK, and Sweden', *Health Policy*, vol 78, pp 39-55.

Raventós, D. (2007) *Basic income*, London: Pluto.

Rawls, J. (1972) *A theory of justice*, Oxford: Oxford University Press.

Rees, M. (2003) *Our final century*, London: Arrow Books.

Regan, T. (1983) *The case for animal rights*, Berkeley, CA: University of California Press.

Regan, T. (1985) 'The case for animal rights', in P. Singer (ed) *In defense of animals*, Oxford: Blackwell.

Reinikainen, J. (2005) 'Social justice by basic income', *Statsvetenskaplig Tidskrift*, vol 107, no 4, pp 351-76.

Renner, M., Sweeney, S. and Kubit, J. (2008) *Green jobs. Working for people and the environment*, Worldwatch Report no 177.

Revell, A. (2005) 'Ecological modernization in the UK: rhetoric or reality?', *European Environment*, vol 15, no 6, pp 344-61.

Richards, D. and Smith, M.J. (2002) *Governance and public policy in the UK*, Oxford: Oxford University Press.

Rincon, G., Cremades, L., Ehrman, U. and Pena, A. (2007) 'Comparative study of environmental regulations in Latin America, Environmental Health Risk IV', *WIT Transactions on Biomedicine and Health*, vol 11, pp 259-68.

Roberts, J.T. and Parks, B.C. (2007) *A climate of injustice, global inequality, North-South politics, and climate policy*, Cambridge, MA: The MIT Press.

Roberts, S. (2008) 'Energy, equity and the future of the fuel poor', *Energy Policy*, vol 36, pp 4471-4.

Roberts, S. (2009) 'Background paper', Presented to *Exploring 'energy justice': Prospects for fairness in UK climate policy*, Working seminar, 30 November, Coin Street Community Centre, Southwark.

Robinson, F. (1999) *Globalising care: Ethics, feminist theory and international relations*, Boulder, CO: Westview Press.

Roland-Holst, D. (2008) *Energy efficiency, innovation and job creation in California*, Berkeley, CA: Center for Energy, Resources, and Economic Sustainability (CERES), University of California (http://are.berkeley.edu/~dwrh/CERES_Web/Docs/UCB%20Energy%20Innovation%20and%20Job%20Creation%2010-20-08.pdf).

Rolston, H. (1988) *Environmental ethics: Duties to and values in the natural world*, Philadelphia, PA: Temple University Press.

Rose, A. (1995) 'Input-output economics and computable general equilibrium models', *Structural Change and Economic Dynamics*, vol 6, pp 295-304.

Rosenbaum, W. (2008) *Environmental policy and politics* (7th edn), Washington, DC: CQ Press.

Rosenbaum, W. (2010) 'Science, politics, and policy at the EPA', in N. Vig and M. Kraft (eds) *Environmental policy* (7th edn), Washington, DC: CQ Press.

Routley, R. (2003) 'Is there a need for a new environmental ethic?', in A. Light and R. Holmes, III (eds) *Environmental ethics: An anthology*, Oxford: Blackwell.

Royal Commission on Environmental Pollution (1994) *18th report: Transport and the environment*, London: HMSO.

Royal Society, The (2008) *Climate change controversies: A simple guide*, London: The Royal Society (http://royalsociety.org).

Royal Society, The (2009) *Geoengineering the climate: Science, governance and uncertainty*, London: The Royal Society (http://royalsociety.org/Geoengineering-the-climate/).

Sachs, W. (1997) 'Ecology, justice, and the end of development', *Development*, vol 40, no 2, pp 8-14.

Sagoff, M. (1988) *The economy of the earth*, Cambridge: Cambridge University Press.

Salih, M. (2009) *Climate change and sustainable development: New challenges for poverty reduction*, Cheltenham, UK and Northampton, MA: Edward Elgar.

Sanne, C. (2002) 'Willing consumers – or locked-in? Policies for a sustainable consumption', *Ecological Economics*, vol 42, pp 273-87.

Satterthwaite, D. (2009) 'The implications of population growth and urbanization for climate change', *Environment and Urbanization*, vol 21, no 2, pp 545-67.

Schnaiberg, A., Pellow, D.N. and Weinberg, A. (2003) 'The treadmill of production and the environmental state', in C. Humphrey, T. Lewis and F. Buttel (eds) *Environment, energy and society: Exemplary works*, Stamford, CT: Thomson-Wadsworth.

Schnaiberg, A., Pellow, D.N. and Weinberg, A. (2002) 'The treadmill of production and the environmental state', *Research in Social Problems and Public Policy*, vol 10, pp 15-32.

Scholsberg, D. (2009) *Defining environmental justice*, Oxford: Oxford University Press.

Schwartz, T. (1979) 'Welfare judgments and future generations', *Theory and Decision*, vol 11, pp 181-94.

Scott, M.J., Roop, J.M., Schultz, R.W., Anderson, D.M. and Cort, K.A. (2008) 'The impact of DOE building technology energy efficiency programs on US employment, income, and investment', *Energy Economics*, vol 30, pp 2283-301.

Selden, T. and Song, D. (1994) 'Environmental quality and development: is there a Kuznets curve for air pollution emissions?', *Journal of Environmental Economics and Management*, vol 27, pp 147-62.

Selin, H. and VanDeveer, S. (2010) 'Global climate change: Kyoto and beyond', in N. Vig and M. Kraft (eds) *Environmental policy* (7th edn), Washington, DC: CQ Press.

Selin, S. and Chevez, D. (1995) 'Developing a collaborative model for environmental planning and management', *Environmental Management*, vol 19, no 2, pp 189-95.

Sen, A. (2009) *The idea of justice*, London: Allen Lane.

SEU (Social Exclusion Unit) (2003) *Making the connections, Final report on transport and social exclusion*, London: Social Exclusion Unit.

Sevenhuijsen, S. (1998) *Citizenship and the ethics of care: Feminist considerations on justice, morality and politics*, London: Routledge.

Seyfang, G. (2003) 'Growing cohesive communities one favour at a time: social exclusion, active citizenship and time banks', *International Journal of Urban and Regional Research*, vol 27, no 3, pp 699-706.

Seyfang, G. (2004) 'Time banks: rewarding community self-help in the inner city?', *Community Development Journal*, vol 39, no 1, pp 62-71.

Seyfang, G. (2005a) 'Shopping for sustainability: can sustainable consumption promote ecological citizenship?', in A. Dobson and A.V. Sáiz (eds) *Citizenship, environment, economy*, London and New York: Routledge.

Seyfang, G. (2005b) *Community currencies and social inclusion*, CSERGE Working Paper EDM 05-09.

Seyfang, G. (2009a) *Low-carbon currencies*, CSERGE Working Paper EDM 09-04.

Seyfang, G. (2009b) *The new economics of sustainable consumption: Seeds of change*, London: Palgrave Macmillan.

Seyfang, G. and Paavola, J. (2008) 'Inequality and sustainable consumption: bridging the gaps', *Local Environment*, vol 13, no 8, pp 669-84.

Seyfang, G. and Smith, A. (2007) 'Grassroots innovations for sustainable development: towards a new research and policy agenda', *Environmental Politics*, vol 16, no 4, pp 584-603.

Shaw, J. and Docherty, I. (2008) 'New Deal or no deal? A decade of sustainable transport in the UK', in I. Docherty and J. Shaw (eds) *Traffic jam: Ten years of 'sustainable' transport in the UK*, Bristol: The Policy Press.

Shaw, M., Thomas, B., Davey Smith, G. and Dorling, D. (2008) *The atlas of the real world: Mapping the way we live*, Bristol: The Policy Press.

Sheller, M. (2004) 'Automotive emotions: feeling the car', *Theory, Culture & Society*, vol 21, nos 4-5, pp 221-42.

Shelton, D. (2002) *Human rights, health and environmental protection*, London: Notre Dame London Law Centre.

Simms, A. (2009) *Ecological debt* (2nd edn), London: Pluto.

Singer, P. (1972) 'Famine, affluence, and morality', *Philosophy and Public Affairs*, vol 1, no 3, pp 229-43.

Singer, P. (1975) *Animal liberation: A new ethics for our treatment of animals*, New York: Avon.

Singer, P. (1986) 'All animals are equal', in P. Singer (ed) *Applied ethics*, Oxford: Oxford University Press.

Sloman, L. (2006) *Car sick: Solutions for our car-addicted culture*, Totnes: Green Books.

Smith, G. (2005) 'Green citizenship and the social economy', *Environmental Politics*, vol 14, no 2, pp 273-89.

Smith, M.J. and Pangsapa, P. (2008) *Environment and citizenship: Integrating justice, responsibility and civic engagement*, London: Zed Books.

Solomon, S., Platter, G., Knutti, R. and Freidlingstein, P. (2008) 'Irreversible climate change due to carbon dioxide emissions', *Proceedings of the National Academy of Sciences of the USA*, vol 106, no 6, pp 1704-9.

SOU (Statens Offentliga Utredninger) (2007) *Bioenergi från jordbruket – en växande resurs*, Stockholm: SOU.

Soper, K. (2005) 'The enchantments and disenchantments of nature: implications for consumption in a globalised world', in J. Paavola and I. Lowe (eds) *Environmental values in a globalizing world*, London and New York: Routledge.

Stavins, R.N. (2003) 'Experience with market-based environmental policy instruments', in K.-G. Mäler and J.R. Vincent (eds) *Handbook of environmental economics. Volume 1: Environmental degradation and institutional responses*, Amsterdam: Elsevier.

Stephan, M. (2002) 'Environmental information disclosure programs: they work, but why?', *Social Science Quarterly*, vol 83, no 1, pp 190-205.

Stern, N. (2007) *The economics of climate change*, Cambridge: Cambridge University Press.

Stern, N. (2009) *A blueprint for a safer planet*, London: Bodley Head.

Stokes, R. (1999) 'Lagging behind', *The Guardian Society*, 24 March, p 10.

Stradling, S., Anable, J., Anderson, T. and Cronberg, A. (2008) 'Car use and climate change: do we practise what we preach?', in A. Park, J. Curtice, K. Thomson, M. Phillips, M. Johnson and E. Clery (eds) *British Social Attitudes: The 24th report*, London: Sage Publications.

Sutton, P.W. (2004) *Nature, environment and society*, Houndmills: Palgrave Macmillan.

Swinton, S.M., Escobar, G. and Reardon, T. (2003) 'Poverty and environment in Latin America: concepts, evidence and policy implications', *World Development*, vol 31, no 11, pp 1865-72.

Talbot, L. and Verrinder, G. (2009) *Promoting health*, Marrickville, Australia: Elsevier.

Taylor, I., Newson, C., Anable, J. and Sloman, L. (2008) *Traffic noise in rural areas*, London: UK Noise Association.

Taylor, P.W. (1986) *Respect for nature: A theory of environmental ethics*, Princeton, NJ: Princeton University Press.

Taylor, P.W. (1995) 'The ethics of respect for nature', in J.P. Sterba (ed) *Earth ethics: Environmental ethics, animal rights, and practical applications*, Upper Saddle River, NJ: Prentice-Hall.

Taylor-Gooby, P. (2009) *Reframing social citizenship*, Oxford: Oxford University Press.

Terry, G. (2009) 'No climate justice without gender justice: an overview of the issues', *Gender and Development*, vol 17, no 1, pp 5-18.

Thaler, R. and Sunstein, C. (2008) *Nudge*, New Haven, CT: Yale University Press.

Thoreau, H.D. (1995) *Walden: Or, Life in the woods*, New York: Dover.

Tickell, O. (2008) *Kyoto 2*, London: Zed Books.

Tisdell, C. (2001) 'Globalisation and sustainability: environmental Kuznets curve and the WTO', *Ecological Economics*, vol 29, pp 185-96.

TN (Transitions Network) (2009) 'About Transition Network' (http://transitiontowns.org/TransitionNetwork/TransitionNetwork).

Tobin, R. (2010) 'Environment, population, and the developing world', in N. Vig and M. Kraft (eds) *Environmental policy* (7th edn), Washington, DC: CQ Press.

Tong, S.L., Hu, W.B. and McMichael, A. (2004) 'Climate variability and Ross River virus transmission in Townsville region Australia 1985-1996', *Tropical Medicine International Health*, vol 9, pp 298-304.

Trzyna, T. (ed) (1995) *A sustainable world*, London: Earthscan.

Tuchman, G. (1978) 'Introduction: the symbolic annihilation of women by the mass media', in G. Tuchman, A.K. Daniels and J. Benet (eds) *Hearth and home*, New York: Oxford University Press.

Turner, R.S. (2008) *Neo-liberal ideology: History, concepts and policies*, Edinburgh: Edinburgh University Press.

UK ITPOES (Industry Taskforce on Peak Oil and Energy Security) (2008) *The oil crunch securing the UK's energy future*, London: ITPOES.

UN (United Nations) (2005) *Millennium Development Goals: Progress up to September 2005*, New York: UN.

UNCED (United Nations Conference on Environment and Development) (1992) *Rio Declaration on Environment and Development, Agenda 21*, Rio de Janeiro, Brazil (http://habitat.igc.org/agenda21/index.htm).

UN-DESA (2009) *A Global Green New Deal for sustainable development*, Policy Brief No 12, March (www.un.org/esa/policy/policybriefs/policybrief12.pdf).

UNDP (United Nations Development Programme) (2005) *Human development report 2005*, New York: UNDP.

UNDP (2007) *Human development report, 2007-08*, New York: UNDP.

UNDP (2009) *Human development report 2009*, New York: UNDP.

UNEP (United Nations Environment Programme) (1972) *Declaration of the United Nations Conference on the Human Environment, 1972* (www.unep.org/Documents.Multilingual/Default.asp?DocumentID=97&ArticleID=1503&l=en).

UNEP (2000) Montreal Protocol on Substances that deplete the Ozone layter (www.unep.org/ozone).

UNEP (2005) *Ridding the world of POPs: A guide to the Stockholm Convention of Persistent Organic Pollutants*, Secretariat of the Stockholm Convention on Persistent Organic Pollutants.

UNEP (2008) *Green jobs: Towards decent work in a sustainable low-carbon world* (www.unep.org/labour_environment/features/greenjobs.asp).

UNEP (2009) *Global Green New Deal. An update for the G20 Pittsburgh Summit*, September (www.unep.org/pdf/G_20_policy_brief_Final.pdf).

UNEP (nd) 'Environment and sustainable development brief' (www.unep.org/civil_society/GCSF8/pdfs/gender_susdev.pdf).

UN ESCAP (2005) 'Seoul initiative on environmentally sustainable economic growth (green growth)', Item 7 of provisional agenda for the fifth Ministerial Conference on Environment and Development in Asia and the Pacific (www.unescap.org/mced/documents/).

UNFCC (2009) (http://unfccc.int/kyoto_protocol/mechanisms/clean_development_mechanism/items/2718.php).

UN General Assembly (1987) (www.un.org/documents/ga/res/42/ares42-187.htm).

Urry, J. (2000) *Sociology beyond societies: Mobilities for the twenty-first century*, London: Routledge.

Urry, J. (2008) *Mobilities*, Cambridge: Polity Press.

US Government (2009) 'Recovery.gov' (www.recovery.gov/Pages/home. aspx).

US Metro Economies (2008) *Current and potential green jobs in the US economy*, Lexington, MA: Global Insight, Inc, Lexington, MA (http:// usmayors.org/pressreleases/uploads/GreenJobsReport.pdf).

Varner, G.E. (1998) *In nature's interests? Interests, animal rights, and environmental ethics*, Oxford: Oxford University Press.

Verrinder, A. (2003) *Human ecology and health*, Bendigo: La Trobe University.

Vig, N. and Kraft, M. (eds) (2010) *Environmental policy* (7th edn), Washington, DC: CQ Press.

Vinz, D. (2009) 'Gender and sustainable consumption: a German environmental perspective', *European Journal of Women's Studies*, vol 16, no 2, pp 159-79.

Voisey, H. and O'Riordan, T. (1997) 'Governing institutions for sustainable development: the United Kingdom's national level approach', *Environmental Politics*, vol 6, no 1, pp 24-53.

Wade, J., Wiltshire, V. and Scrase, I. (2000) 'National and local employment impacts of energy efficiency investment programmes', SAVE contract XVII/4.1031/D/97-032, Final report to the European Commission (www. ukace.org/publications/ACE%20Research%20%282000-04%29%20 -%20National%20and%20Local%20Employment%20Impacts%20of%20 Energy%20Efficiency%20Investment%20Programmes%20%5BVolu- me%201%20Summary%20Report%5D).

Wainwright, H. (2009) *Public service reform ... but not as we know it*, London: Compass.

Waldmeir, P. (2009) 'Car sales in China surge 48%', *Financial Times*, 10 July.

Walker, G. and King, D. (2008) *The hot topic*, London: Bloomsbury.

WCED (World Commission on Environment and Development) (1987) *Our common future* (Brundtland Report), Oxford: Oxford University Press.

Wheeler, S.M. (2004) *Planning for sustainability: Creating livable, equitable, and ecological communities*, London: Routledge.

Wheeler, S.M. and Beatley, T. (eds) (2004) *The sustainable urban development reader*, London: Routledge.

Wheeler, S.M. and Beatley, T. (eds) (2008) *The sustainable urban development reader* (2nd edn), London: Routledge.

White, S. (2003) *The civic minimum*, Oxford: Oxford University Press.

White, S. and Leighton, D. (eds) (2008) *Building a citizen society*, London: Lawrence & Wishart.

Whitelegg, J. and Haq, G. (2006) *Vision Zero: Adopting a target of zero for road traffic fatalities and serious injuries*, London: Stockholm Environment Institute for the Department for Transport.

Whitford, A.B. and Wong, K. (2009) 'Political and social foundations for environmental sustainability', *Political Research Quarterly*, vol 62, no 1, pp 190-204.

WHO (World Health Organization) (1948) *World Health Organization Constitution* (www.who.int/governance/eb/constitution/en/).

WHO (1978) *Declaration of Alma-Ata* (www.who.int/hpr/NPH/docs/declaration_almaata.pdf).

WHO (1986) *The Ottawa Charter for Health Promotion* (www.who.int/healthpromotion/conferences/previous/ottawa/en/).

WHO (1988) Second International Conference on Health Promotion, Adelaide, South Australia, 5-9 April (www.who.int/healthpromotion/conferences/previous/adelaide/en/).

WHO (2002) *World Health Report 2002*, Geneva: WHO.

WHO (2003) *Climate change and human health: Risks and responses* (www.who.int/globalchange/publications/cchhsummary/en/).

WHO (2004a) *World report on road traffic injury prevention*, Vienna: WHO.

WHO (2004b) *Transport-related health effects with a particular focus on children*, Vienna: WHO Europe.

WHO (2005) *Indoor air pollution and health*, Factsheet No 292, Geneva: WHO.

WHO (2009a) 'Socio-economic inequities – scenarios, recommendations and tools for action', Third High-level Preparatory Meeting, 29th Session of the European Environment and Health Committee, Bonn, Germany, 27-29 April, Copenhagen: WHO Regional Office for Europe.

WHO (2009b) *Global status report on road safety*, Geneva: WHO.

WHO/UNICEF (2008) *World report on child injury prevention*, Geneva: WHO.

Wilkinson, R. and Marmot, M. (eds) (2003) *The solid facts*, Geneva: World Health Organization.

Wilkinson, R. and Pickett, K. (2009) *The spirit level*, London: Allen Lane.

Williams, C. (2002) 'The social economy and Local Exchange and Trading Schemes (LETS)', in T. Fitzpatrick and M. Cahill (eds) *Environment and welfare*, Basingstoke: Palgrave.

Williams, C. and Windebank, J. (1998) *Replacing informal employment*, London: Routledge.

Wissenburg, M. (1998) *Green liberalism*, London: Routledge.

Woerdman, E. (2000) 'Implementing the Kyoto Protocol: why JI and CDM show more promise than international emissions trading', *Energy Policy*, vol 28, pp 29-38.

Wolff, J. and de-Shalit, A. (2007) *Disadvantage*, Oxford: Oxford University Press.

Woodruff, R., Guest, C., Gsarner, G., Becker, N. and Lindsay, M.F. (2003) 'Weather and climate as early warning system indicators for epidemics of Ross River virus. A case study in south-west Western Australia', *Epidemiology*, vol 14, p S94.

World Bank (2008) *Global development report. MDGs and the environment. Agenda for inclusive and sustainable development*, Washington, DC: World Bank (www.imf.org/external/pubs/ft/gmr/2008/eng/gmr.pdf).

Wright, E.O. (2004) 'Interrogating the treadmill of production: some questions I still want to know about and am not afraid to ask', *Organization & Environment*, vol 17, no 3, pp 317-22.

Wright, E.O. (2010) *Envisioning real utopias*, London: Verso.

Yearly, S. (1996) *Sociology, environmentalism, globalization*, London: Sage Publications.

Youell, M. (2008) 'Why is Africa still poor?', *SAIS Review*, vol 28, no 2.

Zhang, Z.X. (2008) 'Asian energy and environmental policy: Promoting growth while preserving the environment', International Conference on Staying Ahead of the Energy Scenarios, Bangkok, Thailand.

Index

Page references for notes are followed by n

carless people 232–5
pollution and other health impacts
229–31
Carter, N. 53, 54
causal analysis 253–5
centralisation 64–5
CGE (computable general equilibrium)
models 256, 259–60, 261, 265, 266n,
268–9
Chadwick, Edwin 184
Chapin, M. 106
Chasek, P. 295, 303, 304
Child Poverty Action Group 66
children
environmental citizenship 287
mobility 232–4
transport pollution 230
China
cars 228, 229
environmental policy 253
poverty 305
recovery package 262, 263
chlorofluorocarbons (CFCs) 197–8
Chu, Steven 48
cities
developing countries 222–4
Healthy Cities programme 199
land use and housing 210–14
parks, public spaces and ecosystems
220–1
and sustainability 208–10
citizenship 271–2
environment and care 281–3
environmental citizenship 273–9
policy implications and promising
examples 283–8
work-care-citizenship life balance
286–7
Clean Development Mechanism (CDM)
306, 308–10, 311
clean tech 246–7
climate change 6–7, 17–35, 39, 316–17
causes 19–22
consequences 25–7
definition 18–19
developing countries 296–7, 300
effects 22–5
and health 188–9
and planning 209, 210
policies and politics 31–5
responses 27–31
targets and timescales 73–7
and transport 240–2
Club of Rome project 44
cold 25
Collier, P. 304–5
command-and-control 158–9, 161
Commoner, Barry 45
communitarianism 137–8, 139, 142–4,
319
community participation 195

consequentialism 112, 113, 115–16
conservation 28, 30–1
Conservation International 105, 106–7
conservationist conservatives 10
Consumer Focus 176
consumerist ethic model 42, 43, 49–52,
58
consumption
and environmental citizenship 279
environmental critique 62
sustainable 54–5
and treadmill of production model 47,
48–9
contraction and convergence 77–9, 319
Convention on Biological Diversity 194,
307–8
cooperative management regimes 103
Copeland, B.R. 251, 265n
Copenhagen Summit 12, 34–5
cross-sector policies 193–4, 319
CSDH (Commission of the Social
Determinants of Health) 182
Curitiba 222
cycling 235
Czech Republic 274

D

Davis, A. 231
Davis, California 219
de-Shalit, A. 65
Declaration of Alma-Ata (WHO) 196
deep ecologists 9, 10
deferred enhancement rule 171
democratic pragmatists 9, 10
Denmark 235
deontology 112, 113, 114–15
descriptive analysis 253–5
determinants of health 182, 183, 320
developing countries 310–11
development challenge 298–300
environmental degradation and
development 34, 292–6
environmental ethics 119–22
environmentalism and welfare 103–8
global policy responses 300–10
population growth 46
poverty and environmental degradation
53, 292
unequal effects of environmental
degradation 296–8
urban planning 222–4
development *see* economic development
di Chiro, G. 280
Dickens, Charles 184
Dickens, Peter 50
Dinda, S. 299
direct jobs 248, 261, 320
discounting 76, 320
discourse 56